D1524324

Leadership in a Globalized World

Leadership in a Globalized World

Complexity, Dynamics, and Risks

Frannie Léautier
Partner and Chief Executive Officer of Mkoba Private Equity Fund

First published 2014 by
PALGRAVE MACMILLAN

Palgrave Macmillan in the UK is an imprint of Macmillan Publishers Limited, registered in England, company number 785998, of Houndmills, Basingstoke, Hampshire RG21 6XS.

Palgrave Macmillan in the US is a division of St Martin's Press LLC, 175 Fifth Avenue, New York, NY 10010.

Palgrave Macmillan is the global academic imprint of the above companies and has companies and representatives throughout the world.

Palgrave® and Macmillan® are registered trademarks in the United States, the United Kingdom, Europe and other countries.

ISBN 978–1–137–43120–2

This book is printed on paper suitable for recycling and made from fully managed and sustained forest sources. Logging, pulping and manufacturing processes are expected to conform to the environmental regulations of the country of origin.

A catalogue record for this book is available from the British Library.

A catalog record for this book is available from the Library of Congress.

Typeset by MPS Limited, Chennai, India.

For Thomas-Olivier, Oriane, and François-René

Contents

List of Figures, Tables, and Boxes

Figures

Tables

Acknowledgments

This book evolved from experiences garnered from working around the world and from teaching on leadership at the Sloan School of Management (MIT) in 2005, and in a global classroom at the Paris School of International Affairs (PSIA) at Sciences Po. Participants from several locations (Accra, Arusha, Bamako, Dar es Salaam, Harare, Kampala, Ouagadougou, and Paris) engaged with the manuscript as part of the leadership class during the years 2007 to 2014. As such the book enjoys dynamic input and perspectives from around the world.

I acknowledge the learning environments provided by the Independent Activities Program participants in January 2005 at MIT and at PSIA between 2007 and 2014. A number of partner institutions were critical—Ghana Institute for Public Management (GIMPA) in Accra; Institut International d'ingénierie de l'eau et de l'environnement (2iE) in Ouagadougou, Burkina Faso; Public Sector Management Programme at Makerere University in Uganda; Nelson Mandela Institute of Science and Technology in Arusha Tanzania; and Tanzania Global Development Learning Centre (TGDLC) in Dar es Salaam.

Case study materials come from experiences as a development practitioner in Asia, Latin America, and Africa and from leadership roles in complex situations in the USA, Europe, and Africa. I have benefited from comments by participants in the class seminars. I would like to thank all who took part in the role-plays and case studies.

Many have been tremendously helpful in the success of this book. Melissa Mundell got me interested in teaching at Sciences Po and followed the evolution of the materials with great enthusiasm. Jacques Dechampchesnel was an inspiration in bringing real-world situations. Guillaume Lecaros de Cossio Gauthier made invaluable comments and recommended where case studies should be placed in the book. Dr Coffi Noumon facilitated Ouagadougou participants and worked hard with Paul Giniés and Amadou Maiga to ensure engagement in English. Dr Noumon also enabled people from Bamako to participate, despite the technical challenges of connecting in real time. Dr Kobena Hanson facilitated Accra participants, and, with the leadership of GIMPA, brought the excitement of real-world situations to bear on the dialogue and debate of mid-career practitioners from six West African countries. Dr Dieynaba Tandian facilitated at Makerere University, bringing numerous suggestions for improvement, including how best to balance local and global discussions. Franklin Mutahakana supported all the logistical arrangements and troubleshooting and oversaw the start of the exchanges. The participants engaged thanks to Franklin's tireless efforts to ensure that all had the same reference points even when technical glitches cut off communication. Siaka Coulibaly jumped in at short notice to facilitate in Dar es Salaam. Fasil Yilma and David Flipo provided technology support, allowing cases to be resolved in real time. Marie-Therese Kadurira did everything possible to ensure time in the calendar to write the book, and worked closely with Silvia Duerich-Morandi and Ingrid Desauguste at Sciences Po to ensure that allocated slots were feasible for global learning to take place as planned.

Deep appreciation goes to my editor Christina Brian at Palgrave Macmillan for the very thoughtful comments and patient guidance throughout the process. Ambra Finotello was extremely efficient and kept me on my toes in the run up to publication of this book, for which I am very grateful. I am also very grateful for the editorial team under the leadership of Geetha Williams for their patience and diligence in combing through the manuscript carefully to bring out all the inconsistencies. My family lost many evenings and weekends as I worked on this book. Thank you Thomas-Olivier, Oriane, and François-René. This wouldn't be possible without you.

Introduction

The policy maker's challenge

Simon Compaoré reminisced on 21 August 2012 about challenges overcome and lessons learned as Mayor of Ouagadougou.[1] He became Mayor in 1995 at 42, holding the position for 17 years, during which he witnessed dramatic changes. Ouagadougou's population more than tripled from 500,000 people in the 1990s to 1.5 million by the time he left office in 2012. Estimates attribute two thirds of the growth to migration from rural areas and neighboring countries.[2] Ouagadougou got more connected to the rest of the world during this period.[3] The city witnessed tremendous flows of foreign direct investment since the mid-1990s, fueled by telecommunications and mining. More people came to offer ideas and advice in all sectors, including on city management. Ouagadougou became more complex before his eyes, and he led with full consciousness of this complexity and the ensuing dynamics and risks.

The case of Simon Compaoré is not unique. Indeed, corporate leaders, politicians, and public sector officials operate in an increasingly complex and interconnected world. The degree of interconnectedness affects how they make decisions and the outcomes of their decisions. Deciding on the basis of what is visible (surface phenomena) can lead to costly mistakes and irreversible effects. Understanding the dynamics of what is changing is necessary not only for shaping strategy, but also for developing effective risk management approaches, and selecting from a series of potential courses of action.

Origin of the book

This book was born out of research and experiences from around the world as well as from leading in a variety of contexts. Research findings have been sharpened through dialogue and exchange in global learning environments. The book revolves around typical concerns facing policy makers as they seek to make decisions in varying contexts.

The first concern comes from the observation that policy makers are ill equipped to identify the major changes taking place across the world. Changes may be gradual but can become *tectonic shifts*, with substantial implications for decisions in their spheres of action. The changes investigated cover a variety of spheres, including demography, economy, technology, society, and nature. The challenges faced by Simon Compaoré in dealing with the changes he witnessed as Mayor of Ouagadougou are an example. Youth unemployment, which materialized as a major challenge in the late 2000s, even though patterns of birth rates and life expectancy had been known for many decades before, is another illustration. The book interrogates the spheres that are changing to create awareness of gradual changes leading to significant tremors that shake the very foundations of decision-making in the policy sphere.

The second concern comes from *patterns of change* in the global economy and their implications for decision-making at national or local level. The book identifies the main patterns of change and guides the reader toward the skills needed to detect important archetypes. Attention is paid to the skills that support decision-makers to uncover major trends and spot pattern discontinuities that could influence decisions. Few decision-makers consider data over time and over spatial or geographical areas, using the observed patterns of change to adjust strategy. Scores of decisions in the public sector are static and mired in bureaucratic steps that are not as flexible in adjusting to observed changes. In the private sector, many CEOs and captains of industry are caught by surprise by the changes around them; some even preside over the total collapse of their industries and companies. The speed at which banks buckled during the financial crisis of 2007–2008 is just one illustration of this area of concern.

The third concern comes from observing the underlying *dynamics of change* shaping parameters surrounding important decisions. The book aids the reader better understand the major drivers of change related to people, resources, economies, and technology. Drivers, such as the logistics revolution and its impact on production and consumption around the world, are exposed. The impact of security concerns on the logistics revolution following the September 11th 2001 attacks in the USA is also included to show how change drivers themselves can be impacted by other phenomena.

The fourth concern is *complexity* and its implications for decision-making. The focus is on the types of interaction that matter for decision-making and the adaptive strategies available to firms, industries, public sector organizations, and society. Case studies are used to illustrate the main points.

The fifth concern is the *risks* deriving from the changes caused by globalization. Tectonic shifts and their related patterns and dynamics have increased the complexity of decision-making, in turn causing an increase in the level and severity of the risks impacting society and systems. Case studies are used to illustrate how risks materialize in a globalized world and the implications for policy making and response.

The sixth concern is *governance* and its special role in leadership, with many examples drawn from managing in conflict countries. Governance is a major concern because of the impact that globalization has on the interplay between local, national, and international levels of governance. Lessons from managing development in post-conflict countries are used to illustrate the effect of globalization on governance arrangements leading to conflict and those useful for getting to stability after conflict. Spatial effects on decisions are also covered.

These questions are brought together in a final chapter with application to specific contexts, including the financial sector collapse in Iceland, the political economy of infrastructure provision and maintenance, and the logistics industry and its complexities in a globalized world.

Situating the book in the literature

Supporting theories and lessons aiding decision-makers around day-to-day challenges have been garnered through multidisciplinary research covering a wide range of subjects.

The definition of major changes, known as *tectonic shifts*, comes from management science and particularly from the work of Drucker (1992) and his treatment of the four main forces creating shifts in the ways that economies and societies function. The exposition of tectonic shifts is based on how Drucker (1992) highlights the role of new technologies, particularly in relation to the emergence of the knowledge economy and knowledge worker; the advent of globalization and the appearance of multinational corporations and their role around the world; and the rise of institutional pluralism and the need for collaboration across a variety institutions to solve global problems. Drucker's work is complemented by practical assessments by Fariboz and Peterson (2005).

The data to analyze the *patterns of change* taking place around the world come mainly from the World Bank Development Indicators and the International Monetary Fund (IMF). Analysis and case studies are from years of experience working in development in Asia and Latin America, and from questions by country leaders and policy makers in Africa. Patterns of change related to risks come from experience working on risk management in the private sector in Europe.

Analysis of the *dynamics of change* and their implications on the structure of economies is drawn from fields of engineering, systems control, and development economics. The first lens is *logistics* as a turning point in economic and social interactions on a global scale. How companies adjust their logistics and supply chain activities following shocks relies on engineering systems control (Sheffi, 2005). The global implications of firm-level adjustments to change visible in inventory cycles are taken from economics (Cecchetti et al., 1997). The second lens is *patterns of mobility, connectivity, and productivity*, which are based on analysis of data from the World Development Indicators to uncover the main dynamics. The theoretical basis for mobility and connectivity comes from Bar-Yam (1997), while that related to productivity comes from Lewis (2004). The third lens is *ownership and financing arrangements* around key productive sectors in economies. Lin (2012) is used to frame issues into the "new structural economics" and interpret changes visible across a variety of indicators of economic development.[4] The book exposes a fourth lens, interactions between *knowledge and culture*, building on Drucker (1992) and Bergendorf (2007). The fifth covers *risk management* and implications for patterns of change observed in organizations, economies and society. A variety of sources are used, including Kasperson et al. (1988), to cover risks in the financial system, security, and other threats. Finally, the sixth lens investigates growing demand for *ethical and accountable leadership* around the world, building on the surveys conducted by the World Economic Forum. A case study from the Jamuna Bridge demonstrates how complexity in engineering, natural systems and the environment, social and political systems at national and local levels, and global financial systems challenge leaders in different spheres.

For organizational level implications the book draws on Pritchett (2011) on fine-tuning the structure of public organizations to design fit-for-purpose policies, rather than mimicking what has worked elsewhere. Senge et al. (2004) serves for embedding changes at the societal level in considering transformation at organizational level. Amartya Sen (2006) provides reference points for the impact of changes at individual level, particularly in identity.

For *complexity* the book draws on the science of complexity to extract areas for problem solving in a complex environment (Bar-Yam, 1997, 2005a, b), building on the treatment of complexity theory in the field of strategic management (Anderson, 1999). Complex theoretical concepts such as interaction analysis, variation, and pattern recognition are introduced through practical examples observed in decision-making scenarios. Such an approach allows the reader to focus on the main points and not get bogged down with mathematical complexity.

The inclusion of *risk* is motivated by the fact that despite monumental advances in theoretical foundations and computational capabilities, few decision-makers have tapped into the value-creation potential of risk management (Léautier, 2007). The book builds on the integrative framework on social theories of risk by Kasperson et al. (1988) to bring in the scientific and cultural dimensions of the investigation of risks. The Jamuna Bridge case study shows how a technical assessment of risk can be combined with social and institutional risks to amplify or attenuate responses to risk.

The importance of *governance* is derived from the premise that globalization has made the role of leadership paramount in dealing with risk. However, there are multiple sources of leadership and power, as increased complexity necessitates the engagement of multiple stakeholders. Increased complexity means that real power to take decisions is diffused and a larger number of persons exercise power on any given issue. Cleveland (1972) understood that the social, technological, political, and economic problems facing decision-makers in a complex and interconnected world would require more complicated "bundles of relations" to deal comprehensively with the consequences on human and ecological systems of science and technology.[5]

The book introduces governance concepts and levels, and exposes the learner to tools and frameworks for decision-making. Special attention is paid to the global challenges emanating from a set of collective actions by multiple stakeholders. The importance of collaboration between the private sector, government, and civil society is also covered. The concept of "civil society," developed by Scholte (2001), is used to refer to a political space where voluntary associations explicitly seek to shape the rules that govern aspects of social life. The Scholte (2001) definition allows engaging with the effects of civil society in a globalized world, but also covers the role that civil society plays in shaping globalization. The outcomes of interaction across spaces and cultures that challenge security and social cohesion are also covered, as they are central to many interactions on a global scale. The role of leadership in good governance and links to governance institutions also feature. To understand what is changing in governance itself requires measuring governance. Using Kaufmann and Mastruzzi (2008), the book argues why governance matters in a globalized world, and how to select and examine individual and aggregate indicators for decision-making in the face of globalization.

How the whole is connected to the parts

The frameworks and theories from multiple disciplines are held together by subjecting them to six core questions derived from the principles of complexity and their implications for decision-making (Bar-Yam, 1997, 2005a). Various concepts are stitched together from the point of view of a decision-maker, their intentions, and the results of their work. "Theory U" by Scharmer (2007) is used to acquaint the reader to concepts of complexity and risk, and equip them with skills to lead in an increasingly interconnected world.

Six core questions

Decision-making in complex environments relies on the ability to uncover elements that could influence the outcomes of actions, to observe and interpret the behavior of these elements preceding and following a particular action, and to understand the interconnections that could be of interest in the decision-making process. Bennet and Bennet (2008) argue that this is largely because while there are surely trends and patterns that could be observed, they may very well be enmeshed with other factors in such a manner as to be imperceptible, amalgamated by delayed effects, and subject to change with input or feedback from another constituent. The complexity of decision-making can be reduced if the decision-maker can be guided through a set of questions or considerations that help sequence decisions and actions leading toward an acceptable solution (Bennet and Bennet, 2008).

In a globalizing world, areas of inquiry can help decision-makers to navigate through complex situations. The first area involves observing what is happening and uncovering visible patterns – such as contamination flues in the seawater abutting a nuclear plant. The second is detecting change or discontinuity in a pattern that may have been stable or static before – such as an increase in the toxicity levels and levels of radiation in the seawater abutting a nuclear plant. The third relates to understanding the causes of change in observed patterns – such as the leakage of reactors after an earthquake. The fourth concerns identifying the risks that come from observed patterns – such as when the level of radiation is low there is no risk to fish, but at a certain level the fish are impacted as well as the humans who eat them. The fifth is the governance, accountability, and leadership ethics that guide what actions must be taken – such as informing the community around a contaminated area, engaging in evacuation, and testing people in the area for radiation. Then there are the various actions that can be taken to mitigate the risks uncovered and revert to normal or get back to a non-risky situation.

The book is organized around six areas, defined in a set of questions critical for leaders:

1. What are the principal *patterns of shifts* taking place and what types of *discontinuities* do they generate? The use of shifts relates to "tectonic shifts," which are major changes that are consequential and have an important impact on decisions or outcomes.[6] The setting in which these shifts are taking place is also important, as is the specific environment for decision-making or the instance of action by the decision-maker. It is also important to observe the patterns of shifts, as they may carry information that is useful for decision-making.
2. What are the *dynamics of change* that produce such shifts? The term "dynamics of change" is used in this book to refer to the forces and properties which stimulate growth or decline, development or regression, or transformation within a given system or process. Being able to identify what is causing the observed pattern of change is a critical skill that can be useful in functioning with low levels of certainty or high levels of

unpredictability. The use of intuition and judgment becomes vital in such situations, as does the ability to learn from past patterns of results (whether judged to be a failure or a success). The ability to observe patterns of change and track the link between patterns and decisions is a useful skill to uncover the dynamics of change.

3. What do you need to know about *complexity and risk to* better navigate your specific context? The meaning of "complexity" in this book derives from the science of complexity, and as such it means the study of phenomena that emerge from a collection of interacting objects. The use of "risk" in this book relates to a potential loss resulting from a given set of actions, a specific decision, or lack of a decision. Such losses could be an undesired outcome, an unintended consequence, or an unanticipated result.

4. What is the role of *leadership and governance* in dealing with key risks? The term "leadership" refers to the position or function of a person who guides or directs a group as well as the act or instance of guiding or directing a group. "Leadership" also means the ability to guide or direct a group and to come with a set of actions that influence change or sway a result. "Governance" is used to mean the manner in which power is exercised to manage a country's economy and resources (social, environmental, natural) for the purposes of development.

5. What types of *risk management approaches* exist to handle the key risks that arise with increased complexity? The "risk management approaches" covered are both quantitative and qualitative and include parametric and non-parametric approaches, as well as heuristics.

6. What particular approaches are suitable for your *specific context*? In the book the term "context" is used to mean the setting, environment, or situation that a decision-maker is faced with in trying to solve problems occurring as a result of an event or occurrence that has materialized from the complexities of globalization.

These questions form the basic modules of the book. Each question is treated in a self-contained chapter. Key concepts are illustrated using original data analysis and case studies and the reader is guided through a learning approach for effective decision-making.

Theory U and learning to lead

"Theory U" is effective in walking the reader through the key modules in the book, building skills at each stage, so that by the end of the book the reader is exposed to the key approaches for handling complexities in decision-making. Theory U constitutes a body of work that makes explicit the linkages between the intention of the decision-maker and the results of their work Scharmer (2007) (Figure I.1).

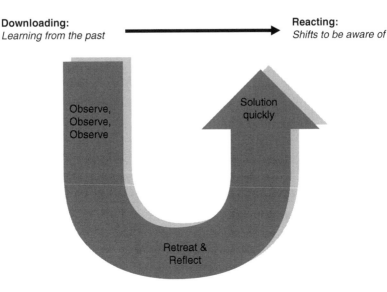

Downloading:
Learning from the past

Reacting:
Shifts to be aware of

Observe, Observe, Observe

Solution quickly

Retreat & Reflect

Figure I.1   Stage I of Theory U: observation and downloading
Source: Adapted from Scharmer, O.C. (2009), p. 33.

The theory also assumes that individuals and work teams can be aided to move consciously from strategy and planning, usually grounded in observation and analysis using existing sources of information, to knowing and visualizing the final outcome of their decisions. As such, the decision-maker is all the time conscious of the vision desired and policies or actions that need to be taken to make the vision real. Theory U also has an advantage of relevance for individual learning, the evolution of organizations, and the development of specific workplace practices.

Scharmer (2007) introduces a very usable approach to practicing the skills needed to manage in a highly complex and interconnected world, based on four stages of leadership. The first stage focuses on the skills of observing what is happening around you and downloading what you know about a situation from your past experience. The second stage relates to being able to see from a different perspective and sense what may be going on underneath an observed pattern of trends or behaviors. The third stage involves the capabilities of working with others to co-create a new reality or vision and to develop pilots or prototypes to test that new reality. The final stage involves embodying the previous stages into day-to-day practice to achieve superior performance. In the first stage, the key skill is keen observation and the ability to identify what is going on, take time to retreat, reflect about the patterns observed and find solutions quickly, using previous knowledge and past experience, which can be easily downloaded.

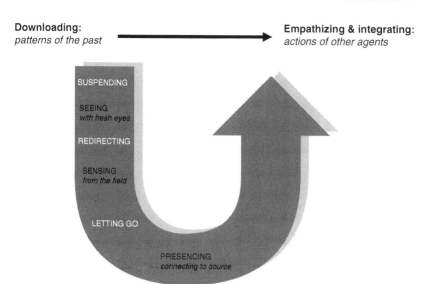

Downloading:
patterns of the past

Empathizing & integrating:
actions of other agents

SUSPENDING

SEEING
with fresh eyes

REDIRECTING

SENSING
from the field

LETTING GO

PRESENCING
connecting to source

Figure I.2   Stage II of Theory U: seeing and sensing
Source: Adapted from Scharmer, O.C. (2009), p. 33.

The second stage relies on ability to suspend prior beliefs or hypotheses and try to see what is happening with fresh eyes, which is key in gaining a new perspective. Indeed, suspending belief does not happen naturally, and is a skill that needs to be learned. As Kahneman et al. (1982) show, people rely on a limited number of heuristic principles to reduce the complexity of making judgments under uncertainty.

In Theory U, the important learned process involves redirecting thoughts, analysis, and interpretations into a new way of thinking, and seeing patterns and combining the new realization with sensing what is happening around you – sensing from the field. It comes from practice and conscious engagement with others and with one's surroundings in a different way (Scharmer, 2007:13–14) (Figure I.2).

The third stage involves the skills to crystallize the newly acquired information or ways of thinking about the issues into a vision and set of intentions that can be acted upon in a series of pilots or prototypes. Such work may include enacting a set of scenarios and co-creating a special place or space where a team can practice, role-play, or test the ideas. Such a place could be a "situation room," a "discussion or collaboration space" on the Internet, or a location or plant where one wants to start. The pilots or prototype tests would generate a set of strategic scenarios that come about by acting together with a group of diverse minded people (Figure I.3).

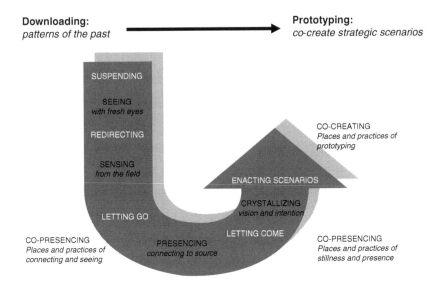

Figure I.3   Stage III of Theory U: co-creating and prototyping
Source: Adapted from Scharmer, O.C. (2009), p. 45.

Many times at the stage of seeing and sensing a decision-maker would have to go beyond suspending judgment or considering new hypotheses to being able to let go of favorite or preferred ways of seeing or doing. In so doing, judgment is required, and that means going back to the source – values, predefined strategy, or set of rules and procedures – in order to make a judgment on how to empathize with the point of view of others or how to integrate one's actions with the actions of other agents. Without specific practice, individuals would go back to what comes naturally, which could result in an underestimation of the impact of evidence (Slovic and Lichtenstein, 1971) or reliance on lessons from a small number of previous experiences (Tversky and Kahneman, 1971).

The final stage of leadership is about embodying desired strategic scenarios into a series of actions that would deliver results through day-to-day practices and supporting infrastructures. In such a manner, the decision-maker introduces a culture of superior performance for results, which is linked to the ability to see with fresh eyes, sense what is happening around you, predict what may happen in the future, co-create a set of actions that could handle the consequences of different future scenarios, create a space for experimentation, prototyping and learning, and embody this way of working in day-to-day practice (Figure I.4).

Theory U is used to help the learner practice the skills needed to manage in a highly complex and interconnected world by practicing along four stages of leadership. The first stage helps the learner develop the skills of

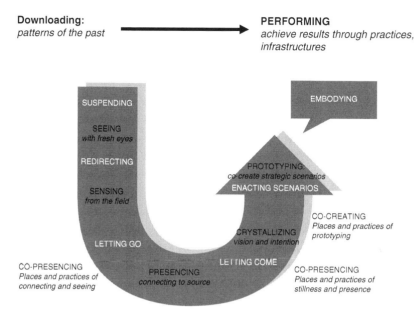

Figure I.4   Stage IV of Theory U: embodying for superior performance
Source: Adapted from Scharmer, O.C. (2009), p. 45.

observing what is happening around them and downloading what is known about a situation from past experience. The second stage helps the learner improve their capacity to see from a different perspective and sense what may be going on underneath an observed pattern of trends or behaviors. The third stage hones the capabilities of working with others to co-create a new reality or vision and to develop pilots or prototypes to test that new reality. The final stage involves embodying the previous stages into day-to-day practice to achieve superior performance.

Theory U, combined with the case studies and examples in the book, helps the learner practice and change unproductive behaviors to become more effective in functioning under a dynamically changing environment that is fraught with complexity and risk.

Objectives of the book

This book is based on the premise that it is possible to learn from experiences in real life using case studies that can be subjected to a structured approach from theories of how decisions get made and how learning takes place. The book brings a practice approach to the theory of complexity, putting a premium on the ability to observe patterns and trends and to uncover the underlying dynamics. Examples from real situations are used to provide the reader with varying contexts. Leadership skills that are needed to be effective in such complex environments are introduced with practice modules built up from multiple disciplines.

Fortunately, complexity can be observed and harnessed. Understanding complexity is the key to identifying and managing risks. Decision-makers need to be conversant with the behavior of interconnected systems to make effective decisions under varying strategic and risk scenarios. They also need to be equipped with values and behaviors to be successful in a specific context.

The purpose of the book is to introduce major changes that are likely to affect decision-making in the public, private, or civil society sphere as a result of globalization and to present the major patterns of change and their implications for decision-making, particularly around public policy. The book shows how the dynamics of change can be analyzed. Using the science of complexity and risk management theory the book's purpose is to guide the reader through useful techniques to handle the complexities materializing from globalization. The guiding principles around leadership and governance are covered to expose the reader to important issues in making effective decisions.

Case studies and lessons from practice are used in the book with the intention of supporting the reader to get the skills needed to solve problems in the complex environments that they may be facing.

Audience for the book

The main disciplines used are development economics, management science, the science of complexity, and concepts from finance and engineering (construction and civil in particular, but also manufacturing). The book offers a lot of descriptions that are useful for those who are not quantitatively oriented. It is rigorous in its approach to self-paced learning, but assumes a basic level of economics and management science. There is no need to be versed in development economics or engineering, even though the book would be particularly useful for practitioners in mid-level leadership positions in such contexts. There are no mathematical prerequisites to understanding the materials in the book, but good logical and analytical skills are needed to make the most of them.

The primary audience for the book is those interested in development economics, international affairs, business, and engineering. The book would be very helpful to academics and mid-career professionals looking to improve their skills on decision-making in a complex interconnected world. It would be particularly suitable for policy researchers and those interested in a self-paced learning environment. The general public would find it useful too. Investors would find it of particular value in deciding on metrics to use when planning investments in developing countries in Africa and Asia.

Structure and approaches in the book

The pedagogical approach used is practice learning from solving problems in a team environment, working with case studies developed from real situations. The reader is encouraged to self-evaluate with tools for self-assessment provided at the end of each module.

Learning by modules and learning by doing

The book is organized along six learning modules, and is grounded in theory but rich in contextual and experiential exposure. An effort is made to evolve applications to specific contexts. Examples come from industries and firms such as logistics, construction, trade, and exports; sectors as varied as transport, energy, and water; geographical contexts including spatial variations embedded in patterns observed within cities, countries, and regions; and policies and their choice implications in terms of education arrangements, science and technology investments, political economy variations, and infrastructure maintenance solutions.

The methodology combines various sources of content. The main principles are exposed using case studies, theoretical and practical illustrations from a rich bibliography list, and stories from practitioners. Theoretical lessons have also been drawn from observing behaviors and tracking skills used in live interactive sessions with policy makers, practice with specific approaches in an advisory role, and the author's own research and experience. All illustrations and cases used in the book come from real-life interactivity. Three cases come from the real-life experiences of the author while leading at a high level over 15 years at the World Bank. These include the Jamuna Bridge in Bangladesh, the case of chicken exports after SARS, and the case of policies for infrastructure finance and maintenance. The Monsanto and Iceland financial crisis cases were developed by the author's students in a Masters and PhD level course in international affairs at Sciences-Po in Paris. The cases from Cameroon, Côte d'Ivoire, and the Great Lakes are an outcome of joint solutions that came from linking up participants in Africa to participants from all across the world. The learning journey of the author over a period of 25 years provides a rich milieu from which to extract lessons and contextualize approaches to a variety of situations. The author has been to more than 100 countries and has led complex organizations in the USA, Asia, Europe, and Africa. As such, the materials presented benefit from deep and often intimate knowledge of the countries, regions, and events taking place around the world.

Holistic, modular, and interactive learning

Learning is important in all contexts, but more so when everything is changing. The complexity in patterns, spheres, and drivers of change makes it necessary to speed up and at the same time simplify the process of learning. Organizing key principles and trends into learning modules helps busy people get access to the material they need when they need it, and also fits well with a style of learning from multiple forms of knowledge, including past experience, case studies, research, peers, and theory. The material is divided into learning modules designed around six critical questions.

What are the principal patterns of shifts taking place and what types of discontinuities do they generate?

The first module introduces trends in globalization and highlights the global discontinuities created by observable patterns of change. This module sets the stage for better understanding of spheres, drivers, and locus of change. Four spheres are covered – people, resources, technology, and economy. Particular emphasis is placed on what is changing, what patterns can be discerned from those changes, and how particular changes are interconnected. The main emphasis is the impact of patterns of change on critical decisions, and the pitfalls when decisions are made on the basis of only what is observable. Changes in the people sphere take up the bulk of the first chapter because of their importance. Patterns relating to the "youth bulge," where the share of population aged under 25 has been increasing in some regions while decreasing in others, are important to bring out what these patterns entail for certain types of decisions. Other patterns covered relate to changing consumption patterns in emerging economies and trends in economic integration. Examples help the learner go from everyday issues, like choosing a brand of shirt to purchase, to longer term strategic decisions, such as deciding whether or not to use genetically modified seeds. Emphasis is also placed on the role of knowledge and learning for public policy and decision-making.

The skill practiced using the first module is developed from Theory U and is aimed at improving the ability to react effectively to tectonic change based on observations of what is happening around you. A case study from Monsanto, which is a multinational, joint-stock company specialized in biotechnology, is used to establish the interconnectedness of decisions and choices, and the impacts created outside of the sphere of influence of the major decision-makers. The Monsanto case study is used to show how a company has reacted to and caused tectonic shifts in how science is used for profit, how farming interacts with science, what people consume and its effects on their health, and how activities are regulated. A set of potential reactions by different groups is provided as a response to the complexities of changes in the global food supply chain.

The reader is encouraged to use the Monsanto case as a starting point for their own reactions, providing them with the possibility of deriving deeper learning as they interact with the case materials. The Monsanto case provides a balance between competition, cooperation, investigation, and regulation, and a set of reactions by different groups active in a complex chain of decisions. This exercise supports self-learning as it guides the learner through a series of challenges and choices made by a company, but leaves the interpretation of the process followed to make choices up to the learner. The case relates to the production and use of genetically modified organisms and the implications for a variety of decisions, leading to a series of diverse reactions by a varied group of decision-makers. The learner goes through the case to formulate and practice their own reactions to tectonic change while interacting with how Monsanto's leadership reacted to the same changes.

What are the dynamics of change that produce such shifts?

The second module goes deeper into the dynamics of change, building on the learner's capacity to observe principal patterns of change. The materials presented help the learner to determine the dynamics of change generating shifts in observed patterns. The dynamics of change are presented through six specific lenses.

The first lens covers the emergence of logistics as a turning point in economic and social interactions on a global scale. The second lens focuses on the dynamics of change coming from patterns of mobility, connectivity, and productivity. Ownership and financing arrangements around key productive sectors form the third lens. The fourth lens is the interactions between knowledge and culture, while the fifth lens provides a picture of the effect of advances in tools for risk management on risk taking and the implications for the patterns of change observed. Finally, the sixth lens investigates the growing demands for ethical and accountable leadership around the world.

In this second module, the issues brought out germinate from the logistics and supply chain area of practice, but are complemented by the behaviors driving increased mobility and connectivity and the changing nature of finance. This module puts a particular focus on the role of culture and the sources and impacts of knowledge and innovation. How individuals, firms and states react to risks in making choices and taking decisions is also an area covered. The special role played by ethics when the outcomes of the dynamics of change are not known in advance is emphasized.

A practice block developed from Theory U provides the reader with the areas of skill needed to deal with tectonic change that rely on seeing with fresh eyes and sensing from others and their experiences to build the foundation for common action. Using a real case of the impact of natural disasters in a country context, from the Jamuna Bridge in Bangladesh, the reader is introduced to what it takes to work with others to understand how they sense problems and relate different perspectives to their own.

The module introduces the learner to the global constraints that impact on strategy and the role of negotiations with different stakeholder groups, as well as the options for dealing with areas that are hard to predict. Other lessons highlighted in the module are the modalities by which the actions of different agents lead to global properties that affect particular decisions. The main skill from Theory U is dealing with change by practicing "emphasizing and integrating actions of others" in a structured setting.

What do you need to know about complexity and risk to better navigate your specific context?

The third module introduces the reader to complexity and risk using illustrations from practice in addition to theory for the reader who is not an expert in complexity and risk. Complexity generally increases with increasing interactions among previously independent systems. Higher complexity has the potential to generate a set of new risks and challenges, and has been known to create more frequent risks and added severity of risk, and can even lead to further synchronization of risks. When complexity is high it becomes progressively more difficult to predict the outcomes of a strategy or a course of action. New approaches are therefore needed to guide leaders, decision-makers, and analysts. Interacting with case materials from the chicken export industry following the SARS epidemic, Theory U is used to introduce the learner to the challenges of co-developing a set of potential scenarios that could play out and their respective courses of action. The relevance of different strategies and actions and how they can be used to develop a prototype to be tested during implementation is one of the key new aspects of the learning from this module.

In addition to general principles of complexity and risk, the third module also covers the skills needed for leaders to be effective in a complex and interconnected environment. These include operating with tectonic shifts and skills for working simultaneously with information from history, actuality, and the emerging future. To operate successfully when there is tectonic change, the science of muddling through can be very effective, including choices about whether to preserve the status quo or seek new technologies or processes. Other skills covered include fighting back or fighting against trends by returning to core values and norms and establishing control of key risks. How to embrace change and undertake transformational change with strategic engagement at individual, family, organizational, and societal level for collective transformation is also covered. Dealing with history, actuality, and the future is covered by providing the reader with a better understanding of how to learn from the past, using case studies, experiences of others, and best practice examples. Interpreting the present from skilled observation, analysis, and assessment is a key area. Sensing what is emerging through effective use of scenarios, possibilities, and options rounds out this module. The module brings together the examples and skill of working with others to sense what they may be sensing and create together an approach for dealing with a common risk with varied but serious implications for all key stakeholders.

What is the role of leadership and governance in dealing with key risks?

The fourth module brings in the dimension of leadership and governance, with exposure to the tools and frameworks that leaders use and the capabilities they need to have to succeed and remain relevant in a changing world. Emphasis is placed on how global challenges emanate from a set of collective actions by multiple stakeholders. The resulting outcomes of violence, hate, terrorism, civil war, poverty, and increased risks of natural disasters require leaders to reconsider their norms and values, as well as their social structures. Interpreting the actions of other agents, empathizing and learning from them, can provide a useful backdrop for better sensing the future and developing appropriate actions and strategies.

Specific leadership skills covered in this module relate to the ability to function in environments with low predictability and the preparedness to handle diverse potential futures. The types of values and behaviors that can guide leaders in making choices in challenging circumstances are also uncovered through a series of practice examples. The learner is introduced to cases and a set of principles that allow them to rehearse for diverse environments, including the ability to function in environments with weak governance and high unpredictability.

Through examples, the reader is introduced to the skill of "presencing" the emerging future and crystallizing a cohesive vision and strategy.

Five sets of skills deriving from Theory U are relevant in this module. The first is the ability to function in environments with weak governance, where the chapter provides opportunities for the learner to rehearse by putting themselves as decision-makers in a post-conflict country setting. Post-conflict settings put a premium on leadership issues related to ethics and values, and particularly on making choices in difficult circumstances. How well you know yourself and your values and how you work towards developing common values is critical as a starting point. Exposure to leadership in post-conflict countries helps the learner be better prepared to lead in conditions of conflict, and to work with tools to function under diverse potential futures.

Second, strategic scanning skills and tools are given space in this module to help the learner enhance their capacity to generate strategic maps of pressure points and risk scenarios.

Third, attention is given to values and behaviors, particularly those that serve as a guide in making choices in challenging circumstances rounds up this module.

A fourth important skill with extensive coverage in the practice examples, is the capacity to identify patterns of change (shifts), extract important relationships (interactions), and select from a variety of approaches (selection) for handling challenges.

Finally, a special case of territorial governance is introduced to help the learner get access to the main strategies for handling spatial challenges.

Cases from Cameroon, Côte d'Ivoire, and the Great Lakes Region are used to introduce the importance of dialogue processes, valuing of contributions of a variety of stakeholders, and bringing different perspectives to bear. The theoretical background relates to crystallizing ideas from multiple stakeholders, which requires skills of sensing what others are sensing and integrating into a strategy for action. It requires a search from the current situation (or what you know) on how to get from an idea to a new vision. It requires the ability to manage tensions and contradictions to arrive at a collage of thoughts from all stakeholders. The module emphasizes the importance of suspending judgment and avoiding cynicism, as well as taking other people's ideas without apprehension. The outcome of doing this right is a vision and collective set of intentions that take note of the future as it emerges from a collage of shared ideas that are related to a set of values derived from a team or from the inner self.

What types of risk management approaches exist to handle the key risks that arise with increased complexity?

The fifth module introduces approaches to risk management, with techniques and examples taken from assessing risk at the firm level using the apparel market and its links to consumer preferences and experiences. The concept of the "experience economy" is introduced while linking changes in preferences to the demands for goods and services and the implications for public policy making. Risk at the level of an industry is also covered using the construction industry, which is a business that is organized and subject to stiff price competition, but is also prone to collusion and corruption. Construction presents a good learning ground for leaders to develop their skills for handling future changes, as project scope and requirements change often in this business, requiring speed and flexibility to adapt without causing harm (a collapsed bridge or building) or ruin (high cost overruns that are not compensated). Managing sustainability risk in the long and medium term is the third area covered in this module, using supporting case material. Sustainability risks are complex and policies to resolve them are not always easy to measure, leaving room for measurement errors. How decisions can be taken, with full knowledge of the potential for errors of omission, commission, or those deriving from unawareness of issues, is a key aspect of learning in this module.

Errors of omission, commission, or from being unaware of important issues can be best understood with lessons learned from perceived risk theory. Slovic et al. (1982) show how judgmental biases enter into risk perceptions and the importance of understanding judgmental limitations for effective decision-making. The approach from Theory U of "presencing" is very useful, especially when working with a "representative group of stakeholders" who can scan a wider sphere of risk and introduce many different perceptions of risk, as a mechanism to minimize biases from perceptions of risk. The concept of a "representative group of stakeholders" comes from the idea of a "representative consumer," derived from discrete choice theory (Anderson et al., 1992).

Case studies are used as a form of problem-based learning to improve the learning experience and encourage self-reflection, as well as to encourage deliberate applicability by the reader to similar risk situations. The book relies on the reader's ability to extrapolate from a representative case study and draw lessons learned from studying the choices made under uncertainty used in this chapter. The work of Wilson (1996) is used to design self-directed constructivist learning environments for the reader to use in interacting with the case studies and theoretical and other materials in this chapter. The assumption in the book is that a randomly selected case study can be the basis for learning if the issues concerned come from a given risk distribution. This idea of learning from case studies originates from the argument that in a continuum of cases with similar characteristics, a randomly selected case could be representative of the options available in similar cases.

The reader is introduced to risk-based approaches for defining and assessing policies. Scenario generation and analysis is introduced, along with examples from practice. A team of participants facing a common challenge would bring different perspectives to the table, allowing them to devise a better set of actions to handle emerging risks. This fifth module is intended to sharpen the skill of co-sensing the key risks and co-creating strategies and actions that could serve as a prototype for handling the challenge. The role of scenarios and testing of prototypes takes on importance, as do learning from others and learning from failure. For risk management, it is important to have at least three potential scenarios, usually referred to as a base case, worse case, and best case. In this fifth module, emphasis is placed on defining such scenarios within a dialogue with multiple stakeholders as an aid to better refining the identification of risks relevant to each scenario, or shaping strategies within a scenario to better manage a given set of risks.

Setting priorities is also covered in the module through guiding questions to ensure that learners spend time on the outcomes that matter most (cost, speed, attribution). By drawing from co-sensing the substance and people, leaders can put together a prioritized set of actions and assign roles, as well as develop a time line by which they would like to achieve their objectives. The most important question in this module is: What can be ignored or where can one afford to see failure?

From Theory U, the skill of "presencing" is of most relevance for developing scenarios that are risk-based, as it helps the decision-maker better understand the emerging future and its implications for risk. Interaction management is also emphasized in this module, drawing from complexity analysis concepts in order to refine scenarios that are risk-adjusted. Using complexity reasoning to define the interactions to expect and their implications for risks is an important lesson drawn in this module. Complexity reasoning also highlights the importance of identifying barriers or constraints (external or internal) or deciding where to create or enact barriers to prevent certain outcomes from materializing. Selection and payoffs can then be useful to define the types of actions and strategies to adapt as the outcomes approach pre-defined patterns. Examples are drawn from industry and policy actors who define risk-appetite statements as tools to manage risks; when limits are reached, a set of actions ensues which brings the risk down to a tolerable level.

What particular approaches are suitable for your specific context?

Finally, the sixth module brings it all together in the application to specific contexts. Leadership challenges vary with context. Approaches to understanding what is going on, developing appropriate responses, or even shaping a potential future are all context-specific. In this module we investigate what approaches are suitable for a particular circumstance. Three contexts are explored: industry, with examples particularly from the logistics industry using the cases of Philips and UPS; geography, with examples of systemic failure in the financial sector in Iceland; and policy, with application to decisions around investment and maintenance of large-scale complex infrastructure.

The logistics industry brings out interactions between tectonic change, risks, and potential outcomes. The special partnership between UPS and Philips introduces the learner to options for dealing with change when everything is connected to everything. Iceland and the financial crisis are used to detail the dimensions from interacting geographies. The case brings out a snapshot of the reality that Iceland was facing just before the crisis and investigates the linkages with other countries through the lens of contagion in the financial sector. The sentiment of non-state actors before the crisis is used to determine what may have been shifting at one level of society but was not detected at another level. Questions around whether co-sensing could have helped predict the outcomes that emerged are considered. The case also brings out the implications and recommendations for learners should they face similar challenges. Investments in large-scale infrastructure are very relevant to bring out the challenges of leadership in changing policy contexts. Concepts of complexity are applied to deferred maintenance – a phenomenon rarely considered when leaders take decisions around complex infrastructure. Operational definitions of deferred maintenance help the learner see what ignorance of the concept can do in generating risks and the methodological challenges of managing such risks once they have materialized. Instruments for controlling deferred maintenance risks and their implications for leadership in other areas are also covered.

A special section is dedicated to the science of muddling through and the potential it has for leadership when very little is known and judgment is at a premium. Learning from failure is critical, and a section of this chapter uses examples to uncover important elements. Resilience and how leaders gain comfort with the concept is covered, as resilience strategies are context-sensitive. The chapter ends with a practice block preparing leaders to embody and prepare for superior performance. The module rounds up the last segment of Theory U, where the learner focuses on the skills needed to perform effectively on a daily basis. The module brings together lessons from previous learning modules.

Using the book in real life

This book was written for academics and practitioners. It provides practice blocks and learning guides and can be used for further research or for choice making in real-life situations.

Part I, particularly the section on identifying patterns of change in the various spheres, would be very useful when handling a context that is undergoing tremendous change. If your situation requires understanding of what is changing as a result of globalization and its impact on your practice and the practices of others, the approach to downloading used in Part I would be particularly useful.

To be effective at uncovering the causes of change in your decision environment, Part II and its practice block would be particularly useful. Reading the Jamuna Case Study and seeing what the complexities of interaction are could also help a great deal in identifying the areas of analysis and process for decision-making that are the most useful to apply. A process of seeking the perceptions and perspectives of others that are critical for decision-making can be learned and applied from the practice block in this chapter.

For a good understanding of the principles of complexity and how to use them for your day-to-day decision-making, focus on Part III, as the issues raised and their link to analysis are very useful for general application. If the complexity you are interested in relates to practice and policy, then the SARS case study is a good one to read. This part of the book is also good for learning the skills of empathizing and sensing the future as it emerges.

Risk management approaches and their application can be gained from Part IV and those interested in governance issues can focus on Part V. To see how the theory and its application changes from one context to another Part VI is key.

Concluding thoughts

What to do when everything is connected to everything

The story of Simon Compaoré and the challenges he faced as Mayor of Ouagadougou during a period of tremendous change opened this chapter. So how did he handle the challenges? As Mayor, he had to balance the vast priorities of the citizens, both local residents and foreign nationals, who flocked to the capital. Decisions needed to be made about how many and what type of schools to build, as well as where. Choices were needed on priorities for hospitals and clinics, policing, firefighting, garbage collection, roads, and other public services. All these services and choices needed to be made within a limited budget. At the end of office in 2012, he had managed to raise CFA 18 billion (USD 35 million) from taxes as well as other sources, including external resources from outside Burkina Faso. To achieve a strategic plan that is understood by the citizens, adopted by the municipal council, and funded by the central government and external aid, requires deep skills.

Simon Compaoré harnessed such skills from a lifetime of learning, including in his role as Secretary General of a political party called the Congress for Democracy and Progress, as a member of parliament in the National Assembly, and in his years as President of the Association of Mayors of Burkina Faso. But his experience also came from lessons learned and networks created as the Treasurer for the International Association of Francophone Mayors and as the host for the CIFAL (Centre International de Formation des Acteurs Locaux), which is a learning network of the mayors from 24 francophone countries. The Mayor harnessed technical and financial partnerships to develop management and implementation capacity at the municipal level. As such, the form of the city, in terms of its infrastructure networks, style of housing as a result of zoning regulations, and flow of activity, took on the character of a globalizing city during this period (see Södeström et al., 2009 and Guggenheim and Södeström, 2010 for a detailed analysis of the transformations that Ouagadougou went through as a result of increased interconnectivity from globalization since the 1990s).

I learned from my experience, he says, that it is important to ensure there is trust in the leadership of the municipality, that you can develop a strategy and plan that would meet the priorities of citizens and get the plan and budget approved by the municipal council, as well as meet expectations of central government. To receive support from multilateral and bilateral agencies and attain financing from the private sector, you also have to be able to convince them about the feasibility and value of your plan. You have to have tremendous will to get things done and see things change, but you also have to be open to learning from others, locally and internationally, to be successful, he adds. The Mayor also highlighted that his approach was to see things from the point of view of an evolving portfolio that can be revised with changes in priorities and availability of financing, but also to address emerging issues and adapt to challenges and shocks. As such, he would have found it useful to have the capacity to define and manage a series of alternate scenarios. He had to do a great deal of adjustment many times – in order to handle the unprecedented flooding that hit Ouagadougou on September 1, 2009, for example. The level of flooding was so severe that nearly 25,000 dwelling houses collapsed, with 150,000 victims and eight deaths.[7] Such flood levels had not been seen since 1919. The city had to call for international aid and asked the Burkinabé Diaspora for help.

This book is rich with examples from decision-making that which cover a full array of sectors and countries, exposing the reader to a variety of applications in each chapter. The reader will find examples from transport logistics, exporting companies, water management, and agricultural production. At the geographical levels, leadership challenges in cities, countries, and regions are also introduced with a variety of illustrations. Finally, examples of policies and their application in economies, within sectors or in dealing with deferred maintenance decisions, are included as learning materials and contexts. Singular importance is given to participation and democracy processes.

I have found it very helpful in the various leadership positions I have held to extract immediate lessons from a situation. This is best done through a set of guiding questions that can be used in practice as self-evaluation questions. I have included such questions in the book with the aim of helping the reader sharpen self-knowledge (what you know and how you download what they know). Investigation and interaction with data and patterns most often relates to logical and analytical capacity. In this book I have also put emphasis on learning how to communicate, which is in the realm of emotion and behavior. Self-evaluation is useful as a complement to materials in the different chapters of the book and can guide day-to-day practice.

A set of guiding questions can help a reader practice. There is a start-up set at the end of each module for practice at each of the stages of leadership. In the first module the case of Monsanto is used to walk the reader through the skills of observing and downloading from the past. The questions help the reader interact with the tectonic changes that have been introduced and develop reactions based on observing what is taking place and downloading from past knowledge and experience.

The modules can be taken together or separately. It is critical is for the reader to identify which part of the "U" they are on in Theory U, and what lessons need to be taken to learn new ways of doing and unlearn old ways. As Simon Compaoré reflected in his reminiscing about the lessons he learned, it is important to have a starting point, or a benchmark, that guides you to see not only how you are doing in bringing others along, and listening to them, but co-creating a common future that can be delivered with visible results. All this while adapting to the challenges that uncertainty brings your way.

Expected learning outcomes include facility in interacting with information from multiple sources, dealing with diverse people and situations, and handling oneself in complex settings. I hope that the book will provide readers with the materials they need but also with the motivation to lead in a different way.

1
Setting the Stage

Key Lessons from Chapter 1: Setting the Stage

This chapter introduces the main spheres, observed patterns, drivers, and locus of change taking place. Detailed illustration is given of the four main spheres of change— people, resources, economy, and technology. Key patterns covered in the people sphere relate to demographic changes (youth, aging, population growth, urbanization, and migration). In the resources sphere patterns of change in water, food, energy, and environmental systems are given special attention. In economics, the focus is on change at the country and global levels such as in finance, trade, and integration of economies and societies, but also at the individual and firm levels as in patterns of production, sourcing, sales, and branding. The patterns of change in the technology sphere appearing in this chapter relate to knowledge, science, experience, and innovation.

The main skills introduced are reacting to tectonic change, using the first stage of Theory U of downloading and observing patterns and trends. A case study of the Monsanto Company highlights the decision-making and choices of a multinational company facing tectonic changes in all four spheres. Lessons from the case are used to draw issues of importance. The reader is guided through practice questions that aid using the material for similar situations.

Introduction

Decision-making in a complex environment relies on a specific set of abilities. Critical amongst them is uncovering the basic elements that could influence the outcome of actions. Once the basic elements have been uncovered, it is important to observe and interpret their response or behavior preceding and following a particular action. Such understanding, particularly of the interconnections between key elements, forms an important input into the decision-making process that allows decision makers to function in a complex environment.

Bennet and Bennet (2008) argue that in any complex system there are trends and patterns that may be observed. However, such trends are often hidden or may be enmeshed with other factors in such a manner as to be imperceptible. Furthermore, delayed effects may render it impossible to see what may be happening to another element that is interconnected but not visible at first blush. Such complexities may combine the independent effects of changes into one element, making observation of the behavior of specific elements difficult to disentangle. The complexity of decision-making can be reduced if the decision maker can be guided through a set of questions or considerations that help to sequence decisions and actions, leading toward an acceptable solution (Bennet and Bennet, 2008).

The first question to guide the decision maker on the main trends in globalization is: *What are the principal patterns of shifts taking place and what types of discontinuities do they generate?* The question is aimed at highlighting the global discontinuities created by the shifting patterns one can observe. While many things are changing as the world continues to become interconnected, there are three factors to keep in mind: the *spheres* of change, the *drivers* of change, and the *locus* of change. It is by observing these factors that the "tectonic shifts" that have an impact on the decisions and actions taken in the face of globalization may be detected.

This module emphasizes the impact that patterns of change have on critical decisions and the pitfalls when decisions are made on the basis of only what is observable. The skill practiced is improving the ability to react effectively to tectonic change based on observations of what is happening around you. Particular emphasis is placed on guiding the reader through what is changing, what patterns can be discerned, and how changes are interconnected. A case study from Monsanto is used to establish the interconnectedness of decisions and choices, and the impacts created outside of the sphere of influence of the major decision makers. A set of potential reactions by different groups is provided as a response to the complexities of changes in the global food supply chain.

Spheres, drivers, and locus of change

There are four main spheres in which to interpret what is going on around us—people, resources, technology, and economy. Drucker (1992) refers to four main forces creating shifts in the ways that economies and societies function: the role of new *technology* and the emergence of the knowledge worker; major changes in the *economy* and the appearance of multinational corporations and their role around the world; the importance of the variety of institutions needed to solve issues impacting *people*; and the use of *resources*. Fariboz and Peterson (2005) sharply highlighted the implications of changes in these four spheres for the strategy and actions of CEOs and leaders in the business sector. This chapter brings together all these threads, which have featured in management philosophy over two decades, to apply them in the public sector and public policy making.

People have long been the main sphere in which change has been visible historically. Measures of change include population growth, as people choose to have more or fewer children; migration patterns based on where people choose to live; aging and youth patterns driven by advances in medicine and health care; urbanization patterns, visible in the level of agglomeration of population in concentrated spaces; and the changes in the disease burden as a result of lifestyle and environmental factors. The person (people as a collective) is the main object of the "social technology" presented in Theory U (Scharmer, 2007: 377–442). It involves using the skills of listening to others with the mind and heart, reflection, and inner knowing, and seeing from the perspectives of others as well as acting with others in an adaptive sense. Such skills are important when facing tremendous change and when imagining a future that has not yet come about. All the questions around fertility, migration, urbanization, disease burden, and environmental factors revolve around individual choices and collective action. Being able to co-initiate policies, co-evolve visions of the future and co-create a set of actions to realize that future is critical and relies on skills learned from Theory U.

Societal choices around preservation, conservation, and use also change over time with impacts on the people sphere. The level of available *resources* in the future, such as water, food, and energy, as well as the friendliness of the climate for human existence, all vary with past patterns of use. Challenges like travel congestion and air quality in a city, which were previously local problems, become global problems when the drivers for travel are orders to deliver shirts from Dhaka in Bangladesh to Los Angeles in the US. Being able to connect the dots, listen, and engage in dialogue with stakeholders involved in the various parts of the interconnected world of using and interacting with resources is an important skill. One can learn from Theory U (Scharmer, 2007: 380–381) how such skills can help evolve global compacts to transform companies to become more socially and environmentally sustainable.

Technology advances and choices are another key sphere of change that is of relevance when observing globalization. What is the level of knowledge being used in a given economy? How are science and technology featuring in a given location or across a set of players? What sorts of experiences are embedded in the processes and products being used by a given society? All of these questions relate to the sphere of technology and its implications as the world globalizes. The skills to innovate across systems require joint leadership of international organizations, global companies, civil society organizations, and individuals. In Theory U this requires leaders (CEOs, executives in the public, private, and civil sectors) to be committed to lead differently and to be equipped with the requisite skills to know what lies ahead of them and how to respond to the challenges ahead (Scharmer, 2007: 381).

Perhaps the sphere most looked at is the *economy*; whether it is in the finance and financial systems, or the degree of trade across societies and how integrated it is, or even in the patterns of production and product sourcing and their link to the evolution of brands and patterns of sales across companies. The economic sphere is perhaps the one receiving the most attention in political choices, as the effects tend to be visible over shorter periods of time. In Theory U, the concept of a global economy that works as a single unit raises many questions that require thinking and acting together in a different way (Scharmer, 2007: 81–104). Innovations that cause discontinuities in how companies behave (net-shaped industries), ethical issues concerning technology and science (e.g. genetic engineering, nanotechnology), and the globalization of governance (World Trade Organization (WTO), World Bank and International Monetary Fund (IMF)), all rely on the ability to co-exist, co-develop, and co-evolve.

The four spheres of change arise as a result of six drivers. The first is the emergence of *logistics* as a turning point in economic and business outcomes, producing both opportunities for success and added risks. Logistics management, as defined by Cooper et al. (1997) is "the process of planning, implementing, and controlling the efficient, cost-effective flow and storage of raw materials, in-process inventory, finished goods, and related information flow from point-of-origin to point-of-consumption for the purposes of conforming to customer requirements." Such capabilities have made it possible for firms, consumers, governments, and civil society to operate in ways that were not possible previously.

Increased *mobility and connectivity* is the second driver, responsible for producing further pressures on productivity. This is mainly due to the simultaneous morphing and divergence of preferences. Consumer behavior differs across countries as a result of national culture, making it necessary for global firms to be conscious of this divergence and to serve these markets in a differentiated manner (de Mooij and Hofstede, 2002). The forces of globalization, such as access to common information instantly through social media, on the other hand, could create a sort of "global consumer," leading to homogeneous consumer needs, tastes, and lifestyles (Bullmore, 2000: 48). The driver of mobility and connectivity can help uncover the reason for observing certain trends in consumption patterns, environmental preferences, or indeed global governance outcomes. Such knowledge is useful for international retailers, but also for regulators and trade negotiators. Using the skills of co-sensing from the field from Theory U can help decision makers who are developing strategy to be better able to anticipate these changes and deal with them in an effective manner (Scharmer, 2007: 133–136).

The third driver relates to *ownership and financing* arrangements, which are creating new risks but also opportunities. In particular, complex financing arrangements generate large information asymmetries between the sources and users of finance, which could lead to an escalation in the level of risks with limited options for mitigation (Sufi, 2007). The motivation for anticipating risky behavior comes from models of agency and moral hazard (Holmstrom and Tirole, 1997) that assume that firms with limited public information require due diligence and monitoring by an "informed lender." But as the "informed lender's" effort is unobservable, the informed lender is forced to retain a larger share of the loan precisely when the borrower requires more intense due diligence and monitoring effort relative to when the borrower does not require such intense effort. Ownership and financing arrangements at a global scale, with more and more stakeholders involved, requiring different levels of due diligence, can generate a very complex web of interactions and interrelations, rendering the systems under-regulated. The risks of such complexity have materialized in the various financial crises that have been seen in the 21st century in particular. In Theory U, the skills needed to anticipate and indeed handle the risk structures that materialize from global capital are related to addressing root questions around equitable societies, more democratic institutions, and cultural sensitivity (Scharmer, 2007: 95).

Interconnectedness is the fourth driver, which puts a premium on the interaction between *knowledge and culture*. Global companies interact with different cultures as they source, produce, and sell around the world, having an impact on culture as well as responding to it, especially in the retail sector (Mooij and Hofstede, 2002). The use of pesticides and genetically modified seeds relies on the interaction between culture and science, which varies from one place to another. In this book, the focus is on the aspect of personal mastery (the use of dialogue as a change method), building from Theory U to handle conflicts and engage in joint inquiry on the issues impacting societies (Scharmer, 2007: 91).

The fifth driver is the evolution of key *risks* affecting decision-making around the world, raising the need for effective tools for risk management. These are the increased financial risks due to information asymmetry, but also increased risks of conjoined failure of financial systems due to the integration of banking and other financial systems. Risks have also evolved to become more severe, with a crisis in one country impacting another. Contamination from diseases as a result of travel also can portend higher risk. Understanding the evolution of risks is a skill that can be helpful as the complexity of decision-making environments increases.

Finally, the growing demands for *ethical and accountable leadership* across the world (even more so after the 2008 global financial crisis) are a driver which links up many of the other drivers, with important interactions on all four spheres of change.

Corporate leaders, politicians, and civil society influencers thus operate in a complex interconnected world. The degree of interconnectedness affects not only how they make decisions, but the outcomes of their decisions as well. Making decisions on the basis of what is observable (surface phenomena) can lead to costly mistakes and irreversible effects. Understanding the dynamics is necessary for shaping strategy, developing effective risk management approaches, and selecting from a series of potential courses of action. Yet the dynamics can be complex, and not all options can be known in advance. Methods for dealing with partial information become necessary. The locus of decision-making also changes, with increased interconnections amongst societies rendering choice making more complex.

The good news is that complexity can be observed and harnessed (Bar-Yam, 1997), and understanding complexity is the key to managing risks. Leaders need to be conversant with the behavior of interconnected systems to make effective decisions under varying strategic and risk scenarios. Leaders also need to be equipped with the right set of values and behaviors to be successful in a specific context.

Patterns of change

The ability to observe change is a key aspect that distinguishes successful leaders from less successful ones. Making good choices usually comes from the responses to a simple question: what are the principal patterns of shift taking place? While the question is simple, the answers and the process for exploring the range of potential answers are not. The patterns that most affect decision-making on a global scale derive from four major spheres of change, introduced in the last chapter.

People: population, aging, migration, urbanization, and disease patterns

The starting point for understanding patterns of change is the sphere related to people. Where and how fast population levels are changing are important, but such changes need to be further viewed in the context of aging patterns and the dependency of the young and old on the working population. The growth in the number of young people, often referred to as a "youth bulge," is a determinant of many related changes, not least of which is the creativity of a society. The risks of conflict may be serious, as when disenfranchised people organize to get change and cause a revolution, as the young people of North Africa did in early 2010.

Where people move to and why is also an important sphere, as migration has a "brain drain" effect if skilled people leave their countries of origin. But migration can also have a benefit if people send money home as remittances. Where people live and the size of settlements they create determine the level of urbanization, including whether settlements are connected to other agglomerations around the world (global connectivity) and how fast cities grow. Patterns and trends in communicable diseases also change with the concentration of people in densely populated areas, which can be the source not only of the spread and speed of infection and contamination, but also of the risk of emergence or reemergence of diseases.

Consider the patterns of population growth and distribution character-ized by the explosion in global population in the last 200 years. Asia has historically been home to the majority of the people in the world (65% in 1800) and is projected to remain so in the near future (57% in 2050). However, Africa is expected to double its share from 11% in 1800 to 22% in 2050. Europe will see its share of world population drop from 21% in 1800 to just over 7% in 2050.

The main question for leadership relates to the capacity to tap into the creative potential of a younger and more concentrated population in regions such as Africa, where the population growth rates are also growing.

The patterns of growth across continents also raise the question of manag-ing the twin challenges of creating jobs and securing food for larger popula-tions, particularly if population growth outstrips the capacity to employ and feed the growing population. Patterns of growth present challenges such as how leaders will deal with the aging and declining population levels (say in Japan and Germany). The balance of power also shifts with the changes in population concentration across the world.

Where people are, or their spatial distribution in a given geography, is also an important pattern to observe. In Africa, the majority of people are con-centrated along the coastal areas and in the central belt from Cameroon to Mozambique. Such a pattern is great for interaction with the outside world through ocean shipping, but presents risks should sea levels rise.

Changes in climate patterns interact with how populations are distrib-uted. Where people and activity are concentrated also matters. The capacity to manage cities and communes at the decentralized level, while at the same time integrating people across regional commons such as water and other natural resources, is stretched when populations are growing unevenly and people are becoming more mobile.

Observing the spatial distribution of populations is important for many decisions in an increasingly globalized world. Where people are going, and the flows of people into and out of specific regions, countries, and spaces, are also relevant when looking at global trends. Patterns of migration have changed over the years as a result of a shift in the reasons to migrate.[1] Prior to 1930 there was strong regulation of migration in most countries and peo-ple moved mostly to look for jobs. Another reason for migration at the time was the search for land for agriculture, with migration mostly across short distances. After the Second World War there was a big effort to recruit guest workers for post-war reconstruction in Europe. Barriers to entering a coun-try were lowered to allow for such migration. After 1973, migration became mostly poverty-driven, from developing to developed nations. Skilled workers were welcomed, but concerns were raised about the increase in unskilled labor and its implications for labor policy and employment.

Table 1.1 Migration stocks and flows

Countries	International migrant stock, total in 2010	International migrant stock, % of population in 2010
Brazil	688,026	0.36
China	685,775	0.05
India	5,436,012	0.47
Japan	2,176,219	1.70
South Africa	1,862,889	3.80

Source: World Bank (2010): World Development Indicators 2010, International Bank for Reconstruction and Development/The World Bank, Washington D.C.

The patterns of migration changed in the 1990s as new pressures developed across the world. Two measures are important when looking at migration—the share and the stock of migrants (see Table 1.1). The top five countries with the highest share of international migrants in 2010 were Qatar (87%), Kuwait (73%), Monaco (72%), UAE (70%), and Andorra (65%). These are countries that largely depend on international migration to meet domestic labor needs and resemble the migration-for-employment trends of the 1950s. In absolute terms, however, the top five countries with the highest stock of international migrants in 2010 were the USA (42.8 m), Russia (12.2 m), Germany (10.8 m), Saudi Arabia (7.3 m), and Canada (7.2 m).

When people leave their home countries they bring in new ideas, skills, and resources, but they also keep connections with the old country. Such connections become more and more valuable in a globalized world, as can be seen by the interaction between trade and migration. When the changes in trade patterns are measured by the growth in exports and changes in migration links to the home country are measured by growth in remittances, a pattern emerges which distinguishes countries that have strong growth in both exports and remittances (Cameroon in the early 2000s) and those that have declines in both trade and remittances (Chad in the early 2000s). Two other groups of countries emerge—those with growth in exports but decline in remittances (Burkina Faso in the early 2000s) and those with declining exports but growth in remittances (Angola in the early 2000s).

How long people live and how many children they have, when they start working, and when they retire are patterns that are important to observe for many global decisions.

Indicators like the age dependency ratio, which measures the share of people who are dependent on those who are of working age, can be helpful in tracking the changing patterns of aging and youth. The working age population needs to earn and generate more to support the dependent population in countries that have high age dependency ratios, or there have to be effective safety nets for those not able to do so. High age dependency ratios are also important indicators of potential future booms as younger people come into the job market with creative ideas, but they can spell trouble if there are not sufficient opportunities for employment. Organizing to deal with an aging population is also a challenge for countries that have a high age dependency ratio that is driven by increasing life expectancy.

Spatial distribution of people in cities around the world shapes many other decisions and is important to observe (see Table 1.2). Agglomerations of people have always been good predictors of where the next innovations will come from or the next set of risks. Migration in the past 2,000 years has mostly favored people moving to cities rather than other rural areas, yet there is a growing trend for people in advanced economies, particularly in Europe, to favor migrating to smaller towns for a better quality of life. Before the 1950s the majority of people who lived in cities were in countries that were developed. By the 1990s that pattern had shifted to where the majority of city residents were in developing countries. The distance between cities is an important indicator when looking at the spatial distribution of population, as is the degree of connectivity of urban zones to the rest of the world.

Patterns of population agglomeration and density are also important because of the spread of diseases. Changes in population concentration and increased mobility impact the emergence and reemergence of infectious diseases throughout the world. Morens et al. (2004) highlighted the patterns of emerging and re-emerging infectious diseases throughout the world. Newly emerging diseases are mostly from North America, such as cycloporiasis, E. coli, hepatitis C, and Whitewater arroyo virus; from Asia, such as SARS and H5N1 influenza; and Africa, such as HIV. Re-emerging or resurgent diseases are mainly from Latin America (dengue fever, yellow fever, and cholera); Africa (cholera, ebola hemorrhage fever, plague, and drug-resistant malaria); and Asia (diphtheria, typhoid fever, and drug resistant malaria). Some diseases, such as multidrug-resistant tuberculosis, are re-emerging in all regions of the world due to travel and increased interaction. Morens et al. (2004)

Table 1.2 Spatial distribution and concentration of population by type of economy

Level of development	Number of countries with large urban populations		
	1950	2000	2030
Advanced economies	11	9	7
Developing countries	17	25	21
Share in advanced economies (%)	65	36	33

Note: Share calculations by author.
Source: Data from United Nations (2011).

also have a category called "deliberately emerging diseases," such as anthrax bioterrorism, which emerged in North America.

The proximity of people to animals is responsible for the added risks of animal-to-human transmission of diseases, but can also have positive effects on immune systems. Successfully assessing the risk of communicable diseases is a key enabler in building readiness for handling emerging diseases and responding dynamically to the data and treatment needs of various risks. There are a number of maps of hotspots for emerging and reemerging communicable diseases that are useful for making important decisions globally, especially around preventing pandemics.

Resources: water, food, energy, and environment sustainability

The distribution of water and how the existing resources are used and managed is a key dimension under the resources sphere of change. Most freshwater in developing countries is used for agriculture. Increases in irrigation of land put more pressure on water resources. When food production rises faster than population growth it may reduce the frequency of famine or persistency of chronic undernourishment. The patterns of water use across the world and their relation to the production and availability of food remains a key aspect of observation for decision makers.

The availability, efficiency of consumption, and sources of energy generation are also areas to pay attention to in terms of patterns of change. During the period 1990 to 2008, China registered a 20% growth rate per year in electric power consumption per person. During the same time period, India registered a 5.6% growth in per capita consumption of electric power (see Table 1.3).

Brazil nearly doubled its per capita consumption of energy, recording a growth rate of 2.1% per year. During this same period, South Africa, which has a higher per capita consumption of energy than China, Brazil, and India, registered a modest increase of 0.3% per year. Increases in the consumption of electric power result from improvements in the standards of living in these countries and are expected to grow as the numbers of people in the middle class in developing countries grow. China registered a high growth averaging 15.9% per year for 30 years (see Table 1.4).

Table 1.3 Electric power consumption (kilo-watt hour per capita)

Year	Brazil	China	India	South Africa
1990	1,457	511	275	4,431
2000	1,897	993	400	4,361
2010	2,384	2,944	616	4,803
Annual growth rate 1990–2010	2.1%	15.9%	4.1%	0.3%

Source: World Bank (2012): World Development Indicators Report 2012, International Bank for Reconstruction and Development/ World Bank, Washington D.C.

Table 1.4   Electric power transmission and distribution losses (% output)

Year	Brazil	China	India	South Africa
1990	14	7	20	6
2000	18	7	28	8
2010	17	6	22	10

Source: World Bank (2012): World Development Indicators Report 2012, International Bank for Reconstruction and Development/ World Bank, Washington D.C.

Changes in the pattern of electric power use in a given country can also be a good indicator of the changes in the modes of production or advances in science and technology. The efficiency and effectiveness of different systems of management can also be detected in the pattern of electric power transmission and distribution losses. Countries like Brazil and South Africa saw a deterioration in the efficiency of their electricity distribution systems in the 30 years between 1990 and 2010, while China was able to remain in single digit losses as a share of electricity produced. India managed to reverse runaway losses that had peaked at 28% in 2000 from 20% in 1990, bringing the losses down to 22% by 2010.

Water, food, and energy are sensitive to changes in climate and choices in technology. The level of use and renewability of water and energy feature in decisions around how sustainable development can be. As the world globalizes and these resources become scarce, the countries and regions that have these resources will have an advantage over those that do not.

Observing the impacts of changes in climatic and weather patterns is a key area impacting global decision-making, as vulnerability to change is a key aspect of risk and, in some cases, opportunity. Africa is a continent facing upside risks related to changes in weather and climatic patterns. Such changes impact mostly the coastal and central regions of the continent, which is where the majority of people live. The observed effects include desertification, deforestation and loss of forest quality, coral bleaching, coastal erosion, and sea level rises, as well as the spread of weather-sensitive diseases like malaria (Balance, 2002).

Economic: finance, trade, integration, production, sourcing, sales and branding

Economic integration has been taking place over centuries. Four key indicators usually measure the level and depth of integration. The first important marker of change in this sphere comes from the relations between firms and people in the trading and commercial relations across countries.

The second is the presence of goods and products that are sold and branded globally or across a wide set of countries. A third marker captures the spread or concentration of production and sourcing locations for a

Table 1.5 Geographical patterns of the top five highest real GDP growth rates in 2010 compared to those in 2009, ranked in decreasing order of 2010 growth rates

Country	Year		Span (change from 2010 to 2009) (%)
	2009 (%)	2010 (%)	
Mongolia	−1.6	12.8	14.4
China	9.1	9.5	0.4
India	9.1	8.1	−1.0
Mozambique	6.3	7.8	1.5
Ethiopia	8.7	7.7	−1.0

Source: IMF Data available at http://www.imf.org/external/data.htm.

variety of firms, which globalizes the process of production and marketing. The final marker relates to finance and the interrelationship between financial systems, including their degree of integration.

The outcome of interactions between these four markers is visible in the geographic pattern of production around the world. Looking at data from 2009 and 2010 (see Table 1.5), which is the period just after the 2008 financial crisis, one can illustrate the pattern of real GDP growth rates across a range of countries. Two subsets of data are of particular interest for discerning patterns—the top five countries with the highest real GDP growth rates in 2010 (representing the fast movers) and the bottom five countries with the lowest GDP growth rates in 2010 (representing the slower movers). The interest in these tail-behaviors comes from a model in the science of complexity known as the "punctuated equilibrium model," which assumes that long periods of small, incremental change are interrupted by brief periods of discontinuous radical change as a result of technological discontinuities (Rosenkopf and Tushman, 1998; Tushman and Anderson, 1986).

A capacity to sustain significant growth patterns over time is a key aspect that distinguishes one country from another, even as all countries are impacted by a global economic slowdown. The long-run patterns of growth and behavior immediately after a shock are also important, as there is a relation between economic activities and the carrying capacity and resilience of the environment (Arrow et al., 1995). A lot can be learned from looking at changes between one year and another—surface phenomena—as well as looking at long run patterns of growth and their relation to environmental resources. Let us focus on the pattern of response to a shock in this analysis.

Mongolia reversed a declining growth pattern of −1.6% GDP growth rate in 2009 to a positive 12.8% in 2010 (see Table 1.6). A general pattern to note in the dynamics is that the period-to-period change is usually higher when coming from a low base, and it is usually harder to grow fast once very high

Table 1.6 Geographical patterns of the bottom five lowest real GDP growth rates in 2010 compared to those in 2009, ranked in increasing order of 2010 growth rates

Country	Year		Span (change from 2010 to 2009) (%)
	2009 (%)	2010 (%)	
Germany	−4.7	1.2	5.9
Italy	−5.0	1.3	6.3
Spain	−3.6	1.7	5.3
Japan	−5.2	1.7	6.9
Congo, Republic	2.7	1.9	4.6

Source: IMF Data available at http://www.imf.org/external/data.htm.

growth levels have been attained. China, for instance, registered a 0.4% gain between 2009 and 2010, compared to Mozambique which showed a 1.5% gain and Mongolia a 14.4% gain.

The pattern holds for both the top fastest growing countries and bottom slowest growing countries, as can be seen when comparing Italy and Japan to Germany, Spain, and Congo. The patterns in trade over time are also a good marker of the level of economic integration. They indicate the differential capacity to transform primary products, manage complex supply chains, and negotiate appropriate trade agreements.

The pattern of exports in the wool value chain provides us with an example to explore the aggregate impact of firm-level changes and country policies on the outcomes in the long run. Compare the export values from 1994 to 2010 of the top ten exporting countries in the wool value chain. Two components of the value chain are relevant—wool that is not carded or combed; and woven wool and wool fabrics. Observe in particular the short run pattern between 1994 and 2004 and compare it to the longer run pattern between 1994 and 2010. In the short run, countries like the UK have succeeded in increasing their exports of un-carded and un-combed wool, going from ninth-ranked exporter in 1994 to number six in 2004. However, the UK could not keep up its position, sliding back to number eight in 2010. While the UK struggled in the area of exporting un-carded and un-combed wool, it managed to maintain its fifth position in the exports of woven wool and wool fabrics throughout the 15-year period of 1994 to 2010 (see Table 1.7).

Italy on the other hand, with a small role in "wool, not carded or combed," was able to maintain its number one position in the value of exports from wool and woven fabrics in the short and long run. Such patterns belie a lot change and decisions at the firm, country, and global level, including the role played by brands. The patterns are also related to the pattern of resource use in the country concerned and the potential effect it has on the use of

Table 1.7 Top ten wool exporters 1994–2010 by value (US$ 000)

Wool, not carded or combed			Wool, woven fabrics		
1994	2004	2010	2001	2004	2010
Australia	Australia	Australia	Italy	Italy	Italy
New Zealand	New Zealand	New Zealand	Japan	China	China
Argentina	South Africa	South Africa	Germany	Germany	Germany
South Africa	Germany	Germany	China	Japan	Japan
Kazakhstan	Argentina	Argentina	UK	UK	UK
Russia	UK	Uruguay	France	Hong Kong	Turkey
Uruguay	France	China	Spain	France	Czech Rep
France	USA	UK	Hong Kong	Turkey	France
UK	Italy	Spain	Turkey	Spain	Spain
Ireland	Uruguay	Belgium	Korea, Rep	Czech Rep	Portugal

Source: FAO, Statistics of Food and Agricultural Trade (2007) and ITC Trade Statistics (2010).

natural resources such as land, water, and forests and the ensuing pattern of pollutants and contaminants released into the environment.

Picking up what is changing is a good starting point to investigate the deeper changes taking place within the said sphere (in this case economy) and across others spheres (people, resources, and technology) as they interact with a given sphere. What matters in understanding the implications of these patterns is the content of growth—not only the inputs of sheep and wool into the production process by firms that result in a volume of production by a firm in a country, but also the preferences of consumers packaged in a brand that show up in the pattern of exports from a given country. All these factors are important and all this information can be seen in the pattern of change at the economy level of a system of interaction. Following all the changes that are visible in the sphere of the economy means not only following the composition of the inputs, but also that of outputs (including waste products). As Arrow et al. (1995) state: "This content (of economic growth) is determined by among, other things, the economic institutions within which human activities are conducted. These institutions need to be designed so that they provide the right incentives for protecting the resilience of ecological systems." How these patterns interact is the subject of the next chapter, where the subject of dynamics of change is covered.

Among the incentive types that impact on behavior is the question of brands. Brands have long been used to distinguish products but also to signal unique value to the consumer. There are theories that link purchasing behavior to information garnered from brands (see, for example, Howard and Sheth, 1969). Analyzing the pattern of brands can help uncover important interactions within the spheres of people, economy, and technology. An analysis of the top 100 brands in use today indicates that the oldest brand is a beer made in 1664, which holds the name of the year it was made. The youngest brands are in mobile communications and motor fuel. Most of the top brands in 2012 are either American or European, but significant inroads have been made by emerging markets in the areas of beer (Mexico) and financial institutions (China and India). Brands have been the subject of much study and have been used to send all sorts of signals. Civil society groups have put pressure on the responsibility of brands, as have the media. Consider an article in the *Guardian*, posted in a blog on September 16, 2011, that argues for luxury brands to wake up to their ethical and environmental responsibility (Birch, 2011 07.00 BST). Looking at how long brands have been around is a pattern that signal resilience and ability to change.

Changes in the sectoral contribution to the economy are also an important marker distinguishing countries and regions of the world as policy choices are made and the impacts of integration felt. Compare Botswana and Colombia. According to the UN statistics for 2010, the share of travel services to overall trade in services was 13.03% in Botswana and 13.77% in Colombia. However, Colombia had a much higher contribution from transportation services of 46.86% compared to Botswana at 40.32%. Communications services in Botswana at 6.63% were higher than in Colombia with 4.49%. Differences in the composition of the service sector could have very significant effects on other spheres, such as whether young people can start up a service business after graduation from school. They also vary depending on the structure of the economy—whether agrarian, manufacturing, service, or knowledge—as we will see in subsequent sections of the book.

The reason for the difference across countries can be as varied as the cost of doing business and its consequences for the start-up of certain types of business, or the pattern of demand in a country favoring a different bundle of goods. When demand patterns across countries are linked, as when preferences for the same brand dominate across countries, or when production is outsourced, all these micro effects gain relevance that they would not do in a less interconnected sphere.

Technology: knowledge, science, experience, and innovation

Technology and knowledge form the sphere that has had the most profound impact on decision-making throughout history. The use of knowledge in day-to-day activities has never been as high as it is today, causing a number of thinkers to coin the term the "knowledge economy" (see Drucker, 1992). The term is used to refer to the production and management of knowledge in firms, or by individuals, but is also used to refer to the use of knowledge itself to create jobs and increase incomes or economic value.

As such, the term "knowledge economy" is closely linked to science, technology, and innovation. The speed at which discoveries are made and rendered economically valuable is another sphere of change in a globalized world, with serious implications for decision-making. The other dimension in the knowledge sphere is more directly related to the consumer, the user, and the firm and the specific experiences they would like, have had, or would want to create, respectively. It is related to knowledge from a very special and distinct sense—the knowledge that comes from experience, practice, or deep understanding and skill.

The concept of the "knowledge economy" has gained more recognition in the sphere of global decision-making from comparisons of the development trajectories—such as between South Korea and Ghana, which had the same level of per capita income when they achieved independence in the 1950s. The countries diverged significantly after that, causing analysts to query the reasons for the observed patterns of divergence. The generation of data and development of tools to better understand the factors driving changes in the knowledge economy was largely responsible for the big investments that were eventually made by countries in the area of information and communications technologies (ICTs). The World Bank took a lead in assessing knowledge economies (Chen and Dahlman, 2005).

Pritchett (2011) made the linkages between knowledge and development trajectories in his famous work on mimicry in development, where he argued why poor countries could not just mimic the things that work in rich countries and see themselves evolve into fully functional states. This type of analysis makes connections between evolution and institutional development, with the tendency of countries to adopt the semblance of good institutions and practices just as natural selection will favor insects that look like other more dangerous insects. Thus, external influence through knowledge and ideas that have worked in other places could cause such forms of isomorphic mimicry (Pritchett et al., 2010).

Pritchett et al. (2010) argue that country development trajectories are visible in their economic prosperity and levels of productivity. One could also see advancement in the level of administrative capacity in a country. How a country treats its citizens could also be observed to make assessments of how well a country is doing. Measures like the degree of social equality, tolerance for diversity, and environmental sustainability would all be indicators of how well a country is doing. Other measures could also include whether the polity represents the will of the citizens.

The link to the knowledge economy relates to incentives for learning, creativity, or innovation, which would lead to effective generation and use of ideas and enhance not only economic prosperity, but also productivity and the quality of public management. Having skilled people who not only create but also use knowledge effectively, including knowing what works and what doesn't, could make a big difference to the quality of administration. Having such people engaged and their talents utilized through consultation and participation for sustainable production depends on the desire for sustainability. For the polity to effectively represent the will of the people, you need organizations that can source local ideas, tap into the stock of global knowledge, and adapt and assimilate it to local contexts in a way that is not "isomorphic mimicry," but in a manner where the talents and perspectives of the citizens are linked to the contexts of application. Having an information infrastructure that facilitates dialogue and exchange, as well as the sharing of and access to ideas, is the final link that drives patterns of change in the knowledge sphere.

The link between information and knowledge can also be seen in the experience dimension. Experiences of a particular good or service are forms of "knowing" that are highly individual and contextualized. Where did the individual get to know about the product or service and where is it located now? Who else is consuming the product or service and do they "like" it or not as expressed in various social media platforms? How has the service been made possible by the advances in communication technologies? A coffee consumer at Starbucks has about the same experience, whether drinking the coffee in Seattle, Seoul, or Saigon. People who go to Starbucks go not only for coffee but also for the company, the ambience, and what it means to them. They share their experiences using social media and their views have an impact on what others do.

What and how people feel about a product or service as well as how they consume and trade it makes a difference in the price. A coffee cup consumed in a tourist hotel or at Starbucks costs more than when purchased at a Coffee Board or on the New York Stock Exchange. Pine and Gilmore (1999) had foreseen this phenomenon and coined the term "experience economy," which distinguishes countries and firms by the economic offering, type of economy, economic function, nature of offering, key attribute, method of supply, type of seller and buyer, and factors driving demand.

Pine and Gilmore (1999) classify decision makers by their ability to differentiate whether they are dealing with commodities, goods, services, or experiences. Producing coffee beans in Colombia puts you in the *commodity* realm, where you are handling players such as smallholder farmers who are extracting value from the land in an agrarian setting. The farmers could be selling their produce to a coffee board or to a series of small traders. Coffee boards could interact in commodity markets, where traders would be setting global prices, or they could sell to unique predetermined customers on the basis of long-term contracts. The key aspect of choice in such a realm is the characteristics of the coffee—Arabica or Robusta, AAA grade or other grade, and so on.

Roasting, grinding, and packaging coffee in a factory positions you in the *goods* area of influence, where you are dealing with industrial processes and functions to make a product that users would like. A coffee drinker would be able to distinguish one product from another and make choices to consume one brand over another. The production process is standardized to produce at scale and the producers inventory their final product. A coffee processing plant would be linked to a manufacturer of coffee and brands would distinguish themselves on specific features of the coffee they sell—drip coffee, instant, roasted beans, flavored beans, and so on.

Offering coffee in a coffee shop puts a player in the *services* field and therefore in a service economy. The key aspect creating value is how the service is delivered, and the nature of service is less tangible. Clients coming to a service point would interact with the provider of service and would get their coffee delivered on demand. A return to the same service provider would occur be because the client sees benefits from the service. In some cases, the benefits of the service would be bundled, as in consuming coffee and a cigarette in the few remaining cafés that allow smoking, or consuming coffee outside on a pedestrian pavement where one can observe and contemplate life.

The *experience* economy has players who are staging experiences for their guests. The guest leaves with a specific experience of how coffee is brewed, the way it smells, how it is served, where they sit, and who else is there. These sensations over a period of time are revealed in the choices the guest makes from a flexible menu of options. The seller of the experience reveals the different ways in which coffee can be consumed over a period time. The key attribute of an experience economy is how personal it is, and the seller of the experience is in the realm of theater, as a stager of experiences.

Moving from an agrarian economy through industrial and service economies to an experience economy allows value to be extracted in different ways. Most countries have all four forms of economy going at the same time. For example, India has an agrarian economy in its rural areas, even as it embraces a service and experience economy in urban areas. The use of mobile communication tools puts India in a place where urban users can use sophisticated services to get just about any information on their cell phones (www.asklalia.com). Another service is GNT, where users are linked to each other by the quality of SMS messages in a GIVE and TAKE form, where you either give information or get information or both (www.gntindia.com). The rating system on amazon.com is a similar service, where users can use the experience of others to help them make choices. The experience economy can have a major impact on how activities are organized and decisions made and is one of the major changes in the pattern of production and consumption driven by the knowledge and experience economy.

Performance can be gauged by how a country is plugged into the knowledge and experience economy through observation of the patterns of a few indicators. Variations in the capacity of countries to tap into the knowledge economy are measured by high-tech exports as a share of manufactured exports, which measures the degree to which a country is straddling the knowledge, goods, and service economies. East Asia leads the developing countries in this indicator, but South Asia has managed to make a big jump in a few years in the share of high-tech exports in manufactured exports. Africa, on the other hand, despite being a strong user in the mobile communications area, seems to be losing out in new idea generation at the goods production phase, having actually seen a big decline in the share of high-tech exports in manufactured exports during the period 2005–2007.

Other indicators for Africa show a different pattern. For example, services in banking, like Safaricom's M-PESA program, indicate that innovation in the use of mobile technology is very high in Africa. This also indicates that Africa occupies space in the service and experience economy, but not necessarily in the goods economy, and raises the question of whether countries can skip the goods production phase altogether and function without manufacturing much.

It is therefore important to analyze patterns of change. Decision makers need to be aware of broad trends. Leaders shape and intervene in spheres that drive the patterns of change and should have the ability to attract "followers" and create "trends."

Reacting to tectonic change

So far the book has covered how to read patterns of change for decision-making in a globalized world. Many of the changes presented are of such important consequence they can be labeled "tectonic." Ghadar and Peterson (2005) presented the revolutions that are shaping the future of every facet of society in a compendium that covered trends including aging and natural resource issues, as well as dramatic advances in technology, terrorism, and immigration. The compendium was aimed at educating CEOs and senior managers on what they need to know to develop and implement good global strategies. The main thesis is that CEOs often overlook small changes or gradual developments and miss out on shifting strategy until it is too late and the changes have become major quakes that shake the very foundations of the companies they lead.

There is an alternative view to waking up to gradual change, which is to embrace change and make it part of the organization's DNA. Brown and Eisenhardt (1997) use an inductive study of multiple-product innovation in six firms in the computer industry to show how organizations engage in continuous change. They show that successful firms rely on a wide variety of low-cost probes into the future, but also on the design of experimental products, hiring futurists into the firm and having them peek into the future, forming strategic alliances that help them leapfrog ahead. Brown and Eisenhardt (1997) develop the ideas that firms can use, such as creating "semi-structures" and deliberate "links in time" as well as following "sequenced steps" to crystallize the key properties of relevance to decision makers functioning in continuously changing organizations. As such, they extend the thinking about complexity theory, time-paced evolution, and the nature of core capabilities in ways that are very useful to use in the workplace.

Scharmer (2007) puts together the types of behaviors that can sustain the constant adaptation into "Theory U." Along with case studies, the work of Scharmer (2007) can be used to highlight the skills of observing what is happening around you and downloading what you know about a situation from your past experience. Theory U is also useful when extant theory does not appear to be useful in explaining rare and unusual phenomena. As such, one has to rely on a grounded theory-building approach, which is more likely to generate new insights into the phenomenon under study. Glaser and Strauss (1967) argue that indeed grounded theory-building could be more useful in generating accurate and novel insights into rare phenomena than either past research or office-bound thought experiments. The reader is encouraged to go along with this grounded theory-building approach in its application to a case study and extension of the work of Scharmer (2007). The key practice skill is one of keen observation and ability to identify what is going on, taking time to retreat and reflect about the patterns observed and find solutions quickly using previous knowledge and past experience, which can be downloaded quickly.

Reacting to tectonic change: Monsanto[2]

This case study assesses the responses of a multinational company to advances in science and technology that have caused tremendous change in the way food is consumed and agriculture practiced. As such, it provides the reader with examples that illustrate the skill of reacting to change and the aspect of Theory U related to adapting to change.

Genetically modified products offer tremendous opportunities as well as risks that cause players involved in this business to adapt their strategies and respond to the issues raised by society. The company concerned is Monsanto, a firm that has a powerful role in the invention of methods of cultivation of genetically modified plants and animals aimed at increasing productivity and reducing the cost of food production.

The Monsanto case is important for assessing reactions to patterns of change around you. The case offers the opportunity to derive deeper learning as you interact with the materials. The Monsanto case is about competition, cooperation, investigation, and regulation; but it is also about interactions between different groups active in a complex chain of decisions. The exercise is useful for self-learning to *observe* the challenges and choices made by the company, reflect on the process followed by its leaders to make choices, and to *retreat and reflect* on the production or use of genetically modified organisms and their implications for a variety of decisions. What are the different types of reactions by groups of decision makers to the choices made by Monsanto? What characterizes these reactions and how did Monsanto formulate and execute a response—in other words, how did Monsanto react to the tectonic changes that come from consumer preferences and regulations in different parts of the world? What has been the role of science and technology, and how have leaders in different spheres of production, consumption, branding, sales, and regulation used such information? How would you *solution quickly* if you were faced with similar challenges? These are the questions explored in diving into the case.

The grounded theory-building approach is used to draw conclusions from the author's perspective that would be useful for the reader. The reader is encouraged to reflect further on these interpretations and lessons and inform their own lessons learned, in a grounded theory-building effort.

Downloading: learning from Monsanto

Monsanto is a multinational, joint-stock company, specializing in biotechnology and organic chemistry for use in support of production in agriculture. It was founded in St Louis, Missouri, in 1901 by John Francis Queeny, a 30-year-old veteran of the pharmaceutical industry. It is the world's leading producer of the herbicide glyphosate, marketed in the "Roundup" brand of herbicides and in other brands. Monsanto is also the leading producer of genetically engineered (GE) seed; it provides the technology in 90% of the genetically engineered seeds used in the US market. Headquartered in Creve Coeur, Missouri, Monsanto controls from 70 to 100% of the market, producing the genetically modified seed grain. Monsanto is a good example of a globalized company intervening in all four spheres of change—people, resources, technology, and economy.

Monsanto and its subsidiaries provide agricultural products for farmers internationally. It operates in Seeds and Genomics and Agricultural Productivity. The Seeds and Genomics segment produces corn, soybean, canola, and cottonseeds, as well as vegetable seeds, including tomato, pepper, melon, cucumber, pumpkin, squash, beans, broccoli, onions, and lettuce seeds. This segment also develops biotechnology traits that assist farmers in controlling insects and weeds, as well as providing genetic material and biotechnology traits to other seed companies. The Agricultural Productivity segment offers glyphosate-based herbicides for agricultural, industrial, ornamental, and turf applications; lawn-and-garden herbicides for residential lawn-and-garden applications; and other herbicides for the control of pre-emergent annual grass and small seeded broadleaf weeds in corn and other crops. The company offers crop seeds principally under the DEKALB, Asgrow, Deltapine, and Vistive brand names; vegetable seeds under the Seminis and De Ruiter brand names; traits primarily under the Roundup Ready, Bollgard, Bollgard II, YieldGard, YieldGard VT, Genuity, Roundup Ready 2 Yield, and SmartStax brand names; seed treatment products under the Acceleron brand name; and herbicide products under the Roundup and Harness brand names. It also licenses germplasm and trait technologies to

seed companies. The company sells its products through distributors, independent retailers and dealers, agricultural cooperatives, plant raisers, and
agents, as well as directly to farmers. It has a collaboration agreement with
BASF in plant biotechnology that focuses on high-yielding crops and crops
that are tolerant to adverse conditions.

Retreat and reflect: the science, its benefits and risks

The DNA of living organisms frequently contains dormant forms of viruses
and bacteria. Putting them into genes which are used in the production of
GMOs may activate hidden forms of microorganisms and cause unpredict-
able recombination and mutation of microbes. This may lead to the development of a new generation of pathogenic microorganisms more dangerous
than SARS and H5N1 viruses. Scientists name such actions "biological
terrorism."

Fragments of altered genes from GM soy and corn penetrated genes,
blood, liver, spleen, kidney, and fetal warm-blooded organisms fed with
genetically modified food. Scientists report that this causes danger to the
health of humans and animals.

BST (rBGH, nourish)—genetically modified growth hormone—increases
milk production in cows. Unfortunately, it also increases the risk of breast,
colon, and prostate cancer in milk drinkers. The use of BST has been prohibited in EU countries. Roundup is an herbicide produced by Monsanto. After
application on an industrial scale in corn, soybean, rapeseed, cotton, and
sugar beets, it formed Roundup-resistant weeds. As a result, farmers must
now use higher doses of herbicides, which mean higher costs.

During the 100-year history of Monsanto, the company has been responsible for tremendous innovation and has driven the inputs into food and
beverage businesses around the world. It has also been the subject of con-
troversy and legal challenges.

The company's first product was the artificial sweetener saccharin, which
it sold to the Coca-Cola Company. It also introduced caffeine and vanillin
to Coca-Cola, and became one of Coca-Cola's main suppliers. The 1940s
saw Monsanto become a leading manufacturer of plastics, including poly-
styrene and synthetic fibers. Since then, it has remained one of the top 10
US chemical companies. Other major products have included the herbicides
2,4,5-T, DDT. In 1945, Monsanto introduced the manufacture of DDT—a
chlorinated hydrocarbon used to control insects. Scientific discoveries on
the effect of these products caused challenges to the safety claims made by
the company. Today it is known that DDT is highly toxic, causes cancer, and
accumulates in the fatty tissues of animals and humans. In the late 1960s
DDT was banned in developed countries, but it is still used in many developing countries to this today. DDT and "Agent Orange" were primarily used
during the Vietnam War as a defoliant agent and are believed to have caused
immense damage to health, not least by genetic modification.

In 1976, Monsanto launched Cycle-Safe—the first plastic drinks bottle—banned a year later because of carcinogenicity. In 1985, Monsanto began selling Aspartame (Nutra-Sweet)—a sweetener suspected of causing brain tumors, and later banned in the US. In 1979, Monsanto conducted a study that stated that dioxins do not increase cancer risk. Later in 1990 it became clear that these results were falsified. In 1997, it came to light that Monsanto had sold 6.000 tons of waste contaminated with cadmium to companies producing fertilizers.

Observe, retreat, reflect: new ownership continues to dominate global markets but faces legal challenges

Pharmacia purchased the Monsanto Company in March 2000, and the new ownership resulted in changes in the structure of the company. On May 19, 2001 Monsanto revealed that the genetically modified Roundup Ready soybeans contain "unexpected genetic fragments." In 2004 and 2005, Monsanto filed lawsuits against many farmers in Canada and the US on the grounds of patent infringement. Agracetus, a company 100%, owned by Monsanto, has a monopoly on the production of genetically modified soya beans sold under the name "Roundup Ready." Monsanto employs 15,000 people worldwide. According to its August 2004 tax return, its gross annual income is US$ 5.4 billion.

Monsanto has delivered superior performance despite the legal challenges. Common stocks of Monsanto have consistently outperformed those of a competitor, *United Phosphorus Ltd.*

Observe and react: highly varied regulations for the production of GMOs in the EU and US

Monsanto operates in a complex legal environment with highly differentiated regulations. The EU has possibly the most stringent GMO regulations in the world. And in fact, people in the EU do not willingly consume GMOs, which renders the EU a tough market for Monsanto. EU legislation after 2003 contained strict rules on labeling, traceability, and risk assessments of genetically modified foods by all the biotech companies.

Legal requirements governing organic production in the EU are set out in regulations enforced in its entirety and directly in each EU Member State. They are:

- Basic COUNCIL REGULATION (EC) No 834/2007 of June 28, 2007 on organic production and labeling of organic products and repealing Regulation (EEC) No 2092/91.
- Implementing COMMISSION REGULATION (EC) No 889/2008 of September 5, 2008 laying down detailed rules for implementing Council Regulation (EC) No 834/2007 on organic production and labeling of organic products with regard to organic production, labeling and control.

The use of hormones in all primary production and in organic production is strictly prohibited in the EU. The only GMO food crop that was approved in 1998 is the GM maize MON810; therefore it can be used for cultivation in Europe. On March 2, 2010 a second GMO, a potato called Amflora, was approved for cultivation for industrial applications in the EU by the European Commission and was grown in Germany, Sweden, and the Czech Republic that year.

The US is the largest commercial grower of genetically modified crops in the world. A lot of GMO products that are forbidden in other parts of the world can be freely produced in America. No single statute and no single federal agency governs the regulation of biotechnology products. The Food and Drug Administration, the Department of Agriculture, and the Environmental Protection Agency have primary responsibility for the regulation of biotechnology products. Each of the laws that exist today in the US was developed before the advent of biotechnology products and reflects widely different regulatory approaches and procedures (Box 1.1).

Box 1.1   Responding to the Promise and Limits of Science

The reader is encouraged to see how differently they would act in the space that Monsanto had to act, where there are links between the knowledge gained from science on how to grow food, which resides in the sphere of *technology*, with the health of *people*, and the impacts on the environment where food is grown, which is the natural *resources* of soil and water. All these are taking place in an *economy* where the leaders of Monsanto have to react to shareholders, who want to see profits.

From my perspective, the main problem Monsanto has faced in using a broad-based GM strategy is the lack of independent, reliable information. Societal concern for contamination of the environment and attention to human health risks demands a tough tradeoff if you are in the GM business. These tradeoffs vary across cultures, and when operating in a global sphere they require differentiated strategies that help a multi-national company like Monsanto, shift to meet the expectations of consumers in local markets that they serve around the world.

The main argument for an expansive strategy such as the one used by Monsanto is that GMOs can be used to produce better and cheaper vaccines and drugs, as well as help to tackle the problem of world hunger. The reality has been challenging, with secondary effects such as plants that produce toxic substances, and toxic plants that are resistant to herbicides. Yields have not universally improved in all cases and farmers cannot all afford the increasing volumes of herbicides and fertilizers.

Modified grains are in fact patented and in many cases cannot re-germinate, causing farmers to change their behavior and having them purchase seeds to sow for the next season. Changing farmer behavior is costly and can cause short-term risks, as productivity is lost until local systems can adjust to having farmers in a cycle of seed-buying from independent seed companies.

When patents are highly valuable, copying and mimicking can take place, reducing the incentive for further innovation by a company. Patent infringement, on the other hand, is a challenge and Monsanto has been the subject of many law suits to defend its patents.

Developing countries in Africa, Asia, and Latin America, with their need to meet nutrition challenges in the short run and their capacity to use abundant land for global food production, are a wide open territory in terms of choices around GMOs and whether to use them or not. A good understanding of the risks and opportunities is needed in order to pair such knowledge with societal preferences to make a choice that is meaningful to developing countries. How easy it is for actors in the whole agriculture value chain to adapt to science and technology is another consideration.

Retreat and reflect: anti-globalization and environmental organizations against Monsanto

Activity in the market for genetically modified seed corn and the production of domestic bovine growth hormone rendered Monsanto one of the most targeted companies by anti-globalization activists and environmental multinationals. They coined the term "frankenfood" (from the reference to genetic modification of humans in "Frankenstein") in relation to food produced using Monsanto's technology, and the name of their group, "Monsatan," means "my Satan" in French. According to the opinion of anti-globalists, Monsanto is a leading example of so-called "corporate terrorism."

Such organizations hold many protests and publish e-articles and in newspapers. But so far they have not joined forces to fight against the products of Monsanto.

Lessons from the Monsanto case

In this case study one learns what happens when changes interact in the common decision space of an organization. Also learned is how to identify reactions by individual stakeholders and the unique strategies they employ to get a desired outcome. The case also shows us that the reactions are not a zero-sum game, and indeed there are winners and losers. However, a special focus on downloading and observation from what is going on can help identify the potential for a common vision and strategy on how to use science for the benefit of farmers, consumers, and companies that make innovative products. The lessons learned are summarized below.

Spheres and patterns of change

The Monsanto case study shows effects in all four spheres of change. In the *people* sphere there is the question of nutrition and feeding the world, but there are also preferences for organic food and non-genetically modified products due to the presumed impacts on the health of consumers. In the *economy* sphere there are many factors, such as the dependence on agriculture and the need for increased productivity that could rely on the use of better seeds and treatments for higher yields. There are also expected returns from science and innovation in the form of patents that need to be protected in a globalized world where patent infringement is serious. In the *technology* sphere are the methods and practices of farming (organic, modern, traditional, and so on) as well as the scientific research that brings in new technologies and the reliance on knowledge systems and knowledge workers. A farmer in rural Africa, Asia, or Latin America may not have the skills needed to use some of the highly scientific products available on the market. Effects on *resources* are also present, such as soil contamination, the use of water for irrigation, and the impacts on the ecosystem, including on the growth of other plants and on animals and their consumption of genetically modified products.

Reactions to change

One may also identify the distinct reactions to change of five groups of stakeholders, each with a different approach to dealing with the tectonic changes facing them, but all interacting in the dynamic decision space for Monsanto. These include the company, governments in different parts of the world, donors engaged in agriculture, civil society, farmers, and agricultural workers.

Monsanto has reacted by rethinking its policies and actions aimed at consumers and farmers. First, it has revised its approach to the dissemination and promotion of their genetically modified products, and works with farmers and farmers' associations to do so. Secondly, the company has been seeking a better balance between patenting its products and sharing research ideas and inventions with farmers in poor countries. Monsanto is also focusing on research in organic and other forms of products that are a better fit to the variety of ecosystems in which the company has clients.

Governments in different parts of the world have started to collaborate to come up with a common set of regulations that match their citizens' demands for purity and safety of the environment, yet allowing other countries to choose on the basis of a localized risk assessment. Legislation from the EU is such an example. The authorities of different countries also conduct educational programs on the potential and actual dangers contained in genetically modified products, including Monsanto's products. Governments deliver useful information to agricultural workers, farmers, and owners and employees of food companies, so they can also be partners in making effective policy choices. There has been progress on an agreed set of penalties and fines for the use or production of harmful genetically modified products. Supporting organic methods of cultivation and managing the farm sector in general is also helping to reduce dependency on single large players in the market of GMOs.

Donors have supported programs of research and finance for smallholder farmers and agricultural workers, providing means and an opportunity to experiment and use organic products in their work. Through financial support programs, farmers have been encouraged to use organic and nature-friendly products, or choose from a wider variety of input producers, including at the national and international level.

Global environmental civil society has concentrated on coordinating its activities on the common dissemination of information on a global scale. It has organized the gathering of voices of citizens in different countries, in order to appeal to the parliaments and governments of those countries, so as to influence their decisions to introduce relevant laws governing food safety. Also, activists have effectively influenced the activity of companies like Monsanto by putting better research in the hands of lawyers in important court decisions. Environmental organizations have worked together to support farmers and agricultural workers, and *ecologists* have provided research, analysis, and product testing to provide independent assessments of the products of companies like Monsanto.

Farmers and *agricultural workers* have started to use alternative products, such as organic solutions and those free of human pathogenic microorganisms and without residues of harmful substances (antibiotics, coccidiostats, or other feed additive products) used in primary production in consumer-ready products. Farmers are blending traditional methods of land cultivation and sowing with recently invented new technologies, with beneficial properties in terms of food and livestock production.

And finally, *consumers* are making better choices in the consumption of genetically modified foods, including choosing to eat organically grown foods when that is a better value-for-money deal.

Implications for strategy

This case study has shown how a company (Monsanto) has been impacted by changes particularly in the spheres of people, technology, and economy, and how the company has reacted to and caused tectonic shifts in technology, economy, and resources. The case is also illuminating in how science is used for profit, how farming interacts with science, what people consume and the effects on their health, and how the use of scientific knowledge is regulated. A set of potential reactions by different groups was considered and their reactions to the complexities of changes in the global food supply chain analyzed. A balance was provided between competition, cooperation, investigation, and regulation, and a set of reactions by different groups active in a complex chain of decisions was highlighted. The implications of this case study for strategy are that it is important to learn from and adjust to the ways that other stakeholder groups see an issue.

Practice Block I: reacting to tectonic change

The case study (Box 1.2) illustrates the wide range of issues to consider when making decisions in complex global world. These include the production and use of genetically modified organisms and implications for a variety of decisions, leading to a series of diverse reactions by a varied group of decision makers. Had you been the leader responsible for making decisions, what would you have done differently?

Box 1.2   Practice Block I: Reacting to Tectonic Change

Premise: Global trends are shifting the topography and environment in which your business and political decisions are made.

Objective: To practice the skill of learning from the past while adapting to major shifts.

Approach: Using the Monsanto case study, identify three key tectonic changes that the company was facing.

Recommendation: Looking at potential challenges presented in the Monsanto case study, use your prior experience (including from reading, internet searches, and your own knowledge) to prepare and present the areas you have identified as critical.

Exercise: Summarize your approach for selecting the tectonic changes facing Monsanto.

Skill: Learning from the past and practicing "observation and downloading" in a structured setting.

Theory U makes a distinction between different qualities of how action comes to be undertaken. Action from one player (say Monsanto) could be subject to blind spots, as the objectives of the company of using science for productivity improvements in agriculture and for profits clashes with that of government, of ensuring healthy food is available to society. The sources of action of civil society organizations also differ from those of government and companies. By mapping the topography of the blind spots, Theory U offers a language and a roadmap for crossing the threshold to authentic renewal and change (Scharmer, 2007: 118). Critical in Theory U is the "source of knowing." The key lesson is to identify the key stakeholder group and see the world from their perspective (Box 1.3). Also, the information to share (download) to these stakeholders could have an impact on how they react to the new science or new knowledge.

Box 1.3   Questions for Self-Development

- Who would you have identified as the key stakeholder group?
- What would you have shared to ensure they understand your perspective easily?
- What would you do to ensure success in having them see things from a fresh perspective?
- What information would you provide them and how would you share it to help them think along with you?
- What reasoning and arguments would you use to support the main direction you wanted to take as well as support your conclusions?
- What array of possible options would you consider and what sources of information would you use to advance the options?
- What stories would you tell, or what metaphors and anecdotes would you use to make your context-setting arguments?
- Where would you use humor to lighten tensions and where would you be serious in bringing in the key issues?
- How would you make your arguments and presentation consistent and where would you try to force your ideas on them?
- What reactions would have made you panic or get emotional and how would you handle criticism?
- How would you make all stakeholders feel comfortable?
- Where would you act like yourself, and where would you role-play?

An important skill in Theory U is convincing other stakeholders to see from your perspective or to see from a fresh perspective. What information to provide and how to provide it makes a big difference in how it is used as people have biases when they make judgment under uncertainty and rely on heuristics and other forms of past knowledge and experience (Kahneman et al., 1982). Getting others to buy in also relies on making convincing arguments and skills in negotiations (Fisher et al., 1991). The sources of information used and the approaches for getting points across also matter. Storytelling can be an effective way to get a common vision and to establish powerful motivators for change and acceptance of an idea (Llewellyn, 2001).

Convincing others to see from a fresh perspective and getting buy-in from others relies on communication skills. This book puts the emphasis on learning how to communicate, which is in the realm of emotion and behavior, also known as EQ (Goleman, 1997). Emotional behaviors are learned. To support the reader, the book includes a set of guiding questions to be aware of in developing one's emotional skills of downloading and observation.[3] The guiding tool is a useful complement to the materials in each chapter in steering through day-to-day practice in similar situations.

2
Dynamics of Change

Key Lessons from Chapter 2: Dynamics of Change

This chapter focuses on the drivers of change impacting on spheres of people, resources, economy and technology covered in Chapter 1. These include: (1) the emergence of logistics as a turning point; (2) changes in mobility and connectivity; (3) ownership and financing arrangements; (4) interactions between knowledge and culture; (5) advances in risk management tools and approaches; and (6) demands for ethics and accountability.

The main focus is openness to dealing with tectonic change. The Jamuna Bridge case illustrates the dynamics of change impacting people, technology, natural resources, and economy. The role of stakeholders in shaping decisions is introduced, including local and international NGOs and local and central governments, as well as multilateral and bilateral aid agencies, and the executing agencies and managers from distributed loci of decision-making. Specific skills introduced are: (1) identifying the global constraints impacting individual stakeholder strategies; (2) extracting the key elements needed for effective engagement with stakeholder groups; (3) identifying the options for dealing with areas hard to predict; (4) capacity to anticipate and respond to actions of different agents, leading to global properties affecting a decision process; and (5) practicing "emphasizing and integrating actions of others" in a structured setting of dialogue and negotiation.

Introducing the chapter

It is important for leaders to determine *"What are the dynamics of change that are generating the shifts in the patterns observed?"* Dynamics of change can be understood through six specific lenses. The first focuses on the emergence of logistics as a turning point in economic and social interactions on a global scale. The second investigates the dynamics of change coming from patterns of mobility, connectivity, and productivity. Ownership and financing arrangements around key productive sectors is the third lens of importance. The fourth relates to the interactions between knowledge and culture, while the fifth investigates advances in tools for risk management on risk taking and its implications for the patterns of change observed. Finally, the sixth lens highlights the growing demands for ethical and accountable leadership around the world. All these drivers impact on the spheres of change and on the approach and final outcomes of decisions made in the four major spheres of change.

The chapter starts with an assessment of how the logistics revolution and its technological dimensions makes possible complex interactions between economy, people, and resources; thereby changing the nature of engagement and risk. Detail is provided on the drivers of individual mobility and networked connectivity, particularly on how changes in levels of mobility and connectivity influence interactions and outcomes at the city, country, and global level. Advances in ownership and financing arrangements are another driver covered in the chapter, with examples from industry and practice to bring out the major dynamics of change from these two drivers. The chapter brings out the influence of knowledge and culture and the theoretical and cultural underpinnings behind them. The evolution of key risks, the sixth driver, is investigated, with the emphasis on shocks in financial systems, fuel and commodity prices, and from security threats. The impact of an increased demand for ethics and accountability is the final driver captured, and the focus is on the global evolution of ethics and implications for decision makers at various levels. The chapter closes by highlighting the main lessons from the Jamuna Bridge case and what is needed to get a good understanding of the drivers of change.

Logistics as a turning point

The *Economist* referred to work by Cecchetti et al. (1997) in its September 20th issue of 2007 titled "Global Economy: The Turning Point." The article highlights what was at the time an important pattern of change driven by a revolution in the field of logistics. The main change turned around the practice of warehousing by firms, which can be measured by the volume of goods stocked before shipping, display, or being dispatched to consumers. The

"For such a tiny part of GDP, the content of warehouses has had a surprisingly big effect on its volatility. When industries cut or add stocks according to demand, that adjustment magnifies the effect of the initial change in sales."

"on average, more than half the improvement in the stability of economic growth in the countries [Mr. Cecchetti et al] studied is accounted for by diminished inventory cycles. That something so workaday as supply-chain management could have so marked an effect might seem a dull conclusion. But dullness is a virtue, because technological improvement is irreversible. This means the greater stability it provides is likely to be permanent."

Source: The Economist: Global Economy: The Turning Point, September 20, 2007

Economist attributed the observed stability in economic growth to the reduction in the size of inventories held in warehouses and credited the workaday aspects of supply chain management to the observed stability in the patterns of economic growth.

There is commonality between the financial crisis—which is a serious shock resulting from decades of small changes at the individual country level—and the emergence of *logistics* as a turning point. Both the financial system and logistics system have visible effects on economic and business outcomes, producing both opportunities for success and also added risks. Logistics management, as defined by Cooper et al. (1997) is "the process of planning, implementing and controlling the efficient, cost-effective flow and storage of raw materials, in-process inventory, finished goods, and related information flow from point-of-origin to point-of-consumption for the purposes of conforming to customer requirements." Such capabilities have made it possible for firms, consumers, governments, and civil society to operate in ways that were not possible previously. The changes in behavior have been gradual and cumulative over time and come from the increased capacity to handle supply chain logistics (Fariborz and Peterson, 2005).

A look at the long-run dynamics of inventory cycles just before a shock, such as the financial crisis, provides us with a good understanding of how a small supply chain effect can propagate into an interconnected set of micro-decisions by manufacturers, sellers, and buyers, to have an effect that takes years to work oneself out of. Consider the period between 1960 and 2000 from which we can learn by looking at "before" and "after" patterns. This was a period of constantly growing changes in inventory, peaking in the 1990s and declining thereafter. Stock levels in the 1980s and 1990s were much larger relative to the size of the global economy. At that time, a small slip in demand for a particular good, like oil or minerals, or aggregate demand at the global level in general, could easily blow up into a recession. Companies during the period 1960 to 1990 were operating with sizeable inventories and started to draw down on those inventories after 1990.

Operating with lower inventories means that companies have few cushions to rely on when something goes wrong. Short-run dynamics in changes in inventory during the period 2000 to 2003 indicate a continued decline, supporting the hypothesis that firms were holding smaller inventories and relying more on just-in-time deliveries. However, that pattern reversed in 2002, shifting to a pattern of increasing inventories. The shock to the global system that took place after September 11, 2001 reversed the declining inventories trend and wiped out the advances that had been made as a result of major improvements in technology. Such improvements had until that point led to faster and better information on buyers, allowed production in smaller batches and better matching of demand and supply. Before the September 11 shock, companies relied heavily on supply chain efficiency and were sensitive to small swings in inventory.

Shocks to the logistics chain not only have an impact on the behavior of firms but can also shift the global balance of trade and manufacturing behavior. Consider what happened to India, which had changes in inventory in the 1960s of about US$ 99 million in current terms.[1] By 1980 that figure had grown to US$ 11.6 million and had ballooned to US$ 18.7 million by 2010. India in the 1980s was not as connected to the global system as it was in 2010. A shock in 2008 therefore shows a greater impact on India than one in 1980. Such dynamics indicate that it is important not only to look at the short-run effects on a global scale, but at the long-run ones as well, and also to identify the specific effects that matter at the local level.

There are four key elements of the logistics revolution driving supply chain behaviors (Cooper et al., 1997; Fariborz and Peterson, 2005). The first is *access*, which can be measured by the extent and density of transportation and communication systems like roads, railways, ports, and harbors, as well as telephone and internet access. The second is the approach taken to warehousing and *inventory*, as has been discussed above. The third element is the arrangements made in the *logistical choices* along a given supply chain. Finally, the approach to *risk management* makes up the final critical element driving the logistics revolution.

While these elements have been around since the days of Hannibal and his logistical feat of crossing the Pyrenees into France (Gabriel, 2011), they are now providing a unique opportunity for emerging and developing economies alike. Many developing countries are still tackling first generation infrastructure and face severe access bottlenecks in basic transport services. Such constraints in access have long forced companies operating in developing countries to hold large inventory. The advent of internet-supported buying and ease of communication using mobile phones is helping such countries remove some of the trade facilitation constraints.

The retail sector is a good one to illustrate changes in logistics practice. Developing countries undergo fundamental transformations in the organization of their retail sector, with implications for other dimensions of their economies. Consider, for example, the rise of supermarkets in Africa, Asia, and Latin America, which have revolutionized the practice of farming and agriculture (Reardon et al., 2003). Increases in income along with reductions in the cost of processing food have combined with the entrepreneurship drive of serving food markets at long distance, aided by supply chain logistics. Global supermarket chains like Walmart and Carrefour have introduced standardized and centralized logistics practices that are changing the behavior of procurement officers in Africa, Asia, and Latin America (Reardon et al., 2003). Such transformations are having a profound effect on how food is grown, packaged, transported, and eventually displayed for consumption.

However, there are remaining challenges, as few firms in developing countries have internalized supply chain management, and the high speed of behavioral change in advanced economies is once again challenging the management of supply chains. Shocks such as September 11 and events such as the Fukushima earthquake on March 11, 2011 remind us of just how important it is to get a good handle on supply chain logistics. Indeed, there is room for countries to learn from each and there are advantages for companies that get it right.

Long-lasting effects of the logistics revolution have been mostly driven by achievements in transport, especially the tremendous improvement in access to local land systems. Growth in individual mobility has paired up with a culture of self-sufficiency among the young people in advanced economies, with important implications for "Do it yourself" solutions. Companies like IKEA have gone from being players in a small town like Jönköping in Sweden to being global players with multiple stores around the world. The re-emergence of rail as a clean and reliable service provider is causing new corridors to be opened up and is forcing a global techno-logical competition amongst countries like Russia, India, China, Japan, and France that have long relied on railway technology. Evolution in the use of air transport systems is allowing flower growers in Rwanda and Kenya to sell their produce in Europe, competing with long-time players who dominated these markets, such as the Netherlands. Scaling up of maritime transport has also allowed shipments to be made in record time aided by transformations in technology for transport and transport equipment, with possibilities to on- and offload cargo from factory to truck to ship to train. All these technological advancements have resulted in increased efficiency in transport services.

But the logistics revolution is also driven by the emergence of new approaches to supply chain management (Cooper et al., 1997) and integra-tion (Bowersox et al., 1999). Supply chain risk assessment is perhaps the single most important advance for identifying sources and sizes of risk. Supported by supply chain risk control methodologies and approaches at the enterprise level, decisions can be made at record speed and with almost instant assessment of the impact, rather than having to wait as was done in the 1990s for a full shipment-transaction to be terminated. Supply chain risk mitigation through dynamic risk management approaches has increased the capacity to manage risk; so much so that companies can now define their partnership strategies using risk management as a guide (Finch, 2004). Where leadership needs to catch up is in the approach to risk taking and the understanding of the distribution of the effects of materialized risks (Léautier, 2007).

Mobility and connectivity

Three aspects stand out in importance with respect to the questions regard-ing how mobile or linked the world has become and the related implica-tions for decision-making. The first aspect is the increase in individual mobility—whether it has to do with the diminishing share of people remaining within a small perimeter of the place they were born, the physical distance traveled by an individual in a given day, or the virtual adventures each person can get into without leaving the confines of their home. The second is the effect of the increased concentration of people in cities or large agglomerations on productivity, while the third is the relation between increased connectivity and productivity. The changes in behavior that are driving the growth in the "do it yourself market" are one of the implications of increased mobility and connectivity. Concepts like mass customization would be impossible without the changes in connectivity, and the dominance of global brands could not be possible if people were less mobile and less linked. Communication is much easier today and is rendering the nature of political interactions more complex as it is shifting business preferences and specialization. Yet such changes in mobility, particularly residential mobility (number of moves for an individual or percentage having moved in a given time frame), are also associated with changes in the behavior of individuals and collectivities with key implications for public policy (Sanchez and Andrews, 2011) and the future of mind and behavior in an increasingly mobile world (Oishi, 2010).

The world has become more mobile, with a steady increase in the number of vehicles per person worldwide.[2] The issues of increased physical mobility, however, are felt most at the local level in growing traffic congestion (NCHRP, 1997). The densest traffic areas in 2010 according to *The Economist: World in Figures* were Hong Kong with 286.7 vehicles per km of road, followed by Kuwait with 267.7 vehicles per km of road. City-states like Singapore also account for the densest traffic areas, with 5.3 km of road per square km of land area in 2010, driven mostly by movements to and from the port. China, being the most populous country in the world, tops the list with multiple dense traffic areas (Macau and Hong Kong for example). Europe dominates in terms of the densest countries, with 24 countries in the top 40 densest countries in the world. Mobility has global drivers and effects, but it is mostly felt at the local level, as people sit in endless traffic in cities from Accra to Hanoi, Paris, Shanghai, and Seattle.

The concentration of population in cities, known as urbanization, has been increasing over the years, along with the increase in mobility. The more inhabitants a city has the more possibilities it has for benefitting from the creativity and interactions of its citizens. The productivity of a city in terms of how much it produces per inhabitant is high when cities are small (less than 500,000 people), but also when they are large (1–5 million people). Megacities (more than 5 million people) are better performing than medium-sized cities (0.5 to 1 million people). The dynamics that drive productivity are at play in these patterns. Megacities have to deal with congestion, which is one of the major causes of efficiency losses in wasted time during travel, more expensive infrastructure, and so on. Medium-sized cities cannot stay medium-sized forever, as when they perform well and are governed effectively they attract the highly mobile youth seeking employment and entertainment, which causes medium cities to grow, becoming large. If they do not perform well in delivering services or they are poorly governed, they lose residents, who migrate to seek better opportunities elsewhere, and the cities shrink, becoming small. Léautier (2006) shows how dynamics at the city level impact governance, city performance, and sustainability.

What most city leaders need to contend with is the provision of services to satisfy a growing population that is ever more demanding. Changes in preferences by city residents drive the demands they make of cities. A growth in preferences for self-sufficiency, as can be seen in the pattern of exports servicing the "Do It Yourself" market, creates inter-linkages between cities across different countries and even continents as a result of the globalization of companies like IKEA (Table 2.1). Because of the integration of supply chains and the globalization of standards (Reardon et al., 2003), practices across cities start to converge, offering the global traveler, and indeed residents in global cities, a common level of service. Indicators of such globalization of preferences are the exports of products that require some degree of assembly, such as prefabricated buildings, which rely on common standards of materials and construction and assembling techniques.

The exported volume of items like prefabricated buildings from France to the rest of the world grew from $79.2 billion in 2001 to $118.9 in 2012. The value of exports from the Netherlands in these same products shrank from a value of US$ 52.2 billion in 2001 to US$ 44.7 billion in 2012. The Netherlands

Table 2.1 The "Do It Yourself" Market: Top 10 Exporters of Prefabricated Buildings (Product Code 9406 in US$ billions)

	Value of Exports			Value of Imports	
Country	2001	2012	Country	2001	2012
France	79.2	118.9	Netherlands	21.58	41.64
Netherlands	52.2	44.7	France	13.11	19.44
Germany	12.3	10.9	Czech Republic	4.27	12.07
Qatar	0.001	5.3	Germany	10.18	7.27
Switzerland	4.4	4.6	China	0.06	4.26
Mexico	0.009	4.25	Poland	0.23	4.12
Sweden	0.003	4.2	Estonia	0.075	2.86
Chad	0.0	2.9	Italy	4.05	2.70
Spain	2.8	2.6	Israel	0.89	2.19
Luxembourg	5.8	2.5	United Kingdom	7.05	2.03

Source: ITC-UNCTAD/WTO Trade Map – International Statistics.

remained the largest importer of prefabricated buildings between 2001 and 2012, while Qatar, Mexico, and Sweden came from nowhere to be in the Top ten exporters of prefabricated buildings in the world by 2012.

Company strategies and risk management decisions to handle these demands have had to adapt to these rapid changes. Understanding the dynamics of change at the city level across the world could help decision-makers develop better strategies and take actions that would render them more competitive. Mass customization is now possible because there is a consumer base that is linked globally and is consuming similar products because of brand recognition (Table 2.2).

An analysis of global brands helps us see the effect of well-integrated company strategies.[3] The brand with the highest value globally in 2007 was Walmart, a retail industry, according to Milword Brown Optimor (2007). IKEA, on the other hand, which is the poster child of the "Do It Yourself" market for highly educated urban residents, had a brand value of US$ 7.4 billion in 2007. By 2013, the number one company by brand value was Apple, at a value of $185 billion, five times bigger than Walmart in 2007 (Milword Brown Optimor, 2013). Perhaps more interesting is that not a single company that was in the Top 15 in 2007 remained in the Top 15 by 2013. Walmart dropped to number 18 in 2013, even as it retained its brand

Table 2.2 Mass customization, mobility, and brands: RETAIL—top 15 by brand value

2007			2013		
Rank	Brand	Brand value (US$ millions)	Rank	Brand	Brand value (US$ millions)
1	Walmart	36,880	1	Apple	185,071
2	Home Depot	18,335	2	Google	113,669
3	Tesco	16,649	3	IBM	112,536
4	EBay	12,927	4	McDonalds	90,256
5	Carrefour	11,710	5	Coca-Cola	78,415
6	Target	11,560	6	AT&T	75,507
7	Marks & Spencer	9,509	7	Microsoft	69,814
8	IKEA	7,373	8	Marlboro	69,383
9	Best Buy	6,674	9	Visa	56,060
10	Amazon	5,964	10	China Mobile	55,368
11	Auchan	5,570	11	GE	55,357
12	Asda	5,540	12	Verizon	53,004
13	ALDI	4,712	13	Wells Fargo	47,748
14	Costco	3,784	14	Amazon	45,727
15	Safeway	3,772	15	UPS	42,747

Source: Milward Brown Optimor available at http://www.millwardbrown.com/Sites/mbOptimor/Default.aspx.

value at about $36.2 billion compared to $36.9 billion in 2007. Home Depot disappeared altogether, while Tesco dropped to number 55. IKEA dropped to number 74 in 2013, even though the value of the brand nearly doubled from $7.4 billion in 2007 to more than $12 billion by 2013.

Advances in ownership and financing arrangements

The shifting roles of the private sector in what gets done, and how, around the world have been driving a lot of the dynamics that have been discussed so far, especially in relation to international standard setting (Haufler, 2001). The shift in the destinations and sectors that attract foreign direct investment (FDI), and the transfer of corporate values that goes along with that, is one of the patterns that most visibly shows the change in the role of the private sector. The other pattern of interest is the fluctuations in Mergers and Acquisitions (M&A) activities around the world, and the related changes in expectations of the role of the multinational private sector in dealing with the side effects on other systems. (Haufler, 2001) Many of the changes seen derive from the emergence of new forms of companies as a result of strategic alliances, integration of activities, or evolutions in company strategy in response to the changes in demographics and other dynamics discussed so far.

An illustration of the new forms of companies being created as a result of the logistical revolution is the integration of logistics into manufacturing for end-to-end solutions (Figure 2.1). Such integration is possible as companies seek to serve their customers better. BASF is a good example to illustrate the impact of logistics on the possibilities of companies to meet customer needs, but at the same time consider the broader effects on society of the behavior of companies. BASF is a significant player in the tire and rubber industry and used its position as a driver in innovation to advance unique solutions in the packaging business (www.basf.com).

BASF manufactures Koresin Pellets, which are produced as an input for tires and other rubber products. The company serves customers who purchase in bulk and those that order smaller packages of about 25 kg. To better serve their customers, BASF integrated the production, packaging, and delivery of these pellets by sending the 25 kg packs in wood containers and delivering the bulk packages in plastic containers that were not only recyclable, but were 1.7 kg lighter (www.basf.com). Such innovations in specialized logistics link the various points in the rubber value chain of production, packaging, and delivery. As a result, BASF has been able to compete in the area of supply chain management and has raised its brand value from $3.5 billion in 2010 to more than $5.6 billion by 2013, while raising its brand rating from AA in 2010 to AA+ in 2013 (http://brandirectory.com/profile/basf). Yet BASF was also a company concerned about the safety of the driving

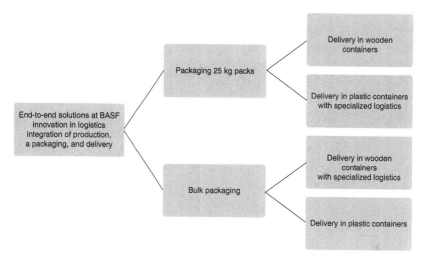

Figure 2.1   End-to-end solutions at BASF
Source: Developed by author from data taken at www.basf.com.

behavior of their drivers around the world, and their behavior as they interact while delivering these unique solutions to their customers (www.basf.
com). They introduced a safety strategy that had important implications
for the company in terms of its own safety record (www.basf.com) and also
for safe driving practices in the countries in which the company operates
(www.basf.com).

Policy makers need to be aware of the advantages but also potential limitations of vertical and horizontal integration. *Advances in logistics make it
possible; advancements in policy and regulation need to follow to allow the best
outcomes from a social welfare point of view.*

The other major dynamic relates to the evolution of the "resilient enterprise," which is one that has managed to build flexibility into the way it
operates and hence secure its activities under varying risk scenarios. Sheffi
and Rice (2007) discuss the main reasons why companies should build
resilience through flexibility, explaining that such added flexibility can
sometimes be seen as a pure cost. They further suggest that "although
necessary to some degree, redundancy represents pure cost with no return
except in the eventuality of disruption." Sheffi and Rice (2007) contend
that significantly more leverage, not to mention operational advantages,
can be achieved by making supply chains flexible. Flexibility requires
building in organic capabilities that can sense threats and respond to them
quickly.

Resilient companies build flexibility into each of the five essential supply chain elements, including the supplier, conversion process, distribution
channels, control systems, and underlying corporate culture. This allows
them to reduce vulnerability by reducing the likelihood of disruption or
increasing the capacity to bounce back after a disruption. As Sheffi and Rice
(2007) argue, this requires creating redundancy or increasing flexibility.
Some ways to do it include keeping some resources in reserve to be used in
case of a disruption (safety stock). Other actions could be the deliberate use
of multiple suppliers even when the secondary suppliers have higher costs.
Firms could also deliberately lower capacity utilization rates to allow for sudden need. Illustrations and in-depth discussion of resilience are provided in
Chapters 3 and 4.

The choices of where to locate activity also drive the dynamics of change
in the global economy. The private sector's interest in developing countries
has shifted over the years as a result of perceived opportunity and risk.
Investments in developing countries in transport and logistics with private
sector participation went from US$ 7.6 billion in 1990 to US$ 31.6 billion in
2011.[4] These investments peaked in 2006 at US$ 75 billion, declining con-
sistently after that to a value of US$ 28 billion in 2010. Private sector invest-
ments recovered in 2011 to US$ 31.6 billion. There does not seem to have
beeen a decline in the total flows to the sector in the US, despite the financial crisis of 2008–2009. Transportation, including logistics, is the fourth
largest sector in the US economy, and the sector saw a resumption in private
equity interest since the lull in deal activity following the 2007 financial crisis (www.reuters.com/article/2010/01/29/us-logistics-privateequity). What
has happened, however, is that the financial crisis has resulted in a decline
in the maximum flows to a given country, as private investors hedge their
risks. The trends in private investment mask large transactions in M&A
activities, particularly in shipping and trucking.

Cross-border M&A was at a high of US$ 299.7 billion in 2000. It was not as
affected as other sectors by the financial crisis of 2007, because private companies saw value in investing in other markets. Cross-border M&A, which
was at US$ 66.3 billion in 2007 declined to US$ 15.3 in 2010, recovering to
US$ 24.4 billion in 2012 (World Investment Report, 2012). Such M&A activ-
ity is based on the very high shareholder growth potential in transport and
logistics sectors (Table 2.3). Consider that an investment in trucking could
expect a return of about 7%, while an investment in shipping brought only
about 2%, and logistics services posted returns of up to 30% (Brooks and
Ritchie, 2006).

Interaction between knowledge and culture

There has been a longstanding debate on the role of culture in development.
Bergendorf (2007) argues that sustainable development is only possible if

Table 2.3   High value of logistics services driving M&A activity
in shipping

Sector	Shareholder growth potential (%)
Shipping	2
Trucking	7
Equipment leasing	14
Logistics services	30

Source: Brooks and Ritchie (2006).

certain aspects of a culture can be changed, and that development projects
fail because of political and cultural aspects. Culture in the Bergendorf sense
is seen as an integrative mechanism within which long-term knowledge of
people is embedded. As such, culture can be conceptualized as a complex
system based on groups and sub-groups that interact in networks, producing cultural traits and local institutions. The policy implications of the
Bergendorf classification would lead to a different approach to handling
change depending on context. Consider for example, the policy decisions
aimed at gender, with an understanding of culture as a complex system
instead of creating new gender roles. One would look at the local interactions between men and women and the rules upon which they are based
before making a recommendation for change. The question of introducing
democracy would be dealt with similarly: which has been shown to be
highly context-specific, with the Arab Spring resulting in democratic movements that evolved in a wide variety of ways from Egypt (Peterson, 2011) to
Djibouti (Manson, 2011). Leaders need to be aware of these interactions in
shaping decisions.

Knowledge impacts on culture via a number of channels. Cho (2012)
considers globalization as the proliferation of economic, political, social,
cultural, and technological interactions across countries—the spread of
ideas, information, and values, but also flows of people, goods, capital, services, and market exchanges. As such, one would expect a differentiated role
or reaction to these flows across cultural lines. Analysis in Léautier (2013)
applied to the issue of gender shows that globalization has had a differential effect on the role of women in enterprises. Léautier (2013) shows that
between 2005 and 2010, the depth of female ownership in domestically
listed companies in Africa was less than 50% in all but three countries (Côte
d'Ivoire, Liberia, and Madagascar). Women found more employment opportunities in societies that opened up more to the outside world, but remained
"occupationally segregated" according to Giugale (2011). Some negative
effects are visible as a result of globalization; for instance women are trapped
in subsistence farming in societies where manufacturing capabilities are
low. Women are also often frozen out of jobs in the flourishing extractive

industries of oil, gas, and mining, and hence could lose out despite the new discoveries of oil and gas and rich minerals in Africa. It is therefore important for leaders to consider cultural aspects in the flow of knowledge and ideas in order to get the desired results.

Evolution of key risks affecting decision-making

Attention to the issue of risks and how they affect decision-making has been heightened in recent years. Among the chief reasons are the contagious effects of financial crises and the escalation in fuel prices, with their knock-on effects on business and society as whole. Heightened attention to security and safety threats has also been brought about by the increased costs of theft, pilfering, contamination, and terrorism. Corruption is seen to be mostly negative in the long term and a key source of instability. An escalation in road accidents has rendered the risk of road safety high on the agenda of decision makers. Unanticipated catastrophes, such as dramatic infrastructure collapses, epidemics and pandemics, natural disasters (tsunami, earthquakes, floods) and climate-related risks all cause worry when looking at activities on a global scale.

Complexity in financial systems

Contagious financial crises come about because financial systems today behave as coupled systems that transfer a crisis from one system to another. Failure in one system changes the probability of failure in the other system. The consequence of such coupling is that the financial system overall is more susceptible to large failures and there is a greater probability of synchronization of financial failures. There are a number of examples of coupled financial systems effects, such as the "Tequila crisis" which started in Mexico in 1994–1995 and spread to Brazil and Argentina, which provided many lessons and rendered Latin America more resilient to future crises (Mishkin, 1999). The collapse of the baht in Thailand in July 1997 was the onset of the Asian financial crisis that went on to impact Indonesia and caused concern for a global financial crisis. Lessons are still being drawn from this, including how to enhance preparedness to deal with periodic socio-economic up- and downturns (Krishnamurthy, 2009).

The US financial system crisis in 2007 started in the banking sector and was triggered by complex interactions between valuation and liquidity problems that spread to cause a global financial crisis lasting from 2007 to 2012. Many of the potential contagion effects were well known, based on the work of researchers in economics such as Bernanke (1983), who studied the non-monetary effects of the financial crisis in the propagation of the great depression. Other scholars investigated the reasons for the banking crisis in the US after it happened and drew lessons for reforms (see, for example, Kregel, 2008).

Lessons learned in various regions of the world had an impact on how the euro area crisis of 2011 was handled, with some arguing that the global financial system was better prepared for a crisis than it was in 2008 (*The Economist* 2012). All these assessments of previous financial crisis and their implications from a point of view of contagion, propagation, and response further emphasize the importance of understanding the underlying complexity and adjusting decisions and policies to the local contexts.

People in positions of authority need to be aware of these dynamics even if they are not experts in finance, so that they can gauge the speed and depth of changes need to handle crisis and put the resources needed to build resilience, as well as build the political coalitions necessary to sustain reforms. Chapter 6 considers the detailed case of Iceland, which helps the learner navigate through challenges in specific contexts.

Evolution of fuel prices

Fuel price shocks have a dynamic effect on a number of systems, not the least of which is the price of basic food and commodities, due to their link to cost of transport. Countries that are net exporters of fuel benefit during an upswing, while those that are net importers hurt. Thus, understanding the long-run dynamics of fuel prices is important to make better decisions around activities that are impacted by fuel prices. Fuel prices are driven by dynamics in other areas, but cause dynamics of their own. India in the period 2008–2012 had the lowest pump price for diesel fuel amongst the BRICS countries listed in Table 2.4, while South Africa had the highest, having grown from US$ 0.95 per liter in 1998–2002 to US$ 1.42 in 2008–2012.

The rising costs of shipping illustrate how the long-run dynamics of fuel prices shape decisions. Many companies, especially small and medium sized players in developing countries, are unable to anticipate the evolution of freight costs, which play an integral part in the final cost of goods and services. For large consumers of freight logistics, freight cost estimation

Table 2.4   Evolution of pump prices of fuel

Country	Pump price for diesel fuel (US$ per liter)		
	1998–2002	2003–2007	2008–2012
Brazil	1.03	1.14	1.02
Russia	0.86	0.72	1.00
India	0.70	0.82	0.86
China	1.01	1.04	1.28
South Africa	0.95	1.14	1.42

Source: World Development Indicators available at http://data.worldbank.org/data-catalog/world-development-indicators.

has become so complex that specialized companies have been created to do freight audits that examine, adjust, and verify freight bills for accuracy (Aberdeen, 2007). Government decisions on taxing fuel are also fraught with complexity, as the added tax on fuel changes driver behavior and driving costs, with knock-on effects on a whole series of other economic and social systems (Schiraldi, 2010). Pricing utilities and setting appropriate rates is also impacted by the dynamics of fuel prices. Fuel price levels even drive decisions made to enhance fuel efficiency—such decisions result in a wholesale change in technologies, impacting energy production, automobile manufacture, or airplane size.

Nowhere is the issue of fuel price escalations felt more sensitively than in Africa's food markets. Africa imports large amounts of grain (particularly rice and wheat) and uses much of its vast resources of arable land for maize production (Cassman and Liska, 2007). Utilization of grains for biofuels not only causes competition for land but also has an impact on the prices of food. Being able to get the right balance in terms of country and global policy on food and biofuel production is a complex business that becomes sensitive when fuel prices are on the move.

Impact of security threats

Security and safety threats are also a key driver whose dynamics have important effects on decision-making. Assets of all kinds can be subject to risk, including people, facilities, equipment, materials, information, activities and operations of companies, governments, and even households.

The types of threats have also changed over the years. One needs to be concerned about insider threats, such as when a trader goes rogue, as was the case at Societé Generale where Jérôme Kerviel cost the bank US$ 7 billion in losses in 2008 as a result of fraudulent activity arising from placing questionable bets that circumvented the sophisticated computer-based risk controls (Kar-Gupta, 2008). Threats could also derive from terrorists, with severe consequences and global shocks, as was the case with the September 11, 2001 plane attacks on the US. Environmental threats are numerous ranging from flooding to drought and earthquakes. The threat to global air travel from volcanic ash coming from an eruption of the Icelandic volcano Eyjafjallajökull in April 2010 was the first of its kind. Risks to aircraft caused the cancellation of some 17,000 flights per day (BBC, 2010) due to the high interdependency of travel and the sheer volume of air travel on a given day. Some threats come from negligence during design, or accidents during construction, such as the dramatic infrastructure collapses reported on regularly on the news (Table 2.5).

Decision-makers also need to understand the motivation, triggers, trends, and methods by which threats can materialize. These could be cyber-based or involve physical assault, as in the case of piracy on the high seas. Attacks can be linked to transport systems and there is a risk from suicide bombers.

Table 2.5 Business costs of threats

Country	Business costs of terrorism	Business costs of crime and violence	Organized crime
Brazil	6.4 (11)	3.5 (102)	4.0 (122)
Russian Federation	4.7 (118)	4.5 (90)	4.2 (114)
India	4.8 (114)	5.0 (64)	5.0 (81)
China	5.1 (102)	4.8 (70)	4.7 (98)
South Africa	6.2 (29)	2.9 (134)	4.3 (111)
United Kingdom	5.2 (98)	5.3 (51)	6.0 (35)
United States	4.4 (124)	4.5 (86)	4.9 (87)

Source: World Economic Forum (2013): Global Competitiveness Report.

Vulnerability can be physical (toughness, strength), technical (energy surge, cyber attack, contamination), operational (policies, practices, procedures), or organizational (business continuity). It is not surprising therefore that when firms were asked about their observation of security cost trends by the World Economic Forum in its Executive Opinion Survey of 2013 they showed varied patterns of costs across countries. There even distinct differences between cost of terror threat and cost of organized crime. Brazil, for example, has a much lower business cost of terror, but has major challenges with organized crime. India does the best amongst the BRICS countries in terms of organized crime and business costs of crime and violence. The US, like the UK, has a big challenge in the business costs of terrorism, but also has challenges in the areas of business costs of violence and organized crime.

Such statistics have prompted the Global Agenda Council on Terrorism of the World Economic Forum to quote on its website that "Al-Qaeda spent US$ 500,000 to attack the World Trade Center. Conversely, the costs of 9/11 to the United States are estimated at US$ 3.3 billion, nearly seven times the investment by al-Qaeda" (for more detail see http://www.weforum.org/content/global-agenda-council-terrorism-2013).

Vulnerability can also increase with changes in weather patterns, as has been observed in the pattern of increase in the type of natural disasters between 1987 and 2012. Floods have increased dramatically in Asia, going beyond the countries that were vulnerable to flooding in a spatial spread of flooding risk.

The consequences of threats can be human (death/injury), economic, environmental, or even threaten national security. Some threats could even be symbolic, like bringing down a company website and leaving a special message. But one of the under-evaluated threats to human and economic systems is the threat of road accidents, which are more risky than malaria, tuberculosis, and HIV-AIDS in claiming the lives of children aged 5 to 14 in developing countries as measured in Disability Adjusted Life Years (DALYs).

According to Licari et al. (2005), because children's health has improved significantly in many countries, the risk of car accidents has risen to become a real threat to child safety, calling for a revision in the approach to policy-making to ensure that it is more evidence-based.

The escalation in the level of road accidents, particularly in developing countries, has coincided with the increase in mobility. The severity of this risk has induced some companies to develop dedicated strategies to deal with the threat (Table 2.6). Accidents cause loss of life and limb, but even when they are minor, with no serious damage or fatality, they cause delays in traffic that have consequences for other systems.

Companies like BASF faced high costs as a result of road accidents during the 2000s and have made special efforts to reduce the risk with significant success (www.basf.com). The decision to act on transportation accidents was a good business decision that came as a result of the dual link to sustainability and to costs per shipment.

A number of ways of reducing risks exist, ranging from the total elimination of a threat, to reducing vulnerability by toughening the assets, or dampening the impact of consequences through well-designed backup systems. Any risk reduction strategy needs to have priorities so that the most severe risks can be targeted first. Cost-effectiveness is another consideration, especially with the increase in interplay across risks: not all risks can be eliminated or reduced at affordable costs. The strategy has to ensure that to a large degree the solutions embedded in action are irreversible and not easy to undo. Choices also need to be made to reduce specific threat scenarios, including assessing the geographical spread of risks and agreeing on acceptable levels of risk. For a complete treatment of corporate risk assessment see Léautier (2007).

Some threats can be in the form of epidemics and pandemics, requiring urgent attention and coordinated solutions. The effect of the severe acute respiratory syndrome (SARS) epidemic on the chicken export markets in both the US and China is quite telling. The threat began in Guangdong, China, in November 2002, when what had been mostly limited to birds crossed over to humans. The impact that this epidemic had on US exports of chicken when the threat had largely been contained in China is an indication of how sensitive interconnected systems can be. Threats do not necessarily have to originate in your market or touch your product, but the impact can be felt across products and markets with similar characteristics.

Ethics and accountability

Business leaders and politicians don't always have the same priorities, especially with respect to policies and programs. Globalization has caused evolution in the perspectives of businesspersons and politicians, especially in the area of ethics and accountability. When the World Economic Forum

Table 2.6   Twenty-year pattern of natural disasters in the world (by number per year)

1987	2012	
11 recorded floods	**70 recorded floods**	
Bolivia – Jan 2007	Brazil – Jan 2012	Philippines – June 2012
Peru – Feb 2007	Ecuador – Jan 2012	Gabon – June 2012
China – May 2007	Bolivia – Jan 2012	India – June 2012
Colombia – Jul 2007	Mozambique – Jan 2012	Uganda – June 2012
Chile – Jul 2007	Fiji – Jan 2012	Sudan – June 2012
Iran – Jul 2007	Papuan New Guinea –	South Sudan – June 2012
Nepal – Aug 2007	Jan 2012	Bangladesh – June 2012
Venezuela – Sep 2007	Tajikistan – Feb 2012	Burkina Faso – June 2012
Guatemala – Sep 2007	Afghanistan – Feb 2012	Afghanistan – July 2012
Jamaica – Nov 2007	Chile – Feb 2012	Nepal – July 2012
Indonesia – Nov 2007	Kazakhstan – Feb 2012	DPR Korea – July 2012
	Occupied Territories of	Nigeria – July 2012
	Palestine – Feb 2012	Central America –
	Colombia – Mar 2012	July 2012
	Haiti – Mar 2012	Niger – July 2012
	Fiji – Mar 2012	Pakistan – Aug 2012
	Kenya – Apr 2012	Myanmar – Aug 2012
	Russian Federation –	Chad – Aug 2012
	Apr 2012	Cameroon – Aug 2012
	Paraguay – Apr 2012	Senegal – Aug 2012
	Rwanda – Apr 2012	Mali – Aug 2012
	Vietnam – Apr 2012	Central African Republic –
	Dominican Republic –	Aug 2012
	Apr 2012	Gambia (The) – Sep 2012
	Comoros – Apr 2012	Somalia – Sep 2012
	Kyrgyzstan – Apr 2012	Benin – Oct 2012
	Nepal – May 2012	DR Congo – Oct 2012
	China – May 2012	Colombia – Oct 2012
	Georgia – May 2012	Haiti – Nov 2012
	Venezuela – May 2012	Congo – Nov 2012
	Honduras – May 2012	Panama – Nov 2012
	Ethiopia – May 2012	Sri Lanka – Dec 2012
	Cuba – May 2012	
	Solomon Islands –	
	June 2012	
	Indonesia – June 2012	
	Guatemala – June 2012	

Source: Data from www.reliefweb.int on July 23, 2013.

surveyed business leaders in 2005, asking them what their top development challenges were, they highlighted good governance and tackling corruption as the number one priority. The international financial architecture made it to the top ten, but was the lowest ranked challenge, despite the ensuing financial crisis three years later. Poverty alleviation and education, peace and security, and human rights were all in the top ten. In 2005 business leaders were very concerned about ethics and accountability.

Similar surveys carried out in 2009 and 2012 showed a much different pattern of risks identified by global business leaders and there were also differences when comparing what African leaders said, indicating a gap between global and regional concerns. Global business leaders ranked access to financing as number one and corruption as number two. So ethics and accountability still made it into the top two challenges of global business seven years later. African leaders ranked the opposite problem of staff retention, which is on the supply side of generating skilled people, picking the fast tracking of education and skills as their top priority. African leaders had retaining skilled youth as a concern as well, because of the challenge of a brain drain in a global labor market. So there was agreement on skills, albeit with attention split between the demand-side and supply-side concerns. They were also concerned about food security and preparing for higher energy costs.

Ethical issues and concerns were also on the top for both groups of leaders, although they saw them with different lenses (Table 2.7). African leaders focused on self—"visionary and self-less leadership" which was ranked 2nd and "direct mindsets to responsibility and ownership" which was ranked 5th. One could also consider "ensure security of person at individual, community and business level" ranked 7th as an ethical concern.

Table 2.7 Differing perspectives of business and political leaders

African leaders top challenges in 5–10 years taken in 2009	Most problematic factors for doing business in Africa in 2012
1. Fast tracking education and skills	1. Access to financing
2. Visionary and self-less leadership	2. Corruption
3. Food security and affordability	3. Inadequate supply of infrastructure
4. Retain skilled youth	4. Inefficient government bureaucracy
5. Direct mindsets to responsibility and ownership	5. Tax rates
6. Prepare for higher energy costs (oil)	6. Inadequately educated workforce
7. Ensure "security of person" at individual, community, and business level	7. Inflation
	8. Policy instability
	9. Poor work ethic in national labor force
8. Capture maximum benefit from foreign intervention into the continent	10. Tax regulations
	11. Restrictive labor regulations
	12. Crime and theft
	13. Foreign currency regulations
	14. Insufficient capacity to innovate
	15. Government instability/coups
	16. Poor public health

Source: World Economic Forum 2009 and World Economic Forum, Executive Opinion Survey 2012.

Openness to dealing with tectonic change

Skills of importance for leaders are related to openness to dealing with tectonic change. A case study and a practice block provide the learner with the areas of skill needed to deal with tectonic change in an open manner that relies on seeing with fresh eyes and sensing from others and their experiences to build the foundation for common action.

The Jamuna Bridge case study is used to illustrate the skill of keen observation to identify what is going on, retreating and reflecting about the patterns observed, and generating solutions quickly using previous knowledge and past experience, which can be downloaded quickly. The reader is challenged to go through what is needed to suspend prior beliefs or hypothesis and try to see what is happening with fresh eyes, which is the key to gaining a new perspective. The process involves redirecting thoughts, analysis, and interpretations into a new way of thinking and seeing patterns and combining the new realization with sensing from what is happening around you—sensing from the field.

The Jamuna Bridge case study is very useful for investigating *"What are the dynamics of change that produce such shifts?"* The case has all the features of decision-making in the face of multiple stakeholders, with engineering, economic, and social complexities. It also posits the dynamic decision-making of major stakeholder groups in the face of shifting patterns of environmental topology and people's preferences, as well as financing and implementation arrangements. As such, it provides a good opportunity to go deeper into the dynamics of change, building on the learner's capacity to observe the principal patterns of change.

The materials presented in the case study help the learner determine the dynamics of change that are generating the shifts in observed patterns. Dynamics of change are presented through various lenses—the need for transport solutions to meet trade needs enabled by the emergence of logistics as a turning point in economic and social interactions on a global scale. The case also provides the learner with information about the dynamics of change in Bangladesh which come from the patterns of mobility, connectivity, and productivity and how these are linked to the outside world. Ownership and financing arrangements that bridge the World Bank, other multilaterals, bilateral aid, and the private sector also feature in the case. The case highlights the interactions between knowledge and culture, especially in the description of the *char* people, and provides a picture of the value that good tools for risk management could have for risk taking and the implications for the decision-makers involved. Finally, the case also brings in information about the growing demands for ethical and accountable leadership around the world.

The Jamuna Bridge case study brings out issues that germinate from the logistics and supply area of practice, but complemented by the behaviors driving increased mobility and connectivity within Bangladesh and in the world at large, as well as the changing nature of finance. This module puts particular focus on the role of culture and the sources and impacts of knowledge and innovation. The case also illustrates how individuals, firms, and states react to risks in making choices and taking decisions. The special role played by ethics when the outcomes of the dynamics of change are not known in advance is emphasized in the case study.

The case illustrates the Theory U concepts of "empathizing and integrating actions of others," by introducing skills for identifying the global constraints that impact on a variety of stakeholders; selecting among options for dealing with areas that are hard to predict; adapting to the actions of different agents and extracting the impact their actions may have on business, political, or development objectives; and dealing with change through negotiating strategies with multiple stakeholders that lead to superior results.

The Jamuna Multipurpose Bridge case study[5]

It was March 1995. Ismail Mubarak gave a final look at the notes he was preparing for the upcoming Jamuna Bridge public meeting, wondering whether he had addressed all the key issues raised by the complainants. "I hope this is the last time I have to run such a meeting," he muttered to himself. "I hope we can once and for all get the concerns raised addressed." The project he was task-managing in Bangladesh was an engineering marvel, but the social and environmental issues it raised were extremely complex—and Mubarak was becoming frustrated by the numerous unanticipated developments that the project raised at each stage. Should the project be completed, he thought to himself, it might become one of the truly amazing development projects of our time, proving that complex infrastructure projects do have a role in a country's development. Being two years from retirement, he was also wondering whether this project would be a feather in his cap or a thorn in his side.

Mubarak's life had been much simpler before he took over as Task Manager for the Jamuna Bridge Project. When his Sector Manager had asked him to take on the project, he had assured him that it would be exciting and rewarding, and one of the most complex things he would be asked to do in the world Bank. "The project is basically sound, though there are a few complex details you need to take care of to ensure that the interests of the people displaced by the project and the environmental concerns surrounding the project—like flooding and soil erosion—are taken care of. And you will have to take care of the technical complexity as well, of having a multipurpose bridge that can carry road traffic, railway freight, a gas pipeline, an electric inter-connector, and telecommunications facilities. All in all, the previous Task Manager has done a good job, and you will have no trouble bringing this project to the Board and to a successful implementation."

The Sector Manager was half right. The technical issues, though intricate, Mubarak had managed successfully in record time. But managing the stakeholders had proved far more difficult than he'd been led to believe. And now he was preparing for a public meeting where he expected discord, disarray, and disappointment—all from those he'd originally thought the project would benefit most.

The Jamuna Bridge Project

The Jamuna Bridge Project was different from the beginning. It was expected to be a winner, even before it was designed and implemented. When completed it was to be the 11th longest bridge in the world and the longest in South Asia, with a multipurpose bridge connecting the east and west of Bangladesh. It was a difficult project that had taken 25 years (1971–1995) and seven studies to convince financiers from outside Bangladesh that it was worth doing. The final report, an appraisal completed in 1993, indicated very high economic returns and manageable social and environmental consequences. Once the bridge location was fixed and appropriate designs made in 1994, the project was ready to go.

The project was to take five years of construction (1994–1999). It was also expensive. It was to cost US$ 800 million to cover the expense of constructing a bridge with access to roads (viaducts), to carry a railway line, an electricity inter-connector, a gas pipeline, and telecommunications facilities. Also included in the project were guide bunds to protect against flooding. All such complex engineering projects also come with complex institutional issues. One per cent of the project cost was to support the strengthening of public administration, the system of Law and Justice and Central Government Administration. Such institutions turned out to be critical in the implementation phase of the project, which involved considerable complex details around property rights (ancestral lands, relocation of people, and compensation).

The project has major stakeholders

As complex as it was from an engineering perspective, the project was complicated even further by the various stakeholders that had a keen interest in the project. Ismail Mubarak, as Project Task Manager, and his Sector Manager were responsible for the project in the South Asia Region of the World Bank. The World Bank was one of four primary financiers of the project through its concessionary finance to developing countries under the International Development Assistance (IDA) instrument. Each financier provided US$ 200 million: the Government of Bangladesh (GOB), the World Bank (IDA), the Asian Development Bank (ADB), and the Government of Japan (OECF). The Government of the UK also had a small stake in the project through its Oversees Development Agency (ODA), now known as the Department for International Development (DFID). The main stakeholder among the group

of financiers was the World Bank, having assumed the role of lead coordinator, whose main responsibilities fell under the oversight of its Board of
Executive Directors. Mubarak, as Project Task Manager and Financiers' lead
coordinator, answered to World Bank Management in both its management
oversight and financier capacities.

Other stakeholders included the Government of Bangladesh, which had
the major responsibility of representing the interest of its citizens, and which
included the Bridge Authority responsible for the planning, construction
oversight, maintenance, and operation of the bridge, known as the Jamuna
Multipurpose Bridge Authority (JMBA). Representing the interests of the
project-affected people (*char* people) was a local Non-Governmental Association
known as the Jamuna Char Integrated Development Project (JCIPP).

Project complexities intensify

When the project was conceived, everyone expected the main complexity
to be the changing morphology of the river, which made it difficult to fix
the final location of the bridge (the final location was fixed in 1994 after
23 years of study and analysis). The best engineers from around the world
were commissioned to design, construct, and supervise the project. Since
flooding and erosion impacts were expected to occur up to years after the
start of construction, there was a special unit set up to analyze the movement of the river and provide real-time input to the contractors.

However, the main challenge of the project turned out to be the effect of
the river migration on the sole livelihood of a group of people. Over centuries, the movement of the river created seasonal islands, known as *chars*,
which were occupied by inhabitants known as the *char* people. They lived
on these ancestral lands, which were made up of 75 seasonal islands (*chars*)
whose location could not be fixed in advance. There were 2 million people
dependent on these ancestral lands for their livelihood when Mubarak took
over the management of the project, of whom over 70,000 inhabited the
project area.

A complaint is lodged

In 1995, one year into the project, the *char* people's representatives, the
JCIPP, lodged a specific complaint. It alleged that the *char* people were not
consulted during the project planning, design, and implementation phase
and that they were seeing major impacts on their livelihoods as a result of
the construction. Not being aware of what the future held for them, they
were very concerned that they would not have much of a livelihood in the
coming years (Table 2.8).

Mubarak looked at the items of the specific complaint and at the
Management Response that argued that the complaint was not valid. The
complaint was being reviewed by the Inspection Panel, an independent

Table 2.8 Jamuna Bridge statistics

Total project beneficiaries: 27 million
Total *char* people: 4 million
Char people living in the project area: 0.5 million
Project's effect on *char* people living in the project area:
• Total loss of property and livelihood: 25%
• Partial or no loss of property: 75%
• It is not known exactly which *chars* will be lost, since the river morphology is not known precisely in advance.
Exchange rate: 40 Bangladesh *Taka* = 1 US Dollar
Measurement of area: 1 decimal = 2.35 square meters
Cost to purchase serviced land: 15 Taka per 1 square meter
Cost to purchase agricultural land: 12 Taka per 1 square meter

body created as a means for increasing the transparency and accountability of the World Bank's operations. The Inspection Panel was an independent instrument responding to claims by those adversely affected by the projects financed by the Bank.

According to the complaint filed by the JCIPP and signed by nearly 3,000 people, "the IDA failed to include *char* people in the process of planning, designing and implementing resettlement and environmental measures that are both preventive and mitigative." Indeed, 74% of *char* people interviewed by the JCIPP said they had never been officially informed that the planned project would have a direct impact on them. As a result, the JCIPP alleged, *chars* and *char* people had suffered damage for which they had not been appropriately compensated and which was likely to escalate. The type of damage cited included loss of a traditional way of life, loss of livelihood (especially from fishing), and other forms of loss from dislocation to other areas.

Mubarak and his colleagues had answered the complaint in their Management Response. Noting the disruption of river life as a result of bridge construction, the Response stated that planning for the bridge had been under careful consideration and examination, and that since building was only allowable during the dry season, a phased approach was adopted to ensure that the erosion and flooding were properly observed. Moreover, although the Requesters alleged that the resettlement areas were too small and did not allow enough room for all of the people to be resettled, the Response stated that the idea for resettlement incentives was in effect and that people would be allowed to resettle themselves on nearby farmland. The Management Response Mubarak prepared allowed for each allegation to be responded to by the Management and the Government of Bangladesh.

Mubarak thought he had all the key elements and was ready for the meeting, where all the stakeholder interests would be represented. But he also knew he would have to convince the Inspection Panel and his own Board of Executive Directors that the project management team had done all that could be done to address the major concerns of the *char* people. All the stakeholders knew that the project was already expected to take a total of six years, a year longer than initially planned, so he anticipated some impatience.

What could have been done differently during the planning stage? Why was it not done? What could be done to address the shortcomings? What would the project management team need to have in place to address the shortcomings in the time that remained? And could Mubarak and the other stakeholders find a mutually acceptable solution to the problems raised without derailing the project entirely? These were all questions running through Mubarak's mind as he entered the public meeting.

Entitlements and entitlement package

Project-affected households depend on a variety of sources such as farm land, tenant farming, wage labor, and trading for their livelihood. Often a single household may rely on more than one means of livelihood through the properties and work of its several individual members. A large number of households suffer different kinds of losses in the process of relocation. The entitlement policy takes this into consideration by linking the entitlement to types of losses and to individuals. This will ensure that households get compensated according to their losses, irrespective of their social composition.

The basic concepts and principles of the entitlement policy include who is affected, what they are entitled to, and how entitlements are distributed. An affected person is referred to as a "Project Affected Person" (PAP), who owns property, lives and/or earns a living in the area to be acquired for the construction of the Jamuna Multipurpose Bridge under the Land Acquisition Law or at the time of the Bangladesh Rural Advancement Committee (BRAC) socio-economic survey of January 1993 (whichever is later). A household, defined as all persons living and eating together (sharing the same kitchen and cooking food together as a single family unit), is the basic record for identifying entitlements to a resettlement benefit.

Entitlements, which include replacement land or cash grants and credits in lieu of replacement land, are on the basis of legal ownership. In the case of joint title deed, the replacement land or cash grants and credits in lieu of replacement land are given to the joint holders (i.e. joint holders will be treated as one unit). In the case of utilities and squatters who do not own land, but are entitled to a homestead plot (or grant to purchase land), the entitled person is the head of the household.

Table 2.9 Entitlement matrix for the Jamuna Bridge Project

Category	Entitlement
Loss of farmland	Monetary grant adequate to buy an equal area of replacement land. Loan up to 50% of the total compensation for purchase of land at commercial interest rates for Project Affected People with per capita holdings less than 40 square meters.
Loss of homesteads	Replacement homestead plot with no evacuation prior to provision of replacement homestead as follows: • 100 square meters or more of homestead lost to a household = cash grant equivalent to cost of replacement for an equal homestead or plot plus cash valued at the same price as the replacement land. • < 100 square meters of homestead lost to a household = minimum compensation of homestead of 100 square meters through private sale land purchase or relocation to resettlement site, plus grant in cash for any difference in value between original and replacement homestead. • No homestead but loss of residence = a homestead plot of 100 square meters through private land purchase or relocation to resettlement site; OR cash grant equal to predetermined replacement value of 100 square meters homestead plot.
Loss of residential structures	Transfer and house construction grant of TK 7000 paid in two installments: • TK 2000 at time of relocation; and • TK 5000 after identification of homestead and evacuation from project area.
Loss of commercial structures	Reimbursement for cost of: (a) dismantling and removing products and materials up to 15% of market value; and (b) building construction grant of TK 25 per sq. ft. of floor area.
Displacement from rental premises	Moving grant of TK 2000
Loss of rental income/share-cropped farm wage/employment	Three compensation categories: • One time maintenance grant of TK 3600 • Vocational training at project cost • Help to find employment or get credit to start a business activity OR • 15 decimals of land or cash to purchase 15 decimals of land, paid only against purchase of land

In the case of house/building construction grants, the entitled person is the legal owner of the structure (one who received the compensation under the law) where legal ownership is established. In the case of utilities and squatters who do not normally own the land on which the structure is constructed, the entitled person is the head of the household as recorded in the BRAC survey.

Maintenance grants and vocational training are provided to persons affected by loss of wage-earning opportunities or rented in/sharecropped land. This entitlement is to the individual (persons above the age of 13) so affected and the criteria of entitlement are loss of primary occupation/primary source of income as reported by the BRAC psycho-economic survey.

If more than one adult in a household is affected by loss of their primary source of income, each such person is entitled to maintenance grants and vocational training assistance. Domestic help, casual employees, and persons not usually residing with or dependent upon the PAP household, however, are not eligible for resettlement benefits (Table 2.9).

Indirectly affected persons are also catered for if they have lost their primary source of income as a result of the project. Disputes and grievances arising out of the definition of a household or entitled person are resolved through a mechanism of formal verification.

Losses compensated include farmland, homesteads, and places of residence, as well as residential and commercial structures. Affected people who are displaced from a rented/occupied commercial premise are entitled to a moving/transfer grant.

Loss of rented in/sharecropped farm wage labor/employment are compensated by getting access to vocational training at project cost and are helped to find employment or to obtain institutional credit for starting a suitable production/service activity. Alternatively, affected people are entitled to alternative land, the cost of which is considered equivalent to the cost of vocational training. Landless tenant farmers and farm laborers residing within areas acquired for the project are offered an alternative option of a cash grant adequate to buy land.

Lessons from the Jamuna Bridge case study

A practice block developed from Theory U provides the learner with the areas of skill needed to deal with tectonic change in an open manner that relies on seeing with fresh eyes and sensing from others and their experiences to build the foundation for common action (Box 2.1).

Box 2.1   Practice Block II: Openness in Dealing with Tectonic Change

Premise: The shifting topography and environment in which business and political decisions are made is shaped by a variety of stakeholders. By better understanding the perspectives, and connecting them to your inner source, you can identify superior actions for your particular context.

Objective: To practice the skill of seeing with fresh eyes and sensing from others and their experiences, building the foundation for understanding the emerging future.

Approach: Using a real case of the impact of natural disasters in a country context, participants will work with each other to understand how others sense problems and relate their perspectives to their own.

Focus of the case: To explore the specific perspectives of project affected people, the government, financiers, and project managers involved in the Jamuna Bridge and expose participants to the basics of risks from agent-to-agent interaction.

Key questions for practice:

(1) Which global constraints can you identify that would impact the strategy you would negotiate with a given stakeholder group?
(2) What options would you use for dealing with areas that are hard to predict?
(3) How could actions of different agents lead to global properties that affect your business?

Skill: Dealing with change by practicing "empathizing and integrating actions of others" in structured setting.

The Jamuna Bridge is a real case of the impact of constructing large-scale infrastructure in a highly populated environment that is subject to natural disasters. The learner is introduced to what it takes to work with others to understand how they sense problems and relate different perspectives to their own. The module introduces the learner to the global constraints that impact on strategy, the role of negotiations with different stakeholder groups, and the options for dealing with areas that are hard to predict. Other lessons highlighted in the module are the modalities by which the actions of different agents lead to global properties that affect particular decisions. The main skill from Theory U is dealing with change by practicing "emphasizing and integrating actions of others" in a structured setting.

Evaluation can serve as a guide for further learning and practice. To achieve efficiency, focus on what you know and exploit it; make an effort to meet the demands of the various stakeholders; demand accountability from the different decision-makers involved; and aim to improve on the process and structure of decision-making based on lessons learned and observed patterns of change. For creativity think outside the box; focus on what you don't know; anticipate what could emerge in the future; let things emerge; allow for maximum freedom and flexibility; and avoid process, rather focusing on unstructured interventions (Box 2.2).

Box 2.2   Evaluation Block II: Strategic Innovation after Seeing and Sensing: Practice Codes

Code A: Efficiency

- Stick to your knitting
- Exploit what you know
- Meet current client/customer/ guest needs
- Demand accountability
- Improve process and structure

Code B: Creativity

- Think outside the box
- Explore what you don't know
- Anticipate future needs
- Let things emerge
- Allow freedom and flexibility
- Avoid process, encourage unstructured interventions

Source: Developed using concepts from Govindarajan and Trimble (2005).

3
Complexity and Risk

Key Lessons from Chapter 3: Complexity and Risk

This chapter focuses on concepts about complexity that are useful in any decision setting. This includes identifying the nature and types of interactions surrounding a decision and understanding their implications. It is critical to observe the variations in the pattern of behavior after action in an interconnected system and the ensuing pattern of risks and their severity. This chapter also introduces the role of learning from the past and reacting rapidly to changing situations, as well as the role of values and the behaviors that serve best in choice making under uncertainty.

Specific skills introduced in the chapter are useful for guiding decision-making under increased complexity. These include: (1) the ability to observe and adapt to variations in the operating environment; (2) skills for assessing and selecting from a variety of options with little or partial information; (3) options for functioning in areas with low predictability about the future; (4) approaches for adjusting to the range of actions of other stakeholders; and (5) methods of engaging in actions to shape the global properties of decision environments for a common future outcome.

The dynamics of change may lead to complex outcomes defying the beliefs that people hold concerning the likelihood of ensuing actions. It is human nature to rely on a limited number of heuristic principles that reduce complex decision-making processes or tasks to simpler judgmental operations (Tversky and Kahneman, 1971). When making decisions in the presence of multiple alternatives, decision makers employ search strategies designed to eliminate some of the available choices as quickly as possible (Payne, 1976). The process of elimination to reduce the complexity of choices is done on the basis of limited information—hence introducing judgment by heuristics into the process. As such, the characteristics of the decision process determine the approach to choice making (Payne, 1976). It is important to have a better understanding of complexity so that the final choices made in the face of dynamics of change may be understood with the appropriate knowledge of what risks might be introduced by the selected method of decision-making.

This chapter expands on the issues of complexity and risks that come from the dynamics discussed earlier. The purpose is to support leadership learning in understanding *"What you need to know about complexity and risk to better navigate your specific context?"* The chapter starts with a few general concepts and outlines the specific skills set that is needed to navigate uncertain and risky scenarios. The analytical skills required are illustrated through examples and tools available to support decision-making in this area. There is also a focus on the behavioral skills desirable to succeed in risky and uncertain environments.

Introduction to complexity and risk

Few general concepts about complexity are useful in any decision setting (Bar-Yam, 2005a). Complexity generally increases with increasing interactions among previously independent systems. A failure or an effect in one system is transferred to other interconnected systems. Higher complexity has the potential to generate a set of new risks and challenges, and has been known to create more frequent risks and added severity of risk, and can even lead to further synchronization of risks. A small initial perturbation can dissipate, propagate, or be enhanced with long-ranging effects. When complexity is high it becomes progressively more difficult to predict the outcomes of a strategy or course of action. New approaches are therefore needed to guide leaders, decision makers, and analysts to select among competing strategies and outcomes.

The specific skills that are useful when operating under risk and increased complexity have to do with adaptability to *variation* in the environment for decision-making. Other skills relate to the degree of comfort in the *selection* of options with little or partial information, and where predictability about the turn of events or the future is low. Leaders need to be aware of the potential range of actions of other agents and the nature of their *interactions* in shaping the global properties of the decisions they are about to make.

Globalization is expected to increase the degree of synchronization of business cycles, enhancing global spillovers of macroeconomic fluctuations, particularly in industrial countries (Kose et al., 2003). Macroeconomic fluctuations of particular import include an investment or consumption boom in one country generating demand for increased imports and hence boosting economies abroad. Fluctuation in trade flows could induce increased specialization of production across countries, resulting in changes in the nature of business cycle correlations. As consumers benefit from global trade and preferences drive manufacturing, aided by smoother logistics, the speed at which changes are transmitted from one country to another and one system to another could increase.

Another example comes from transport. Consider the case of the volcanic eruptions in Iceland in 2010 that resulted in the largest air traffic shutdown since the Second World War. A volcanic eruption of this level previously would have been limited to Iceland and a small section of its airspace. Because of the volume of air travel and the degree of interconnectedness between airlines and countries through travel, the volcanic ash had severe impacts on an extended part of the world. Large parts of European airspace were closed completely for nine days (April 15–23, 2010) and intermittently thereafter until May 17, 2010.

Volcanic ash incidents indicate how a small event in one country can have an impact on a series of decisions in an interconnected system. A challenge and failure from the European airspace system caused delays and closures of other airports around the world, over and above the travelers in the specific aircraft caught in the ash crisis. Passengers who were stranded needed to select from alternate air routes or other modes of transport like rail and road to make it home. Meetings were held by video instead of face to face, and travel plans were canceled or changed. The incident resulted in a speeding up of the integration of European national air traffic systems into a Single European Sky (SES) (see European Commission, 2011).

The crisis of volcanic eruptions and the delays and losses to airlines resulted in a change in attitudes toward an integrated airspace system and resulted in decisions that would be different had the crisis not occurred. European lawmakers had to adapt, reacting to citizen demands and reality on the ground. Delays in travel with stranded passengers required swift decision-making by airline and airport managers to feed, house, and accommodate those caught in this unusual event. Such adaptability was very useful when the Icelandic ash disruptions manifested again in later years. European airspace leaders had learned how to manage such large disruptions. Leaders in the airline and airport business had "practiced" under a previous scenario and were ready for the outcomes of a more serious one.

These two illustrations show that decision-making in one setting is increasingly impacted by choices made in another setting. In the absence of total control, and without past experience in handling a particular scenario, one needs to make the rules as you go along. An example would be the decision to coordinate central bank activities to attenuate the effects of the euro crisis, as happened in 2011 (Hilsenrath and Sparshott, 2011). Other choices are to react rapidly to changing situations, as in the case of volcanic ash blown from Iceland. With limited experience in handling crises and little knowledge of the effect of choices, values are what remain as the true guide. The behaviors that serve best in choice making in the face of complexity and risk need to be learned and practiced and perfected over time.

Adapting to global constraints: the challenge of sustainable development

Many interactions are made more complex because of the desire by society to control some of the outcomes of those interactions. So, for example, while all countries are deeply in search of the means for higher economic growth, choices of strategies across countries and within specific periods of time constrain or enable the range of strategies to be selected from. Sustainable development is a concept that encapsulates such complexity of decision-making in very deliberate ways, by considering issues like irreversibility of ecological change, fundamental uncertainty, and system complexity (Faucheux et al., 2013). One key question about sustainability has to do with the concept of economic growth, which is a critical requirement for raising the welfare of billions around the world.

Countries have been growing at different rates over time, with countries like China managing to attain multiple years of very high growth rates and other countries growing in bursts of high growth followed by slower periods of growth, as in Ghana and Tanzania. At the same time, other countries like France and the Netherlands showed low levels of growth. As countries interact more, they depend on the level of growth attained in their neighbors' or trade partners' economies and this dependency calls for common decision-making on a series of policy choices, rendering economies even more integrated.

The level of interactions is increasing for many reasons, but migration is one of them (Castles and Miller, 2009). Migration patterns across countries are uneven and are driven by different forces. Patterns of migration have implications for how societies and economies integrate and also for how stable such integration may be. More people live in cities in the 2000s and they are more connected. They live in common spaces, but they do not necessarily have commonality of purposes, as individuals with commonality of purpose need not live in the same geographic space, but can find each other across long distances through social media channels like Facebook and Twitter. There is a varied rate of connectivity and globality across cities in the world, with some cities being open to outside ideas and influences while others remain closed, with implications for the evolution of democracy and choice. Taken together, these long-range social influences have an impact on economic behavior and vice versa. Other effects of increased interaction are disease burdens and global medical capacity, managing scarcity of water and food, and the implications of changing weather patterns on the prices of food. Scholars have come to question whether trade and globalization is a good or a bad thing when looked at from the lens of sustainability.

Kellner (2002) articulates a critical theory of globalization that brings out the contradictions brought about by the fundamental transformations in the world economy, politics and culture. He places particular emphasis on the directionality of globalization from above (through technology and capitalism) and from below (through local reactions and democracy), and the implications of such forces of change on the final outcome of globalization. Choices about sustainability are at multiple levels—global, regional, national, and local—and can benefit from the science of complexity. O'Brien et al. (2004) bring out geographical differentiation in vulnerability to climate change in a methodology applied to India which uses vulnerability mapping, and local-level case studies to assess the varying nature of vulnerability for any particular sector in country or region can be used as a basis for targeted policies and decisions.

Learning and the speed at which ideas spread are also causing fundamental shifts in the behaviors of individuals and economies alike. Arnett (2002) investigates the psychological consequences of globalization, with a particular focus on identity, arguing that globalization results in the development of bicultural identities whereby young people join self-selected cultures to maintain an identity separate from the global culture. Young adults and adolescents tend to have more interest in music, movies, and global social media, and tend to be more influenced by global movements and brands. This interest, argues Arnett (2002) tends to stretch the period of learning well into adulthood. It is not surprising therefore to see that a sustainability approach to complexity would be superior to other approaches in embedding not only the financial, economic, and technological aspects, but also the psychological effects of globalization.

Mobility, migration and urbanization

The effects discussed of interaction are most visible in urban areas and in geographical locations with high mobility, both physical and virtual. Shifts in patterns of migration tell us a lot about the various dimensions of complexity discussed so far. In the 1960s the majority of immigrants went to developing countries, but by 2005, the majority (60% of flows) were going to high-income countries (World Development Indicators). There have also been tremendous variations in the regional patterns of migration: only 0.2% of the population in countries in the East Asia and Pacific Region is made of migrants—Vietnam has the smallest immigrant population. Despite changes in the patterns and trends of migration, there has been stability in the rate of migration: a steady percentage of the world's population is immigrating (about 3% between 1960 and 2005). In 2005, the data show close to parity in the gender distribution of migration: 95 million female and 96 million male.

While there has been stability in the rate of migration, there has been an increase in the volume of migration, growing from 70 million in 1960 to more than 190 million in 2005. Migration flows are also concentrated, with some countries receiving more people than others. There are five countries that have immigrant populations making up more than half of the total population—Andorra, Kuwait, Monaco, Qatar, and United Arab Emirates. However, large volumes of people go to a few countries, making these countries have very large migrant populations; like the US, which tops the list, followed by Russia, Germany, Ukraine, France, Saudi Arabia, India, United Kingdom and Spain. The world has also seen a reduction in refugees: 8.4 million in 2005, down from 14.9 million in 1995 (United Nations, 2005).

The majority of migrants go to the big cities, which makes providing services to incoming residents a critical question. Similarly, when there is an economic downturn and there are fewer jobs to go around, there are negative impacts on recently migrating families, who find it difficult to get jobs and access to services.

There is a strong interaction between urbanization and increased mobility, with consequences for decision-making in a range of areas of policy—mainly because migration can also take place within a country (rural to urban). Such patterns have resulted in an archetype of urbanization, with cities of all sizes growing, but with a predominance of small cities and towns. The leadership capabilities to manage the provision of services in small towns and cities are often overwhelmed as the sizes sometimes triple or quadruple in a short space of time.

Consider Gaillac in the South West of France, which had a population of 10,315 residents in 1968. By 2007 the population had grown to 12,939 residents (CartesFrance.fr). Such a city falls under the last category of size used to capture city population dynamics of less than 500,000 people. The growth of Gaillac masks large transformations in the population; there were 5,692 people (46% of the population of Gaillac) aged less than 44 years in 1999, just before the boom in population growth. The number of people less than 44 years old grew to 6,509 (50% of the population of Gaillac) by 2007. There was a long period of time (15 years) where the population of Gaillac had actually been stagnant and even declined between 1975 and 1990. The challenge for decision makers is also to see how to manage such fast growth in a regional setting.

City managers perform vastly differently in their approaches and success levels in managing cities. Small cities tend to be better managed, with higher quality of life. Large cities are more challenging and few of them offer the same quality of life as small cities. Megacities, while even more challenging to manage, also have more resources and can compensate for the deterioration in quality of life by offering alternatives, like underground metro systems that reduce pollution levels, or green spaces and entertainment facilities that offer variety for their residents in terms of quality of life. Mid-size cities have all the complexities of large cities but not enough of the resources and they tend to have a challenge in meeting the quality of life expectations of their residents. Mid-size cities that succeed in maintaining a good quality of life attract more residents and become large cities. Such patterns of performance result in migration toward small or larger cities, making mid-size cities quite unstable in their population levels, with ebbs and flows depending on the cycles of opportunity for jobs and other such drivers.

Simon Compaoré, the former Mayor of Ouagadougou, organized utilities services to meet evolving population sizes. Having more people means providing more services like water, electricity, and waste collection, which is a severe challenge to day-to-day as well as strategic management. More people may also mean more revenue and therefore provides a chance for technological breakthroughs and major jumps in service levels.

A higher demand for services than the leadership is capable of providing could lead to governance challenges, where the services are captured by those with more economic or political power, or when moving up the queue for services only happens when a bribe or a favor can be given. The complexity of interactions between political leaders, city residents, and service providers can result in a wide range of outcomes. Some outcomes are positive, with cities evolving to become well governed and with the capability to provide a high quality of life for their residents. Others deteriorate into weakly governed places with poor quality of life, where to get service you have to bribe or take measures into your own hands.

The pressure of globalization, which allows residents to be aware of the quality of life in other cities through increased travel and interaction, can lead to other outcomes. Kaufmann et al. (2004) show that indeed global cities that are well connected to the outside world are better able to control bribery in utility services, but also exhibit state capture by a few powerful interest groups. Well-governed cities outperform poorly governed ones, whether local or global, indicating the premium that good leadership offers in solving the service conundrum as city sizes evolve.

Disease burden: global responses to shifting patterns

Shifting patterns of disease are another area of complexity that leaders need to be mindful of. The appearance of epidemics over time has historically challenged leaders. The outbreak of typhoid in Greece during the years 430 BCE–427 BCE, known as the "Plague of Athens" had complex results on social norms and behavior, with lasting implications for governance (Finley, 1985; Zippelius, 1986). People stopped saving and investing and went into a consumption spree, believing they would not live long enough to enjoy the fruits of their hard work and earned savings. Respect for human life and courteous and honorable behaviors also declined according to historians. Such plagues occur even today, with some emerging and new strains reemerging. In August 2012 there were typhoid outbreaks in Harare and Chitungwiza in Zimbabwe, Kabwe in Zambia, and Kikwit in the Democratic

Republic of Congo. The source of the disease is contamination with fecal matter that happens when water and sewer networks are not properly maintained or when there is weak governance preventing important priorities from being addressed.

Shifts in the patterns of disease burdens also have important policy implications that leaders need to be aware of. Comparing the global disease burden between 1990 and 2020 indicates that lifestyle diseases like ischemic heart disease and unipolar major depression will rise to become the top disability creating diseases, while diarrheal diseases, lower respiratory infections and measles will decline, and tuberculosis and HIV will remain flat or decline slightly (Murray and Lopez, 1996). The accuracy of these predictions depends on whether new strains of diseases appear or if infections reappear because they were not treated in all locations in the world. Increased mobility and interconnectedness means that leaders need to be aware of any appearances and keep a watch, as they could turn into epidemics and catch countries unaware.

Leaders need to be aware not only of the conditions that lead to an epidemic or pandemic, but also of the best way of responding, the cost of responding, and the approach to managing cross-border effects of epidemics. Such disease patterns put a premium on balancing global and local leadership roles in ways that were not as necessary when there was less interaction across societies.

Water, food, and climate change: implications for development patterns

Water, food, and climate change also have implications for development patterns. Countries need to work together to manage water scarcity, and regions of the world need to collaborate to manage common water systems. Water is also a critical input for food production and agricultural productivity and competes for other uses like industry and energy production. Climate change has the potential to shift the patterns of available surface and underground water, with serious implications for choices to be made locally and globally.

Leaders need to develop regional strategies and policies for water basin management, as well as approaches to handle the suite of risks related to water shortages. Developing such strategies is necessary because water is at the nexus of many risks. Infectious diseases like cholera are waterborne. Pandemics like typhoid have their origins in water systems, as seen in the case of ancient Athens. There are numerous chronic diseases that are related to water—as seen in the impact of dehydration on bladder, prostate, and kidneys, as well as coronary heart disease according to Chan et al. (2002). Risk factors driving the availability of water come from external weather events like flooding or drought, or changing patterns of biodiversity. Human actions that can alter the availability and quality of water include urbanization and migration and infrastructure provision. Changing patterns of available water can impact food prices and agricultural productivity.

Leaders need to decide whether or not to build secondary networks and have some redundancy in systems of water supply to avoid risks of water unavailability. Other decisions depend on analytical capabilities to identify and remove obstacles in the critical path, like maintaining embankments and inspecting sewer lines to avoid major disasters. Leaders need to have a set of actions to hedge against water-related shocks, like silos to store grain in the event of an elongated drought period. Some choices revolve around controlling for natural or induced risks, like avoiding leakage of sewage water into drinking water, which could cause a typhoid epidemic. Some decisions, like managing flood plains and managing secondary effects on food prices, require that countries work together and select amongst a suite of actions at the local and global level.

Investing in science and technology can render locations that are water-scarce viable. Desalination, making use of abundant sea water, and growing genetically modified drought-resistant crops can also transform deserts into fertile lands. Such use of science and technology is more important in countries where land scarcity and water scarcity co-exist.

According to the World Development Indicators and the World Atlas, arable land makes up 11% of total global land area (1.4 billion hectares globally). Europe and Central Asia have the highest level arable land per capita (0.57 ha per person). However, arable land per capita has declined by 19% in low-income countries over the past two decades. Africa is home to the largest amount of unused arable land in the world and has great potential, but has challenges in terms of the availability of water.

From a technology perspective, fertilizer use per hectare is highest in East Asia and Pacific and lowest in Sub-Saharan Africa (by a factor of 17). Using modern technology for agriculture in Africa could help deal with the effects of drought, as during the past 30 years Africa has experienced at least one major drought each decade.

The pressure on political leaders is high, as water is becoming an increasingly scarce natural resource, as can be seen in the increase in the number of water-vulnerable countries in Africa. Country leaders need capabilities that include the ability to raise agricultural productivity, find innovations that can work in drought stricken areas, manage food security, create regional food markets and improve the functioning of agricultural supply chains.

A good example of how leadership can transform agriculture, even in water-scarce zones, is the case of the African shea tree (*Vitellaria paradoxa*) which grows in the Sahel with limited need for water. The nuts from the tree, also referred to as karité nuts, are crushed to make butter or oil for all sorts of uses in cosmetics (creams, shampoos, moisturizers), cooking (as an oil), medicinal purposes (as an ointment), and to increase the durability of wood and leather (see Dei et al., 2007; Dennie, 2012; Warra, 2011). Much of the production in Africa is now for sale in terms of exports and there is a lot of research ongoing on the uses of the nut. It is not surprising therefore to see that many countries have invested heavily in the production of shea butter. The top producing countries include Nigeria, Mali, Burkina Faso, Ghana, Côte d'Ivoire, Benin, and Togo (Table 3.1).

The example of karité nuts, coming from a low water use plant, is not unique. Some countries have focused their attention on transforming agriculture and its relationship to water, with spectacular results. The cotton supply chain is a good indicator of the choices countries have made and their results. China, India, and the US have been able to effectively increase the value of cotton by focusing on improving productivity levels from farm to export point.

Other countries, like Burkina Faso, have made major jumps by better utilizing science not only for cotton production but also for products as varied as karité nuts, okra, dried cow peas, and goat's milk. The production of goat's milk for export grew in value by 25% between 1967 and 2007. The seven highest karité nut-producing countries by value are all in Africa, with Burkina Faso ranking at number three by value of production (Table 3.2).

Burkina Faso has taken the lead since the 1990s in making major transformations in agricultural production. The country took advantage of the growing "green" and "health" movements to increase their annual production of critical lifestyle products like goat's milk, fresh fruit and vegetables, cotton lint, and karité nuts, amongst other products (Figure 3.1). Policy decisions in agriculture rendered cotton lint its number one commodity in 2007, coming from a ranking of 12 in 1967 (FAOSTAT, 2010). Karité nuts went from number 18 to number 15 during the same period. Fresh goat's milk went from a non-tradable good in 1967 to 13th in rank by exported value of the commodity in 2007 (FAOSTAT, 2010).

Table 3.1   Top producing countries of karité nuts in 2007 by value

Rank	Country	Value (US$ millions)	
		2007	2010
1	Nigeria	61	118
2	Mali	27	38
3	Burkina Faso	10	17
4	Ghana	10	16
5	Côte d'Ivoire	4	3
6	Benin	2.2	2
7	Togo	1.4	2

Source: FAOSTAT, 2013. Data for 2010 or latest available year can be found at http://faostat.fao.org/site/291/default.aspx.

Table 3.2 Top 20 producing countries of cotton lint (current million US$)

Rank	Country	Value ($ 000)	Rank	Country	Value ($ 000)
1	China	9,700	11	Turkmenistan	460
2	India	9,099	12	Egypt	415
3	Turkey	5,645	13	Argentina	412
4	USA	5,432	14	Kazakhstan	406
5	Australia	4,068	15	Mexico	201
6	Pakistan	1,234	16	Greece	174
7	Uzbekistan	1,677	17	Benin	161
8	Brazil	1,484	18	Burkina Faso	146
9	Nigeria	643	19	Tajikistan	145
10	Syria	541	20	Mozambique	28

Source: FAOSTAT, 2010. Data for 2010 or latest available year can be found under Food and Agricultural Commodities Production at http://faostat.fao.org/site/339/default.aspx.

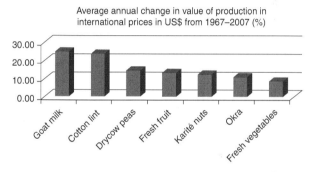

Figure 3.1 Transforming agriculture: Burkina Faso's capacity to tap into the "green" and "health" movements
Source: FAOSTAT, the data used in these tables are from 1967 to 2007 and is available at http://faostat.fao.org/site/291/default.aspx.

The ability of countries to make such transformations depends on how they manage the water cycle. Ethiopia is a relatively water-rich country, but its GDP is still tied to yearly annual rainfall variations. The leadership of the country selected agriculture as a key sector for transformation in an effort to address this dependency on rain-fed agriculture and even to export food in the coming years (Berhane, 2012). Ethiopian leadership has taken the role of transforming the link between agriculture and climate change at the global level, as seen in the role played by Prime Minister Meles Zenawi at the Copenhagen Conference in December 2009, with an effort to come out with a common African position (http://www.youtube.com/watch?v=ZK6EDUQBO7A). President Jakaya Kikwete of Tanzania used an initiative from the World Economic Forum to push transformation of agriculture through the private sector in Tanzania, including the use of private investments for irrigation and effective use of available water (Elinaza, 2013).

Global trade: social and political implications

Global trade is another aspect of globalization that leaders need to be comfortable with in decision-making. Global trade patterns and their evolution are critical, not only for global brands and global companies, but also for leaders at the local, community, and country levels, if not regional or continental levels. Questions that loom large include whether globalization will lead to convergent or divergent tastes amongst consumers and its implications for particular brands. Other questions relate to the social and political implications of convergent or divergent preferences in society.

The case of beer is illuminating. Beer is one of the oldest products to be branded and one of the earlier ones to go global. Furthermore, while the beer market is highly consolidated globally, with four brewers dominating the global market,[1] beer consumption is influenced greatly by local tastes.

The top beer brands by value are Budweiser and Bud Light from the US. Corona, from Mexico, has managed to increase its value to the rank of number five in the world, coming from a country brand to become a global brand in less than 10 years. The rise of Corona has also had an effect in the rise of another Mexican brand Cruzcampo, which was ranked in 2007 at number 10, but did not manage to maintain its position in the top 10 by 2013. The oldest branded beer in the world is Kronenbourg 1664, which has been around, as its brand says, since 1664. Kronenbourg 1664 was ranked number 13 globally in 2007 and has managed to stay a top brand for nearly 350 years (Table 3.3).

Table 3.3   Global brands in specific product markets: Beer—top ten by brand value

	Brand	Brand Value (US$ millions)	
		2007	2013
1	Budlight	4,419	10,840
2	Budweiser	5,558	9,458
3	Heineken	3,699	8,238
4	Skol	1,283	6,520
5	Corona	3,286	6,620
6	Stella Artois	2,940	6,319
7	Guinness	2,718	4,473
8	Beck's	1,039	3,831
9	Miller Lite	2,104	3,093
10	Amstel	1,272	1,516

Source: Milward Brown Optimor and Brand Directory available at http://brandirectory.com.

Changes in brand value drive export volumes and vice versa. Of relevance to leaders from these trends are the roles that knowledge and access to ideas have on preferences and the role of learning in transforming societies. Consider that in 2013 beer brand values improved 36%, the greatest percentage brand value rise of all categories, including consumer and retail, food and drink, financial institutions, commodities, and technologies. Of particular relevance is the strength of beer brands in developing countries. Changing consumer preferences and habits, including concerns about health as more knowledge becomes available, in addition to economic pressures, all contribute to shaping the outcomes of individual decisions and their implications for company performance. Leaders need to be aware of these interactions and beer is a good brand to illustrate the effects.

Complexity and approaches to risk: options for functioning with low predictability

Skills for adapting to global constraints and taking advantage of the opportunities that come along with complexity and change are important, but so are capabilities to function with low predictability. There are two broad options for functioning in areas of low predictability: a cascading model that relies on probabilistic reasoning, and dynamic complex system modeling. The approaches are unique and their usefulness depends on context.

The cascading probability model

In the cascading probability model, failures in one system drive failures in the other, and risks are interrelated over time. A severe drought causes a sharp increase in food prices when the drought country is a net exporter—like wheat in the US—or if the commodity is a major staple in human and animal diets—as maize is. With the cascading probability model, the cross effect is weak below the critical points of failure. If a drought lasts for six months and causes farmers to miss a whole planting cycle it could have an impact on the prices of maize until the next planting cycle. If food prices remain high for more than six months, civil unrest and even revolutions can occur.

The frequency of cascades increases with the strength of the coupling between the systems—food prices are strongly coupled to drought levels, and hence the presence of severe droughts increases the probability of sharp increases in food prices. The speed of the cascade is higher when the system is close to the critical point—an extra week of drought in a food-sensitive region could make the difference between political and social stability and civil strife if the drought has already been going for several months.

Feedback of one system to the other shifts the critical point downward as a function of the strength of coupling between the systems—if the government is successful in controlling food price spikes due to policy interventions then the effect of a longer and more severe drought on social stability may be reduced or attenuated.

At the critical point both systems become strongly coupled, acting more like a single system—severe and long periods of drought render a region incapable of producing food at affordable prices, famine sets in, and the region begins a cycle of dependency on food aid.

The dynamic complex system model

In the dynamic complex system model formulation, the behavior of systems is understood in a different manner from the cascading probability model. When the coupling is strong and two-way, there are constant failures in both systems—severe drought causes maize prices to spike; higher maize prices result in a switch by farmers to growing wheat instead of sunflowers; wheat requires more water than sunflowers; farmers consume more underground water for irrigation and increase the severity of drought on the replenishment of underground aquifers; and the soil gets drier and is unable to support higher food production, leading to a shortage of wheat and potentially severe famine and hunger in wheat-dependent countries.

When individual elements in one system are coupled to fewer elements in the other system, or when coupling is weak, cascading failures are self-limiting and there is a low probability of propagation. If some farmers switch from feeding maize to animals and feed them hay instead, they depend less on water-intensive maize farming, thereby shielding maize farmers from the impact of severe drought on food production levels.

When systems are coupled there is a possibility of multiple paths to failure. A severe drought can lead to a spike in wheat prices, thereby inducing farmers to grow more wheat. Higher wheat production leads to a decline in wheat prices, which causes farmers in the next planting cycle to switch to sunflowers. The next year wheat production is low since fewer farmers planted wheat and the severity of the drought reduced even further what little was produced, causing wheat prices to spike sharply.

The critical point of failure depends on increased nearest-neighbor coupling and increased cross-system coupling. Farmers in America grow maize to feed animals and small volumes are traded on the global market. A drought impacts maize farming in America, but has little effect outside due to the low levels of trade, and maize prices remain stable on a global market—the effect of low cross-coupling between drought and maize prices. If farmers in America were to sell most of their produce on an international market (strong coupling) and there were a drought that led to lower maize production, there would be a sharp rise in maize prices globally.

Synchronization of failure across systems increases with the size of the system and the number of interacting elements across systems. The introduction of maize for ethanol is a good example to show the complexity of multiple potential failure paths and the introduction of new dynamics.

Farmers in America grow maize for animal feed locally, for export markets, and for ethanol production in America. Fossil fuel prices go up globally, causing an increase in demand for ethanol. Farmers sell more maize for ethanol production than for food exports, and maize prices spike sharply. Ethanol becomes expensive and fossil fuel prices—which are weakly coupled to ethanol prices—remain high. High maize prices cause famine in other parts of the world that are net importers of maize.

All these examples illustrate that there is a higher possibility of really large failures when systems are coupled and the cross-coupling is strong. Such effects can be seen in maize and fuel prices, and also in the spread of epidemics.

Options for functioning in areas of low predictability: role of scenario analysis

Scenario analysis is needed when predicting the outcome of interactions is difficult or impossible. This could be because decision makers are facing sudden collapse after long periods of stability—for example, inflation levels were low and manageable and the economy starts to face high inflation rates all of a sudden. Difficulty in prediction can also occur during periods of rapid change, especially when followed by periods of little or no change, and it is not clear what is likely to happen next. Alternatively, there can be visible but small initial variations leading to large differences in later outcomes—a young vegetable vendor sets himself on fire on December 17, 2010 in Tunis in protest against the confiscation of his wares and for being harassed and humiliated by the municipal officials. His act becomes a catalyst for the Tunisian Revolution between December 2010 and January 2011, and the more widespread Arab Spring,[2] which resulted in the ousting of leaders from power in Tunisia, Egypt, Libya, and Yemen and civil unrest in other countries (Al Jazeera 2010-12-20). These examples also illustrate how a small change in one place could lead to large change in other places.

Scenario analysis helps define the actions and strategies to adopt as outcomes approach pre-defined patterns. Evolving scenarios helps decision-makers find leverage points—how to meet the demand for jobs for young people before they result in a revolution? Scenarios can also aid in finding the most significant trade-offs—short-term job creation versus longer-term structural change to address youth unemployment, for instance. Scenarios can help leaders develop adaptive strategies that change as the reality on the ground changes, allowing them to know in advance which zones of outcomes to avoid, as they are irreversible or the consequences very severe. Scenarios also help leaders select from a series of approaches—among types of agents (individuals, groups, young people), location of agents (cities, rural areas, borders), capabilities of agents (self-motivated change makers or good organizing skills), and types of strategies (sharp and targeted change through messages on YouTube or slower long-term change through Wikipedia).

The probabilistic models and dynamic complex system models can be used to select the most appropriate set of actions.

A good scenario will rely on analysis of what is probable from history and from case studies. When the historical or case study outcomes have been mapped out, they can be assessed against a range of possible futures: relevance, plausibility, and logical consistency. Leaders can then form hypotheses about what might happen and the implications of alternate outcomes, as well as considering outside-in and divergent options. Leaders can subsequently decide whether they act as if the probable outcome from history could be worse, with the situation or outcome deteriorating further, improving, or staying the same. The actions can be to seek to reverse or improve the outcome, muddle through, or speed up and escalate the deterioration or decline.

Three key factors are important in identifying a good scenario. The first is to seek a good balance between *variation* and uniformity—provide enough options that assume patterns will remain the same or change, for example. Types and patterns of *interaction* are also important factors to include in any scenario. Approaches for *selection* amongst successful strategies and agents would involve choosing from the types of strategy, location, and capabilities of different agents (Figure 3.2).

Defining the interactions is always a good starting point for building effective decision-making scenarios. The first level of choice relates to the *types of interaction* mechanisms: what structures and processes govern interaction between agents and agent types—for example between farmers, markets, food prices, and water use?

The second choice to make is the *level of interaction*: at what level are the key interactions taking place (agent to agent, agent to environment, agent

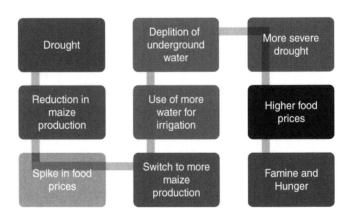

Figure 3.2 Interactions in agriculture, economics, and environment

to instance)? Are farmers directly interacting with food markets and global good prices?

The third choice relates to policy: what *types of policies* would influence the interactions (external, internal)? Should there be price controls for key staples like maize? Should maize be used for ethanol production? Should farmers be allowed to irrigate their maize crops during drought periods?

Finally, decision makers need to have measures: what *types of measures* would be used to assess the impact of the interactions identified? Is it the level of maize production, the price of maize on the global market, the share of maize going to ethanol production, or the number of incidences of famine and hunger?

Once the interactions have been detailed out and choices made as to what types would be retained in the scenarios, leaders need to build redundancy or slack to limit failure frequency in the event of negative outcomes. Another critical exercise is to identify and then remove or avoid critical paths, or paths that would lead to failure and bad outcomes. Identifying and hedging against sources of shocks is also important and needs to be built in. Decision makers can then decide to increase or reduce coupling to better redistribute stress or prevent cross-element transfer of stress. Control for natural or induced failure cascades is also needed. For a detailed review of the behavior of complex systems, see Bar-Yam (1997).

Finally, there is a need to seek balance between local actions to postpone failure versus longer-run coordinated actions to handle failure more permanently. The credit market squeeze of 2008 is an example that needed coordinated actions in the short run by all central bank governors to manage the crisis. The euro crisis of 2011 required a combined series of short-term coordinated actions—like the fiscal pacts signed by member countries—but also coordinated actions in the long term, such as the role of the European Central Bank and the degree of autonomy that needs to be given for it to act on behalf of member states, bringing the system to a tighter coupling.

Managing the level of interactions is also important for a good scenario to work. Starting with the types of agents, decision-makers need to manage the interactions amongst people (central bankers in a fiscal crisis, population growth in a resource depleting world, aging and youth to better manage retirement and job creation). Agent types could also be companies (choosing to support particular industry types in a structural economic setting with defined industrial policy, managing the size of an industry to control monopolistic tendencies). Agent types could also be countries (neighbors and their effect on a local economy, trading partners, competitors, states at war) or associations (of key stakeholders like labor unions, farmer organizations).

Once the agent type is defined, it is important also to look at the location of agents. For example, in migration and emigration policy the agents are mobile, as they are in cases of urbanization and city growth. Population concentration in coastal areas could also be an agent location-sensitive area to manage if what you worry about is effects of climate change on rising sea levels. The capabilities of agents in terms of communication, knowledge, and learning, as well as mobility, are also key factors for the building of effective scenarios.

Strategy is the next thing that decision makers need to have in mind. What types of strategy would be used: trial and error, experimentation and learning, or some other approach? The type of response to a set of actions also forms part of the strategy component of scenarios—what to observe; how to evaluate and shape different strategies; when and how to react and respond to a set of outcomes; and how to learn, understand, and adapt to materializing effects.

A strategy will evolve with the type of environment, instance, or context in which it is applied. The environment of application could be stable or volatile; open or closed; long history, little or no history; shifting preferences, identities, behavior; and shifting nodes of control. For example, in an agriculture-dependent economy, price controls on maize can have a serious effect on production (as farmers make local decisions on what to grow) and hence GDP and incomes. Similar maize price controls in economies dependent on services may have limited effects, such as on milk (due to the knock-on effects on animal feed prices), and attenuate before they impact the overall economy (as consumers adjust to consume non-dairy products).

Within a strategy, decision makers can also build in controls or external policies that govern what outcomes are going to be or should be permissible. These policies relate mostly to barriers to movement, permeability, or sequencing of barriers. On barriers to movement, decision makers make choices of policies that could be physical, such as immigration and national borders or physical walls (which controlled entry and exit in medieval times, fell in the sweep of democratization in Berlin, or are to be erected in modern times, as at the Mexico–US border); trade barriers (import fees, quotas, agreements); membership requirements (G7, unions, associations, clubs); and channeling exchanges through communication and infrastructure (roads, telephones, Internet). Barriers could also be conceptual, such as ideas (human rights) and beliefs (democracy; citizenship, castes, and clans). Permeability of barriers is also a decision. Religious organizations choose the degree and possibility of conversions as a sort of permeability into the system. Email filters that block out spam are an example of the degree of permeability. Immigration policies are also an exercise of policy that limits or allows permeability into a country's borders. Decision-makers can sequence the barriers, deciding to use different barrier types sequentially, or may make parallel use of some barriers, and so on.

In addition to external policies, decision-makers can also rely on internal policies for a good scenario. Internal policies could include creating followership through varied forms of apprenticeship, defined work practices, select trading partners, elaborate religious ceremonies, refined musical forms, or even the norms around social roles. Other choices of internal policy are signaling devices, like prices, brands, fashion and trends, tags, or peace agreements. Boundaries are also a form of internal policy that can be used to define political and ideological clustering, religious concentration, social clustering, or levels of ethnic integration. The time scales for action or decision are internal policies that can be used to decide whether strategy and vision should be driven at the top or using a bottom-up approach; whether actions need to be slowed down or speeded up to get the desired effect; and whether it is preferable to have slower or faster action at the bottom or at the top. Stress distribution is an important internal policy, including choices like the risk management strategy to use, how much redundancy to build in, how much independence or coupling to create or allow between systems, what actions to use to build up to criticality where large scale change takes place, managing the size and frequency of change (by exploiting the power law if possible), and inducing correlated shocks or not. Policies at the internal level could also include routines and schedules like total quality concepts, feedback loops, and work manuals. Internal policies may be designed to interact with external policies as varied as restructuring physical and conceptual spaces by introducing censorship, engaging in trade, and encouraging or discouraging tourism.

How do you measure success to get adaptive change? How do you define success? How do you evaluate payoffs? These three questions are important to include in any scenario. To get adaptive change, performance should be measured within the system of interest to decision makers. This is because the measures can be modified to adapt to the lessons learned, adopted, or disregarded by the agents based on the reliability of the measures as indicators of success. How success is defined affects the chances for effective learning. If the purpose of a scenario is to learn easily, then there should be more *tolerance* built in for failure. If success is intended in the long run, then *patience* needs to be built in the scenario, compared to searching for quick wins in the short term that may jeopardize the chance for deeper success in the long run. Decision makers can consider a short-term criterion that may not include *winning* in the near term and that requires having the stomach to tolerate failure. Traders in the stock market make such choices on a daily basis. Other measures of performance are related to assessing or evaluating the payoffs for a given set of actions. Is an action too expensive to do? Do you have to wait too long for a result? When the result is achieved, will it be easy or difficult to attribute reasons for success?

Table 3.4   Selection and payoffs

Level/Criterion	Cost	Speed	Attribution	Application
Agent	Expensive	Slow	Low	M&A, spinoffs, restructuring, elections
Strategy	Cheap	Fast	High	Stock market, social mobilization
Tradeoff	Acquire agent or copy strategy	Do it yourself or buy	Context preserving or action preserving	Country strategy, trade negotiation

High selection pressure: excellence but less diverse (exploitation)
Moderate selection pressure: average but more diverse (exploration)

Building all the options defined above into a scenario-generating process results in a set of scenarios to choose from. So how do you select from among a set of credible and well thought out scenarios (Table 3.4). Three aspects aid the decision maker in choosing amongst a set of credible scenarios. The first is the degree of variability in the scenario: what will be changing and how (people, economy, environment, technology, institutions)? The second is the type of anticipated strategic shifts: what should you change; what should you keep uniform; and what should you vary in your approaches? Finally, the important question of experimentation and learning: how much should you exploit what you already know and how much should you invest in new areas of exploration and learning?

Typically, agent-level criteria are expensive and slow to generate results, and when results happen it is difficult to assign or attribute cause for success. The Arab Spring is a good illustration of the agent-level change and its payoff—the change was sparked by the action of a single agent (the vegetable vendor's decision to set himself on fire in protest)— and was sustained by a group of agents using strategies that were physical (through rallies, marches and demonstrations) and virtual (through communication and organization using Twitter and Facebook). It is not easy to attribute the result of the Arab Spring to a single agent or strategy. Agent-level change has useful applications in areas such as mergers and acquisitions, where a single company or business line can be selected to drive the process of change; managing spinoffs from companies in order to encourage innovation; and restructuring economies, where a specific group of agents (say agribusinesses) are used to drive structural change (building small-scale manufacturing capability using the food industry). Election strategies typically use a combination of agent-level strategies, such as relying on student support in universities, labor unions, business associations, and so on.

A strategy-level criterion is cheap and fast, with a high level of attribution, and can be used in a wide variety of practices. Social mobilization to get increased use of contraceptives is an example, or strategies to reduce malaria by supplying bed nets, where in both cases there is a direct link between strategy and result. Stock market trading strategies also fit in this category of cheap to do, fast to see, results, with high attribution of success or failure to the type of strategy.

When using tradeoffs to choose amongst criteria, a decision-maker needs to respond to a series of questions. Is it easier for you to acquire an agent or copy a strategy in order to reduce the cost of the scenario? An illustration of whether to acquire an agent or copy a strategy is the choice Africa needs to make to restructure its economies and become more sophisticated and industrialized. Should it do so by picking its own companies (agents), which have some sort of rudimentary mechanization and industrial capability, and support them to grow in the way South Korea did (copy a strategy), or should it buy light manufacturing capability from China (acquire an agent), as suggested by Lin (2012).

Another key question is around the speed of change. To get speedier results should you do it yourself or buy the service from another agent? Following the end of the Rwandan conflict in July and August 1994, the country embarked on a capacity-building strategy to get rapid results (see Majeed, 2012). It engaged the Ministry of Local Government in a pilot to reduce poverty in Gashaki in North Rwanda. The focus on rapid results improved the ability of local officials and leaders (agents) to help their families raise their income, and it also improved the ability of public servants (agents) to deliver services effectively. Therefore the rapid results approach is a strategy with high attribution and fast speed of attaining results, but it was considered a high-cost approach for getting change (http://resourcecentre. pscbs.gov.rw/content/reports-and-studies-0).

The Rwanda case raises another key question to consider in selecting scenarios on the basis of payoffs, particularly if you wish to get the right attribution. Should you seek to preserve the context you are intervening in or the actions you are engaging in? In the case of Rwanda, the interventions were with communities that had just come out of severe conflict, and the intention was not to preserve previous behaviors, but to seek change in behavior in a short period of time (not context-preserving). The agents intervening in the process were public servants and the rapid results strategy was aimed at preserving their service delivery functions while speeding up the attainment of results (action-preserving).

Adapting to actions of other agents

Being aware of the actions of other agents is critical in shaping the global properties that affect your decisions. The microcosm of decisions made by city leaders helps us understand the role of complexity in shaping decision-making strategies. In particular, how citizens interact with mayors and firms in a variety of city types is a rich source of learning how to adapt to the actions of other agents. One may also look at choices made at a continental level and the variety of scenarios possible at that level, as illustrated in this section by looking at the evolution of cities and urbanization as well as the potential for different scenarios in Africa.

Cities and scenarios

A measure of a successful city could be its size. A well-functioning city would attract migration and location choices of firms and the city would grow. City size over time could be the criterion for judging the success of a strategy. Long-run patterns of city size indicate that this is a very dynamic process of change, with cities starting off small, growing steadily, growing and then shrinking, or not growing at all, and even dying (see Léautier, 2006). As seen in Léautier (2006), the number of small cities over time grew dramatically between 1975 and 2015, but so did the number of megacities. However, the number of medium-sized cities has not grown as much and the shape of the curve of city population over time has become sharper over time, with a bigger differentiation between small and megacities. Such patterns belie a differentiated set of dynamics, depending on size or a varied set of actions that lead to different outcomes on size. Since size was selected as a performance measure, it is used for the latter interpretation.

Ouagadougou went from a small city in 1960 (where it had a population of 59,000) to a large city by 2012 (with a population of close to 1.5 million). Ouagadougou became attractive to people who moved in, companies that located there, and to international and regional agencies that also located there. The city performance outcomes observed in Ouagadougou and other cities like it, which can be referred to as attractiveness, derive from a series of interactions. Political interactions between residents and their leadership (mayor, city manager) drive the internal policies that govern city management. The commercial interactions between residents, politicians, and the firms who choose to invest in those cities shape the productivity outcomes at the city level. Communications between and among residents as they pursue their cultural and social interests determine the quality of life of city residents, which has an impact on city size in the long run.

A wide variety of scenarios can be built using three agents (citizens, firms, mayor), the level of interaction amongst them (local or global), the type of interaction (service, political), and the selected payoffs or performance measures (size, productivity, quality of life).

Regions and scenarios

Scenarios can be built at continental level. Consider the case of Latin America, where you could build three potential scenarios. In one there is more coordinated effort at the continental level, with continental owner-ship of policies and decisions, and leadership that shapes the choices made for the whole continent. Another scenario could be where sub-regional enti-ties, like the members of MERCOSUR (the economic and political agreement among Argentina, Bolivia, Brazil, Paraguay, Uruguay, and Venezuela), work together in a mosaic. Finally, one could consider a continent that is shaped mostly by decisions from outside, in a sort of externally driven nation states scenario.

Scenario 1—Coordinated Effort   Choices can be made in the first scenario to define the internal and external policies. Under the continental leadership and ownership scenario, efforts could be made to ensure Latin American leadership and ideas on a global scale. This can be secured by ensuring that the polity owns the economic growth agenda through participatory techniques. Latin America could lead innovation in key sectors such as agro industry, petrochemicals, and metallurgical industries. Home-grown solu-tions to drugs and crime would be built on traditional principles and would flourish, and there would be no outside intervention in domestic crimes. Latin America would wield leadership and would be represented in inter-national institutions and debates. An outcome from such policy choices would be to drive Latin America faster towards international parity. Latin American standards of governance would be internationally accepted and there would be no need for institutions such as the United Nations Office on Drugs and Crime, with Latin Americans trying their cases using domestic judicial systems and processes. Latin America would be contributing in a sig-nificant way to the international architecture in areas such as trade, finance, environment, migration, and debt. At the country level, Latin American institutions would be resolving conflicts and preventing violence and crime (including the drug trade) using domestic, regional, and continental institu-tions. Services would be provided effectively in the areas of health, gender parity, water, and education.

Scenario 2—Sub-regional Mosaic   Under the second scenario, there would be some models of success, as in some of the members states of MERCOSUR (say Argentina and Uruguay), but limited learning from each other at the continental level. There would be a large variety of outcomes in the quality of democratic and economic governance, with some countries doing better than others. Performance would also be differentiated under the sub-regional mosaic, which would be more realistic, focused on performance and results and managing interdependency while mastering strategic planning.

Under the second scenario, countries would engage in bilateral strategies (say Bolivia and Venezuela) with *ad hoc* cooperation, and a few prominent countries (say Brazil or Mexico) would drive the external agenda. Outcomes would be visible but uneven, with isolated successes in service provision in the health, education, gender parity, and water sectors. External aid would be driven by external security needs and donor-based evaluations of capacity and need.

Scenario 3—Externally Driven States   This scenario is gloomier. It requires attention to adaptability and resilience, focus on managing uncertainty from conflict, dealing with climate change and managing external conditionality on development aid. In such a scenario Latin America would be reacting to external threats, such as new technologies and business models, threatening domestic production. Governance standards for the continent would be externally set and Latin America would be severely underrepresented in international forums and debates. Countries would have weak capacity to manage, having trouble dealing with ethnic, drug-related, and political violence.

Weak country institutions under Scenario 3, caused by lack of capacity to analyze and implement policies, would react to international imperatives rather than drive them. Access to the benefits of globalization would be determined by bilateral and multilateral organizations with little input from Latin American countries. Country conditionality would be the norm for allocating aid to aid-dependent countries. Service provision would vary across countries and would be heavily dependent on the international civil society. Donors would practice selective aid provision with specific conditions going to specific programs.

Values and behaviors as a guide in the face of complexity and risk

When faced with complexity and risk, it is difficult to make choices. In the absence of any previous strategies or lessons to learn from or case studies of relevance, what remains as a guide is the set of values and behaviors deemed appropriate at the time of choice making. The first step in building the right values and behaviors comes from better knowing the self. How do you form judgment from observation and self-knowledge? How do you build awareness of blind spots? Is the truth what you can observe or does it come from challenging observations with new information? How do you learn to endure the pain of knowing what the outcomes of your actions will be? What would be most useful to use, facts and evidence or a set of mysteries and beliefs, to get results in a particular setting?

The skills needed to define the values and behaviors that can serve as a guide in making choices can be arrived at through reading, through case studies, as well as through lifelong learning in the real world. This book covers mostly what you can learn from cases and simulated practice sets.

A leader will ultimately have to choose from a set of scenarios, policies, actions, and so on. Any outcomes from those choices remain the responsibility of the leader. Choice is therefore value-ridden and leaders need to have not only the freedom to choose from a set of actions, but also to bear the responsibility that choice brings. Leaders need to go beyond faith and engage in active choice making. They have to push themselves to replace their prior beliefs with reason, in order to engage in the right scenarios. Leaders need to make choices in the face of suffering, knowing that their choices could cause harm to others.

Decisions move very fast in a globalized world, and leaders have to constantly learn and adapt, which calls for constant attention to self-development. Some tools can be useful for self-development. I have personally found 360-degree feedback very useful in learning about my blind spots. Client feedback and dialogues with peers can also sharpen your skills and allow you to test your value system against others. Practice and experimentation, as are encouraged in the case material and exercises in this book, are very helpful in leading you through a learning process with results. Discussions with friends and family as well self-learning and reflection and reading are all tools that can be enormously helpful in shaping and honing a set of values and behaviors that are necessary to navigate in a complex decision setting.

The nature of leadership is also quite unique and it is important to know the limits of the self and the challenges that leadership presents. One cannot build a scenario without a good understanding of the nature of human conflict. While reading and reflection are useful for learning, one has to sharpen learning through practice and experimentation. The following series of practice blocks and cases support the learner in their journey with practice sets that build skills and sharpen insights.

Co-sensing and co-creating a superior risk management strategy

A practice block providing a case study on the SARS epidemic offers practice of the skills needed to lead in complex and fast-changing risk scenarios.

The SARS epidemic case study[3]

As globalization increases it is more likely that an infectious disease that emerges in one country will be transmitted rapidly to another. The severe acute respiratory syndrome (SARS) is a recent example. What started with a "small notice" in the *Weekly Epidemiological Record* of the World Health Organization (WHO) in early 2003, reporting five deaths from an unknown acute respiratory syndrome,[4] turned out to be a highly contagious disease that managed within a matter of weeks to spread from the Chinese province of Guangdong to the rest of the world – eventually infecting individuals in 37 countries.[5] The first case outside China had been reported on the 26th of February, rising to 8448 cases by July 2003, with a total of 774 human deaths.[6] Although many people had feared that SARS would rival the influenza pandemic of 1918, which killed around 40 million people, it did not lead to the devastating health impact that many feared.[7]

SARS originated in China in 1996, when a highly pathogenic virus was isolated from a farmed goose in Guangdong province. By 2003, events in humans had been reported in China and events in animals reported in the Republic of Korea, Thailand, and Vietnam. In 2004 other countries reported events, including Japan, Cambodia, Laos, Indonesia, and Malaysia. By 2007, SARS events in animals had been reported in nearly 60 countries:

Afghanistan, Albania, Austria, Azerbaijan, Bangladesh, Bosnia-Herzegovina, Bulgaria, Burkina Faso, Cambodia, Cameroon, China, Côte d'Ivoire, Croatia, Czech Republic, Denmark, Djibouti, Egypt, France, Georgia, Germany, Greece, Hungary, India, Indonesia, Iran, Iraq, Israel, Italy, Japan, Jordan, Kazakhstan, Republic of Korea, Kuwait, Laos, Malaysia, Mongolia, Myanmar, Niger, Nigeria, Pakistan, Poland, Romania, Russia, Saudi Arabia, Serbia-Montenegro, Slovenia, Spain, Sudan, Sweden, Switzerland, Thailand, Turkey, USA, Ukraine, UK, Vietnam, West Bank Gaza

Twelve countries have reported cases in humans:

Azerbaijan, Cambodia, China, Djibouti, Egypt, Indonesia, Iraq, Laos, Nigeria, Thailand, Turkey, Vietnam

At the time SARS appeared, I was working at the World Bank and had been traveling quite regularly to China. On a cold February morning in 2003, Lystra, my special assistant, rushes into my office with a piece of paper in her hand. "Sorry Lystra, you need to wait for a while as there is a whole set of meetings the Vice President needs to go to and I cannot have you coming in here without an appointment" says Alice, my Executive Assistant, firmly shutting the door behind her as she exits the office with a bunch of files in her hand. A few minutes later Alice buzzes me saying, "I really think you ought to see this." Lystra walks in with an anxious look on her face still clutching the piece of paper in her hand. "I am not one to be alarmed, but this looks like something we need to worry about as you plan your trip to China." She hands me the piece of paper and looks at me as I read it (Box 3.1).

Box 3.1   Outbreak News[a]

Acute respiratory syndrome, China—Update

On 20 February 2003, the Chinese Ministry of Health reported that the infective agent in the atypical pneumonia outbreak in Guangdong Province, which affected a total of 305 persons and caused 5 deaths, was probably *Chlamydia pneumoniae*. Further epidemiological studies are underway and are coordinated by the Guangdong provincial health department."

It was an article from the *Weekly Epidemiological Record* No. 9, 2003, p. 57. "Lystra, this sounds like the outbreaks that appeared before, perhaps as far back as the 1990s in Taiwan." "Take a look lower down at the third record on the bottom of the page." she says anxiously. I read on:

Influenza A(H5N1), Hong Kong Special Administrative Region of China—update

As of 20 February 2003, the Department of Health in Hong Kong SAR confirmed that a 33-year old man, who died in hospital in Hong Kong on 17 February, had been infected with a strain of the influenza A(H5N1) virus. A nasopharyngeal swab taken from the man and tested in the Government Virus Unit was positive for influenza A(H5N1).

The 33-year old man is the second case of influenza A(H5N1) virus related to this outbreak in Hong Kong SAR. The man is known to have been the father of the 9-year old boy reported as testing positive for influenza A(H5N1) on 19 February. Both cases had traveled to Fujian Province (China) in January. Two other members of the family who accompanied them to Fujian in January have also been unwell. The mother of the family has now made a full recovery; the other affected member of the family (an 8-year old girl) died on 4 February in Fujian Province.

[a]The two excerpts are taken from *Weekly Epidemiological Record* No. 9, 2003, 78: 57–64 http://www.who.int/wer.

I remember the feeling in my stomach as I looked up at Lystra and saw her grave look. There was indeed reason to be alarmed back then. The reported cases were to have an impact on travel around the world as the reports made by the WHO in that *Weekly Epidemiological Record* of deaths from an unknown acute respiratory syndrome would turn out to be a highly infectious disease that would spread out from Guangdong to the rest of the world. By 2007, SARS events in animals would have been reported in nearly 60 countries, and 12 countries would have reported cases in humans. But I also had to be cautious of the potential impact that officially sanctioned information (such as by the WHO in the case of SARS) could create panic and could boost the profits to the pharmaceutical industry.[8]

Epidemics and their effects

The SARS epidemic served as an important opportunity for a number of stakeholders to study and test the existing strategies and information systems on a scenario the global community had not yet known before at this scale. A previous pandemic in 1918, which killed 40 million people, was foremost in the minds of policy makers and researchers at the outset of the

SARS breakout, as many feared a similar scale of impact. Indeed, the pattern of emerging and re-emerging infectious diseases was made more serious with the increase in globalization, as it is more likely that an infectious disease emerging in one country could be rapidly transmitted to another. Frequent travel across countries and the increased export of food and other products across the world have made the risks that were limited in the past to be orders of magnitude more serious. The SARS case was a sharp reminder that an obscure event in one country could easily have serious global consequences.

The experience of SARS was also to test the functioning of collaborative and multi-centered research and policy decision-making bodies to identify causative agents and develop diagnostic tests.[9]

In addition to the concerns about human health, many other stakeholders in industry were equally concerned. There was immediate concern about travel and tourism, impacting primarily the airline industry as people changed destinations or preferred to stay home. News reports on passengers being asked to exit aircraft due to wheezing and coughing symptoms abounded, and many who did not need to travel cancelled their trips. Those like us who had to travel into infected zones had to go through temperature scans at arrival in Beijing, for example, and witnessed fellow passengers being pulled aside due to the slightest indication of a fever. To this day passengers are scanned as they enter global city airports like Johannesburg. The panic reaction to the epidemic has also been blamed for the collapse of Asian tourism in 2003 and provides a good case for caution about transnational crises and the approaches to reacting to them (McKercher and Chon, 2004).

The chicken export market was affected directly as the world market for meat exports had grown dramatically since the 1990s. Health impact studies reveal that the global macroeconomic impact of SARS was at $ US 30–100 billion,[10] affecting a wide range of sectors, but particularly travel and tourism. The SARS outbreak had far-reaching implications for other industries, as seen by the sharp decline in the export of products related to the chicken value chain. The big producers of chicken meat for export—China and the USA—were impacted, as can be seen in their export patterns as the epidemic took hold.

There were a variety of responses from industries and countries to the SARS epidemic, with some benefitting and others losing out in the chicken export business. Effects could be seen in all the key economic indicators, including the volume of chicken exports, the value of the exports derived, and the price per ton.

As I was reading an article in the online version of the *Guardian* at www.guardian.co.uk on my iPad on June 1, 2011 while waiting to board a flight from Johannesburg to Harare, a small headline caught my attention. "*E. coli outbreak in Germany adds 365 more confirmed cases*" Germans warned against eating raw lettuce, cucumbers, and tomatoes as the cause of the outbreak, centered on Hamburg, remained a mystery. The mysterious German *E. coli* outbreak that had killed 16 people showed no sign of abating, with 365 new cases confirmed on Wednesday.[11]

I remembered the day Lystra rushed into my office in 2003. I thought about how at the time we responded to the demands by country clients in dealing with the SARS epidemic. The capacity needs were indeed complex, with some of the issues having relevance at the levels of the national health systems, and others stretching across countries and requiring international and coordinated responses. Then there are the complexities of the interactions between farmers, meat factories, meat exporters, butchers, supermarkets, consumers, and policy makers. Each of them had a complex set of actions they needed to take to manage risk, whether at the production, export, packaging, or consumption levels. All sorts of policies were also at play. The policies had differential impact on the outcomes.

Globalization, and particularly the ease of transport, had caused an expansion of the world market for chicken prior to the SARS epidemic. The appearance of SARS was close to a nightmare scenario for chicken farmers and meat exporters. Brazil, the US, Germany, and the UK saw their exports of chicken meat increase, despite the SARS epidemic. China, Thailand, and the Netherlands witnessed a sizeable decline in their exports following the epidemic (Table 3.5). France had a slight decline in its exports. What was different about their approaches and why was the pattern of responses so different?

The different reactions and the national contexts were largely responsible for the variation in the domestic responses across the affected countries. Some countries switched strategies, to enter the market for live animals rather than selling meat. Other countries, such as Germany, France, and the UK were able to absorb the decline in exports seen in other countries (such as the decline in American and Chinese exports[12]) with less devastating effects.

Because SARS originated in Southern China, the mainland's chicken-farming hub, poultry exports in the region were badly hit. As an immediate result, for example, Thai exports were boosted[13] for a couple months,

Table 3.5 Country responses: chicken meat exports 1984–2004 (value in US$ millions)

Year/ Country	Brazil	US	Netherlands	France	Germany	UK	China	Thailand
1984	264	225	239	299	17	13	35	60
1994	607	1249	757	640	85	114	357	382
2004	2454	1785	536	623	332	284	123	44

Source: FAOSTAT (2007) or latest available year can be found at http://faostat.fao.org/site/291/default.aspx.

though unfortunately they ended up in an even more devastating decline when the first Thai chicken was diagnosed with SARS in November 2003 as a result of the spreading of the pandemic.

What was common to all countries was the immediate need for individual as well as collective responses of a variety of stakeholders, including the media, consumer groups, and business associations, in order to address the political, economic and diplomatic challenges of such a worldwide issue. The "small notice" from February 15th 2003 had turned into a problem to be dealt with internationally.

These were the sorts of issues running through my mind as I saw an email come in with a request to the Fezembat Group to summarize the lessons learned from the SARS case for application to other infectious outbreaks, such as the *E. coli* outbreak in Germany. I responded to the email with some advice on the questions they could ask while seeking the lessons learned from the SARS case, asking Serge, the young researcher, to look particularly at how stakeholders can be ready for small events that end up becoming global crises. What techniques can be used to speed up information, analysis, and action across multiple stakeholders when faced with low-probability–high-impact events? Are there ways in which stakeholders can act that would make them better at handling these types of events? When I arrived in my office in Harare I dug up the information I had about the SARS epidemic to see what could be gleaned from it and sent it off to Serge. Alas, other pressing matters at the Foundation prevented me from doing more. The young researcher would have to carry out the analysis and be ready for the client request that had come in, with limited support. The guidance I provided Serge is outlined below for the learner to use for his or her own purposes. This guidance has also been tested in a classroom setting and has proven very useful in soliciting multi-stakeholder groups to co-develop an approach to a crisis.

Lessons from the SARS case study

The practice block Box 3.2 below can serve as a guide to the learner for broader applications.

Box 3.2   Practice Block III: Co-sensing and Co-creating a Superior Risk Management Strategy

Premise: A team of stakeholders facing a common challenge would bring different perspectives to the table, allowing them to devise a better set of actions to handle emerging risks.

Objective: to practice the skill of co-sensing the key risks and co-creating strategies and actions that could serve as a prototype for handling the challenge.

Lessons: the case of the chicken export industry shows the value of co-developing a set of potential scenarios that could have played out and their respective courses of action. Looking at how different agents adjusted to the same epidemic can be helpful in assessing the relevance of different strategies and actions. Such information is critical when designing prototypes to pilot with in similar situations.

Skill: The main skill of value in this case is working with others to sense what they may be sensing and creating together an approach for dealing with a common risk with varied but serious implications on all key stakeholders.

The outcomes of the SARS epidemic

In reality, the chicken industry was deeply affected by the crisis, because of the gravity of the disease and because of the patterns of the globalized economy. It was the biggest crisis of its kind that had occurred in the developed world in contemporary times. SARS was the first new disease of this millennium, and in some ways the most dramatic of all. It rapidly achieved notoriety through outbreaks in Hong Kong, the rest of China, Vietnam, Singapore, and Canada as a readily transmissible infectious disease with a significant mortality rate (11%) and global economic consequences. The outbreaks in early 2003 spanned 30 countries in six continents, causing estimated losses to the countries of $30 to $150 billion. Yet by July 2003 they were largely controlled, appearing thereafter in minor ways with less global disruption.

In the form of SARS, Asia endured its greatest economic challenge since the currency crisis of the late 1990s. The chicken export industry that was hit saw a sharp decline in exports—specifically service exports, such as tourism. Prior to the SARS outbreak, the region's airlines, hotels, and restaurants were already experiencing soft demand as a result of slow world growth during 2001 and 2002. That slump turned into a catastrophe for the region, as vacationers diverted their travel to safer destinations. Furthermore, the direct impact of reduced traffic yielded significant negative multiplier effects. Initially, hotels and restaurants required fewer housekeepers, waiters, and maintenance personnel. Thus, service employment, which had been growing strongly in the region and had helped to diversify Asia's economic base, suffered.

Aside from travel and tourism, amongst the first effects was a reduction in household consumption. Retail establishments were reporting a dramatic fall in foot-traffic as shoppers ventured out only to purchase necessities. Discretionary and leisure shopping were being eliminated as people in hard-hit countries avoided public gatherings, where the disease could be contracted.

Thus, the initial impact was to undermine sources of growth that are related to discretionary spending—vacations and nonessential consumption. Of greater concern was the potential of SARS to disrupt trade patterns. Economists anticipated that intra-Asian trade would suffer as a result of SARS, reality was that East–West trade only experienced a mild decline. Trade between Asian economies decreased insofar as there was a fall-off in spending on Asian-produced goods. The primary channel was the disruption to discretionary spending. Thus, to the extent that residents of, for example, Beijing, purchased fewer televisions produced in Korea, intra-Asian trade slowed appreciably.

Much in the manner where growth in US business travel permanently slowed following the disruptions that ensued after the September 11 terrorist attacks, a fair amount of business travel to Asia was permanently replaced by Internet conferencing and the like, as cost-conscious firms adapted to the new means of international exchange. Also of great concern was the effect of SARS on foreign investment in the region. Over the near term, foreign investment was delayed, but not cancelled. Manufacturers were still keen to take advantage of China's cheap labor, its admission to the WTO, and its currency peg with the US dollar. Multinational firms waited, then, for more evidence on the extent of SARS in China and other low-cost Asian countries. Some projects were delayed before firms decided to proceed with relocating to China, or were diverted to another Asian or non-Asian destination.

In 2003, the extent and longevity of the SARS outbreak was still highly uncertain. Multinational firms adopted a cautious approach before responding to the disease by shifting production locations or redirecting investment. Although the disease's impact was not permanent, and in fact there was a progressive and rapid return to normal levels of business, the short-term impact was unprecedented.

One main cause of the rapid spread of the crisis, with so many economic consequences, was globalization. Multinational companies, which are both strong and weak when they have to deal with this kind of threat, link every producer and consumer in multiple countries. They are strong because they can easily change their supply chains, and weak because they are connected with many countries, so are directly concerned by any crisis that occurs somewhere in the world.

Emerging infectious disease outbreaks have a tremendous negative economic impact on trade, travel, and tourism, but in the case of the emergence of the SARS crisis and after, despite major losses, the industry showed good capacity to adapt to this kind of threat. In addition, many sectors showed that they had learnt from the SARS case. For instance, the pharmaceutical sector understood how to take advantage of this kind of crisis. If it seemed not to be much concerned by the SARS crisis and reacted slowly, the last H1N1 crisis was instead a great economic opportunity for many pharmaceutical companies. Criticism of the WHO and how it has created opportunities for such pharmaceutical companies coexists with praise for the WHO.

In conclusion, the industry, irrespective of its sector, now shows a good capacity to react and control the crisis, or (for some) even to take advantage of it.

SARS: an epidemic affecting multiple domains

The issues in the SARS case study fall into three aspects: (a) health of humans and animals; (b) economic effects on the market and market responses to crisis; and (c) political effects on governmental relations and their reactions. All these effects are closely linked and must to some extent be considered as a whole.

(a) *Health Aspects*: The epidemic concerned the health systems of all countries and the WHO. The first challenge is to identify the virus and the origin of the epidemic. Is the country in which the outbreak occurs able to identify the risk and notify the WHO and the other nations? What should be the reaction of the WHO? Should it wait for further confirmation or take the initiative to investigate on its own? If the country in which the crisis occurs is not forthcoming with information or has challenges in gathering and verifying information, what should the reaction of the international society be? In this situation, sovereignty can be an obstacle to solving a global crisis, yet the efficacy of a solution depends on local capacity and local approaches. So before dealing with the epidemic, international organizations have to first settle relations with other countries and achieve some level of cooperation. After the SARS crisis, numerous lessons were learnt, many of which became useful when other epidemics occurred, as in the case of H1N1. After SARS one can say that in a globalized world, an infectious disease in one country is a threat to all. Infectious diseases do not respect international borders. SARS helped the world learn that disease outbreaks can reveal weaknesses in the public health infrastructure of a country and indeed even globally. SARS also shows that even in the absence of a curative drug and a preventive vaccine, emerging infections can be contained if there is a high level of government commitment; however, it is also important to strengthen epidemiological and public health services and to beef up international and inter-country collaboration. Communication with the public, media, and other stakeholders is a key element and lesson learned from the SARS epidemic. Global partnerships to share data and information can enhance the level of preparedness and efficacy of responses to epidemics. Such sharing needs to be rapid to have the needed effects. SARS has also shown that the WHO and other international technical agencies can play a critical role in catalyzing international cooperation and support.

(b) *Economic Aspects*: The major questions relating to the economy are: what is the impact on the market? And what will be the market's response? There are three groups of economic stakeholders: producers, exporters, and consumers. They all need to know whether they must stop producing, trading, or eating chicken. There are also many shared decisions: where to stop production and how to anticipate the reaction of the public, and hence how to gauge the effects on and patterns of consumption. Ultimately, the main question relates to reorganizing production and trade systems.

(c) *Political Aspects*: The political issues revolve around the reaction of the government, in particular where the epidemic originated. The role of government must be one of regulation, supporting industry and trade, while abiding to international commitments. Should imports from affected countries be banned or could other control measures be used? If bans were imposed, what would be the reaction of the concerned country? Is there a risk of retaliation? This reaction was seen in the response to the *E. coli* outbreak in Germany, when many countries banned products from countries feared to be the source of the outbreak. Furthermore, what role could be played by international organizations, such as the WTO, and how do these roles relate to country-level decision-making and sovereignty? Finally what would be the diplomatic consequences of each state's reactions?

The economic issues usually dominate the concerns. The many actors with an economic stake sometimes push for downplaying the fear about spreading the disease. Producers want to continue producing chicken, and traders want to import, export, buy, and sell chicken. It is interesting to note that many countries banned imports of chicken meat from China, and even those that did not called for better labeling to identify the origin of products so that consumers could make their choices. Many countries weighed the possibility of prohibiting consumption of chicken altogether, but were prevented from instituting bans due to the reactions of other actors. Importers focused on the possibility of replacing imports from China. The US, UK, France, and Brazil gained from the loss of China. In general, mediation between the different actors ensures that overreaction to a crisis is avoided.

Drawing up scenarios

The SARS case could include consideration of possible scenarios: best, realistic, and worst case.

Worst-Case Scenario—International Shutdown: In a worst-case scenario, the disease could disrupt production schedules and trade, as well as inducing a crisis of confidence that could re-orient international investment patterns. The worst-case scenario, in which SARS degrades the quality of the labor force in afflicted countries, brings manufacturing activity to a halt. This is most likely to occur in the countries where the health system is poor, and could even cause and faster transmission of the disease. In the worst-case scenario, not only would foreign direct investment (FDI) be redirected, but the country would also experience an exodus of multinational firms that utilize it as an export platform. The WHO could react too slowly in such a scenario, not providing sufficient information or guidelines for countries to implement. Diplomatic relations could break down, and the lack of cooperation could lead to closed border policies, with the result of a dramatic reduction of travel. Ultimately, the final result of the crisis could be a new status quo, as returning to the old state of affairs would no longer be possible.

Base case scenario—successful containment In the realistic case scenario, cooperation between governments, international organizations, and economic actors occurs, but with a time lag. In this realistic prototype, countries ban live chicken imports, resulting in diplomatic and trade tensions. Imports and exports of the concerned product fall. Information strategies become important regarding the safety of chicken meat cooked at high temperatures, although the presence of multiple sources of information could sometimes cause consumers to be confused. Chicken consumption plummets, but then returns to normal levels relatively quickly when international cooperation takes place. The effect of the fall in consumption is mostly felt in the countries originating the disease. In the long term, tensions might be created, but eventually cooperation can be achieved and a return to the previous status quo is possible. There is no complete breakdown of international relations nor are there significant steps towards the creation of an international framework of cooperation and reaction to a global crisis.

Best-case scenario—international crisis management The epidemic could also be successfully contained through cooperation and internationally planned responses. The WHO could play a more important role in negotiations, all member countries could implement anti-panic campaigns and substantial regulation and a containment system could evolve. Affected countries would cooperate and chicken exports would be temporarily suspended in order to avoid a major spread of the disease. In the long term, the economic and political status quo would be restored whilst resulting in a strengthened framework for international crisis management, communication, and transparency. More attention would be given to regulating health issues and providing support in developing countries, recognizing the global effects that such issues can have. Farmers in affected countries would be subject to health standards. The international community as a whole would result in improved access to information and improved capacity for joint decision-making.

To achieve a shared vision on a global scale it is necessary to have certain conditions in place. First, leadership is about building trust and identifying and communicating issues clearly (what to do with facts and how facts are confronted). Indeed, one of the leadership's roles is to define reality and to mobilize stakeholders into action. This requires commitment to work on different aspects of the crisis. A demonstration of this is a quote from Prime Minister Goh Chok Tong of Singapore in 2003 that "SARS may not kill everyone in Singapore. But it can kill the Singapore economy. Therefore, it can kill the livelihood of Singaporeans." Reputation, transparency, and accountability are all important measures to reflect one's standing in the global hierarchy. In its initial mishandling of SARS, China squandered precious political capital that it had built up over the past years, which it later regained and used in future years.

Setting priorities

The SARS phenomenon had a worldwide effect on the volume of chicken meat exports, quasi-similar to the oil shocks of the 1980s. It is important to consider as a top priority, in any shared solution, the establishment of regulations to avoid the breakdown of a whole system based on trade, cooperation, solidarity, and transparency; a system that impacts on all the individuals in their safety and quality of life. The consequences of regulatory failure can be huge.

In times of crisis, especially when there is a risk of contamination, countries tend to close their boundaries and take unilateral measures. That's why dialogue is fundamental to try to reconcile the divergent interests of the respective stakeholders.

Among the divergent interests of stakeholders are farmers who want their governments to take concrete measures to solve the problem of imports and exports, but also want the implementation of a national policy that takes into consideration the situation at a national level, for example, through the demand for subsidies for their losses.

For example, one of the Chinese government's top priorities was the circulation of the right information for safe consumption, whilst contemporaneously dealing with the effects at the industry level to ensure that exports would not be affected. They wanted to learn more about the disease in order to control it. As a corollary to such concerns the Chinese government showed a willingness to resolve conflicts of interest and to take strict control measures like ensuring inspections of the farms or establishing disease prevention campaigns. But China focused on and stressed mostly the importance of continuation of exports.

Worldwide exporters, from their side, wanted an international database to confirm that the exported chickens were safe to consume. They wanted to secure their exports; thus they were in favor of external interventions with standardization of norms. Consumers want to continue consuming chicken, as it is cheaper than other meats, but not to the detriment of their health. In addition, they argue for the "right to know" especially seeking information about health risks. Advocacy groups were keen to suggest the creation of a vaccine. But the challenge is that poultry vaccines available may not be effective against a virus that is constantly mutating. All actors would benefit from the WHO tackling this challenge on a global scale. This requires international support to fund the WHO and to support calls to fund collaborative research.

One can distinguish a national dynamic (for example between government and farmers) and an international dynamic (for example between health organizations and governments). It is more difficult to solve situations like the SARS epidemic because of the need to coordinate what is done on the national level and what should be done on the international level.

To manage the risks at the production, export policy, and consumption levels is also critical. For example, on the health level, it implies avoiding the spread of contamination by setting up, among other things, hygiene criteria. On the economic level, controlling prices for consumers is important, because a chicken labeled as safe will be more expensive.

Some measures for a worldwide policy are: inventory of the cases; strict measures for biological security in agricultural practices (recourse of subdivisions, control of animal movements and so on); intensify collaboration between sectors of the government; use "antivirus" for national use in the beginning to protect exposed people; support comparative research to know more about the conduits of transmission and the group at risk and to find effective treatments. And that leads to the final priority, but before that it is important to stress the value of preparing an action plan in case of a worldwide pandemic (for example closing schools).

Developing the relevant data and measures is also very critical: How is SARS spreading? And how is the disease evolving? This objective needs the reinforcement of cooperation between countries at the international level (declare the cases and find solutions together). Data is essential to know what is going on and to limit the panic effect of uncertain consequences. Many scholars have argued the fact that the public health responses to SARS and also to pH1N1 were hampered by compromised decision-making as a result of a failure to understand the true nature of the events. Lack of understanding derives from over-reliance on assumptions rather than epidemiological intelligence to guide responses to threats from novel pathogens (Schabas, 2003).

Not all priorities can be tackled at once and in a short amount of time. A process of triage, classifying areas of least and high priority, is needed. Actions that can be done directly are usually accorded high priority (export bans for example), as they can be explained by the need for speed. Some of the major players could also be weak—such as the relative weakness of the WHO at the time of SARS—a fact that forces decision makers to afford them least priority because it needs time to resolve. Co-developing shared futures through reflection and collaboration to give the organization the means for its actions could result in making strengthening the WHO the top priority. Indeed, the WHO ended up having a very important role in the SARS solution process. Existing international law on infectious disease control is archaic, formed half a century ago before mass global travel. The WHO can only issue "soft law" recommendations, rather than binding obligations. Many governments see disease prevention as an internal business; but in a globalized world, any disease is just one airplane away. That's why it is not a provincial or national issue; it's a global one. In addition (and unfortunately), the WHO lacks the authority to investigate outbreaks without an invitation. For SARS, the WHO did issue the first travel advisory in its 55-year history. The backlash over lost trade and tourism may explain some of the deference to member nations in somewhat downplaying the immediacy of the current pandemic threat. Finally, one could question whether the WHO is under-funded; is an annual core budget of $400 million sufficient to be ready for all pandemics?

In the long term, building an international health system and developing more collaboration between the WHO and the World Trade Organization (WTO) may be needed. Such a solution explicitly recognizes the interrelationship between health and economy. The financial crisis of 2008 is a good example; it appeared that the WHO did not react directly because it had insufficient background on the effects of economy on global health.

Evaluating risks involved

The major risk involved at the core of crisis management in the SARS case is that of deteriorating global public health, i.e. the risk of widespread infection and propagation of the epidemic. Such a risk focuses the attention of all the players (whether global or local stakeholders) of the private sector and of public policymakers. In fact, the interests of all parties concerned converge in instances such as SARS with regard to the necessity to join their efforts to find a scientific and medical solution to the situation. In order to have a clear picture and to assess the risks of widespread pandemics, it is essential to allow researchers and scientists to determine scientifically the nature of the virus, its origins, whether it mutates, how quickly etc. Measures of importance include the number of cases concerned, the likelihood of finding adequate treatment for infected people (such as a vaccine) and understanding of the virus' mechanisms of action on human organisms. All such measures can be used to assess the global health-related risks mentioned above.

This chapter has identified considerable divergences in view of political, economic, and reputation-related positions, corresponding to responses to real or perceived risks by the various agents involved in the crisis. For instance, any state's tendency to view crisis management as a matter of domestic concern is particularly worrying knowing that the WHO does not have any means of enforcement of legislation at its disposal. However, in practice "unilateralism" has been successfully avoided in the face of the gravity of concerns and of the interdependence and interconnectedness prevailing in today's world; the governments of countries affected by the pandemic did cooperate to a satisfactory extent. Looking at the internal affairs of the countries at stake and analyzing their public discourse and specific health management during the crisis can best assess the latter risk of having uncooperative government behavior. A country that is not willing to cooperate will typically have a very "independence-based" discourse, emphasizing national sovereignty and principles of non-interference in a very ideological fashion. Examining diplomatic ties with international key actors, i.e. the WHO and strategic member states, and state behavior in general, also evaluates in a qualitative way the probability of non-cooperation on behalf of a member country of the WHO.

Activities such as tourism experienced a highly negative impact due to the SARS crisis. This impact was very dependent on the way the crisis was dealt with and how long it took for people's mistrust to disappear. Risk can be measured through the evolution of parameters such as trust in public authorities and their information, the quality of media information, and the image conveyed by the press, as well as the efficiency of global WHO campaigns to position the problems in rational terms. These parameters, which can be qualitatively assessed, provide insights into the dimension of risk for tourism and leisure industries, as well as for the travel industries. To assess these same risks quantitatively one may take the figures of flight tickets sold, possible cancelled flights, and profits/losses of airline companies, or evaluate the drop in governmentally provided figures relating to tourism and tourists' spending in one country.

Similarly, declines in the export of goods and products and in diverse private investments constitute economic middle and long-term risks for countries affected by the pandemic—which can be measured by comparing figures on financial investments and import/export balances published by governments or by international organizations, e.g. WTO. A possible collapse of the chicken farming and exporting industries constitute a serious risk that will orient many countries' policies as it would have a major impact on jobs and incomes, and raise political risks as well. This explains why the US and the EU temporarily blocked their imports from China to reassure and revitalize local production and consumption at the request of farmers and consumers.

All these risks depend on the way the crisis is dealt with internationally and on how information is conveyed. An important aspect is the attempt to rationalize the issue in people's minds so as to generate rational responses, which are hence predictable and easier to deal with. The amount of trust that individuals manifest toward their own authorities is a defining factor, as seen in the drastic reduction in chicken consumption due to a lack of trust in the information provided. Social trust is in fact an important component of the phenomenon of social amplification of risk, in that distrust distorts the overall risk perceptions and amplifies risk signals. This is especially true in risk situations like health epidemics, in which people are expected to trust the scientific information they are given. Complex risk management and communication and the lack of trust distort our perception of reality and, as it is typically self-reproducing, it is much easier to entertain than trust, which can be easily lost.

Achieving outcomes

In challenges such as SARS, it is the capacity for rapid reaction in the public and private sectors to adapt to threats that makes a difference. For businesses and other interest groups, it means organizing one's self and exercising pressures on government and companies to ensure that stakeholder concerns are taken into account. This implicates trade-offs and compromises, but also the constitution of perhaps eclectic and informal alliances.

Mutuality and reciprocity are necessary principles for transparency, responsible state behavior, and accountability toward the international community. These principles turn out to be a condition for trust, which is in turn necessary for other sovereign states to take less drastic steps toward contaminated countries. So it is in the interest of any country facing a pandemic to disclose and fully cooperate, in order to gain credit. Otherwise, non-complying governments will, at least, be informally sanctioned by public opinion and consumer choices, and will eventually even suffer exclusion from international decisions. Communication is in everyone's interest. Instead of entering a phase of mutual economic "threats" or direct coercion, diplomatic relations seem to be sufficient and effective instruments.

Theory U shows us that dialogue is essential to identify convergent interests and adopt a fair consensus on the objects of negotiations at the international and national levels, and also at the level of interactions between internal public debates and international commitments.

In the situation of SARS, options were designed within a dialogue structured at various levels that advanced very quickly to deal with the crisis and that addressed, managed, and controlled the risks of policy-making, market failures, asymmetric information systems, and communication, as well as international cooperation. However, a huge part of the risks resulted directly not from the rational and objective quality of observation, but rather from highly emotive reactions, namely "perceived risks," which operate as rumors and spread in societies.

Because formerly national or regional problems are increasingly dealt with through international cooperation, different actors with unique backgrounds are forced to cooperate in order to achieve a common solution. The SARS case emphasizes co-sensing to allow a deeper understanding of each stakeholder's concerns. By bringing in the perspectives of all stakeholders one can learn how others receive their arguments and how to define and refine their arguments. As a practical social technology, Theory U suggests that the way in which one attends to a situation determines how a situation unfolds. It therefore seems logical to reflect on one's own not necessarily impartial cultural background when working in groups. In order to handle an emerging risk it is necessary to look at an issue from different angles. *The lesson learned is that more powerful international players could learn more and become more effective if they were to listen to a broad array of stakeholders before determining a course of action.*

Tensions arise when a response seems too unrealistic for others, although it opens a window to address issues that have not been considered. Immersion in an unknown field requires leaving behind an environment that in the past has provided a sense of security (what Theory U calls "letting go" and "letting come in"). Another important issue to pay attention to is the mood of multi-stakeholder groups, which swings between highs and lows and is not always at the optimal level of energy. One needs to address these issues of motivation for energy to be restored and the work continued with high involvement. *The lesson learned is that it is important to take time to ensure different approaches, so that understanding of the problem can be sorted out before going to the solution stage, and it is important to engage as many stakeholders as possible to arrive at superior performance in terms of shared outcomes.*

Pulling it all together

As in the previous modules, it is very useful to self-evaluate. What I suggested to Serge, and which he used with the client, was very helpful for the team leaders of each stakeholder group and for Serge himself. You will find in Box 3.3 a summary of the self-assessment questions that were helpful to Serge and which can serve in assessing learning-while-doing in a similar crisis.

The first assessment relates to downloading and sensing from other members of the team, which is the first stage of Theory U. It involves starting off in areas of personal expertise and exploiting what you already know. Negotiation while sensing what other stakeholders may want is also an important skill. Shared accountability that comes from ensuring that all have a role and agreement on the final approach helps to ensure success in implementation. Keeping track of what worked in the process of reaching agreement and the steps followed helps the learner hone this skill over time. The approach is also aimed at getting to a final agreement with as much efficiency as possible (Code A from Chapter 2).

The second set of questions revolves around thinking outside the box and seeking innovations. It is important to take note of the actions, instances, or triggers that led you to think outside the box (Code B from Chapter 2). Negotiation can be very useful to explore what you don't know.

Empathizing with other stakeholders can help you become more effective in anticipating follow-up demands during a negotiation. Listening carefully and trying to see things from their perspective is also very helpful in shaping areas where you can be flexible and where you have to fight to ensure that your perspective or preference makes it to the final agreement. New information garnered from co-sensing a solution with a wide range of stakeholders could also result in a shift in your behavior and introduce areas of new flexibility. Tracking where you evolved and became more flexible helps you learn when next to use such a strategy. Sometimes detail can come in the way of a attaining a grand bargain and it is important to note when this happens and to ensure that a process is used that allows you to get out of the weeds. Encouraging open and structured interventions is a good way to get out of narrow perspectives, but you sometimes need to pay attention to the big picture or common objective in order to avoid being bogged down by details that may derail from a shared final agreement (Box 3.3).

Box 3.3 Evaluation Block III: Self-Assessment Tool for Seeing and Sensing

Did you focus negotiation on your personal area of expertise?	Code A
How did you exploit what you already know?	Code A
Were you able to meet needs of your negotiating partners?	Code A
How did you ensure accountability for the final agreement?	Code A
What steps did you follow to improve the final agreement?	Code A
What steps did you follow to improve negotiation process?	Code A
What forced you to think outside your preliminary position?	Code B
How did you use negotiation to explore what you didn't know?	Code B
Could you anticipate follow-up demands of negotiators?	Code B
How did you allow other ideas to emerge?	Code B
Where did you have flexibility?	Code B
How did your areas of flexibility evolve?	Code B
How did you avoid getting bogged-down (detail, process)?	Code B
Did you encourage open and unstructured interventions?	Code B

The role of learning during a crisis cannot be underestimated. Reflecting with Serge on what worked best at the end of the engagement some months later, we learned that the process of asking each individual participant to write a report on the group work, developing the perspective of their stakeholder group further using other sources of information from outside the group work session, was invaluable. Each participant included a short observation note on the process employed in the group work to come collectively to a common strategy within the primary stakeholder group and during the multi-stakeholder dialog, as well as on the lessons learned from the sharing at the plenary sessions. These reflections have become tremendous learning opportunities and I have used them in subsequent classes and for client work in similar situations. Such a process replicates what happens in a real crisis, as shown by Bennett et al. (2011) in their study of how information is spread at the community level and the effect the behavior and opinions of peers have on public reactions to crisis. This form of social learning is critical when managing crises. The ability to track and disseminate information faster using social media presents capabilities that can render the reaction to crisis more effective in the future.[14]

4
Leadership and Governance

Key Lessons from Chapter 4: Leadership and Governance

The chapter investigates the role of leadership in good governance and the relationship between leadership and institutions. The important question of territorial governance is also covered, as are the pressures that geography puts on leaders in all spheres of action.

The main skills introduced derive from Theory U and complexity science, including: (1) "presencing" the emerging future and crystallizing a cohesive vision and strategy; (2) the ability to rehearse for diverse governance environments and function in environments with weak information and high unpredictability; (3) strategic scanning skills that build the capacity to generate strategic maps of pressure points and risk scenarios; (4) lessons learned from leadership in post-conflict countries and preparedness to lead in conditions of conflict; and (5) approaches for working with tools under diverse potential futures.

Through examples, the learner can investigate the values and behaviors that serve as a guide in making choices in challenging circumstances. There is exposure to the special cases of security and cohesion as well as territorial governance. Three case studies help the learner to extract leadership and governance lessons from post-conflict countries. These include Cameroon, Côte d'Ivoire, and the Great Lakes Region. The chapter brings out theoretical materials on the approach to crystallizing ideas from multiple stakeholders, which requires skills of sensing and integrating into a strategy for action. Questions about the nature of leadership, ethics in public life, and how to practice in different governance settings round off this chapter.

What is the role of *leadership and governance* in dealing with key risks?

This chapter considers the role of leadership and governance in dealing with key risks. General concepts around governance are introduced and the learner is exposed to the tools and frameworks that leaders use to make decisions. The levels of governance that are critical for decision-making are introduced, as are their implications. Special attention is paid to how global challenges emanate from a set of collective actions by multiple stakehold-ers. The resulting outcomes that challenge security and social cohesion are also covered, as they are at the heart of many interactions on a global scale.

The chapter starts off with the levels of governance and their implica-tions for decision-making. The sections expand on the role of individual leaders, but also on how institutions, particularly institutions for economic governance, can support them. Human geography and the role of space in a globalized world are covered and the learner is presented with a practice block to rehearse the skill of "presencing" and crystallizing different ideas and perspectives into a cohesive vision and strategy.

Levels of governance and their implications

Globalization has made governance more complex and brought in stake-holders who interact in ways that change the process of decision-making and the outcomes of decisions. Heywood (2011: 125) defines governance as the various ways in which social life is coordinated, of which government is merely one. He defines good governance as the "standards for the process of decision-making in society, including (according to the UN) popular par-ticipation, respect for the rule of law, transparency, responsiveness, consen-sus orientation, equity and inclusiveness, effectiveness and efficiency, and accountability." As such, Heywood (2011) recognizes the different levels of governance and the complexity that comes from interactions between local, national, and supranational bodies.

There are two critical levels to be concerned about. The first is global, where the global balance of power and global governance are of importance. The second is country, where national governance and sub-national issues are of interest. The governance approach to political science offers a new perspective on the role of the public sector at the national level and the interrelations between states at the international level (Pierre, 2000). A vari-ety of strategies are needed for decision makers in the public sector to handle challenges deriving from urbanization, service delivery, unemployment, and regional integration. All of them depend on the effective functioning of governance at multiple levels.

Any discussion on governance in the context of globalization cannot ignore the influence of civil society. Civil society is defined by Cohen and Arato (1992) as "the sphere of social interaction between economy and state, composed above all of the intimate sphere (especially family), the sphere of associations (especially voluntary associations), social movements, and forms of public communication." This is an operational definition that has been rendered even more potent with the advent of social media. Groups based on common interests can be formed almost instantly using Facebook or other social media platforms, and issues can gain global currency on Twitter, which feeds into international networks like Al Jazeera, BBC, CNN, and France24. Rooy (2004) argues for the need for global supplementary mechanisms that take into account the representation, rights, experience, expertise, and moral authority emanating from civil society action on a variety of global issues.

Civil society can be strong or weak in a given country context, and the varying boundaries between the public sector and private sector could be tight in some countries and loose in others. Experiments that countries have undergone in privatization policies and public policies around subsidies, social spending, and infrastructure also provide a rich environment for learning.

Starting with the levels of governance—global or country—we note that any decision maker would need to be conversant with the question of the global balance of power. Measures of global power typically include military expenditures as a proxy for military prowess, the share of global GDP, which is a measure of economic power, and diplomatic or soft power (Table 4.1), which includes moral authority, the power of ideas, and the influence on values and culture (Nye, 2004).

National governance concerns approaches to governing at country and local level. Trends in democratic systems of governance at the country level and their evolution over time are useful for uncovering pattern changes. The

Table 4.1 Diplomatic, economic, and military power

Country	Diplomatic power		Economic power	Military power
	In-country embassies in 2000	Change since 1995 (%)	Rank in GDP in 2010	Expenditure as a % of GDP in 2010
BRICS countries				
Brazil	88	+19.3	7	1.6
Russia	140	0.0	11	3.9
India	101	4.1	9	2.5
China	130	10.1	2	2.0
South Africa	95	46.0	29	1.2
Former colonial powers				
USA	172	+3.0	1	4.8
France	154	+4.1	5	2.3
UK	149	+4.1	6	2.6
Spain	96	+5.5	12	1.1
Portugal	67	+11.7	37	2.3

Source: A.T. Kearney/Foreign Policy available at http://www.foreignpolicy.com/articles/2007/10/11/the_globalization_index_2007.
Data on GDP and military spending as a share of GDP are from World Development Indicators available at http://data.worldbank.org/data-catalog/world-development-indicators.

degree and speed of devolution to local governments is also an indication of change and transformation of governance at the country level. Countries have differentiated the size and scope of the state, which vary with policies on nationalization, the nature of inserted clauses in contract renegotiations when the private sector is involved, or even patterns in divestiture. Tax and expenditure management are good indicators of the strength of the state as the ability to manage public spending is a key state capability. The level of access to the media and information are also indicators of transparency of the state—a measure of the degree of confidence that the state can explain its behavior to its citizens and civil society at large, including the press. The ability of a state to maintain law and order and protect its borders is also an important indication of the level of country governance.

Civil society can be measured through elements of individuals, organizations, and institutions as proposed by (Anheier, 2004). Looking at the range of issues that civil society is involved in at the country level and globally could help assess its influence and importance. For example, a measure of the influence of civil society on advancing the objectives of transparency and accountability through a campaign on freedom of expression, press, association, and assembly could be based on the number of organizations (CSOs) working on the subject or the number of activists or participants engaged in the subject. (Anheier, 2004) takes this analysis further to look at the media as an institution of civil society and how freedom of the press exists in a given country. Such freedom of information could vary with access to the Internet and indeed the degree of control of the Internet. The number of individuals who use the Internet could also provide information, including how many web users there are, how often they use the Internet, which sites they visit, and so on. The level of public trust for civil society is also another measure of the moral influence of civil society. Other measures are also important, including the levels of autonomy and independence, such as in the amount of funding civil society has from domestic and outside sources. Engaging and forming partnerships is also important in terms of the level and quality of partnerships between civil society and government. Does civil society engage with business? Does it engage locally or internationally? All these are important measures of the spheres of influence of civil society (Anheier, 2004).

Changes in governance can be garnered from looking at the evolving roles and responsibilities of the public and private sector in practices around the world. Globalization of industries like construction, manufacturing, and transport is a rich sphere for study in understanding the shifts in governance that have enabled a different way of working between the public and private sectors. Grimsey and Lewis (2004) provide a detailed review of the experiences in public–private partnerships (PPPs) from engineering practice, academic literature in economics, finance, and public policy, as well as from government and independent reports. Public–private boundaries can be seen from the perspective of the relative size of the private sector and the mix of functions between the public and private sectors. The structure, degree, and quality of cooperation or partnerships between the public and private sectors are also of interest in gauging the influence of the private sector on local and global governance. PPPs have also brought unique risks whose management requires a shift in governance structures around the world.

Experiments at the country level offer a good window of opportunity to assess the quality of governance across state and non-state actors. When the Russia Government decided between 1992 and 1994 to engage in voucher privatization, whereby assets formally owned by the state were distributed equally among the population, including minors, it embarked on an experiment in public–private boundaries on a scale never tried before. The vouchers could be traded for shares in the companies to be privatized, and most of them ended up in the hands of the management of the enterprises who bought them from citizens who were not ready or willing to take a risk and invest in the newly privatized companies (Appel, 1997).

Other experiments in shared governance include the definition of the hierarchy of roads in countries like France, where there is a category of roads known as *routes communales* (communal roads) that are owned and maintained by the commune, which is the smallest level of settlement, some with as few as 10 people. The segment of road that goes from the communal road to a private residence is private, but in rural areas communal roads serve many residences. Such roads are different in their ownership structure from *routes départementales,* which are managed by the 100 local governments at the department level, and are thus publicly owned by the respective local governments. Other road networks are public, such as the *routes nationale,* which are the main roads maintained directly by the state. The highest level of shared ownership is the *autoroutes,* which are mostly tolled motorways that connect France to the rest of Europe. This hierarchy for the road network sets the boundaries between what is national, departmental, or communal, and what is private. The road system has been classified and reclassified several times as the appetite for public or private ownership has changed over the years since Napoleonic times. (For a good discussion on the rationale for and changes to the French road classification system, see Beyer, 2004).

There are many examples that stretch the definition and role of the public and private sectors when it comes to governance. Consider for example the issue of human rights, as when civil society organizations can exert influence on the labor practices of a company in a given country by holding them to account in social media over child labor or unfair labor practices. Leadership in this case comes from pressure by individuals who are organized to raise concerns. Reactions by CEOs of companies to resolve problems singled out by civil society, even when the shareholders of the company have not considered them as a priority, is another manifestation of leadership in a complex governance setting. Fair wages is another concept that can be stretched across boundaries, with organizations such as the International Labour Organization (ILO) having the ability to change the level and practice of labor standards across boundaries even in countries that do not have minimum wage laws. In the provision of public services, the concept of condominium security in gated communities is an illustration of the shift in boundaries where there are shared security and access control systems (instead of police services by the municipalities), shared services such as electricity and garbage collection (in place of public utilities), and common road maintenance (in place of those services being provided and overseen by municipalities).

Governance has become more complex with changes in the supervision of borders across countries. Borders are not only national or linked only to states; much more complex and diverse borders exist at other scales of action, and are not always easy to identify on maps. The border of a big city is a complex and changing territory, transformed by peri-urban dynamics, with some cities fusing into others in a continuous urban space—such as the New York–New Jersey corridor. At the regional level the discovery of natural resources that overlap formal borders can cause tensions between countries—such as the tensions between Tanzania and Malawi from the vast gas resources discovered under Lake Malawi in 2012. Such natural resources may initiate territories not coincident with the administrative boundaries of countries, as a private enterprise exploiting the resources would have to work across borders. At the macro-regional level, a new international territory emerges if several states enter a regional economic community (as has happened in Europe with the European Common Market (ECM) and in West Africa with the Economic Community of West African States (ECOWAS); the external borders enclosing these large territories have a different value compared with the internal borders. It is the case for the European Union, where internal borders have a markedly different weight compared to the external borders of the Schengen area. It is also the case for the ECOWAS Region when other African nationals come to visit and need visas.

Special case of security and social cohesion

Security and social cohesion get special treatment because of the impact that war, terror, and crime have on global activities. Decision makers need to be vigilant in assessing the status of major conflicts and wars and the trajectory they are likely to have. These could include extra state and inter-state conflicts and wars or civil wars and ethnic strife or conflicts. Stresses in important borders or boundaries are also of interest, as are the effects of resource constraints and resource-related conflicts.

Terrorism has reared into the forefront of risks since September 11, 2001, when there was an attack on the World Trade Center in New York and coordinated attacks in Pennsylvania and the Pentagon, aimed at the USA. Since then, decision makers have kept track of the number of terrorist events around the world and the types of events, and use the information to consider the likely impact they would have on the economy nationally or domestically. Firms do similar assessments to decide on their location and security strategies.

Global crime impacts citizens and firms alike, whether in the form of money laundering, pirating of goods, illicit drugs, human trafficking, illegal arms trade, antiquities theft, or gemstones trade. Trade in prohibited products, such as rhino horns and other items from endangered species also falls into this category. Coordinated action at border posts is a key capability to handle these kinds of risks and they require highly specialized tracking and monitoring systems to succeed.

Firms also invest a good amount of work into better understanding the presence and outbreaks of terrorism by looking at the evolution of the returns to terrorism (see Collier, 2006). Such studies also investigate the causes of civil wars and coups, which have been found to range from poverty to the effect of slow economic growth on the risk of civil war. Long-run analysis also shows the patterns of conflict that could have implications for decision-making. Consider for example the period between 1946 and 2001 in Africa, where there have been a series of conflicts, particularly in Chad, where more than 41% of the conflicts have taken place during this period (Table 4.2).

Collier (2007) shows that a 1% increase in economic growth reduces the risk of civil war by 1%. Natural resources tend to increase the risk of strife, as it is possible to strike deals between rebels and extraction industries. In some situations, Collier (2007) and Chua (2002) found that the presence of a large

Table 4.2   Conflicts and neighbors: armed conflict incidents 1946–2001

Country	Conflicts	% of total
Cameroon	3	17.6
Central African Republic	1	5.9
Chad	7	41.2
Congo, Rep	2	11.8
Equatorial Guinea	1	5.9
Gabon	1	5.9
Nigeria	2	11.8

Source: World Bank Database on countries in conflict published by UCDP/PRIO in Norway and can be found at http://www.nsd.uib.no/macrodataguide/set.html?id=55&sub=1.

dominant ethnic group could lead to instability. The size of the country is also a potential source of tension, as large countries with dispersed or diverse populations (Bar-Yam, 2005b) or those with sharp edges or mountains are hard to govern.

How long a conflict lasts is also of importance and Collier (2005) found that it depends on the level of income of the population, with conflict lasting longer in low-income regions. If there are valuable exports to finance a war, the conflicts last longer, which is also the case if there has been a previous war. The costs of conflict are numerous and include disease, mass rape, mass migration, increased poverty levels as economies are destroyed, and deterioration of political rights. Collier (2005) finds that the risk of falling into civil war or having a coup in any five-year period is 1 in 6 if these conditions exist.

There are a number of actions that leaders can take to deal with risks from security and social cohesion. These include security responses, such as increasing defense and security spending, including cyber security. Other actions relate to the control of money laundering and the illicit flow of finances. Immigration and border policies are also an important set of actions to manage increased security risks.

There are also some actions that can be taken to deal with cultural, ethnic, and religious tensions. Many such tensions arise from identity and whether people associate themselves with national, continental, global, religious, or specific ethnic groups or groups to which they feel similar (Sen, 2006). Tensions could also arise at the boundaries between traditional communities and newcomers. Responses could range from insulation of the traditional communities by instituting indigenous people policies that can be embedded in the operational policies and practices of multilateral, bilateral, and private actors as they engage around the world. World Bank (2011) provides a review of the application of such policies around the world.[1] Other responses could include supporting traditional communities in their efforts to adapt or embrace change, as shown in the Jamuna Bridge case study presented in Chapter 2.

Language barriers are at times a source of tension and misunderstanding. Challenges emerge when working at a continental level between the need to use Arabic, English, French, Portuguese, Spanish, and Swahili in official African Union proceedings, which is costly and slows down decision-making processes. In some cases, local dialects can be unifying factors as in the common use of Wolof in Senegal, the Gambia, and Mauritania.

The resulting outcomes of violence, hate, terrorism, civil war, poverty, and increased risks of tension among groups require leaders to reconsider their norms and values, as well as their social structures. Being able to interpret the actions of other agents and to empathize and learn from them can provide a useful backdrop for better sensing the future and developing appropriate actions and strategies.

The specific role of leadership in good governance

Professor Klaus Schwab, Founder and Executive Chairman of the World Economic Forum (WEF) said in January 2006: "The assumptions, tools and frameworks that leaders have used to make decisions over the past decade appear inadequate. It is imperative for leaders of all walks of life to develop new capabilities if they expect to be successful and to maintain relevance." Professor Schwab signals the need for new leadership skills that include better knowledge of how leaders form assumptions, what frameworks they use for analysis and what tools they have available to decide. This section examines the assumptions, tools, and frameworks in the context of varying governance and institutional settings to extract what changes in those environments. Emphasis is placed on the special situation of post-conflict countries, where things are in flux and decision-making is very fluid, making it a testing ground for leadership.

The nature of leadership

A typical leader in today's world would have faced difficult choices that range from how to balance work and life, how to accept a change in status, or how to avoid corruption. Ms Indra Nooyi (CEO of PepsiCo) stated famously in a YouTube interview that "work is life and life is work," as she recounted how she struggled to balance work and life and the choices she had to make along the way (http://www.youtube.com/watch?v=J7lCOLDRnKg). This interview brings front and center the reconciliation of private needs and desires with public responsibility and the desire for excellence. Whether in a good or bad governance setting, the leader's challenge is to find a way to make that reconciliation. In so doing, the leader needs to make choices on a daily and even hourly basis on what to do. Do I attend to my daughter's piano recital or do I finalize the key points in my telephone conversation with the Chairman of my reelection campaign? Do I take my full entitlement for maternity leave or do I go back to work and make a head start on difficult organizational reforms? Do I take time for that much needed visit to the dentist or do I read one more time the strategy presentation scheduled for the Board meeting tomorrow? All these are questions about which leaders make different choices. In my own case, family and friends called me after an interview was published in a management journal where I disclosed the choices I had made and some of the regrets I alluded to (Areba, 2012).

A leader needs to curb the desire to benefit from the bounty of position, or of the state, corporation or entity they preside over. Corruption is one form of benefitting from the bounty of position. Staying too long in power is another manifestation, as deposed leaders face challenges in accepting an average life after holding high positions of power. Hence aspiring to leadership positions needs to be decoupled from the tendency afterwards of relying too much on position. Leaders have to remind themselves of the unique skills and abilities that propelled them to leadership, ensure they remain sharp in those, and not rely on the crutch of position, as situations can suddenly change, leaving the leader who did not hone in their skills incapable of action without the authority that their position bestowed on them.

Heifetz (1994) proposes two key distinctions from which to understand the challenge of leadership. The first is the type of problem confronting the leader, where Heifetz recognizes the difference in decision-making when facing a structured technical problem as opposed to deciding in complex and adaptive problem situations that demand learning and innovation. The second distinction drawn by Heifetz relates to the level of authority, and how to exert leadership in contexts where one does or does not have authority. His work focuses on a governance framework steeped in the US constitutional system, at a specific time in the governance of the US where there was a presidential election being organized and challenging riots got out of control in Los Angeles. Helfetz (1994) provides a wonderful background from which to draw out the specific governance environments and their challenges for leadership, but also how to develop the skills needed to act in such situations.

The challenges mentioned above give us an indication that there may be specific attributes needed in a leader to function under different governance arenas, and that the process of selection and development of leaders needs to be designed with these attributes in mind. One key aspect that stands out in the face of globalization is the complex nature of decision-making and therefore the need to have a team of leaders with differing abilities who can manage under highly varied scenarios. Only a few people can lead in highly varied contexts, as they can withstand the burdens of choice—Indra Nooyi missing her daughter's recital—yet abilities are allocated through democracy and chance. A given context renders you a leader—the vegetable vendor in Tunis whose protest of burning himself sparked the revolution and the Arab Spring did not wake up saying I am going to start a revolution. People reacted to his act and followed in less dramatic ways his protest against the corruption in the municipal leadership in Tunis and the lack of opportunities for jobs for the youth.

Even though only a few can lead in all contexts, and individuals come with different abilities, research shows that leaders are sharpened through challenge and observation and shaped by feats of accomplishment (Plato, *The Republic*, Book III). As such, there is room for succession planning models to embed the challenges of managing in a complex environment when developing a series of people who can take over a position of President, Minister, Member of Parliament, or CEO and Chairman of the Board. When leaders are putting together a team for a task they can consider the specific abilities needed to meet the goals intended and ensure that the team as a whole has these abilities. As you consider developing yourself, you can consider seeking experiences that sharpen your abilities in a variety of leadership settings to get better at leading in different contexts. Similarly, when managers of Human Resources are seeking to develop individuals in their organizations they can consider the challenges of managing complexity as the starting point before recommending training and development actions or assignments for specific individuals.

During the 2012 Olympic Games in London I happened to be seated next to Jean-Christophe Rolland, a rower from France who is the holder of multiple Olympic and World Rowing Championship medals. I started to chat with him about how he selects a winning team for competition, whether it is for a team of two rowers or four. He said to me that he had learned that some rowers are excellent on their own but when rowing in a team they cannot translate that personal excellence into a win for the team. Other rowers are not so good and may not even win in a single rower competition, but form the missing ingredients for a win in a team of two or four rowers. The lessons learned can be seen in Jean-Christophe's own career history, which shows how he has learned over time. He just missed an Olympic medal by coming in fourth in 1992 in Barcelona. He went on to win a bronze medal in Atlanta in 1996 and then won a gold medal in Sydney in 2000. The same learning curve can be seen in the World Rowing Championships, where he won two gold medals (1993, 1997), two silver medals (1991, 1994) and one bronze medal (1995), having risen from 9th place in 1989, 8th in 1990 and 5th in 1991.

Jean-Christophe Rolland's story is a good illustration of the leader's obligations to learn and discover and the role that time and working in diverse environments plays in shifting an individual's capabilities. But what was unique in Jean-Christophe's story is that he continues to teach and impart wisdom to others in a unique way through his own process of knowing from experience. This presupposes the value of an art to speed up the process of learning, which Jean-Christophe did through daily practice. A leader is obligated to guide and mentor and to compel the best minds to attain knowledge and impart it to others. All these lessons can be applied in self-learning, in helping people you lead develop, and in developing the next generation of leaders. Developing ethical leadership through role models and mentoring is very critical, especially when seeking to curb or reverse behaviors such as corruption.

Ethics in public life

We cannot introduce the question of governance environments without first introducing the issue of ethics in public life. In a complex world, leaders are faced with ethical choices in areas that may not have been previously defined. The key question then is whose ethics should be in play: those of the leader (which come from self-interest) or from some form of leadership ethics? To answer this question presupposes knowledge of what your values are. Where do they come from? What responsibilities do you have as a leader and what ethical framework applies to your work? Pellegrino (1989) argues that there is a firm philosophical foundation that can be used to develop appropriate professional ethics, and that what deficiencies there are in professional morality come from deficiencies in the character and virtue of the individuals in the profession.

Pellegrino puts full responsibility for developing and practicing the appropriate public ethics on the professionals in their respective fields—be they doctors, lawyers, religious leaders, or political figures. This means that the character of the leader is central in terms of intent and how the leader balances the objectives of others with the objectives of self. Taking from the public coffers to benefit private expenditures is a form of preferring self to others—aka corruption. Shirking at work and not putting in the effort desired to get good outcomes is a form of preserving self over others—aka public sector inefficiency.

Motivation and its source —whether the leader is motivated by altruism or self-interest—are also of relevance. Pellegrino (1989) argues for characteristics like selflessness, compassion, empathy, and fairness. But for a leader to have these traits means that they have conquered their blind spots and are able to overcome self-deception (The Arbinger Institute, 2000). How well you know yourself and your values and how you work towards developing common values is critical as a starting point.

Experimentation is critical in a complex world and it challenges the leader to find a way to balance the negative effects of experiments on people or the environment, while spearheading learning. Leaders need to be aware of when to start or stop an experiment or a pilot. Where and how to define experiments for results is also important. How to scale up results in an ethical matter takes on even more importance. The skill of learning to see the whole and to see with a set of ethics in mind, a term that Senge et al. (2004) referred to as "seeing our seeing," becomes paramount, and leaders who lead in innovation and experimentation need to have these skills at their highest level.

Governance and institutions

Important as individual leaders are, they are shaped by and shape the institutions in which they work, and are shaped by the governance arrangements in use at a particular point in time or location. Institutions impact on people's lives in a myriad of ways, not least of which is the performance of an economy. Economic growth can be impacted by governance arrangements, as can the benefits and distribution of such growth (Kaufmann et al., 2008). Interactions between individuals and institutions form the very foundation of governance, and weak governance has impacts on the performance of multiple systems, including economic systems. This section exposes a definition of governance, the impact of institutions on economic performance, and the role of the leader in structuring effective institutions. The learner is introduced to a set of factors that generate diverse governance environments. Knowing these factors is critical for improving the ability to function in environments with weak governance and high unpredictability.

Institutions and economic growth

A number of channels link basic governance institutions to macroeconomic performance. One channel works through the motivation systems that leaders put in place at political, social, or economic levels and how the incentives impact on the effectiveness of policy options for society and shape the collective outcome of individual decisions by citizens and entrepreneurs. Leaders define the set of rules and norms, whether formal or informal, by which activities take place. Formal rules include the constitutions of countries, regulations in the financial sector, or the protection of property rights during acts of civil unrest. Informal rules come from the trust relations in society or within an organization, and are shaped by the norms, conventions, and codes of conduct in use. Formal and informal rules, and how they are managed, determine the effectiveness of the rule of law. The third element of relevance that is shaped by leaders in an institutional setup is the definition or setting of limits on the choices that an individual can make. Such limits have an impact on the practice and tolerance of corruption, and also on the accountability of individuals in their functions to a broader set of objectives.

One can measure the effects of a leader's decisions on the quality of governance institutions. The process effects of a bad setup can be seen in high transaction costs. Reducing uncertainty and better structuring interactions can reduce transaction costs, as can a better definition of what choices are available or allowed in the work setting. Outcome effects could include the protection of human and property rights, where a poor definition of incentives, rules, and allowable choices could result in inadequate protection of property and human rights.

Measures of governance

Leaders play an important role in defining governance arrangements and there is a need for a common understanding of measures of governance. Kaufmann et al. (2008) use a set of measures based on the traditions and institutions that determine how authority is exercised in a particular country. These measures include the process by which governments are selected, held accountable, monitored, and replaced, as represented by two indicators of (1) voice and accountability and (2) political stability and no violence; the capacity of governments to manage resources efficiently and formulate, implement, and enforce sound policies and regulations, as assessed by

(3) government effectiveness and (4) regulatory quality; and the respect of citizens and the state for the institutions that govern economic and social interactions among them, as judged by (5) rule of law and (6) control of corruption.

How can leaders create an environment by which voice and account-ability can matter? Creating an environment for involvement in political processes can elicit and aggregate local knowledge and preferences, thereby not only helping to build better institutions in the long run, but making better resource allocations in the short run (Evans, 2004; Rodrik, 1999). Public discussion of key issues in open forums and the general exchange of ideas, information, and opinions offer the only way to adequately define the desirable developmental outcomes (Sen, 1999). Dialogue can help corporate and political leaders alike get a better sense of the collective will and become better able to shape choices within a risk-aware scenario.

Empirical evidence shows that when political leaders handle inclusion correctly it can have positive consequences for the welfare of citizens in terms of income growth, as countries that score high on governance and accountability also score high in growth in per capita GDP. Consider the case of Tanzania, which made a big jump in economic growth between 1996 and 2007 when the traditions of consultation at the village level were matched with a bold political decision to open up to market competition (Figure 4.1). Tanzania was propelled into a high-growth environment, seen by the sharp movement of the placement of the country on a curve relating governance to economic performance.[2]

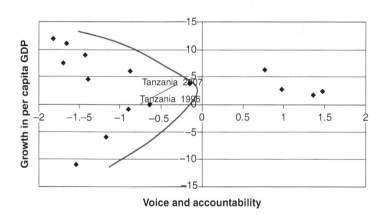

Figure 4.1 Income growth and governance: steady improvements in voice and accountability versus rapid deterioration
Source: Per capita GDP growth data from Heston, Summers, Daten (2008) calculated by author into three year moving averages for periods 1994–1996 and 2002–2004; governance data on voice and accountability from Kaufmann et al. (2008).

The choices made by leaders can also shape the trends in political stability and the levels of violence in a country setting. The world is largely divided into wealthy and generally peaceful countries and those that are poorer and subject to instability, conflict, and war. A steady rise has been observed between 1946 and 2001 in the number of civil wars, which have become more frequent and affect close to one quarter of all countries in the world. Civil wars last longer, with the victims of war, now more than in the past, being economic producers rather than military targets. Fighting groups have to act as economic agents in order to survive, controlling industries, regulating production, and providing services or plundering and looting to finance the war.

A number of factors cause conflict and drive achievable levels of political and social stability, many of which are in the control of political and industry leaders. The first factor is economic growth, where evidence suggests that growing economies are less subject to conflict and war (World Bank, 1998).

The second factor is inequality between ethnic groups or between regions (sometimes known as horizontal inequality), which is thought to matter for conflict (Macartan Humphreys, 2003). Demographic factors are the third important element as in how population growth can lead to scarcity and a fight for resources, and how migration can put ethnic groups together, thereby creating tensions (Macartan Humphreys, 2003). Natural resources are the fourth factor, and, in particular, reliance on natural resources for export is seen to relate to conflict, especially when the resources' regional distribution is uneven or when they are usurped by special interests (Collier, 2007; Macartan Humphreys, 2003). Finally, geography seems to matter, as being landlocked or with difficult access to trade due to unfriendly neighbors may lead to conflict (Macartan Humphreys, 2003; Sachs and Warner, 1995). In the 1990s conflicts were concentrated in Africa and Asia, having escalated steadily since the liberation movements in the 1940s and 50s.

Leaders can shape the trajectory of economic growth by having the right policies, and can avoid conflict and civil unrest by concentrating on generating economic growth. Inequality distributions can also be controlled by policy decisions in terms of how tax burdens are distributed and subsidies organized, as well as by ensuring fair access to opportunities is afforded to excluded groups and across gender lines. Leaders can devise rules for managing under scarcity to avoid the negative effects of demographic pressures, and supporting newly immigrating families can reduce the tensions coming from ethnic rivalry in cities. Natural resources do not have to be a curse; they can be a blessing if leaders set rules on how they are extracted and how the proceeds from extraction are shared.

Cameroon has six neighbors, two of which are landlocked (Central African Republic and Chad). Leaders in landlocked countries can seek alliances with neighbors in a regional integration setting or choose to excel in producing services (communication and banking) that do not rely on long-distance

Table 4.3   The case of Cameroon—neighbors' population and economy

Country	Population	GNI per capita in US$	Share of population (%)	Share of sub-regional per capita GNI (%)
Cameroon	16,682.772	1,080	9.2	6.5
Central African Republic	4,095,142	360	2.3	2.2
Chad	9,987,027	480	5.5	2.9
Congo, Rep	4,105,127	927	2,3	5.5
Equatorial Guinea	514,889	8,250	0.3	49.3
Gabon	1,405,766	5,000	0.8	29.9
Nigeria	144,719,953	640	79.7	3.8

Source: World Development Indicators (2006), available at http://data.worldbank.org/data-catalog/world-development-indicators.

transport. Cameroon has used its relationships with its neighbors to support its development strategy. Cameroon is a member of the Economic Community of Central African States (ECCAS), which includes Angola, Burundi, Democratic Republic of Congo, Rwanda, and São Tomé and Príncipe, in addition to its physical neighbors of Central African Republic, Chad, Congo Republic, Equatorial Guinea, and Gabon. Nigeria, which is the most populous nation in Africa, is a neighbor to Cameroon, but the country does not hold membership in ECCAS. As such, the leaders in Cameroon balance physical boundaries and virtual ones (as in the ECCAS members who are not geographically contiguous with Cameroon) (Table 4.3).

The formation of ECCAS is helping further the choices by regional leaders in handling the constraints of geography, and giving countries like Chad an opportunity to support its large population through reliance on neighbors like Cameroon. There is a remaining challenge that leaders still have to face in the ECCAS region, including appropriate policy design following the construction of the Chad–Cameroon Pipeline. The pipeline was intended to reduce poverty and ameliorate the resource curse by breaking the cycle of resource extraction plus bad governance. Pegg (2006) shows that the policy interventions selected had yet to show tangible results in reducing poverty and breaking the resource curse.

Another example of leadership in landlocked countries comes from Rwanda. After the end of conflict in 1994 the country chose to focus on building up the Information Communication and Technology (ICT) backbone to exploit its ability to produce knowledge services. Such a choice shielded Rwanda from competition on physical space, where the country would lose (being landlocked), and instead focus on competition in cyberspace, where talent, efficiency, and innovation drive outcomes. Similarly, the formation of the East African Community, with the joining of Rwanda and Burundi in July 2007, allowed these landlocked countries to benefit from regional integration (IPAR, 2009).

Political instability and the presence of violence can have severe effects on society, which compels leaders to seek ways of reducing their causes. Consider the growth in per capita GDP of a country like Ethiopia, which has gone from –4.9% in 2003 to 10.8% in 2004 after political stability was achieved, and has held at stable high levels of between 7–10% each year, only dropping to 5.0% in 2011 following the effects of the financial crisis of 2008–2009.[3] In general, lack of political stability and the presence of violence have many effects that can be measured and seen directly in the economic trajectory of countries.

With the onset of violence, the first manifestation is a loss of physical capital: destruction of existing physical capital and reduced investment in future physical capital. There are effects on people and the availability of labor, with deaths due to battle, famine, disease, and the destruction of health services, resulting in distortions to the labor market. Human capital is impacted due to brain drain, decline in the health status of workers, and reduced investments in education and health during wartime. Total Factor Productivity is usually affected through delays to technological innovation and interruption of production and market transactions (trade). Some sectors are more impacted than others, and the asymmetric impacts press harder on vulnerable groups like the landless, urban poor, women, and children. Construction, transport, distribution, finance, and manufacturing are severely impacted when countries are going through periods of violence and instability. Government expenditure patterns change during crises, with resources going to military spending, starving other sectors.

Institutions and economic growth

Leaders in government have a special role in determining whether government institutions are effective. Countries with high government effectiveness like China are able to sustain multiple years of high or steady economic growth. But at times, improving government effectiveness can come at the expense of higher performance of the economy. This was the case in Chile between 1996 and 2007, where massive gains in government effectiveness came at some cost to growth in per capita GDP. Common measures of government effectiveness include the capacity of government to define and implement policy relating to macroeconomic management (fiscal and monetary), social insurance (policies and safety nets for employment, income, social benefits), and public investments (infrastructure, human capital). The role of the leader in ensuring a good institutional design is in ensuring there is a set of well-functioning critical institutions (markets, regulation, rule of law, conflict management).

Regulatory quality is another area of importance for leaders to set the stage at the country level by first ensuring that the process of how regulations are produced is right. Regulations need to be constantly evaluated and adapted to changing situations, and a good process for such renewal impacts the quality of regulation and its positive influence on economic performance. Countries need the capacity for effective regulation, which depends on the capability to assure high-quality regulations. There are three key elements of the regulatory process defined by the OECD relating to policies, tools, and institutions. The OECD defines the dimensions of regulatory policies, provides a set of guiding principles for regulatory quality and performance, and assesses achievement across OECD countries in a number of areas (OECD, 2010). The report provides the outcome of leadership decisions on how regulations should be defined and managed in the OECD countries.

There are different pathways for moving towards common goals, with country contexts driving the design of regulations for a common final goal. Complexity is embedded in the design of regulations and any assessment of outcomes needs to bear in mind that the outcome of such complex processes can be difficult to predict in advance. The use of complexity models can also help critique other studies, such as the World Bank's Doing Business Indicators (Du Marais, 2008), which suggest a set of potential indicators that can be used to measure regulatory quality, for example dealing with licenses, protecting investors, and enforcing contracts. The empirical analysis of the Doing Business Indicators finds that heavier regulation (as measured by a greater number of permits, certificates, and documents that the law forces businesses to comply with in order to legally constitute a firm) does not help solve market failures (Benedettini and Nicita, 2010). Instead, they find positive correlations between the burden of regulation and the level of corruption and autocracy of a country and a negative relationship between regulatory burden and economic development (Djankov et al., 2002). Such analysis shows not only the importance of the context of the country—like inherited legal systems—but the role of leadership in ensuring smooth, efficient, and non-corrupt conduct by the public servants responsible for ensuring that regulations work.

An analysis of the achieved levels of the Doing Business Indicators by a group of countries in Central Africa and their large neighbor Nigeria shows the early warning signals that can signal the triggers for civil unrest. Cameroon suffered civil unrest due to high youth unemployment and high cost of living due to escalating food prices, coupled with demands for political reform. Cameroon had seen no change in its ranking in "Doing Business" between two consecutive years of assessment, while all its neighbors had seen a deterioration. Its large and populous neighbor Nigeria also had a steady ranking in "Doing Business" during the same period. The presence of a large stable neighbor helped mitigate the risk for Cameroon, whose leaders soon had the unrest under control.

The short duration of unrest in Cameroon could also have been due to stability in policy, which meant that the crisis did not touch the very important middle class, who are the main players in the business sector, allowing the leadership to focus on youth unemployment and high food prices. The crisis did, however, have an effect on trading across borders. All countries in Central Africa suffered, with Cameroon showing the sharpest deterioration. Sequencing policy reform is an important choice in any scenario at the country level. Political leaders constantly have to juggle multiple variables, some of which require tough political choices with serious effects on the potential to stay in power. The values that guide leaders in sequencing policy changes as they adapt or react to emerging crisis are paramount.

Leaders who face multiple constraints have an even bigger challenge, such as those managing small landlocked economies or highly populous and ethnically diverse countries. Leaders of landlocked countries have managed to achieve superior performance in "Doing Business" indicators compared to peers in other regions. Landlocked economies rank lower on the ease of doing business in every region except sub-Saharan Africa, where landlocked economies perform better (World Bank, 2009). Leaders in landlocked countries outperform those in non-landlocked countries in employing workers, registering property, and enforcing contracts. These three indicators happen to be the key drivers of macroeconomic effects of the rule of law. The protection of human rights in general and labor rights in particular is a key channel by which the rule of law impacts on the macro economy (Kaufmann et al., 2008). Property rights and how they are defined and protected have been central to the effective performance of economies (Benedittini and Nicita, 2010). Ensuring that investors are protected and that contracts are honored have been found to be very important drivers of performance and many times failure in these areas is due to corruption (Djankov et al., 2002).

Controlling corruption is a key responsibility for any leader. Corruption impacts investments in a variety of ways (Kaufman et al., 2008; World Bank, 2000). Bribes and the misguided allocation of scarce resources lead to lower effectiveness of governments in general and of regulation in particular. Distortions in public expenditure allocations could lead to neglect of important priorities, like infrastructure, with severe long-run implications for economic growth trajectories. Corruption can lead to unprotected property rights and can produce obstacles to private investment (Table 4.4). All of these factors could lead to low economic growth and insufficient levels of much needed investment flows from the domestic private sector or from foreign investment.

State capture of government policies by the elite as well as extortion of bribes paid to officials by small firms and poor households could lead to unequal benefits from economic growth, further deepening inequality. Nepotism could lead to poor quality of labor inputs, whereas a focus on meritocracy can increase productivity and creativity (Kaufman et al., 2008). Badly targeted services because of powerful interests can sway who gets service and how, and may impact consumption patterns. Slower accumulation of human capital or unequal accumulation across groups because favors are

Table 4.4   Control of corruption—macroeconomic effects

Causes of poverty	Effect of corruption
Low economic growth, insufficient investment	Vested interests leading to bad policy choices Distortions in public expenditure allocations Unprotected property rights Obstacles to private investment
Unequal benefits from economic growth	State capture by elite government policies and resource allocation and regressive public expenditure and investment Regressive effect of bribes on small firms and poor households
Impaired access to services	Political capture by elites of access to services and regressive effect of bribes on quality of basic services
Poor outcomes in health and education	Low human capital accumulation Lower quality of education and health care

Source: Adapted from World Bank (2000), Chapter 2: The Economic and Social Consequences of Corruption in Transition Countries at http://lnweb90.worldbank.org/eca/eca.nsf/Attachments/Anticorruption2/$File/chapter2.pdf.

made to particular individuals could lead to poor outcomes in health and education, as well as causing stubbornly weak capacity and potential instability in the long run.

Specific skill sets to function in diverse governance environments

Five skills are important in functioning in diverse governance environments. The first is ability to rehearse in and learn from lessons of leading in weak governance settings. Post-conflict settings put a premium on leadership, ethics, and values, and particularly on making choices in difficult circumstances. How well you know yourself and your values and how you work towards developing common values is critical as a starting point.

Rehearsing for diverse governance environments

Governance and policies matter, depending upon opportunities in different settings and at specific periods of time. Immediately after conflict one needs a vision and strategy for the future that help the country to move away from the behaviors and choices that led to conflict and to imagine a new future for the country. For Rwanda it was the use of "*agaciro,*" a Rwandan word meaning self-dignity. *Agaciro* was used as an organizing principle to bring the population to a new set of relationships that center on what is common, decent, and focused on getting things done

(Karasanyi, 2012). Rwanda took this concept to a new level in creating the Agaciro Development Fund to receive donations from Rwandans, including those living abroad, to finance development projects (http://www.agaciro. org/Agaciro-Development-Fund-raises-1). The fund focuses on priorities for development proposed and financed by Rwandans. Oversight is through an audited independent non-governmental agency. *Agaciro* is an example of developing effective vision and communicating it, starting from the kind of society one wants, a vision of peace in the region, and a knowledge of self and own priorities.

States that are on the brink of failure are difficult to rescue and it is hard to reverse the negative effects of chronic conflicts. It takes an average of 59 years for a previously failed state to succeed (Collier, 2007). Therefore, post-conflict states present a major opportunity for leadership, as change is relatively easy during periods immediately after conflict. During these periods, one can learn and evolve skills like getting support from the authorizing environment, which includes the wide array of stakeholders needed for success. Such a skill relies on the ability to listen, learn from others, and be open to sharing what you know with a wide range of stakeholders. Post-conflict countries present a rich opportunity to learn, share, and communicate, as they have the preconditions for a turnaround that can be transformed into sustained change. Leadership is born out of seizing reform opportunities related to approaches for motivating others, including especially how to motivate young people to engage and participate, and how to present role models for wide-scale change. Preconditions for major turnaround depend on how well a leader engages technical and political skills and uses the country's income opportunities and population diversity to get major changes in social outcomes (education and health), as well as negotiating shifts in the terms of trade.

How to organize for delivery of important results in the short and medium term is also critical, as is the ability to build platforms for success in the long term. What will be the "rules of the game" by which stakeholders will interrelate and abide? What combinations of stakeholders and interest groups, but also of particular individuals, will make effective teams for delivery on key objectives? What technical and people skills and talents would be needed to succeed? How can such talents be nurtured and selected and how can the inclusion of important stakeholders and groups, including women and other under-represented groups, be ensured? How can the development of leaders at different levels be supported to oversee the delivery of results? How can results be achieved that will impress in the short run yet last and remain sustainable in the long run? How can small experiments and test pilots be designed and how can they be scaled up to successes across entire organizations, society at large, or countries and regions? All these are important questions that require a set of skills that ready the individual to lead and succeed in post-conflict environments.

On ethics and values in post-conflict settings, understanding the nature of human conflict is paramount, as is knowing how stakeholders see equality and freedom, the role of civil and human rights, and leadership ethics. Historical issues would have been at play to generate conflict, which could have come from corruption and how it was handled (Tunisia in 2011), high levels of inequality leading to conflicts across groups (South Africa and Zimbabwe), or poor regulations and weak enforcement of rules (Democratic Republic of Congo). Such conflicts would mostly emanate from justice and knowing how to govern and follow rules. Reconciliation would be of great importance and would rely on knowing the past (Truth Commissions), understanding roles today, and having hope for the future. Dealing with conflict in the future, including early warning systems, would be of critical importance as a skill that is widely needed in post conflict settings.

How do you create a chain of positive obligations rather than the dread of punishment? How do you use reason to engage people rather than terror, as was done during periods of conflict? How do you delegate responsibility and recognize good values and performance? All these are questions that need to be practiced in the field and learned for successful management after conflict.

Globalization renders some post-conflict challenges even more severe. For example, communities that coexist over a wealth of natural resources stretching beyond the administrative boundaries of a country could present challenges in managing conflict. Increased mobility creates communities beyond the geographical aggregation of families and presents challenges in dealing with conflict for those who choose to return at different points in time. Communication technologies connect people to each other and can be used to bring them together or tear them apart, and the role that these technologies play after conflict is particularly critical, with the simultaneous need to manage freedom and privacy versus risks from misuse and security concerns. Dealing with the effects of globalization at the community and country level and even within organizations takes on a premium in post-conflict settings.

Strategic scanning

Strategic scanning—the capacity to generate maps of pressure points and risk scenarios—is another skill that it is important to hone. A typical strategic map would assess the quality of existing leadership in an area, analyze the demographic and economic interface and the challenges and opportunities they present, and develop a typology of existing traps or conundrums. What risks are there and how can they be managed? What factors are unique and present an opportunity to lead in a unique way? What do external stakeholders think? What tools can be used to mitigate risks?

The type of political leadership at the top is a good starting point according to Collier (2007). In addition to the type of political leadership, one needs to look at political parties—number, size, geographical and ethnic representation, role in parliamentary or presidential elections, and so on. What is the power of opposition if it exists—strength, level of influence at the community, local, national, regional or international level? What is the level of diversity, in terms of languages, religions, and other factors that could drive dynamics? What is the nature of power distribution between groups, including economic and political power (Chua, 2002). Is there a market-dominant minority or market-dominant majority? Is there a good size middle class participating in politics, or does a poor democratic majority drive politics? Are there positive social outcomes from development programs? Is there a small population with poor social outcomes or are social benefits well distributed across society? Are incomes increasing or declining? Is there substantial economic growth or stagnation and declining rates? All these factors could be important in making choices in strategy, and selecting amongst outcomes and leadership lessons can be garnered from a diverse set of cases with different starting points in these factors.

Points of irreversibility and traps are also important to note in strategic scanning. Collier (2007) identifies four major traps: conflict which comes from protracted civil war, plague or disease, and ignorance; natural resources and the degree of resource wealth and dependency on a narrow array of resources; the type of neighbors to a country and whether it is landlocked or not; and the size of the country and level of governance. Countries that are prone to conflict, dependent on a single or few natural resources, landlocked with neighbors that are not performing well, and large and poorly governed, have a hard time getting out of conflict. According to Collier (2007) this is because poverty increases the risk of civil war. As noted earlier, economic growth reduces the risk of conflict, with 1% growth reducing the risk of civil war by 1%. Natural resource wealth allows deals to be made with extraction industries to finance conflict. A large dominant ethnic group can effectively constrain minor groups, and this leads to conflict. Dispersed populations in large countries with sharp boundaries or edges are usually prone to conflict, as they are challenging to administer. The risk of falling into civil war or having a coup in any five-year period is 1 in 6 if certain conditions exist— poverty and low incomes, valuable exports from natural resources to finance war, existence of a previous war or conflict, slow economic growth, and the other factors mentioned earlier.

Special case of territorial governance[4]

One cannot discuss post-conflict challenges without looking at geography. Managing a landlocked country, planning and managing a city, developing environmental protection policies, putting in place a strategy for development, and dealing with unemployment, gender equality, criminality, or social exclusion, are just a few of the most well-known and widespread issues directly related to contemporary societies and to the globalized contemporary world. Leaders, in the course of their duties, no matter the context in or level at which they operate, are regularly forced to confront geography directly or indirectly.

Consider landlocked countries in Africa, where 30% of the continent's population lives. People in landlocked countries are hostage to the investment and political behavior of their neighbors. A country with a coastline can serve the world, while a country that is landlocked is almost always destined to serve its neighbors, unless it can develop a strategy of deploying air transport and information and communications technologies that expand the space in which a country can have influence or trade.

Uganda is a landlocked country whose neighbors include Kenya, South Sudan, Rwanda, Democratic Republic of Congo (DRC), and Tanzania. Its friendly relations with its neighbors in the East African Community have been attributed to an increase in its total trade. Trade with Kenya and Tanzania grew from 5.4% of GDP in 1994 to 6.6% in 2004, mainly driven by manufacturing exports, which grew from 4.1% of GDP in 1994 to 5.4% in 2004 (Walkenhorst, 2006). The share of merchandise exports to Rwanda, which joined the East African Community in July 2009, grew from 4.4% of exports in 2005 before the country joined to 9.2% in 2010 (WTO, 2012). Merchandise exports to Kenya during the same period grew from 8.9% in 2005 to 11.8% in 2010 (WTO, 2012). The opportunities for regional integration and the potential for economic growth in Uganda depend on the status of peace and stability in Northern Uganda and the security situation in the DRC and South Sudan. Merchandise exports from Uganda to DRC grew from 7.4% in 2005 to 11.4% in 2010, even before the peace agreement in February 2013.

Landlocked countries use geography to their advantage by relying on transport infrastructure, regional integration, and trade policy, as Uganda has done in the East African Community. Infrastructure bottlenecks, particularly energy and transport, have been identified as major binding constraints on economic growth in Uganda, as only a quarter of the road network is paved and there is insufficient energy generation capacity, while transmission losses are high (WTO, 2012).

Countries like Niger have pushed for improved economic policies in their large neighbor Nigeria. Yet others have gone for effective resource prospecting services (Botswana) or attracting large amounts of development aid (Burkina Faso). Countries that are landlocked could also learn from non-landlocked ones by developing into regional service hubs, offering sophisticated financial services (Lebanon), developing air services (Dubai, Singapore), developing an effective urban-rural symbiosis (Brazil), or encouraging remittances (Philippines). Other successful strategies include improving the link between coastal access and the effectiveness of coastal shipping by creating in-land export processing zones or dry ports, as Bangladesh has done with the port city it relies on, Chittagong, and its relations to interior regions of the country such as Dhaka.

Small and landlocked countries present geographical challenges needing special consideration. Governments in landlocked resource-rich countries need to be capable of doing good (Bhutan, Botswana) and those in resource-poor coastal access countries need to be capable of doing no harm (Bangladesh), according to Collier (2007).

The issues mentioned above are directly connected and tightly linked to territories, not only because activity takes place in territorial contexts (where spaces and places are scenes of reference), but more importantly because territorial attributes are an intrinsic part of the processes and outcomes driving decision-making. Leaders need awareness of the relevant territorial data and attributes and have to develop specific geographical or territorial knowledge, allowing them to take into account territorial effects. Such knowledge allows them to minimize risks and better cope with the uncertainty, rapid changes, and crises so typical in globalized contexts.

Leaders and territorial knowledge

Territories are not only scenarios, but also actors with specific and refined roles. In common usage, territories are considered to be locations in which social actions take place. Characteristics like size, shape, borders, and the absence or presence of resources that condition actions and vary through time are also attributed to territories. Yet territories cannot be reduced to passive elements, simply enduring the actions performed on them by a variety of actors over time. A different approach for what are termed "non-human actors" has been developed by the sociology of science and subsequently by geographers to consider territories as non-human actors. This is not only a theoretical approach: it has huge consequences, and is strategic for leaders and their decision-making. For example, the presence of a border, or the creation of one, dividing a territory at a certain time in history, makes a huge difference in the actions and strategies for the actors involved.

The recognition of a border separating Sudan from South Sudan, since July 9, 2011, for example, has produced a huge difference for the actors involved in this region. On the other hand, the fact that Somaliland is still unrecognized today, even if it is a *de facto* sovereign state, establishes a different scenario for the actors and leaders who are concerned in some way with this territory. As a third example, the institution of a trans-border area for environmental purposes, such as the Great Limpopo Transfrontier Park (GLTP) in Mozambique, South Africa, and Zimbabwe, produces new actors, like the Peace Parks Foundation, but also the Transfrontier Conservation Area (TFCA) coordinator, managing the park. The GLTP changes the geography of the entire region, and this first Peace Park introduces a new type of territory in the African landscape, with huge economic and political consequences. Borders are not only linear nowadays; zonal borders become more and more frequent in the globalized world, originating new types of territories. Buffer strips surrounding administrative territories may create unique realities, which change quickly when the economic and political conditions vary.

Additionally, borders are not limited to national scale and linked only to states; much more complex and diverse borders exist at other scales of action, and are not always easy to identify on maps. At the local level, the border of a big city is a complex and changing territory, transformed by peri-urban dynamics. At the regional level, economic processes, like the discovery of a resource that overlaps formal borders, for instance, may initiate territories not coincident with the administrative boundary. At the macro-regional level, a new international territory emerges if several states enter a regional economic community; the external border enclosing this large territory has a different value compared with its internal borders. This is the case for the European Union, where internal borders have a markedly different weight compared with the external borders of the Schengen area.

The challenges facing a country like Côte d'Ivoire have involved its neighbors, some of which have immense territories, such as Mali, with a size four times that of Côte d'Ivoire. Instability in northern Mali causes instability threats to its neighbors. The neighbors can be near the capital of a country and cause important pressures to national political decisions from a variety of factors, including border migration. The capitals of all five neighbors of Côte d'Ivoire are less than 720 km away, the closest being Mali, followed by Burkina Faso (Figure 4.2).

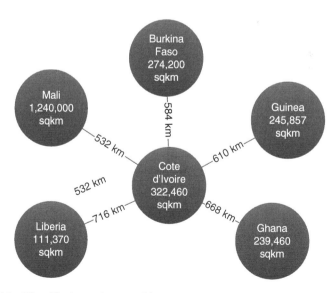

Figure 4.2   Côte d'Ivoire and its neighbors

Territorial issues within Côte d'Ivoire itself and between the country and its neighbors have been at the heart of the conflicts the country has faced in recent decades. This includes severe deterioration in political stability following elections, with bloody civil war and unrest, followed by external intervention since 1996. A short period of stability reigned, with some signs of recovery, until elections were organized in 2010.

Connectivity, traffic, and geography have also been found to determine how diseases spread through the air transportation network. Statistical physics and network theory have been used to understand how infectious diseases can spread through the air transportation network (MIT, 2012). Such models can predict quite accurately where and how fast a disease might spread through an air transportation network in the early days of an epidemic. Analysis can be used to guide decision makers across countries, industries, and sectors, including whether to control mobility through quarantine approaches of infected persons, or whether to use disinfectants and other measures on airplanes and other transport vehicles. Spatial data, while easy to analyze, present challenges for decision-making across different stakeholder groups, putting a premium on the skill sets and techniques that render decision-making tractable.

These examples help to highlight some difficulties related to territories. The behavior of territories as non-human actors cannot be reduced to the simple existence and relative weight of their attributes. In fact, as non-human actors, territories play an active role in situations, and acting through spokespersons, give them voice. This is particularly evident in controversial situations where opposing groups of actors are called "collective actors." Discourses are built by collective actors (stakeholders) to shape and support their actions[5] and, in these contexts, territories are called upon to support one or another group, and they literally "speak," becoming active parts of the conflict.[6]

Issues like migration and mobility, analyzed previously by geographers almost uniquely or predominantly from a quantitative point of view, are considered today from a territorial point of view. Migration and mobility cannot be reduced only to figures and statistics, trying to capture the size of human flows. In contrast, they are complex dynamics, for which the intermediate places of transit and stopover, the activities taking place (e.g. trip to work, trip to drop kids at school, trip to go shopping, trip to get cash at an ATM, possibly one trip with several stops with the same mode or a change in the means of transportation) as well as the involvement of the actors enabling mobility, are fundamental.

The urbanization process is also a crucial territorial issue as it involves spaces, territories, and networks of spaces and actors. People migrating from rural areas to cities need a job, shelter and other facilities. They establish themselves in a neighborhood, eventually moving to another, as their earnings increase their social status improves. Cities have to be considered within their region and by taking into account the networks they facilitate and develop with the surrounding countryside at different levels. These relations are not only economic—they are also social, cultural, historical, spatial, and political—and evolve in different kinds of spaces (territories, places, networks).

Territorial factors are also necessary to analyze the quality of life in cities, which is so closely related to and dependent on territorial resources, opportunities, and networks. They also frame the consequences of phenomena as population growth. Even if, at the continental level, Africa is subjected to a fast-growing population, the spaces and regions within the continent show a great degree of heterogeneity. There are reasons for such heterogeneity—for example the patterns of resource endowments, political and administrative borders, and benefits engendered by neighborhood effects. But within Africa one can also find less attractive "empty regions," where people have left or are attempting to migrate from, to reach big cities or more attractive spaces.

Even water availability, which can seem a purely physical matter, related to hydrology, pedology, and climatology, is in reality a social issue very much linked to its use by individuals and groups. Water shortages are certainly linked to weather and climate change, but are also related to the capacity of societies to adapt to changing availability, meaning that the level of development is central, as well as the quality of institutions and related legislation. The same could be said for food availability; not only is it related to soil quality, but also to such factors as land rights and farm management, which are territorial issues.

Markets and trade place an emphasis on social and territorial networks. The circulation of goods involves different scales of commerce and a hierarchy of places, related through flows. This circulation underscores the fact that some spaces are not continuous; discontinuity is their principal attribute, one that is more and more common in a globalized world. Two or more territories are discontinuous when there is an entity (another territory, a place or some kind of space) separating them. This is the case for urban networks (there is a given distance between cities), networks of marketplaces, and global stock exchanges. In the same network, places or territories remain strongly connected by a common function.

These examples shows that terms like "leadership" and "territory" can have different meanings and have to be defined carefully to emphasize their particular use in human geography, which does not necessarily correspond to the common usage of the terms, or to their use in other social sciences. Human geography, being a social science, develops an understanding of the world-focused territories, as built and transformed by social dynamics.

Theory U functions on a set of three epistemologies that help us make sense as leaders when confronted with territorial issues (Scharmer, 2009).[7] The first relates to explicit knowledge, which is knowledge about things that we can gather from observation and reflection, and to which there is a verifiable truth—such as the snow cover (icepack) around Mount Kilimanjaro's summit that is now measured to be at approximately 15% of the levels measured in 1912 (*New Scientist*, 2010). When Secretary General Ban Ki-Moon flew over Mount Kilimanjaro on February 27, 2009 he "was able to see for himself how ... there are now only a few patches of snow on the mountain" according to a UN News Report.[8] Mr Ban was verifying the state of knowledge about Mount Kilimanjaro.

The second relates to tacit embodied knowledge that comes from experience of doing things, from action, and from reflection on action. The experience of a leader such as Secretary General Ban Ki-Moon, who reflected upon his flight over Mount Kilimanjaro during a press encounter in Dar es Salaam, led him to suggest that by 2030 we may not be able to see any snow on top of Mount Kilimanjaro, adding "That is an alarming situation" (United Nations, 2009). The article in the *New Scientist* in 2010 contributed to the debate on whether the cause of snow disappearance on Kilimanjaro is global warming—hence a shared responsibility of importance to Secretary General Ban Ki-Moon—or from deforestation from aggressive tree felling around the mountain—and hence a local or national factor and the responsibility of the leadership in Tanzania. Tanzanian leaders such as President Kikwete, whom the Secretary General visited, would need to go beyond their territorial accountabilities in Tanzania to find solutions to tree felling at an East African level, as Kilimanjaro is at the border with Kenya, and at a global level if the causes are beyond tree felling and come from general shifts in climate patterns.

The third type of knowledge is self-transcending and comes from deep awareness about the origins for actions. It anticipates the future and is based on the ability to reflect in action and presence reality. On March 5, 2012, President Kikwete flagged off a special team of delegates from 75 countries on a Kilimanjaro mountain climbing expedition (Daily News, 2012). The expedition was a protest gesture in support of the fight against violence on women and girls. The climbers were to issue statements when they reached the peak of the mountain over a period of three days of climbing, on steps taken or to be taken in their respective countries to put the brakes on cases of violence against women and girls, which were on the increase in Africa at the time the climb took place. Each of the climbers would be able to see with their own eyes the state of the snows on Mount Kilimanjaro, which is verification by observation of explicit knowledge. Each participant would be able to reflect on their effort in climbing Kilimanjaro, the view from the summit, and the purpose of the climb, linking them to the actions taken or to be taken in their countries on violence against women and girls. They will be in the realm of tacit knowledge, with their climbing experience forever linked to the set of actions to reduce or curb violence against women and girls in their countries. President Kikwete's speech, and the public awareness raised and increased political will and resources for preventing and responding to the violence against women and girls that came out of this effort, are working on the self-transcending aspect of knowledge. Awareness levels are shifted, a better future for women and girls is anticipated, and the climbers and those listening to the speech of President Kikwete are moved to action. The sign of snow on the summit is forever linked to the actions needed to get results.

Leadership and territories: a human geography perspective

In the previous section we focused on space and leadership, but as seen from the point of knowledge and verification of what is around the visible sphere versus what is in the sensing and reflection sphere, or in the imagining and presencing sphere. This section turns to the geography of leadership, particularly as it relates to power and influence.

Among the numerous possible approaches to leadership, the definition introduced here emphasizes social influence, a kind of authority or *government*; meaning the act or process of governing, the capacity to exert a power. Leaders need to secure the support of others, with power being contingent on the ability to organize people surrounding them. Even if the goal of a leader were to accomplish at least one common task, the power to act would many times differ depending on situations, whose variations in part are due to territory.

The focus on *power* as a legitimated authority initiates the complex relations between power and politics. Geographers have not often raised this relation between power and politics, the core of political geography; and when it has been raised, it has often been reduced to the simplistic idea of the influence of a state on a territory. Only a few geographers have developed an original theory of power, not limited to the national level, to geopolitics and to military objectives. It is impossible to develop a comprehensive theoretical perspective of power in this book, so the choice made is to adopt a vision of power (Raffestin, 1980) where power is not a property by itself, but a relation between actors (individuals, social groups or institutions). Power is at the same time a form of energy (an intellectual capacity to form a vision and to realize it in the best way possible), information (the ability to create and use discourses), and an organization (material and symbolic distribution). The immediate consequence is that power cannot be isolated; there are only fields, combinations, and a network of powers, underlining imbalances and asymmetry, instead of continuity and homogeneity, as is commonly imagined.

Raffestin (1980) develops the example of population; it is not only a question of distribution, as considered by demography, but more a matter of the spatial dynamics of population, with the effects of domination and uneven competition among social groups, firms, cities, and the rural countryside, as well as the neighborhoods of a metropolis. Population is then a question of relations or networks of powers, with winners and losers according to situations and dynamics.

As a consequence, the "geography of leadership" is not only the description of a context, investigating the role of places in shaping leadership, but also the analysis of powers related to the phenomena with which leaders are confronted. Powers are nevertheless in essence territorial powers; they are linked and defined by, with, and within different kinds of territories.

As for leadership, there are many diverse definitions and approaches of territories in human geography. It is impossible to present all the possible definitions of a territory in human geography, as well as the many insights that each of them suggests. A definition focusing on some major attributes and issues related to leadership more relevant for leaders on a day-to-day basis is better.

A *territory* may be defined as a distribution of material and symbolic resources, able to influence the existence of an individual or a social group and participating to build its own identity.[9] A territory is a controlled and limited space. Human and political geographers have for long directly linked territory to the state and its administrative divisions, especially in the Western world, where the state is the archetype of total and hierarchical territorial control. Additionally, the existence of linear limits, the border where state authority ends, easily renders the state as an exemplar for territory.

Individuals and social groups always appropriate a territory. This appropriation may be cognitive or symbolic, but it is a relation built between human beings and the territory that they are related to for some reason; most likely because they live in it or they use its resources (for example: a place where a person works or an itinerary made every day for commuting from work to home, or again a vacation place visited once a year or more or less frequently). In fact, societies produce territories in reproducing and for reproducing themselves, and the territory serves to make available to the society the material resources needed for the social reproduction. Leaders also appropriate territories related to their spheres of responsibility. The examples we provided earlier of the spread of communicable diseases by air transport is a case in point, where leaders of airline business have to stretch their jurisdiction to impose decisions on others to manage the risks of passenger concerns and reduced travel as a result of infectious disease epidemics and their spread through infected travelers.

Appropriation of territory is directly related to a spatial configuration of resources and places at different levels and of multiple sizes. A territory may be discontinuous or may be networks of places or archipelagos. Every territory is built with material networks (roads, infrastructures, etc.) but is also made of social networks. Continuity is not obligatory for territories; it is only one of the many possible ways to organize places and areas related through a network. In this case, some geographers prefer to use the expression *territorial system*, instead of territory, to underline its complexity and its networked form.

In human geography a *network* is the interrelation of places (or spaces) through lines and flows. As with the territory, the network has material and symbolic dimensions. Maritime routes are common networks of the past that today, along with roads, air routes, and railways, are the material essence of the worldwide circulation of goods, human beings, and information. Networks of cities, urban networks organized in a hierarchic system, also concern human geographers. Cities are "located" at different levels in a network, according to their functions. For example, a city may have an important industrial sector, or a very competitive tertiary sector, or a political national or worldwide role (the city capital of a state or a global city).

Flows within a network are strategic, because they create the physiology of the world. With the new industrialization and the correlated construction of new economic powers, the old pattern of exchange of natural resources from the South with manufactured goods coming from the North is no longer realistic. Commercial exchanges are polarized in some countries of new industrialization (e.g. Taiwan, South Korea, Hong Kong, and Singapore). Nevertheless, Africa remains a large supplier of natural resources and only marginally an exporter of manufactured products. This unbalanced relationship between Africa and the rest of the world is a good example illustrating that flows are strategic not only in their density and intensity, but also in their complex characteristics.

Leaders have to deal with the specific and changing resources of territories, not only for their economic value, the commercial value being fixed by market regulations, but also for the peculiar (sometimes symbolic) value they have for the people who live in them. This matters when the natural resources of a given territory are protected and the territory becomes a protected area, a park, with regulated access to resources, restricted or denied to inhabitants. Leaders are confronted with the mechanisms of appropriation of territories, which are historical and political processes, and may encounter conflicts between social groups over resources. Identities are also crucial issues for leaders, because social groups developing some kind of identity more often than not use a territory, the "land," to create their feeling of being part of the same group. Additionally, processes of identity are conflicted, because an identity defines any one group in opposition to others, to the rest of the world, to the "strangers" or the other "nations."

A perspective on how territories work in the contemporary world

In the contemporary globalized world, *dynamics* are the engine of change. Numerous dynamics operate simultaneously, sometimes in an opposing manner, and thus have positive or negative consequences for societies, social groups, and individuals. They also affect territories, with direct or indirect consequences. Direct consequences could include natural disasters, wars, or exploitation of resources. Indirect consequences affecting territories could be widespread viruses, which not only kill a large proportion of a population, but at same time reduce the ability to work and performance at school, and thereby affect the long-term transformation of a given territory or state.

The dynamics include *drivers of risk*. Territories are confronted with multiple and diverse types of risk. It is often more profitable to investigate how risk works, including the role the territory plays, rather than referring to the "original" causes of risk. A risk of flooding, a fire risk, or an industrial risk for instance, engender social dynamics of cohesion and conflicts between actors, using a territory to support their discourse and transforming the given territory according to the actors' perception of danger, their power, and their capacity to attract other groups to their position. Globalization and rapid widespread circulation induce a multiplication of the number and variety of risks and also of networked information and action; as a result it increases the weight of these phenomena among the existing dynamics.

Even if risks tend to transform territories in a much more rapid way than in the past, nevertheless territories are *resilient* entities. They resist changes; they keep traces of inheritances of the past for a long time, even when some material objects are no longer used and are not part of the actual dynamics any longer. Abandoned factories are still present in many landscapes even when they are not seen as part of an historical heritage. One just needs to look at the legacies of old mining towns like Pittsburgh to see such traces. Leaders concerned with sustainability, especially in continents that are mineral rich yet are not as urbanized, need to be mindful of these traces when developing urban policies and industrial regulation.

Territories do not have a unique scale; they are *multiscalar*. Smaller spaces are contained in larger ones, either partially or totally superimposed. Borders may be agreed upon lines held in common or may be zonal. Some borders may also be in conflict, as is the case of China and the Philippines in the South China Sea. A place can be included in different ways in many territories. Every territory is a complex reality, even the smallest: for the relations it shares with others, for the dynamics it is submitted to, for the actors involved in its transformation, for the phenomena of diffusion or distribution it can engender, or for the effects of scale. If complexity is evident for large territories like a state, it may be less obvious for a city square, but in this latter case many dynamics may take place. Even at this fine scale, the territory has a different meaning for different actors and it can be part of different set of larger territories or networks (Figure 4.3).

This way of representing territories and their generation shows them as continuously transforming in a cycle: territories are transformed by societies, social groups, and individuals and in return they produce changes through their way of functioning, creating a continuous cycle of dynamics with changes and interrelations, knowledge of which is strategic for leaders.

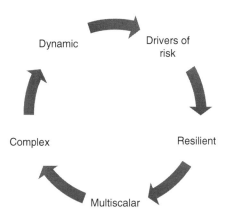

Figure 4.3   Territories as continuous cycles

Leaders facing territories: knowledge and understanding of geographic issues

Leaders and geographic knowledge

Leaders need to possess *geographic (or territorial) knowledge* and have the capacity to understand and handle relations between a society and its territory. The first type of knowledge relates to territorial data and attributes, meaning the quantitative as well as the qualitative comprehension of these phenomena. This is particularly difficult, as it necessitates a thorough knowledge of historical, social, and cultural as well as economic and political insights. National agricultural production, for example, cannot be limited to the statistics of harvesting, to the products and their economic value in the market. These results have to be interpreted in correlation with data related to physical conditions (quality of soil, climate, water availability, etc.) but also with the understanding of how a given society is related to its territory (why in a given place people prefer to produce maize instead of rice, the balance between commercial products and subsistence crops, how the harvest is stored, if and how products are transformed or processed, etc.). Within the same conditions of climate (and even in the same territory) societies make very different choices, because every social group has a particular relation to its territory, conferred by history (what is commonly called "tradition"), but also by contemporary social, political and economic conditions.

This is also true for issues not immediately seen as geographical, such as the adoption and use of a given technology: new information and communication technologies for example. Human geographers studying the way that technologies diffuse have emphasized the collective appropriation and use of these technologies (as opposed to their individual way of functioning) and also the huge consequences that technology has for economic activities (agriculture, fishing, etc.), social networks, political processes, and many other social activities.

The examples show that understanding territories is crucial for leaders in the contemporary world. Leaders have to deal with globalization, which means with societies, social groups and individuals, so leaders need a deep geographical knowledge related to the issues addressed. Leadership includes awareness and understanding of territorial issues. This understanding is crucial for decisions and actions, and mistakes can come from geographic ignorance. Geographers like Paul Pélissier and Jean Gallais (see Antheaume et al., 1989) have shown how huge, repeated, and dangerous mistakes have been made in Africa under the guise of development from the 1940s to the 1970s because of the ignorance of geographic factors. They argue that mechanization and technical progress have been considered as a priority of development (and are now a measure of it), instead of considering the geographical local knowledge held by every society and adapting development strategies to it. This failure to take into consideration local or indigenous knowledge explains many failures, numerous conflicts, and the outright waste of resources, as well as the feelings of misunderstanding and discontent of many actors involved, inducing negative responses to development projects.

Three steps are important in dealing with territories:

1. *Awareness*: leaders need to have geographical knowledge and take note of the importance of territories on given actions; territorial reaction to action has to be evaluated and accounted for. Leaders need to know how, what, where, and how to access territorial information and build their territorial knowledge for a given situation or context.
2. *Capacity to handle powers and governance*: in building geographic knowledge and investigating territories and their complexity, leaders are confronted with the map of powers involved in their action and become aware of governance issues. Actions have consequences for the relations between the actors and powers involved and possessed by each actor. The capacity to transform powers is related to territories, because territories generate power and actors use territories to create or increase power.
3. *Interaction and reaction to territorial matters*: Leaders need awareness of the interactions of actors and powers engendered by their actions and of the possible reactions in return. Territories react positively or negatively to action and such reaction should be integrated in potential scenarios of action.

Territories and patterns of change

Territories and their related geographic knowledge are therefore part of the complexity, interconnectivity, and risks with which leaders have to be conversant, but they are a very special component with their own way of functioning. More precisely, territories are part of the four major spheres of change: territorial issues are evident in the spheres of *people* and *resources*, as well as *economy* (especially for issues like trade and production). A territorial dimension is also fundamental in the sphere of *technology*, because technologies are rooted in societies and transform territories, and the relations engendered by individuals or social groups with technologies are also geographical.

Demographic data is about the spatial distribution of people (youth and aging patterns), the dynamics of transformation in space (like migration) and spatial economic and environmental effects (on job creation, securing food, and managing natural resources). These qualitative and quantitative data need consideration within the related territories: cities, regions, states, and continents. Geographic knowledge has to be well thought out to fully understand and make effective decisions. For example, the spatial distribution of people in Africa is in part a consequence of colonization—such as the concentration of population in coastal areas and along big rivers. However, the patterns of change are linked to the changing patterns of exploitation of natural resources (the continuous discovery of oil fields, metallic ores, etc.) as well as to urban growth and to urban networks (the presence, number, and distance between cities in the same state). Cultural factors are also at play and can be seen in the patterns of activity and population concentration linked to the places where communities want to live, to state policies related to work opportunities and livelihoods, and to the dynamics of conflict, both internal as well as those between states. All these issues and many other possible concerns should be considered, not only from sociological, political, and economic perspectives, but also by the relative weight of territories in these dynamics, the most appropriate scale for analysis, and how territory is used by people (not only for its resources, but also for building the discourses justifying their action).

The sphere of resources is one more evidently linked to territorial issues, but the artificial division between physical (distribution of water and climate change) and social concerns (efficiency and consumption of energy, food production, and distribution) should be avoided. All these issues are socially embedded and require geographic knowledge; water availability is related to hydrology, and increasingly nowadays to the use of water by societies (e.g. the quantity and type of irrigated surfaces, industrial use of water, and private use informed by cultural patterns). Even climate change is not only related to climatology, but has an impact on territories depending on the relative degree of development and resilience. Climate change modifies the way a society interacts with its territory, which is evidently the case for agriculture for example.

For the sphere of economic integration, relations through trade are clearly territorial, as physical and symbolic networks make them so. These patterns should be considered for efficient decision-making. The situation is similar for flows of finance, which are deeply territorial because of their concentration in some places (global cities and central business districts) or action in particular places (stock exchanges). The dynamics of production, as well as the presence of goods and products, are territorial issues and need to be inclusive of the data related to the specific territories where they take place.

In the sphere of technology, knowledge related to the consumers and users is related to territories and is associated with people's location, how society functions, and what is available and needed by others. Product innovation and discoveries are also linked to places. The place where a discovery is made is not neutral in the subsequent dissemination and impact of an innovation. The use of technology in day-to-day activities is also territorial, because it takes place in geographical spaces, and this dimension has to be taken into account by leaders.

Geographic knowledge impacts on decision-making in ways related to Theory U. Territories are directly present in Stage I, where they are an important part of observation, being integrated in the ability to identify what is going on and to reflect about the patterns observed. At this stage, leaders should remember that territories and the geographical dimension of situations and realities are strategic to their capacity to make effective decisions. Territories are also crucial in Stage III, where they have to be taken into account in prototyping strategic scenarios: these scenarios have to have a strong territorial dimension to be fully realistic.

Territorial governance

The term "governance" is frequently used in its economic sense. The expression "territorial governance" is not coincident with this approach and is a recent and rather controversial concept in human and political geography. Although it has been defined in many different ways by geographers and planners, *territorial governance* is defined here as the coordination between public sector actors and socio-economic actors in transforming a territory. With this definition, leaders are present in three ways—in public administration, economic management, and coordination of key sectors for transforming territories.

Territorial governance relates to the capacity of local actors to exert influence on a given process—to get involved at different stages and levels (with different powers) and participate in transforming a territory. When "local actors" are referred to here the sense of the adjective is not the immediate one; the term "local" indicates the size of a situation, a phenomenon or a reality which may vary from the most local level to the global, generating a proportional variation in territorial governance, with the related consequences.

Territorial governance has often been inspired by theories of urban governance. In this case, territorial governance is the capacity and shared responsibility for decision-making for a project or program, the possibility to establish a collective framework of action and strategic reflection, linking the actors through political decision-making. In a globalized world, decisions around projects, at every level from global to local, require partnership between actors with varying territorial jurisdictions. Such actors give birth to a common strategy and framework of intervention, as well as a decision space that incorporates all major stakeholders. This is the contemporary way of planning, especially in large cities and metropolises.

In the case of Africa, aspects related to the informal sector are not managed by traditional governments, so cannot be addressed only through the channels of traditional planning, but they are certainly central dynamics of change that need to be included in urban governance. Le Galès (2010) notes that, in the Western world, the operation of urban governance depends upon the population that is governed, emphasizing that as large cities have such diverse and fluid populations, urban governance becomes ever more complex. Urban governance is part of the world of overlapping powers within global, regional (such as European), and local governance in the making; municipalities, metropolitan authorities, regions (sometimes), the state, the EU and sometimes the OECD urban group, and the UN (Habitat Summit) international rules comprising environmental norms can play an important role in urban governance.

Governa and Salone (2004) present another example of territorial governance, in the case of territorial pacts for local development in Italy. Inspired by a bottom-up vision of development, territorial pacts involve a large number of actors within a common framework, based on a thorough analysis of local resources, potentials for, and obstacles to the territory's development. "The territorial pact is, therefore, an integrated group of activities, planned at the local level, to promote the territory's sustainable development, subscribed to by the principal territorial actors, with precise definition of commitments, time frames, and processes. [...] Within this profusion of practices and experiences, the territorial pact has undergone a partial modification of its role: from intervention instrument for the promotion of development in depressed areas of southern Italy to policy instrument for the entire national territory, becoming firmly established as actively engaging with a variety of economic-territorial situations and with a range of issues, not solely with initiation of development in contexts traditionally excluded from economic growth" (Governa and Salone, 2004: 810).

With a world that is being reassembled by new dynamics, including a tendency to decrease the power of centralized actors, the nature of powers and changes in governance spheres become more frequent and important especially at the urban and intra-urban levels. The dynamics of urban fragmentation are emphasized, as are contemporary nomadism, metropolitization, and communitarianism. Regional governance becomes more relevant, especially in international contexts, like the trans-frontier regions (in Europe encouraged by the European Union, but also in Africa with the various regional economic organizations).

Territorial leadership

Territorial governance, if used as an operational approach, allows leaders better control of available resources and ensures better economic redistribution. By redistributing power from a unique entity to a plurality of leaders, territorial governance decreases state fragility, reduces the chance of conflicts exploding, and engenders transformative change. These strategies support collaboration in public sector management of a variety of actors (civil society, professionals, citizens, trade unions, informal actors, etc.) through participation and negotiation, producing common objectives and projects. This approach is particularly effective in contexts where state capacities are low and consequently the government apparatus is more fragile. This is the case in Africa and more generally in all developing countries. Moreover, the presence of territorial governance highlights the fact that the government of territories is not only in the hands of local government, but can impact on national and even global decisions across the world.

For a leader, the most appropriate scale of action is not immediately evident: it depends on the specific case and on a variety of factors. The choice of the scale is strategic and has, as a direct consequence, the entitlement of a *territorial leadership*, possessing the competence and power to act in a given situation. This territorial leadership, best adapted to act in a given "local" reality, is also linked and related to a configuration of many actors (public actors, private actors, NGOs, CSOs, informal actors, etc.) ensuring this leadership. Leaders should take into account the relative weight of these processes, considering the influence in territorial governance, as related to a given situation. This is a first strategic step for establishing real national, regional, and global governance.

The ultimate challenge for leaders is the territorial governance of a given space, and the capacity to establish solid links between different levels of governance. A leader concerned with an urban context has to be able to consider it within its immediate peri-urban area, within its larger region, and even further in the national, international, and global perspectives. This has to be made through institutions and institutional policies, but it cannot be reduced to this one aspect alone; leaders have to be able to mobilize other forces and put them together through territorial governance.

Leadership in political and administrative settings needs to be able to handle territorial disputes, such as those that arise from land grabs by central government authorities for use in providing public services like roads or rezoning for industrial uses. China is a country that presents many challenges in territorial leadership as it transforms into an industrial and knowledge economy from a rural and agricultural origin. Countries in Africa and Latin America that are on the path to rapid urbanizing while shaping their national and regional governance structures have an opportunity to use territorial leadership to their advantage in a globalizing world. The case of Cameroon illustrates the challenges of territorial governance when considering regional and global trade and the institutions that need to be in place for good leadership to emerge.

The case of Cameroon—territorial trade performance

Cameroon and its development path present a wonderful example to illustrate the features developed in the challenge of leadership in a territorial setting. The capacities needed to perform effectively under a territorial setting are extracted from Theory U. These include integrating economic theory, social science, values and multi-stakeholder processes that can lead to transformation.

Cameroon's demography presents key risks and opportunities as they relate to territorial governance. Seventy per cent of the population of the country is under 30 years old, and the country has escaped the demographic transition faced by many of its peers at the same level of development, as it still has high fertility and high infant mortality (World Development Indicators). The leadership of the country, on the other hand, is in the hands of older people, with a President who is much older than the average age of the population. The leadership of the country could benefit from the foundational capacity of Theory U of listening to others, particularly the youth, and listening to what is emerging from the collective groups (multiple ethnicities).

At the same time Cameroon is urbanizing very fast, with the percentage of people living in cities going from 16% in 1960 to 50% in 2000, and an expected 70% in 2020 (World Development Indicators). Such population pressures have challenged urban governance, which remains weak, with political power still relying on organizations based on ethnic roots, with little link to the increasing demands for services like electricity, water, and transport from the urban residents. Despite these governance challenges, the country has had a historically low level of conflict due to the formation of multi-ethnic coalitions that have held over time and a stabilizing public sector with highly motivated civil servants. There have been short-lived risks and turmoil as the country has transitioned to democracy, including food price-related riots in 2007.

Theory U can be extremely helpful in helping the country craft a strategy that can bridge the generations and the geographies, including not only the rural and urban but also the Cameroonian diaspora that lives in countries distant from their place of origin.[10] Particularly helpful would be the capacity to observe and analyze what is changing in the country's make-up and how that relates to the challenges the country is facing.

In the Chua (2002) classification, Cameroon is a large lower middle-income country but with significant poverty (68% rural and 45% urban). The country has enjoyed periods of good growth, but has not really sustained high economic growth for very long. Growth was 1.2% between 1960 and 1975 when the country was organizing its productive sectors; 6% between 1976 and 1985 when it had a period of sustainable and high growth; 4.6% between 1986 and 1994 during the period of economic crisis; a return to growth in 1995, with challenges due to a budget deficit; and low growth averaging 3.1% between 2007 and 2011 (World Bank, 2012). Local firms have difficulty getting licenses, and contracts are not always enforced. They complain about a heavy tax burden and corruption when they are legally registered, all factors that push them to stay small and informal (World Bank Doing Business Report). The country could benefit from Theory U by actively "sensing" together as a society, bringing in voices and experiences from local communities, the private sector, civil society, and government to identify and prioritize emerging problems together. Such an approach could help curb the challenges presented by the sales of land to agribusiness to grow the oil palm for example. Such sales are considered as land grabbing from the local population by the government for sale to agribusiness (Ramzi, 2013).

There is little financial sophistication and depth in Cameroon with high reliance on family networks for growth. The country trades with its neighbors in the sub-region and has opened up its borders to a certain degree for such trade, but most trade is along the borders and external. Export of paper and paperboard and articles made out of pulp from the rich wood resources with which the country is blessed stood at US$ 1,1 million in 2012. The biggest markets for these exports are the Central African Republic (US$ 758,000), the US (US$ 189,000), and France (US$ 107,000). This compares well in value with the exports of furniture, lighting, signs, and prefabricated buildings, which have been growing over time as the country built its manufacturing capability. The main markets for exports of processed wood products like furniture are the US (US$ 458,000), Ghana (US$ 458,000), Central African Republic (US$ 240,000), and Switzerland (US$ 109,000). Governance of the forests remains a challenge, with illegal logging and damage to the eco-system. Theory U could be useful for the country in building the capacity to connect to values of preservation and care for future generations, in order to preserve natural resources (tropical forests) and use them responsibly for current and future generations.

Manufacturing capability in supply chains around cocoa and cocoa-based preparations has increased with the intended increase in export performance of these supply chains as measured by the value added of exports. Cocoa beans had export values 400 times higher than wood-based exports in 2012, with the biggest markets being the Netherlands (US$ 270 million), Malaysia (US$ 55 million), Spain (US$ 35.1 million), and Germany (US$ 30 million). The geographic pattern of exports varies with the level of processing. Chocolate exports go mostly to Malaysia (US$ 3 million), Central African Republic (US$ 0.5 million) and the rest to Mozambique (US$ 8,000),

Canada (US\$ 4,000), and the US (US\$ 2,000). Similarly for the supply chains around milk, cream, butter and cheese which all go to the Central African Republic (the nearest geographical neighbor). This pattern contrasts with that of unwrought aluminum, which is exported mostly to Italy (US\$ 33 million), France (US\$ 23 million), Luxembourg (US\$ 10 million), the Netherlands (US\$ 8 million), Germany (US\$ 7 million), Spain (US\$ 1.95 million), India (US\$ 1.9 million), and Republic of Korea (US\$ 1.5 million). Manufactured aluminum products like tables and kitchen and household articles mostly go in small quantities to the Central African Republic (US\$ 5,000), Czech Republic (US\$ 3,000), Canada (US\$ 2,000), Slovakia (US\$ 2,000), Ghana (US\$ 1,000), and Luxembourg (US\$ 1,000) (Table 4.5).

Trade performance is highly varied in supply chains like cotton, textiles, and yarn, which posted declining value added during the period under comparison. Cotton that is not carded or combed goes mostly to China (US\$ 174 million), Malaysia (US\$ 10 million), India (US\$ 2.6 million), Turkey (US\$ 1.2 million), and Indonesia (US\$ 0.8 million). Woven fabrics from cotton mostly go to a near neighbor, Burkina Faso (US\$ 39,000), and a small amount to a further neighbor Belgium (US\$ 1,000). Women are mainly responsible for trading cotton products across Cameroon's borders with its neighbors, where yarn and textiles move freely across borders. In addition to good performance in the primary metals area, the country did well in the supply chains related to aluminum, and structures and parts of structures made from aluminum as well as in the paper, paperboard, and wood manufactures. Some supply chains (like cotton and textiles) provide benefits to

Table 4.5   Cameroon's pattern of exports in 2012

Code	Product name	Export value in 2012 (US\$ 000)
1801	Cocoa beans, whole or broken, raw or roasted	424,106
1806	Chocolate and other food preparations	3,631
48	Paper and paperboard, articles of pulp, paper and board	1,138
94	Furniture, lighting, signs, prefabricated buildings	1,489
0401	Milk and cream, not concentrated nor sweetened	0
0403	Buttermilk and yogurt	2
0405	Butter and other fats and oil derived from milk	11
7601	Unwrought aluminum	86,121
7615	Aluminum table, kitchen, household articles	14
5201	Cotton, not carded or combed	192
5212	Woven fabrics of cotton	40

Source: Constructed using data taken from the International Trade Center (2013), available at http://www.intracen.org/itc/market-info-tools/trade-statistics/

a wider segment of society. Theory U could be used to convene the right sets of stakeholders (farmers, traders, manufacturers, policymakers, community leaders, trade ministers) and engage in a social technology that allows the country to shift to a pattern of growth that is more inclusive.

Performance with near and far neighbors is notable given the key risks that the country faces. Cameroon is a large country with access to the sea and reasonable interior transport. However, the port does not function as efficiently as it could and the road networks are poorly maintained, making trade across borders with neighbors not as easy for small players who can move products that are not perishable through short distances rather than through export trade. Such trade takes place with Chad, Central African Republic, Republic of Congo, Equatorial Guinea, Gabon, and Nigeria. The poor transport network connecting Cameroon to its neighbors hurts its trade performance and challenges its ability to function effectively in a regional economy within the ECOWAS states. On the other hand, Cameroon has retained relationships in trade developed during colonial times (such as with France and Germany) and has also developed new patterns of trade with other players on the basis of globalization and global demand (as with the US and more recently with countries in Asia).

Theory U could be helpful in sensing the emerging patterns of relationships as well as the shifts in consumption patterns and consumer preferences in Africa and the rest of the world would greatly aid decision makers looking to make policy on trade, whether bilateral, regional, or global and whether on exports or imports.

Case of Côte d'Ivoire—territorial governance

Territorial governance can be explained by looking at the perspectives of Côte d'Ivoire's neighbors on key agreements and prospects for peace, as well as views on fundamental causes of conflict in the period following the signing of the March 2007 Ouagadougou Peace Agreement (OPA). The OPA was a result of a conflict resolution process that witnessed a rare synergy between a regional entity, ECOWAS; a continental organization, the African Union (AU); and a global international organization, the UN. The role the media played in shaping the views of internal and external actors has also had a territorial dimension, with consequent effects on regional stability. Radio and newspaper reports analyzed the outcome of the OPA and debated whether OPA was a victory for insurgency grounded in the logic of war (Africa Report, 2007) or whether it was an agreement by the two belligerent parties to power and wealth sharing (Ayangafac, 2007). Côte d'Ivoire's progress towards democracy was determined not only by national factors, but also by those related to specific regions within the country (north versus south) and by its relations to its neighbors at a given point in time. Radio and newspaper reports on violence and human rights violations have also shaped the territorial nature of the conflict and have even globalized the conflict.

Territorialism can be seen in the process towards the signing in March 2007 in Ouagadougou of a peace agreement between the two belligerent parties in the Ivorian conflict—the Forces Nouvelles (FN) and the government of President Gbagbo. Skeptics in 2007 from outside the country pointed to unresolved issues and the exclusion of the traditional political opposition in the peace deals. Most Ivoirians were hopeful at that time that the agreement represented a first step towards elections, stability, and peace. Many analysts thought there was a high likelihood that the 2007 peace agreement would succeed (Africa Report, 2007; Ayangafac, 2007). Previous attempts (Marcousis, Accra 1 and 2, Pretoria) had failed. The OPA had an impact on preparing elections, which were held in November 2010, but President Gbagbo and his main opponent Allasane Ouatara were sworn into office in parallel, leading to a resumption of conflict in April 2011, as the outcome was contested by both parties.

Territorial analysis can be used to look at what were the fundamental causes of the conflict in Côte d'Ivoire and the roles that were played by external actors in the peace process. Such analysis can be used to uncover the challenges in involving external actors (such as the UN Peace Keeping Forces and the French Forces Licorne). How does the media coverage of the conflict influence the prospects for a peaceful solution? What is the role of leadership in telling stories about a country and in shaping expectations? Territorial interests were also at the heart of the concerns about negative effects on regional stability in West Africa. Reports on political violence and human rights violations were dealt with on global and local scales, with the airing of disputes on nationality and voter registration prior to the elections and an end to impunity by the arrest and trial of Laurent Gbagbo in April 2011. Could a better territorial analysis be helpful in gauging the risk during preparations towards elections and the move towards democracy? Could such considerations have resulted in a reduction in the number of internally displaced people during the conflict, many of whom spilled over territorial boundaries in Liberia, Burkina Faso, and Ghana?

Theory U could be helpful in co-sensing the future, by bringing together people from multiple regions of a country to co-imagine and co-develop a vision for the future. Malaysia, for example, has been praised for its approach to coming up with its 2020 Vision, which envisages a united country with a confident society filled with moral values and desirable behaviors, that include "living in a democratic, free, economically equal, successful and thriving society enjoying a competitive, dynamic, strong, and growing economy" (Shoraka et al., 2009). The same country has been criticized for the international restructuring of the spatial economy and of spaces of identity in the 1998 Kuala Lumpur Commonwealth Games (Kuala Lumpur 98) where powerful groups are alleged to have used this sporting event in an initiative to reshape and refurbish the ethnic core of the Malaysian people in order to attract global capital (Silk, 2002). The criticism by Silk (2002) was mainly around the use of cultural producers to mask the class, racialized, ethnic, and gendered polarizations that characterize Malaysian culture. The Malaysian example and the outcome of the 2010 elections in Côte d'Ivoire indicate that countries could benefit from the effective use of Theory U in their governance processes.

Economic performance is also of interest from a territorial point of view. Côte d'Ivoire exports cocoa, coffee, timber, petroleum, cotton, bananas, pineapples, palm oil, and fish. When economic performance deteriorates due to conflict, effects can be seen in the prices of cocoa beans in the sub-region with countries that also export cocoa in the neighborhood—like Ghana and Liberia—benefitting. There is a similar situation with cotton exports and prices between Côte d'Ivoire and its neighbors Mali and Burkina Faso (Table 4.6).

Exports from Côte d'Ivoire to Burkina Faso declined from US$ 360,393 in 2011 to US$ 343,931 in 2011. Exports to Ghana also declined from US$ 783,135 in 2010 to US$ 303,859 in 2011, while exports to Guinea improved from US$ 56,076 in 2010 to US$ 58,418 in 2011 and those to Liberia improved from US$ 56,864 to US$ 183,912 during the same period. The impacts of peace and conflict on neighboring countries can explain many of these patterns. Where refugees went and the patterns of interactivity they created there have had an influence on patterns of trade following conflict.

Table 4.6   Côote d'Ivoire's exports to neighbors in 2011

Country	Export value US$	Exported products
Ghana	303,859	Fish; dairy products; fruits and nuts; coffee and tea; cereals and flour; animal and vegetable oils
Mali	241,819	Edible food preparations; animal and vegetable oils; cereal and flour; milling products, malt, starches; vegetables and tubers; dairy products
Guinea	58,418	Edible food preparations; sugar; animal, vegetable fats and oils, oil seed; fruits; dairy products
Liberia	183,912	Fish; milling products; cereal and flour; beverages
Burkina Faso	343,931	Tobacco; cooking oil; milling products; cereal and flour; sugar; dairy products; edible food preparations; vegetables and fruits; beverages; cereals;

Source: Data taken from Trade Statistics published by ITC and can be found at http://www.intracen.org/itc/market-info-tools/trade-statistics/.
The ITC data are supplemented by statistics on trade from the World Bank that can be found at http://data.worldbank.org/data-catalog/world-development-indicators.

The case of the Great Lakes—territorial considerations

The challenges seen in Côte d'Ivoire during a prolonged conflict and in Cameroon while shaping regional trade strategies with its neighbors come together as twin challenges in the Great Lakes Region. The Great Lakes Region case brings the concept of governance in a spatial setting (territories) and interplays with other aspects of governance that relate to identity (ethnicity, religion, gender), as well as themes like corruption and human rights. We can study the Great Lakes Region to identify what needs to be in place for the preparedness of leadership in conditions of conflict and to work with tools that support leaders in diverse potential futures. Such tools include benchmarking and the assessment of performance (Table 4.7).

Benchmarking is a useful tool to define a starting point and track with objective measures in an environment where there are few principles and theories to support decision-making. In the case of a region such as the Great Lakes one can compare the demography, geography, and nature of conflict in the region as well as assessing resource dependence and the histories of conflict and peace. Such benchmarking relies on the analysis and thinking built up in previous sections and is due to Collier (2007) and Chua (2002). Assessing post-conflict performance allows the tracking of complexity features such as stability after chaos, performance (say of an economy) after conflict, and shaping the future (through long-term policymaking).

In terms of demography, the Democratic Republic of Congo is the largest in size and faces what Collier (2007) highlighted as the challenge of geography and sheer size. Large countries are difficult to govern. The Democratic Republic of Congo is also the most populous country in the territory,

Table 4.7   Great Lakes Region's demography, geography, and conflict

Country	Area in million square kilometers	Population in millions	Population growth in 2006
Burundi	0.028	7.8	3.7
Central African Republic	0.622	4.1	1.4
Democratic Republic of Congo	2.34	59.3	3.1
Republic of Congo	0.342	4.1	2.6
Rwanda	0.026	9.2	2.3
Uganda	0.241	29.9	3.6
Great Lakes Region	4	114	4

Source: Data taken from Trade Statistics published by ITC and can be found at http://www.intracen.org/itc/market-info-tools/trade-statistics/.
The ITC data are supplemented by statistics on trade from the World Bank that can be found at http://data.worldbank.org/data-catalog/world-development-indicators.

Table 4.8   Great Lakes Region's resource dependence

Country	Main exports
Burundi	Coffee, tea, sugar, cotton, hides
Central African Republic	Diamonds, tobacco, coffee, timber, cotton
Democratic Republic of Congo	Diamonds, copper, coffee, cobalt
Republic of Congo	Oil, timber, plywood, sugar, cocoa, coffee, diamonds
Rwanda	Coffee, tea, hides, iron ore
Uganda	Coffee, fish and fish products, tea, tobacco, cotton, corn, beans, sesame

Source: Based on export rankings in 2006 taken from the ITC data, available at http://www.intracen.org/itc/market-info-tools/trade-statistics/.
The ITC data are supplemented by statistics on trade from the World Bank that can be found at http://data.worldbank.org/data-catalog/world-development-indicators.

presenting the twin challenge of managing a large population dispersed over a large territory. Burundi is the fastest growing country and such growth is taking place in the smallest country by size in the territory, and all its subsequent challenges of managing high-density populations concentrated in a single city of Bujumbura. Issues around urban governance and service delivery become central in this case.

Economic analysis could also be benchmarked in terms of resource dependence, which shows the Democratic Republic of Congo as the most dependent on natural resources and hence more likely to have long-term conflict according to the Collier (2007) analysis (Table 4.8).

An analysis of the history of conflict and peace, however, does not support all of the Collier (2007) hypotheses. The countries in the territory being analyzed with the longest history of conflict in terms of number of years of internal conflict are Burundi, followed by Uganda. However, in terms of severity of conflict it is the Democratic Republic of Congo, which has seen such severe fighting as to be referred to as the "African world war" (McLaughlin and Woodside, 2004). Such patterns support the analysis done earlier in section "Leaders Facing Territories: Knowledge and Understanding of Geographic Issues" on territories and patterns of change (Table 4.9).

Post-conflict stability can be benchmarked to see what sort of complexities lurk behind observed patterns. Consider the Great Lakes countries in 2006 and the status of achieved demobilization, reinsertion, and reintegration of combatants. The Central African Republic had made the most progress and ended up organizing a peaceful election five years later in 2011. Uganda had made tremendous progress in demobilizing and reinserting combatants, but not as much on reintegration. It held elections in 2011, which had rough patches, but the incumbent President Museveni prevailed. Republic of Congo had made no progress on demobilization and reinsertion and little on reintegration, but held elections three years later in 2009. The speed at which

Table 4.9   Great Lakes Region's history of conflict and peace

Country	Years of internal conflict	Signed pact on peace and security	Election	Source
Burundi	31	5	2010	Ethnic
Central African Republic	10	1	2011	Minerals
Democratic Republic of Congo	11	2	2011	Ethnic
Republic of Congo	10	2	2009	Ethnic
Rwanda	12	2	2010	Ethnic
Uganda	20	2	2011	Land
Great Lakes Region	**16**	**2**	**1**	**1**

Source: Own analysis using data from Wikipedia such as the one for Cote d'Ivore which can be found at http://en.wikipedia.org/wiki/Elections_in_Ivory_Coast and from Election Guide that can be found at http://www.electionguide.org.

Table 4.10   Great Lakes Region's post-conflict economic performance

Country	Main exports (#)	GNI per capita in 2006	GDP growth 2006 (%)	GDP growth 2011 (%)
Burundi	5	100	−8.4	4.2
Central African Republic	5	360	3.5	3.1
Democratic Republic of Congo	5	130	5.1	6.9
Republic of Congo	7	950	6.4	4.5
Rwanda	4	250	5.3	8.6
Uganda	9	300	5.3	6.7
Great Lakes Region	**6**	**348**	**6**	**7**

Source: Own analysis from Wikipedia and Election Guide (electionguide.org).

elections were held after 2006 depended on the speed at which the countries managed to demobilize, reinsert, and reintegrate combatants (Table 4.10).

Assessing economic performance shows that all countries other than Burundi managed to grow immediately after conflict, but that in 2011 Burundi surpassed the Central African Republic in its growth performance. Following Collier (2007), Burundi and Democratic Republic of Congo should have been more likely to have a resumption of conflict due to their poverty levels as per GNI per capita in 2006. However, the resumption of GDP growth has reduced the likelihood of conflict in all countries, with some risks in the Central African Republic and Republic of Congo, which have lower levels of growth in 2011 compared to 2006 (Table 4.11).

The long-term ability to make policy is a potential measure of sustainability of peace. Using such indicators as the time to start a business (because business leaders invest when there is stability) indicates that the Central

Table 4.11   Great Lakes Region's post-conflict economic policy

Country	Time to start a business 2006(days)	FDI net inflows in 2006 (US$ millions)	Merchandise trade 2006 (% GDP)
Burundi	43	0.585	58.9
Central African Republic	14	6	22.2
Democratic Republic of Congo	155	402	59.7
Republic of Congo	71	724	116.2
Rwanda	16	8	24.9
Uganda	30	257	38.5
Great Lakes Region	**155**	**724**	**116**

Source: Data taken from World Development Indicators.
The ITC data are supplemented by statistics on trade from the World Bank that can be found at http://data.worldbank.org/data-catalog/world-development-indicators.

African Republic and Rwanda have the best long-term policy performance post-conflict, while the Democratic Republic of Congo has the worst. However, it is the Republic of Congo, which has average performance in the conditions for business, that has attracted the most foreign direct investment and lost the least (highest net FDI). Both the Republic of Congo and Burundi had healthy merchandise trade performance.

Benchmarking and assessment need to be balanced by the values and behaviors that can serve as a guide in decision-making, as discussed in previous sections of this chapter. The exercises that come next help the learner to practice and get a good understanding of the factors that are important to build good leadership and governance.

Conclusion

This module introduced the dimension of leadership and governance, with exposure to the tools and frameworks used to make decisions. Illustrations highlighted the capabilities needed to succeed and remain relevant in a changing world. Emphasis was placed on how global challenges emanate from a set of collective actions by multiple stakeholders, including how such challenges become more complex, with changes in the territorial space impacting decisions. The chapter has shown through case studies that the resulting outcomes of violence, hate, terrorism, civil war, poverty, and increased risks of natural disasters require leaders to reconsider their norms and values, as well as their social structures. Being able to interpret the actions of other agents and to empathize and learn from them can provide a useful backdrop for better sensing the future and developing appropriate actions and strategies. A practice block provided at the end of the chapter aids the reader in identifying the skills needed to lead in a post-conflict or challenging post-reform or post-merger environment.

Through examples, the learner is introduced to the skill of "presencing" the emerging future and crystallizing a cohesive vision and strategy. Five sets of skills deriving from Theory U are noteworthy. The first is the ability to function in environments with weak governance (as in Côte d'Ivoire), where opportunities are provided for the learner to rehearse by putting themselves as decision-makers in a post-conflict country setting. Second, strategic scanning skills were given space to help the learner enhance their capacity to generate strategic maps of pressure points and risk scenarios. The case of Cameroon and its economic relations to its neighbors were used to demonstrate the type of analysis useful for making decisions on policy with territorial concerns in mind. Third, attention was paid to values and behaviors, particularly those that serve as a guide in making choices in challenging circumstances, as when facing corruption and dealing with issues of labor rights. A fourth important skill covered is the capacity to identify patterns of change (shifts), extract important relationships (interactions), and select from a variety of approaches (selection) for handling challenges. Many illustrations were used to underline the skill set needed. A special section on territorial governance was introduced to help the learner with strategies for handling spatial governance challenges.

Case materials introduce the importance of dialogue, valuing multi-stakeholder contributions, and bringing different perspectives to bear. The risks of not including the right stakeholders were also introduced as in the case of identity and space in Malaysia. The theoretical background from Theory U covers crystallizing ideas from multiple stakeholders, relying on skills of sensing and integrating into a strategy for action. The chapter introduces the skills needed when functioning in space to better manage tensions and contradictions and arrive at a collage of ideas from all stakeholders (Box 4.1).

Box 4.1   Practice Block IV: Empathizing and Crystallizing Co-senses into an Emerging Vision

Premise: Global challenges emanate from a set of collective actions by multiple stakeholders. The resulting outcomes of violence, hate, terrorism, civil war, poverty, and increased risks of natural disasters require leaders to reconsider their norms and values, as well as their social structures. Interpreting the actions of other agents and empathizing and learning from them can provide a useful backdrop for better sensing the future and developing appropriate actions and strategies.

Objective: To practice the skill of "presencing" the emerging future and crystallizing a cohesive vision and strategy.

Approach: Using cases of Cameroon, Côte d'Ivoire, and the Great Lakes Region, the learner is encouraged to think about elements that have allowed leaders in these cases to crystallize a vision of their countries and regions and make decisions using territorial and other governance related information. A new vision of what these countries may look like could emerge if such information is used in a multi-stakeholder setting.

Exercise: Using Theory U cases of Cameroon, Côte d'Ivoire, and the Great Lakes Region are used to present ideas; analysis and assessments help the learner see the value of better territorial governance.

Questions to consider when using governance and territorial considerations:

What kind of alternative visions could emerge if one uses a different set of starting points and considerations (levels) from a territorial perspective?

What sort of strategic map of the current pressure points can emerge and where would there be areas that prevent a vision from being realized? Would a different set of territories have a different outcome on the realization of a vision?

Which set of values and behaviors would need to be harmonized to help move the country or region towards a particular vision?

Recommendation: In practice in a similar situation, the learner can—through a process of dialogue with other stakeholders, where every contribution is incorporated without pre-judgment—develop a collage of ideas that brings everyone's perspective to bear.

5
Risk Management Approaches

Key Lessons from Chapter 5: Risk Management Approaches

This chapter introduces the types of risk management approaches used to handle risks arising with increased complexity.

The specific skills introduced are: (1) sharpening the ability to co-sense key risks and "presence" the future as it emerges; (2) co-creating strategies and actions that serve as a prototype for handling emerging challenges; and (3) setting priorities.

The learner is introduced to complexity reasoning, which involves identifying barriers or constraints, deciding where to enact barriers to prevent certain outcomes from materializing, and how to define and select payoffs from a suite of strategies. A case study from the evolution of brands in the beer industry is used to draw out the main lessons for leadership. Other cases used are from the construction industry and policies surrounding maintenance of infrastructure. The cases involve a varied set of actors as well as their definition of risk and appetite for risk. Tools that are helpful for decision-making are also introduced, including the value of risk-appetite statements. The role of scenario generation and analysis is critical, and the chapter revisits the concepts introduced in earlier chapters to help the learner bring all the learning together in a practical way.

Risk and Complexity

What types of *risk management approaches* exist to handle the key risks that arise with increased complexity?

Leaders need the approaches most suitable for their context to better handle the risks arising from complexity within an industry, managing sustainability risks in the long and medium term, as well as using risk-based approaches for designing policies. The chapter begins with the important role perceptions and ways of viewing the world play on decision-making processes and outcomes, and hence on risk. The influence of perception and perspective is particularly relevant to the concept of the "experience economy" where the link between patterns of change in preferences and the demand for specific goods or services has important implications for public policy.

Unlike previous chapters, there is no single case study used to illustrate Theory U. Rather, various illustrations from multiple areas of practice help the learner embed the concepts of Theory U in real-life situations. The case of beer branding is used to hone the skill of managing multiple preferences over long periods of time. The case of the construction industry, as an integrated production system, is used to provide the learning ground for skills that are useful for handling future changes, with speed and flexibility to adapt, all within a framework of ethics and values. The construction industry provides many lessons because it is a business subject to stiff price competition and is also prone to collusion and corruption. Sustainability risks feature, with a special focus on errors of omission, commission, or those deriving from lack of awareness. The case of infrastructure illustrates the complex interface between politics and policy and the role that Theory U can play in shaping decisions that bridge science with politics and consumer preferences.

Perceptions and perspectives on risk and possibility

Perception is very important in assessing risk. As Slovic et al. (1982) state: "When laypeople are asked to evaluate risks, they seldom have statistical evidence on hand. In most cases, they make inferences based on what they remember hearing or observing about the risk in question." So how does one observe risk? An illustration from the art world could be helpful to the reader.

Risk can be seen in a "Monet" fashion, as an impression, before it hits the markets or society, and decision makers can react to this perception by using the basic tools that can be useful in handling such perceived risks. Designing different strategies or scenarios for action would be of great use if one sees risk as an impression, before it really happens. Risk can also be seen in a "Cézanne" fashion, after it hits the markets and society. In this case, the key elements of risk would have already been made visible through scenario analysis, and the aggregation of tools needed to render the problem holistically visible and resolve it becomes important.[1]

In addition to the time at which risk is perceived, before or after the effects of a particular risk are known, the stage at which risks can be observed and handled is also important. Risk can be perceived at the stage of the outcomes that would result from a course of action and what needs to be done to avoid undesirable outcomes or react should a certain outcome materialize. Risk can also be perceived at the process stage, where the actions that generate particular risks are the object of interest. Alternatively, risk can be perceived at the stage of contemplation and strategy, where the values and visions driving strategy are at play. At this stage the choice set for decision-making can be designed to avoid particular scenarios, based on a vision and values that drive options away from particular considerations as a matter of preference.

These concepts are best understood when looking at specific applications. For a firm, risk can be perceived in the size of market a firm controls, the trends in the demand for particular products, and the key players in the product market in which the firm competes. A "Monet"-like assessment would look at identifying the type of shocks that could impact the market, including the entrance of new players, competition, or shifts in the preference of consumers for the firm's main product market. A "Cézanne"-like assessment would look at the type of effects that would happen from a particular type or series of shocks, with impact assessed, for example, from the impact on the level of exports of the firm's products to a particular country, the choice of whether a firm can position itself or should remain in a particular market segment or production location, or whether a firm should continue to source its inputs from a particular supply source. A response strategy to manage potential shocks can then be developed that would include an entry or exit strategy, a location plan, or a sourcing policy.

Branding, preferences and risk

This chapter provides a constructivist-learning environment (Wilson, 1996) supporting the learner in a self-directed way to perceive the risks that come from observing what is happening around them. A case study assessing brands illustrates the concepts in a real-world setting that challenges the learner to construct explanations of what has been happening, why, what could be done to have an alternate outcome, and what should be extracted from the experiences of particular brands.

The chapter builds and uses risks scenarios such that a "representative group of stakeholders" can have a rich environment from which to learn. This is possible because the discrete product characteristics (Anderson et al., 1992) embedded in each of the product groups selected are distinct enough to provide good indices for the learner to recall and reuse (Wilson, 1996) the materials in the book for similar situations in their work and life environment.

The first product group considered is beverages, including beer and wine as well as non-alcoholic beverages like coffee, soft drinks, and bottled water. Beverages are context-specific, but based on a common input (water) that could have varying degrees of scarcity. As such, shocks to beverage products could come from the input side and also from changes in the preferences of consumers that are sensitive to brand.

The second group is retail, with a special focus on fast food. Fast food is linked to internal supply chains and is sensitive to minor fluctuations in the supply chain, as it depends on the efficiency of cold-chain logistics. It is a good sector to investigate the effect of brand when production can be hampered at various levels of the supply chain.

The third group is apparel, with special focus on garments and textiles and a deeper assessment of sweater and knitwear woolen garments. This sector was selected as, prior to globalization, most societies made their own clothing. The apparel sector is sensitive to global sourcing decisions and to fashion and other trends that drive the evolution of brands.

All of the three product groups should be familiar to the learner's real-world setting and hence can be cross-referenced to the learner's own experiences (downloading from Theory U) and used for sensing alternative outcomes (presencing in Theory U). The learner can also use the product and brand evolution outcomes to sort out the important aspects for future use in real life (crystallizing from Theory U) and be prepared to design pilots or prototypes for a situation they are facing (prototyping and performing in Theory U).

An assessment is also done for products in the following sectors: automotive (cars and motor fuel); technology (general technology and mobile communications); financial institutions; and personal consumption (personal care and luxury). This analysis helps the learner to handle risks that come from shifts in product preferences and the link to product differentiation (Anderson et al., 1992) that is so critical in understanding the policy and sustainability implications of discrete consumer choices of brands. Preferences for cars and motor fuel shift with the desires for a given level of pollution, a specific driving experience, utility, and other factors that interact in the complex spheres of social, economic, and political choices. Technology changes also drive many other choices and hence the evolution of technology brands underlies a complex array of individual, firm, and societal decisions. Financial institutions have intense linkages across countries and are a critical set of institutions for economic development. Changes in the performance of financial institutions or choices made within one institution can have repercussions with far-reaching effects in society and over time. Personal choices for consumption of personal care and luxury products are sensitive to culture and also to influence from external signals, especially in a world that is more interconnected, where trends and fads drive choices. All these outcomes of brand evolution therefore should provide the learner with a rich milieu from which to extract indices for future use.

An analysis of 14 product markets indicates that the oldest brand was beer, with one brand dating from as long ago as 1664. Beverages in general have been branded for many years, including coffee (since 1753) and water (since 1789). The youngest brands are in mobile communications (since 2001), which is the technology that has done the most to speed up the pace of globalization and enhance complexity by increasing the number of potential interactions in a given space and time. Brands related to apparel, financial institutions, personal care, retail, soft drinks, and technology are concentrated in the US as a point of origin for the brand (Table 5.1). Europe dominates in the areas of beer, coffee, mobile communications, and luxury

Table 5.1 Evolution of brands—patterns from 1664–2001

Sector	Youngest (year)	Oldest (year)	Span (years)	Avg. age (years)	USA (%)	Europe (%)	Other (%)
Apparel	1990	1853	137	55	67	33	0
Beer	1990	1664	325	123	27	53	20
Cars	1989	1871	118	85	27	47	26
Coffee	1938	1753	185	134	40	60	0
Fast food	1971	1940	31	49	50	0	50
Financial institutions	1998	1799	199	115	55	25	20
Mobile communications	2001	1983	18	13	20	60	20
Motor fuel	2001	1879	122	64	50	30	20
Personal care	1980	1806	174	81	56	15	29
Retail	1995	1884	111	58	53	47	0
Soft drinks	1982	1885	97	73	70	30	0
Technology	1998	1847	151	55	66	15	19
Luxury	1975	1743	232	141	0	100	0
Water	1999	1789	210	84	40	60	0

Source: Calculated using data from Company Websites, Milward Brown Optimor, available at http://www.millwardbrown.com/Sites/mbOptimor/Default.aspx. These were supplemented with data taken from *Financial Times*, April 26, 2007.

products. Other countries, including emerging markets, have an important presence in fast food brands, and have made inroads into brands in the beer, cars, financial institutions, mobile communications, motor fuel, personal care, and technology markets.

The brand evolution patterns represent shifts over time in brand value, which is the amount of profit generated by the brand for a given manufacturer, which changes with new entrants with similar brands (Wood, 2000). Samsung, from South Korea, has challenged the dominance of Apple in the market for smartphones for example, and displaced an older player, Nokia, from Finland, in this market (Samama, 2013). In order to compete on the basis of the perceived penetration of brands, firms at times choose to shift their cost structures through global sourcing or procurement strategies aimed at global efficiencies in production. Such shifts can be seen as final outcomes not only in the market share of the firm in a given product market, but also in the export competitiveness of countries. Competitiveness in this context is the ability of a firm or country to sell and supply goods and services in a given export market. Such competitiveness is affected by the presence and strength of brands with which a firm and its country of origin or location are competing.

In this analysis risk is perceived as the potential loss of brand value or export competitiveness. Strategies to handle the risk relate to making the brand more visible, changing the cost structure supporting the brand through global sourcing, or intervening to improve the competitiveness of a firm or country through a series of policies. A " Cézanne"-like assessment is used based on the long-term evolution of the brands, after the dynamics have played out. Strategies can then be developed looking at the potential impact of this evolution in a "Monet"-like assessment to develop options to select from or scenarios to anticipate. All these assessments are done at the outcome stage, when all the dynamics of choice and preference have been taken place.

Beverage distribution markets are sensitive to social norms around consumption of alcohol and would hence have different evolution patterns for alcoholic beverages like beer, wine, and spirits as well as non-alcoholic beverages like water and coffee. Retail markets for household products, food (pastries and yogurt for instance), are sensitive to consumer preferences and location. Apparel markets in which garments and textiles are traded are influenced by culture and fashion. Products like men's and women's sweaters and knitwear (men's woolen garments and wool tops for women) are also sensitive to location and weather patterns. Looking at these product markets, one can further illustrate perspectives on risk and the key elements for selecting amongst management approaches.

Global preferences and risk: the beer industry

Beer has been selected to illustrate global preferences and local tastes. As beer is one of the oldest products to be branded, there are many deep markets around the world to study, and it is a product that is steeped in history of humanity yet flexible enough to adapt to evolving tastes and technologies. The evolution of the Mexican beer market offers a good case study to explore the impact of all these factors from a local to global scale and to highlight the differences in the perception of risk at the firm or country level.

Hornsey (2003) argues that ever since man became sapient he has devised means of creating intoxicating drinks like beer from plants. Grain-based alcohols have been brewed in different parts of the world for centuries and the Maya and Aztecs did that in what is today Mexico before the arrival of the conquistadors in America. The art of brewing beer as is now known in Mexico today however came from an influx of European immigrants in the middle of the 19th century. The first lager beer brewery in Mexico (La Pila Seca) was founded in 1845 by a Swiss immigrant, 181 years after the 1664 brand of beer made an appearance. In 2012, two big beer companies dominated the market for beer in Mexico, mainly, FEMSA and Grupo Modelo. FEMSA (Fomento Economico Mexicano SA de C.V.) was founded in 1890 and is the largest beverage company in Mexico and Latin America, employing nearly 180,000 people with a revenue base of US$ 15.8 billion in 2011 (www.femsa.com). The Mexican beer market shares characteristics with the European beer markets, as the technologies and techniques for production arrived in the tacit knowledge of immigrants to Mexico. However, the Maya and Aztecs also manufactured alcohol, with local tastes building on the history of fermented drinks like *pulque*, which has been brewed for centuries (www.larousse.fr). As such, beer manufacturing in Mexico has fused and merged tastes, preferences, and technologies from different parts of the world.

Grupo Modelo started in 1922 and by 2011 had a revenue base of US$ 6.5 billion, employing more than 40,000 people. Its activities expanded rapidly from a small firm when it opened in Mexico City in 1925 of the Cerveceria Modelo. The brands of Grupo Modelo were greatly aided by prohibition in the 1920s in the US, which boosted the Mexican brewing industry (www.grupomodelo.mx). By 1928 sales of Modelo and Corona brands reached 8 million bottles. Grupo Modelo launched the Negra Modelo brand in 1930 and made its first sporadic exports to the US in 1933. The brand beer Corona, which is a flagship beer of Grupo Modelo and the number one imported beer in the world, first began to be exported to Japan, Australia, New Zealand, and some countries in Europe in 1985. Corona went on to become the second most popular beer in the US in 1986 and the number one imported premium brand in the US market in 1997; by 2012 it was available in 180 countries (www.gmodelo.mx, August 28, 2012).

Beer sales are affected by the preferences of society, which have shifted over time. According to a Gallup Poll (www.gallup.com) in 1993, about 47% of Americans of drinking age preferred beer, drinking it more often than other beverages, but by 2008 this share had come down to 42%. The preference for wine went from 27% to 31% during the same period, while that for liquor went from 23% to 21%. Preferences are sensitive to age. Americans between the age of 30 and 49 shifted their preference of beer, which was at 48% in 1994, dropping to 40% in 2004, and bouncing up to 47% in 2008. Preferences for wine for the same group went from 31% in 1994 to 37% in 2005, only to drop to 27% in 2008. In Britain, in the 1990s 70% of 16-to-24-year-olds claimed to have had a drink in the previous week, whereas in 2010 just 48% had (*Economist*, 2013). Non-alcoholic beer sales grew by 80% to a volume of 2.2 billion liters in 2012, to become the fastest growing category in a mostly static beer market in 2013 (*Economist*, 2013). A manufacturer of beer has to be on top of the understanding of preferences in order to develop and protect a beer brand over a long period time, or to penetrate and gain market share from more established players. The skill from Theory U of "sensing from the field" to know what is driving tastes is critical, as is the ability to crystallize a strategy for making a prototype beer that can be branded to last over a period of time.

Risk management strategies for protecting a beer brand need to be informed not only by the preference for beer but also for other alcoholic or non-alcoholic beverages and the overall norms around drinking alcohol in general. Beer sales out of Mexico would move with the trends in wine exports from other countries. During the period 1984–2004 wine exports were dominated by a small group of countries, including France, Italy, Australia, and Spain. New entrants in the market included Chile, USA, South Africa, New Zealand, and Argentina, while Portugal and Germany served select niche markets. Today, there is a vibrant market of non-alcoholic beers serving Asia, the Middle East, and North Africa, but also health conscious consumers in Europe and America. The drivers for the growth in consumption of non-alcoholic beer are an issuing of *fatwas* by prominent Saudi and Egyptian clerics, declaring it permissible to drink zero-alcohol beer (*Economist*, 2013); the growth of income that allows consumers in countries where alcohol is prohibited to consume alternatives at home or in restaurants and bars; and the advances in technology that have made it easier to derive zero-alcohol beer, among other potential drivers.

The entry of new players in the beer market normally coincides with a general increase in the consumption of alcohol worldwide. In the US alone, sales of merchant wholesalers of beer, wine, and distilled alcoholic beverages more than doubled from a US$ 50 billion business in 1992 to about US$ 110 billion in 2010 (www.statista.com). Brands like Heineken, Guinness, and Becks have all entered the non-alcoholic beer market, and participate and shape the beer consumption trends.

Looking at the overall market for alcohol can also help us see the risks and opportunities facing a beer manufacturer.[2] A few players, including the UK (spirits), Canada (beer), and France (wine) dominated exports of alcoholic beverages in 1984. By 1994 new players emerged to dominate the global scene, including the Netherlands (beer), Germany (beer and wine), Ireland (beer and spirits), the US (mostly beer), and Mexico (beer). The pattern of dominance in exports shifted in 2004, with Ireland, the US, and Mexico surpassing Canada in the value of exports from alcoholic beverages in general. New players like Grupo Modelo built brands that were able to usurp market share from established players, who were focused on brands that could not go global.

Scharmer (2009), Anderson et al. (1992), and Bar-Yam (1997) help us see the critical risk factors of import when dealing with products like beer, which are impacted by local and global factors at the same time; have local as well as global preferences and tastes driving patterns of consumption or use; and are impacted by products in the same family with which they share similar characteristics (beer brands), but also by products that similar (other alcohol brands) or very different (non-alcoholic brands).

Risk assessment at the firm level: brands in retail

The retail sector is a good case to illustrate the link between perceived risk and real risk, and the approach for developing a response strategy at a firm level within a globalized context. The retail sector has traditionally been of local relevance and has only recently become globalized. As such, firms in the retail business provide a rich array of opportunities to learn from the variety of strategies they have employed to manage risks and the differential responses they have had to similar risks.

The oldest retail brand by date of founding that featured in the top 15 by brand value in 2007 was Marks & Spencer from the UK, ranked at number 7. Retail brands from the US represented 53% of the top 15 global brands in 2007 with Walmart at the top of the list with a brand name valued at close to US$ 37 billion in 2007. Home Depot came in at number 2, with a brand value of more than US$ 18 billion. Home Depot competed with IKEA from Sweden, which was ranked at number 8 in the sales of outdoor furniture, indoor décor products, cabinetry, fixtures, and lighting, as well as other retail products like kitchenware. Home Depot carried exclusive brands like Martha Stewart Living and Sur La Table in household retail products, while IKEA carries its own brand.

IKEA was founded in 1943 with a revenue base of close to US$ 30 billion in 2010, while Home Depot was founded in 1978 and had a revenue base of US$ 68 billion in 2011. IKEA succeeded in its strategy to compete in the US market by extracting value from the shift in preferences from buying fully assembled furniture to "doing it yourself" as well as minimizing its costs by employing a global sourcing strategy for key inputs. In addition to entering the US market, IKEA established its presence in other markets around the world, including fast growing markets like China (Table 5.2).

By understanding the shift in preference for retail products like furniture, IKEA was able to manage the risks of competition and create a niche to enter as a new player in 23 countries, where it owns 196 stores, but also through a franchise model to have a presence in 15 countries by 2007. Germany topped the list of sales countries, while China was on top as a source for inputs. In 2007, IKEA was a global brand with sales to 410 million people in 33 countries, employing 90,000 people in 44 countries and trading with 32 countries through its global sourcing strategy (Table 5.3).

Some retail products are harder to penetrate due to their dependence on inputs that are sensitive to branding in a different way, such as branding from country of origin or by level of freshness. This applies to food products like buttermilk and yogurt. In 1994, Germany and France dominated the markets for exporting buttermilk and yogurt (yogurt concentrate is used as an input into making yogurt and other foodstuffs as well as in some phar-maceutical products). In 2004, new entrants emerged including from Spain, Greece, and Finland, but Germany and France remained at the top of the

Table 5.2   Location and sourcing strategies—IKEA

Top 5 sales countries	Share (%)	
Germany	19	196 stores in 15 countries operated by franchise
USA	11	90,000 employees in 44 countries
UK	11	46 trading offices in 32 countries
France	9	1,300 suppliers in 53 countries
Sweden	8	Sales to 410 million people in 33 countries
Top 5 purchasing countries	**Share (%)**	
China	18	
Poland	12	
Sweden	9	
Italy	7	
Germany	6	

Source: IKEA.com available at www.ikea.com.

Table 5.3   Export performance in buttermilk and yogurt (US$ 000)

Country	2008	2012
Germany	948,223	874,946
France	805,641	807,257
Spain	234,068	171,856
USA	49,509	146,727
Netherlands	64,562	138,292
Russian Federation	114,452	98,408
Finland	49,439	73,057
Denmark	42,889	35,912
Portugal	7,076	33,618
South Africa	9,917	26,749
Mexico	7,944	15,475
Nicaragua	50	2

Source: ITC international trade statistics, available at http://www.intracen.org/itc/market-info-tools/trade-statistics/.

market for exports in terms of value, even in 2012. The presence of a bigger European market clearly acted as a win–win for the established brands in Germany and France, while Mexico could have benefited from the regional market in the North American Free Trade Agreement (NAFTA).

Competition from emerging markets in terms of exports of buttermilk and yogurt began in earnest in 1998, with countries like South Africa, Nicaragua, Mexico, and Russia entering the market. By 2008, Russia had grown its exports of buttermilk and yogurt from a value of US$ 114 million in 2008, but these declined to a little over US$ 98 million in 2012. Here again once could see the beneficial effect of branding in a regional context for South Africa and for the European Union. A buttermilk and yogurt exporter in Nicaragua has a more challenging risk profile for branding its product than one from Mexico under NAFTA. The influence of territories on risk is very clearly demonstrated in this case, and seems to be independent of consumer preferences (Table 5.4).

The economic downturn that started in 2007 following the financial crisis had an impact on the risk profiles of companies that relied on the yogurt business. Not only were they facing competition from new entrants, but they were also facing a declining potential for sales at home, despite the increase in the consumption of yogurt as a result of health studies that indicate the value of consuming yogurt.

In 2009, a French dairy food firm, Danone, ventured into a new territory outside its habitual market of selling in Europe and the US, starting a business in Bangladesh (BBC, 8 July 2009 00:05 UK). The venture was jointly conceived by Danone and Grameen Bank, and manages risk by changing

Table 5.4   Apparel—top ten by brand value 2006–2013

#	Brand	Year founded	Brand value 2006 (US$ millions)	Brand value 2013 (US$ millions)	Country
1	Nike	1972	10,290	15,817	USA
2	H&M	1947	8,711	12,732	Sweden
3	Zara	1974	6,469	20,167	Spain
4	Esprit	1968	5,411	Not in top 10	USA
5	Next	1982	2,888	4,121	UK
6	Ralph Lauren	1990	2,765	5,618	USA
7	Adidas	1949	2,748	4,882	Germany
8	Puma	1924	1,855	Not in top 10	USA
9	Gap	1969	1,831	Not in top 10	USA
10	American Eagle Outfitters	1977	1,609	Not in top 10	USA
11	Old Navy	1984	1,470	Not in top 10	USA
12	Abercrombie & Fitch	1892	1,172	Not in top 10	USA
13	Levi's	1853	1,041	Not in top 10	USA
14	Banana Republic	1968	937	Not in top 10	USA
15	Timberland	1952	831	Not in top 10	USA
NR	Uniqlo	1949	Not in Top 10	4,627	Japan
NR	lululemon	1998	Not in Top 10	3,764	Canada
NR	Hugo Boss	1924	Not in Top 10	3,524	Germany
NR	Calvin Klein	1968	Not in Top 10	1,801	USA

Source: Millward Brown Optimor, Company websites, Wikipedia, available at http://www.millwardbrown.com/Sites/mbOptimor/Default.aspx.

the perception of risk. First, it focuses on serving poor people and particularly children by providing them with 30% of their daily nutrition needs through yogurt products. Second, it works with a network of women who supply bags of yogurt to local villages, instead of the network of retailers and wholesalers Danone typically works with. Third, it is small in size, to minimize the risk of entry into a new market, and does not pay dividends to shareholders but benefits the community in which it is created. The joint venture has a special brand of yogurt that is local—Shoktidol—and it uses local market techniques, such as a lion that appears in costume to attract the interest of children (BBC, 8 July 2009 00:05 UK).

The apparel market is also useful to illustrate how the assessment of risk can be adjusted to changes in perception and preferences. The oldest apparel brand is Levi's, which has been around since 1853. Most apparel brands used to be from the US, which was responsible for 60% of the top 10 brands by value in 2007, but it has suffered in terms of brand loss as only 30% of US apparel brands were in the top 10 in 2013. Ralph Lauren, which was founded in 1990, was the youngest brand in the top 10 in 2013, and its brand value had doubled between 2006 and 2013, with its ranking going up as well, from 6 to 4. The top apparel brand in 2006, Nike, had a value (US$ 10 billion) that is about a quarter of that of the top branded beer, Corona (US$ 36 billion) in the same year. The company managed to grow its brand (US$ 15 billion) in 2013 but could not maintain its position as the number one brand. Nike was replaced by Zara, which was ranked number 3 in 2006 and grew to over US$ 20 billion in value to usurp the number 1 rank from Nike in 2013.

It is tough to survive and manage risk in the apparel business in a complex globalizing world. The fact that the share of US-based brands in the top 10 fell from from 60% to 30% between 2006 and 2013 shows how tough it is. But it is possible to have staying power and to grow. Nike managed to stay in the top 10, as did H&M, Zara, Next, Ralph Lauren, and Adidas. Zara, Nike, H&M, Ralph Lauren, and Adidas also managed to grow during this period, with Zara showing the most impressive growth. But new players came into the top 10, like Uniqlo, lululemon, Hugo Boss, and Calvin Klein. Some lost out and dropped out of the top 10, like Esprit, Puma, Gap, and American Eagle Outfitters. Interestingly enough, none of the next five (ranks 11–15) in 2006 moved up to the top 10 in 2013, and all of them got overtaken in value by brands that were not in top 15 in 2006.

According to Milward Brown Optimor, apparel is rated the most "sexy" category in research on brands, alongside luxury goods, and that the brands that did well since the recession of 2008–2010 are considered strongly "creative."[3]

The evolution of brand value in the apparel business is closely linked to the strategies utilized by multinational firms for locating their businesses overseas or expanding their overseas activities (sourcing, manufacturing, and sales) and also to their marketing and R&D activities (Kotabe et al., 2002). Even more particular is the fact that companies take risks in locating activity in new markets, but only gain benefits in a lagged manner. Kotabe et al. (2002) found that companies tend to enjoy improved operational environments (i.e. positional strength, including brand strength) from foreign expansion before financial improvement as they increase their R&D activity (such as research to better understand consumer preferences in new markets, production technologies, sourcing strategies, and researching on new ways of doing business). That means that strategy leads to improved financial performance, but is not visible initially, as operational strengths show up first, and only later are financial strengths seen. Managing the dynamics underlying the risks becomes important. Knowing what the emerging preferences are is paramount to success. Sensing the future of demand for apparel before it emerges is an edge that companies can have over others—all lessons from Theory U. Knowing where to locate on the product or service differentiation scale is also important—such as how to make day-to-day wear apparel look like luxury brands through creative input in design and advertising. This is something one can learn from Anderson et al. (1992).

These dynamics are illustrated by patterns of change in how garments are made and textiles manufactured, as a driver of brand value and performance. In 2007 there were 6,368 suppliers of fabric selling on the global market and 10,426 suppliers of men and women's apparel. The market was characterized by stiff competition, with a global sourcing model to manage risks. Following on (Kotabe et al., 2002) one would expect such patterns to have an effect in a lagged manner and explain what was seen in brand performance three to five years later (Table 5.5).

Men and women's sweaters and knitwear manufacturers are of particular interest due to sensitivity to fashion on the one hand, and the need for warm clothing in cold weather, which limits the extent to which fashion

Table 5.5   Global sources for garment and textile manufacturers

Category of manufacturer	Products (#)	Suppliers (#)	Countries (#)
Fabric	2,455	6,368	66
Fiber and yarn	135	1,582	48
Garment display supply	358	1,026	32
Garment trimming supply & accessory	5,202	4,014	57
Men's and women's apparel	7,153	10,426	85
Non-fabric material	138	1,123	49
Textile packaging & printing	262	464	26
Textile supply & service	22	434	28
Underwear & swimwear	1,638	2,605	51

Source: Globalsources.com posted week of April 23, 2007, available at www.globalsources.com.

trends dictate individual preferences. This segment also depends on a supply chain that goes from live animals, to scoured wool, to yarn, and to knitted or manufactured products. Advertising on the Pendleton website encapsulates the transformation in consumer preferences and their impact on manufacturing and marketing of wool shirts: "In 1924, a man could have a wool shirt in any color he wanted—as long as it was grey. Wool shirts were utilitarian items; warm, durable, an excellent first line in the defense against the elements" (http://www.pendleton-usa.com). Pendleton Woolen Mills is a private apparel company founded in 1863 in Portland, Oregon, to manufacture woolen blankets and garments (http://en.wikipedia.org/wiki/Pendleton_Woolen_Mills).

The company would go on through experimentation in weaving and other innovations to ride the market with the emergence of sportswear after the Second World War. Today Pendleton is featured with other brands like Nike, Adidas, and Levi's (http://www.pendleton-usa.com). The company is unique, as it remains privately held, still located in Portland but with a manufacturing plant in Bellevue, Nebraska. It sells its products in the US Canada, Europe, Japan, and Korea. It chose to manage risk by creating a niche market with global appeal, neither embracing the trend for locating its manufacturing outside its country of origin, nor sourcing from outside.

While there are fewer players in the business of manufacturing men's and women's sweaters and knitwear than those in garment and textile manufacturing, there is still stiff competition. There are many suppliers for women's pullovers and sweaters and many countries engaged in the business of making similar products for men. The complexity of product choice is higher for women than for men, as women have up to three times the number of products in sweaters than men. Differentiation of brand and sourcing strategy is critical to survive in the sweater business. In addition, well-established manufacturers compete with niche players, including the grandmother knitting for her family (Table 5.6).

Table 5.6   Men and women's sweater and knitwear manufacturers

Category of manufacturer	Products (#)	Suppliers (#)	Countries (#)
Men's and women's winter knitwear	254	359	11
Men's pullovers	93	862	40
Men's sweaters	101	913	40
Men's woolen garments	10	462	21
Women's cardigans	269	779	34
Women's pullovers	368	1,314	44
Women's sweaters	314	1,378	44
Women's woolen garments	15	465	21

Source: Globalsources.com posted week of April 23, 2007, available at www.globalsources.com.

Table 5.7 Exports of men's shirts, knitted, or crocheted (value in US$ 000)

Country	2008	2012
China	1,745,613	1,894,061
India	488,121	574,463
Germany	289,420	325,457
Italy	245,106	289,422
France	252,317	214,045
UK	122,031	120,828
USA	66,046	92,724
Brazil	6,895	3,961
Australia	5,164	3,827
South Africa	2,529	3,715

Source: ITC International Trade Statistics, available at http://www.intracen.org/itc/market-info-tools/trade-statistics/.

More complexity in manufacturing thins out the competition space and the related risk, as can be seen in the pattern of wool shirt exports between 2008 and 2012. France dominated the export market in the 1980's reaching over US$300 billion in the value of wool shirt exports in 1988. By 2012, a number of countries in addition to France saw a sharp and sudden decline in their exports. These included the UK, Brazil and Australia. Exports grew during this period from China, India, Germany, Italy, USA and South Africa.

Stiff competition from new entrants has become easier due to the possibility of relocating manufacturing activity around the world or sourcing inputs more broadly. Alternatively, selling to local markets or creating a niche brand on a global scale through customized mass supply, as done by Pendleton, can also be used as a strategy to manage risks. Pendleton worked on the preference sphere to manage risk, because entering new markets is also risky. Few new entrants can make it, as can be seen by the sharp decline of wool shirt exports from Thailand, falling to US$ 149 million in 2012 from exports worth more than US$ 212 million in 2008. Argentina, Brazil, and Malaysia saw their export value decline steadily each decade, while Korea struggled to get global space in this market. The Czech Republic, India, and China fared very well, with sharp growth in their exports of wool shirts.

Assessing risk in industry: the construction industry

Risk at the industry level depends on the overall character of the industry as well as the key actors involved. The types of decisions made can also create or reduce risk, and different decision sequences or profiles determine the pattern of risk. The sources of risk can be varied in terms of their impact on a series of decisions, with some decisions being less sensitive to a given source of risk. Choosing the right tools to manage risks, whether formal or informal, is more of an art than a science. The advantage of assessing industry-wide risks is the ability to develop recommendations for the entire industry.

The construction industry is used to develop the concepts to master skills for a good assessment at this level. This is an extremely risky business, because it involves multiple players and depends on many interrelated actors and processes. Furthermore, construction is a business with large fixed assets and repeated transactions, and faces uncertain demand. Tasks in this industry are interrelated, with high interdependency over time. Failure in one task or process can easily spill over to impact other tasks.

Construction is a business that is subject to stiff price competition, and it is also prone to collusion and corruption. There is significant literature on risk management for the construction industry, but with the exception of a few multinationals it is little used in practice. The industry presents an opportunity for industry-wide risk management culture change if common interests can be outlined at the industry level, as is done in other industries through business associations.

The construction industry is a good learning ground for leaders to develop their skills for handling future changes, as project scope and requirements change often in this business, requiring speed and flexibility to adapt without causing harm (a collapsed bridge or building) or ruin (high cost overruns that are not compensated). Working in the industry is also a humbling experience and one needs to deal with mistakes and omissions, with clients making frequent input on design choices. The industry is also a good place to hone skills in defining roles and responsibilities and allocating accountabilities for results. Failure is visible and many times attributable, with some exceptions. A young leader can also learn how to be good at making hiring decisions, as the contracting business requires effective on-the-job skills review and the ability to rate experience. Furthermore, this is an industry in which the differentiation between general and specialized knowledge is at a premium, with the need to have superb knowledge of local conditions to succeed. Technology plays a very important role and choosing the right materials and techniques makes a huge difference. But perhaps the most important skill for a leader to hone by working in or studying the construction industry is the ability to relate to other project actors.

The main causes of construction risks come from a single actor's knowledge and practice, with poor managers of risk causing tremendous losses to a client. Such risks can come from a lack of risk management knowledge, insufficient experience, or a weak employee skills base. These causes are also relevant in other industries, but are more visible in the construction industry due to the highly networked multi-actor nature of the business. Another major category of risk has to do with business culture and industry practices, including contract-awarding processes, the quality of subcontractors one has to rely on, and the application of codes and standards. Corruption can lead to massive risks, as when codes and standards are not followed due to corruption infrastructure can collapse and lead to massive human loss and suffering, as well as physical damage. The multiplicity of actors in the sector makes it difficult to apportion accountability. Risks come from an inability to supervise subcontractors properly and from weak communication and information sharing amongst all the actors engaged in the industry. Uncertainty contributes its share of risks in construction, as surprises and hazards are encountered during the various stages from design to commissioning.

The importance of risk management in all aspects related to infrastructure construction can be seen in a quote from Thierry Mayard-Paul, Haiti's Chief of Staff and Minister of Interior, Territorial Collectivities and National Defense: " The 2010 earthquake demonstrated that development will never be successful if we don't build risk reduction at our core" (PR Newswire, April 17, 2012).

To be successful at risk management in the construction industry requires systemic action that starts with industry practices with efforts to improve the risk management skills of the key actors in the industry, especially the main contractor, but also the subcontractors, suppliers, regulators, insurers, financiers, and legal entities supporting the industry. Clients of the industry can also become more risk-aware to improve their demands and requirements for oversight of the industry. Managing the chain of decisions and the flow of information amongst key players would go a long way to reducing the impact of poor risk management in the industry. Investing in improving industry knowledge and skills is also an important action to manage risk in the industry better, which requires effective ways to build experience of companies and individuals, improve on the quality of designs to minimize risk of collapse and failure, and to embed risk management knowhow in the entire industry. Working on the whole industry environment will allow related and correlated risks to be addressed more effectively through appropriate policies and regulations, codes and standards, and responses to hazards.

Risk management tools include a combination of formal and informal methods. The value of informal tools should not be underestimated, as construction is an experience-based industry where tacit knowledge is critical for success. Informal tools include identifying and using experience as a source of risk identification by looking at past history and assessing the role of previous judgment. This requires effective use of the Theory U techniques of observation and downloading introduced in previous chapters. Second, we need to analyze the challenges at hand using a structured approach, by clarifying objectives and identifying uncertainties. The skills of listening from the field in Theory U play an important role at this juncture, as listening to the multiplicity of actors in the industry could uncover and support the identification of the types of uncertainties that need to be managed.

Such listening can be accompanied by structured dialogue to refine the risk categories and sources, as is done at the crystallizing stage.

Formal tools for risk management can also be used in practice. Engineering standards and technical specifications can reduce risks in the design and construction phases. Having appropriate contract and clause negotiation, and managing these contracts and clauses, can reduce legal and accountability risks. The capacity to manage complex contracts is one of the key bottlenecks that impede achievement in implementing large-scale and complex infrastructure projects. Liability and claims management is another area that can not only reduce the risk of projects being delayed, but also cut the cost of projects. Effective tools for insurance and risk transfer techniques at the industry level also improve the apportioning of risk and enhance the ability to better manage such risks.

Developing management systems to identify, manage, and control risks, including communication, decision-making, and reporting systems, relies on appropriate use of informal tools. Such systems can be developed in prototype and improved with use as the industry practices on a day-to-day basis to deliver better performance. Management systems are most effective when they are customized for the appropriate level of action—actor-specific, between actors, or for a network of actors.

Actor-specific tools include tacit knowledge-sharing at the stage of supervising works, including the use of guidance and mentoring systems. Such informal tools would improve the industry level of knowledge and motivation for risk management. These could be combined with formal tools, such as courses on risk management for all construction industry workers. Formal tools could also link these learning-based risk management approaches, such as the use of financial risk reserves to handle emerging risks due to poor skills and experience at the actor level.

Informal between-actors tools can be used to enhance the outcomes of contract negotiation and management as well as to improve quality standards. These include the use of mandatory meetings and formal partnerships across actors in the industry to revise contractual design and provide incentives for better risk sharing and management. Increasing inspection and supervision effort and proper guidance and mentoring by the main contractor of the subcontractor could effectively hedge against less reliance on contractual clauses and litigation. Supported by pooled financial reserves, such informal tools could bring risks down significantly in the industry.

Many informal tools could be useful amongst the network of actors in the industry. Using business associations to influence industry standards, sharing good practices, undertaking industry-wide training, and certification of skills are some possible actions. Alternatively (or additionally) the network of actors could also agree to use client satisfaction surveys and use the results for common reforms. Pushing for a collective sanctions environment would help tackle difficult problems, such as corruption, collusion, and unethical behavior in the industry. Transparent and repeated partnerships could lead to better management of risks. Combined with formal tools, such as industry-wide financial reserves, these informal tools could go a long way toward managing risks in the construction industry. Theory U calls for continuous dialogue and interaction amongst multiple stakeholders. Used over time, Theory U could induce cooperation amongst a network of actors to develop an industry-wide shared risk management process, managed by an association of actors in the construction industry or through a formal industry development corporation.

Managing sustainability risks to society

Sustainability risks impact not only firms and industries but also society as a whole. Actors at the firm and industry level, however, are the ones with the largest toolkit for response when aided with the right framework of policies and regulations by government. Most actors at the firm and industry levels approach sustainability risks by first identifying the key aspects of sustainability that touch their business. Second, they assess the contribution of specific factors of risk to the core business. Third, they select a strategy for response and areas of focus. Fourth, they categorize potential options. Finally, they highlight the key issues to consider and develop a strategy on how to handle such risks in the long term.

Considering what is external to the firm or industry's influence is the best starting point for identifying key aspects of sustainability. How does the economy impact the industry and what is shifting that needs to be accounted for? What aspects of governance go beyond the boundaries of action of the industry or firm, but have a significant impact on the actions and outcomes of the firm? What is happening to the environment for finance overall and its implications for the firm? What shifts in the trade environment will impact on the expected outcomes for the firm? How are changes in society impacting choices and preferences, and what do they mean for the firm or industry? Will changes in preferences translate into political action and policy changes that would impact the firm? These are some of the questions that are critical at the level of the external environment from a sustainability perspective.

Sustainability can also come from analysis of the internal structure of the firm. What sort of supply chain is the firm relying on and what are the risks related to sustainability embedded in that chain? What is the environment in which the firm is operating and the implications for sustainability? What is happening to labor and employment within the firm and how is it affected by what is happening in society as a whole?

The partnership a firm engages in is also a source of assessment for sustainability (Figure 5.1). What local or international actor is the firm engaged with that is operating in the sphere of non-state actors? Does the industry

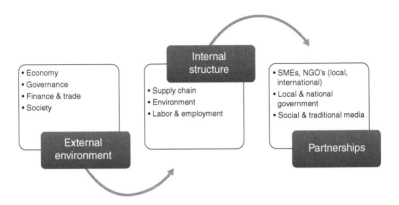

Figure 5.1   Assessing sustainability risks at the firm level

have a small or large share of small and medium enterprises and how is the firm engaged with them? What is likely to happen to the partnerships with non-state actors or small and medium partners? What is the level of engagement and capacity of local and national governments? How active and effective are social media platforms and how do they relate to the local media in the firms area of influence or operation?

Assessment of sustainability can range from investigating the risks to profitability or the financial bottom line and embedding key aspects of a response, to managing such risks into company strategy. Risks can also be to reputation or business operations, and changes in management or fundamental operational processes may be needed. Risks could also provide new opportunities, akin to how businesses have interpreted societal preferences for less pollution by engaging in green energy production and use. Sustainability risks could also be a platform for doing business differently: many firms have sought to reduce their energy use, thus doing good and benefitting through lower cost structures. What are the potential sustainability risks and how can innovation solve them? Firms like Danone have used risks of backlash against a large external industry, edging out small players, to innovate and create a new type of company engagement that works with local actors and serves local needs, without the traditional shareholding structure that pays out dividends.

In addition to embedding actions into company strategy, there is also a potential response of engaging in a multi-stakeholder industry-wide process that minimizes risks for all—as we have discussed in the construction industry. Yet another response is to sharpen the communication strategy at different levels.

A wide array of choice is possible to manage sustainability risks. Many firms use philanthropic activities like charitable contributions, community

Table 5.8 Assessment phase

Sustainability aspect	Strategic response
• Profitability and financial bottom-line (outcomes) • Risks to manage (reputation, business, operation) • New business opportunities, doing business differently • Potential for innovation	• Embedding key aspects into company strategy • Changing fundamental operational processes • Engaging in a multi-stakeholder industry-wide process • Sharpening communication strategy at different levels

work, or employee participation to manage risks of reputation, but also to learn how to handle critical risks. Risk management to manage reputation can be done in partnership with non-state actors, through commonly agreed codes of conduct, or through multi-stakeholder activities to define a common set of rules, share risks, or shape opinion. Actions can also be conceived as an opportunity to create unique value, such as embedding sustainability in core operations, making it part of corporate strategy (Table 5.8).

A number of issues are relevant for consideration for successful sustainability risk management. The most critical one is the capacity of government, in the sphere of the firms operations, to set and enforce rules.

Government capacity and sustainability loss areas are the two most important constraints that firms' face, often with little ability to intervene effectively for a solution. Government capacity can be measured in various ways, but for purposes of sustainability three aspects standout. The first is the quality of political and administrative governance; the second is the ability of government to create a good business environment; and finally, there is the approach and capability government that has to deal with environmental issues, such as regulation, standard setting, and enforcement. Weak government capacity is a risk for sustainability and firms need to develop strategies for how to operate in diverse governance environments (Table 5.9).

Sustainability loss areas are also of relevance in shaping risk management strategy. To assess the value of sustainability strategies, three issues are important. The first is the cost of each initiative pursued and a ranking by level of effort to get the initiative off the ground. The second is the impact of each initiative in its contribution to reducing sustainability risk. Finally, there is the bottom line of each initiative, which combines the cost versus the value in some form of cost-effectiveness assessment or value for money analysis.

Supply chain risks are a category that requires special attention in a globalized world, where information flows instantly and risks can materialize

Table 5.9 Making choices

Actions	Issues

• Philanthropic activities (charitable contributions, community work, employee participation)
• Risk management (reputation management, partnership with civil society, codes of conduct, commitments to transparency, multistakeholder activities to define common rules, shape opinion, share risks)
• Opportunity to create value (embedding sustainability in the core business of the operations, making it part of corporate strategy and implementation)
	• *Government capacity*: to set and enforce rules:
	  • Is the country in conflict?
	  • Is there corruption?
	• *Loss leaders*: initiatives generating losses or diminishing profits more significantly than handling risks?
	• *Supply chain risks*: approach to assess risks in the supply chains?
	• *Competitors and stakeholders*: how are competitors and other stakeholders incorporating the issues of sustainability? Is there room to lead? Is there opportunity to partner? Is there a risk of being overshadowed?

in real loss of brand or position. A good analysis of supply chain risks requires identifying who the players in the supply chain are and how the company communicates and engages with them. Is there a code of ethics signed with players in the supply chain? Is there a discussion on what is expected of them? Are such expectations embedded in contractual clauses? How is compliance with the code of ethics and clauses in contracts audited? What are the results of audits and assessments? How is enforcement handled? (Figure 5.2)

Awareness of the actions of competitors and other stakeholders is also of importance. Key areas relate to human and labor rights regimes in the company sphere of operations and their potential risk to the activities and bottom line of the company. How are other actors reacting or responding to these human and labor rights regimes? What is the quality of infrastructure investment and what are the future prospects? Are competitors engaged in self-production or influencing the production of critical infrastructure? What stakeholders need to be engaged for an effective resolution of infrastructure bottlenecks? Are competitors signatories to codes of ethics and do they abide by them? Is there a possibility to partner with competitors and other stakeholders to get to a common code of ethics, or should the company strike out alone and lead by adopting a code? What is the level of transparency in reporting on ethical issues and sustainability actions and outcomes? Can the level of transparency be improved and is there room for collective action at the industry level? Can partnerships be built with government to improve governance? Should the firm engage in community development? What opportunities exist for bottom of the pyramid

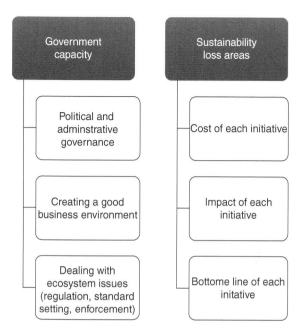

Figure 5.2   Government capacity for sustainability

approaches, including partnerships with non-state actors to reach poorer communities? Is there an active conflict in the country or region? Is there corruption? How is the firm going to respond to the situation on the ground with respect to conflict or corruption?

Questions can serve as a guide to developing effective sustainability risk management strategies, and are employed by various actors in practice. Illustrations throughout the book by way of case studies have indicated the degree of success and challenge in adopting such strategies in different environments.

Risk-based approaches for policies

Policies, and how they are designed, implemented, and enforced, can have a significant impact on the sustainability risks facing an industry actor. It is critical to identify all the areas of risk that can be solved, not through individual or *ad hoc* action, but through a systemic policy solution.

Evolving links between key policies and economic and social impacts would typically rely on a good understanding of measurability, moral hazard, preference myopia, accountability and incentives structures, and measurement errors. Measurability is the observable relationship between policy and economic performance. Information asymmetry relates to impacts of policy that are not immediately visible yet would materialize in the long run. Moral hazard is mostly at play when policy makers are rewarded for visible results rather than for avoided costs or risks. Preference myopia comes from weak links between what voters experience and the real pattern of policy effects. Accountability and incentives regimes get worse when combined with poor reporting practices on what policies are needed and when. Measurement errors come from poor information on what to do and when to implement policy.

Measurability is important, as it is determined by a number of factors that actors in industry need to be aware of to manage policy risks effectively. The first factor is the degree to which there is information asymmetry between the various actors in the policy sphere. Does the government know the constraints that the industry is facing? Does industry discuss policy designs with government? What is known about the real impact of different policy options? What is the gap between policies as designed and as implemented?

Moral hazard is another factor of relevance. Do policymakers have incentives, political or administrative, to delay taking a policy decision or prefer a short-term to a long-term policy solution? Are policy reversals possible and could decisions to reverse policies be of benefit to politicians, to the detriment of industry? Are policy makers accountable for their policy decisions or can industry be blamed when things go wrong during implementation? Information asymmetry, such as when policymakers do not engage with business and are hence not knowledgeable about the constraints faced by business, can cause moral hazard problems or render them more severe (Figure 5.3).

Preference myopia is of particular concern, for example when voters prefer lower taxes, and investments in infrastructure are thus delayed due to financing constraints that then impact the performance of business and its ability to create jobs, leading to the need for higher taxes in the long run and even fewer jobs. What is an effective strategy to deal with identified areas of preference myopia by voters or policymakers?

Arrangements for accountability and the incentive structure the public sector faces to ensure certain policies are well designed, implemented, and evaluated is also an area that can impact sustainability risks. Industry has an interest in ensuring accountabilities around policy are well defined and clear and that there is an incentive system that embeds such accountabilities into day-to-day practice.

Sustainability risks are complex and policies to resolve them are not always easy to measure, leaving room for measurement errors. What aspects of non-compliance come from measurement error? How can one hold actors accountable in the face of measurement errors? Can competitors hide behind measurement errors to get ahead? What partnerships with other stakeholders can reduce the risks of measurement errors?

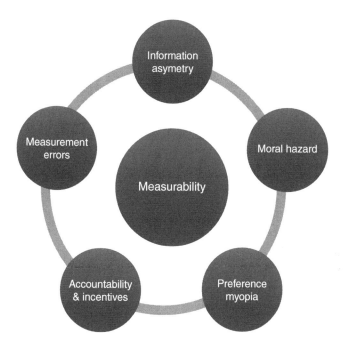

Figure 5.3 Links between policies and their impacts

There are strong links between politics and policy that industry actors use to develop effective policy risk management strategies. Election cycles are subject to their own form of myopia, where voters may prefer a policy arrangement that does not completely resolve sustainability risks for industry actors. Pollution standards that require technology shifts are an example.

It is important to evolve the links between policies and politics. Election myopia is of importance to track. Such myopia can be seen in media reports or other sources of information, such as when voters reward politicians for visible projects (capital) and whether the administrative hierarchy punishes policy makers for visible failures. In such environments, only major projects are easily funded and media coverage is limited to the signing of big financing agreements for large projects, or when large projects are commissioned (Figure 5.4).

Information asymmetry can be gauged by checking whether budgets approved are for pressing and visible priorities or whether they also include instances where technical arguments have been made for particular policy spending.

Budget cycles and how budgets are approved and managed are also of relevance in policy-politics linkages. Information asymmetry as to the real cost

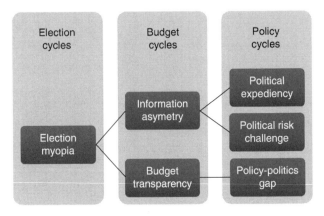

Figure 5.4 Links between policies and politics

of actions can render approved budgets insufficient to handle sustainability risks, or political preferences may delay the presentation for approval of components of the budget aimed at tackling certain risks. How transparent the budget process is and how it is tracked and reported on during implementation is a consideration that impacts on the relations between politics and policy. Most governments go through policy cycles that vary for reasons of political expediency, managing political risks, or due to genuine gaps between the policymaking and political processes.

Political expediency can result in deferred policies and programs that cause unplanned major spending at a later date. Such spending taps into current budgets, putting further pressure on prioritization. Evidence of political expediency would be seen in short-term budgets that are revised often, with limited long-term financing approved in the budget. Political risk challenges occur when there is stiff competition for funding between policies and other programs, leading to appropriations going towards other priorities. Policy–politics gaps are evident when one observes underdeveloped approaches to link policies and programs to the political decision process.

Policy risk can be measured through parametric and non-parametric means. A parametric measure can trace the observed or observable impact of a given policy on an industry actor and sketch the trajectory of such impacts over a period of time and explore the pattern of impacts over a space of influence. Parametric measures do not capture all relevant risks, which leaves room for handling residual risk, which comes from what cannot be measured or controlled. Non-parametric measures are usually useful for handling what you cannot see or what you don't know.

Selecting an approach to assess policy risk and choosing between parametric and non-parametric methods depends on the potential types of policy failure and their link to the key impact areas of an industry actor. It is always best to select simple methods for assessing these risks, including simple parameters that can be tracked or a set of heuristics that can be tested at different stages. Highlighting residual risks due to weak knowledge of the effectiveness of policy action under different implementation conditions becomes easier when what can be measured is removed from the choice set.

Risk management and scenario generation and analysis

Previous chapters have covered the main elements needed to develop good scenarios. For the purposes of risk management, it is important to highlight a few aspects of general scenario generation and an analysis concept, as practicing them in order to manage risks gives them added learning relevance.

It is good practice to have at least three potential scenarios, usually referred to as a base case, worse case, and best case. Defining such scenarios within a dialogue with multiple stakeholders can aid in better refining the identification of risks relevant to each scenario, or shaping strategies within a scenario to better manage a given set of risks. From Theory U, the skill of presencing is of most relevance for developing risk-based scenarios, as it helps the decision maker to understand better the emerging future and its implications for risk.

Interaction management, from complexity analysis concepts, is of most relevance in refining scenarios that are risk-adjusted. Complexity reasoning is used to define the interactions to expect and their implications for risks. Also from complexity reasoning comes the importance of identifying barriers or constraints (external or internal) or deciding where to create or enact barriers to prevent certain outcomes from materializing.

Selection and payoffs can then be useful to define the types of actions and strategies that can be used to adapt as the outcomes approach pre-defined patterns. Some industry actors define risk-appetite statements that are then used as tools to manage risks. When limits are reached, a set of actions ensues which brings the risk down to a tolerable level.

Conclusion

This chapter was aimed at supporting the learner in understanding how to go about identifying and managing risk, and the role of skills like co-sensing and co-creating a superior risk management strategy from Theory U. If you have made it this far, you will by now have a wide range of cases and illustrations to hone the skills that can support development of superior risk management strategies in your specific context.

The material presented covered the stages of co-creating and prototyping in the Theory U framework and used case studies presenting a common challenge to the average person in a globalized world. The lessons to retain from the cases of beer branding, the construction industry, and infrastructure maintenance are multiple. The foremost is the need to work with a team of stakeholders. Such multi-stakeholder exercises are superior in getting the best outcome from the "downloading" work needed to gather relevant information about the challenges faced and from identifying the sources of "knowing." Each stakeholder brings a specific perspective and role, and such a perspective is superior in "sensing from the field" whether in real-life or in a simulated setting. One can set the case materials up as a game to see what comes out of role-plays and scenarios in a multi-stakeholder setting. Multi-stakeholder exercises force participants to clarify the main issues they want to put on the table and bring to the attention of other stakeholders. Such approaches work best if each stakeholder comes prepared with a list of questions they would like to ask the other stakeholders. Listening to the issues raised by other stakeholders during a process of observation and downloading makes the decision maker better able to stake out the risks and opportunities, including those that may be just emerging or would emerge in the future.

Leadership emerges as a stakeholder makes a decision to seek partners to initiate a meeting with (co-initiating), or to implement particular solutions. As such, one can create a lab-like environment that mimics the way coalitions are formed to solve common problems in real life. When participants attend a co-initiated multi-stakeholder meeting, they listen more intently to the other stakeholders, as they own the meeting, while being forced to be clear of their own values and preferences. During the meeting each participant seeks to connect with the other players in the group, using lessons on effective listening. Participants use the meeting to share their core ideas and values (initially at the level of general impressions), aiming to paint a picture in a "Monet"-sense without judgment or prejudice.

Early sharing of impressions should form opportunities to define coalitions amongst the players that need one another to move forward. Coalition members can work together to paint a picture that is not necessarily complete—in the " Cézanne"-sense—and use a process of dialogue to refine the picture of risks and opportunities they collectively see. This part of the multi-stakeholder process helps participants practice the skill of co-initiating by attending joint meetings, connecting with other stakeholders, and co-defining a common set of issues that need cooperative resolution to manage risks.

Participants from a multi-stakeholder exercise of downloading and co-sensing the field usually work together more keenly afterwards to identify the substantive agenda—what, why, who, when, and where? A series of questions is helpful at this stage. What do you want to create together? Answers to this question can uncover common ground as each participant shares the context and story that comes from their choice of role-play. At this stage, participants need to observe, observe, and observe keenly to gather all relevant information that is being downloaded by other stakeholders.

It is important during multi-stakeholder work to ask why it matters to you as a group? Dialogue around such a question can spark inspiration for what you want to create together. It relies on the ability of each participant to suspend judgment, dream, and connect with other stakeholders on what could be possible. How are you going to achieve your creation and what process will you use to get there? Using dialogue and deep listening skills, participants can extract ideas from the group. Dialogue around the "how" also supports an individual participant to connect to others and to their starting values. Who is going to do what and how are you going to allocate responsibilities across your team? Working with other stakeholders could result in a plan of actions, identification of contexts to explore, and a set of core people to lead or champion a set of ideas. Participants need to be mindful to have a healthy balance between efficiency and creativity at this stage. When do you want to achieve your goals by and where do you see yourselves in the future? Responses to this question help participants develop a road map for moving forward, with the necessary timelines and set of outcomes. It results in a sort of "first feel" from the coalition of stakeholders.

Once goals have been defined and the future vision mapped out in a multi-stakeholder process, it is usually helpful for participants to break up and pair with one other stakeholder. This allows a new process of creation to take place, but also a better sensing of the substantive and perceptive issues that may have been skipped during the "first feel" analysis. Important questions to engage in pairs that come from Scharmer (2009) include: what is your most important objective, and how can I help you realize it? What criteria could help you assess whether my contribution to your work has been successful? If I were able to change two things in my role with respect to our group, what two things would create the most value and benefit for you? What if any tensions or systemic barriers have made it difficult for people in my role or function to fulfill your requirements and expectations? What obstacles do you think will get in our way? Such deeper analysis helps the stakeholders co-sense the people side of things and the immeasurable (or not easy to parameterize) set of issues. Stakeholders also learn how to balance their needs with what is relevant to others and how to balance their values with those of others. Also identified in such a process are any barriers that need to be removed for common success.

Checking back after a multi-stakeholder dialogue, to refine the understanding in smaller groups or even with a single peer, is critical. What you learn in paired dialogue can be sharper and serve to answer collectively a series of questions in another setting with more stakeholders. The first question in paired dialogue should be around inspiration: what in the dialogue you have undertaken so far got you the most excited, got you really inspired and for which you can apply your best sources of energy and creativity to resolve?

A question that can sharpen a multi-stakeholder dialogue comes from complexity science and relates to *interconnections*: consider the aspects of the dialogue you all found energizing as small seeds or building blocks of the future: what might a possible future look like in which these small seeds and building blocks are interconnected and grow into an inspiring whole? What aspects of the building blocks resonate with your best vigor to go and get them done?

The learner can consider questions that go at the *barriers*: if you were to take this on, to bring that future into being, what do you need to let go of (types of interaction), stop doing (behaviors), or do differently (policies, practices)? What is the old "stuff" that must die? The level of preparedness is also important: if you took a risk and your project failed, what would be the worst case, and would you be ready to face it?

Answering these questions in a group helps the learner practice co-presencing, seeing the future as it emerges (Scharmer, 2007). Once co-presencing is done, the next important task is to crystallize. This involves putting the ideas from all the stakeholders together into a collage of what you would collectively like to see. Using art and theatre at this stage becomes very helpful to ensure that all aspects are captured, including those difficult to put in a figure, a number, and a chart. The group can come back to reality by analyzing the probable history from the current reality, by putting the group's understanding of the current reality into a collage. Any aspects that stand out are acknowledged in what is a process of identifying creative tension. The best way to do this, according to Scharmer (2007), is to put both images together (as a split screen) and note the main differences between them. Co-crystallizing a range of possibilities is the last exercise to round off this phase of learning. Participants would benefit from hypothesizing together on what might happen and the relevant implications if they could not bridge the gap between vision and current reality.

Selection of scenarios and developing prototypes for testing and eventual scaling up are important. Selecting scenarios is made easy by addressing a number of questions. It is important to identify at least three potential scenarios using a vetting group process on most likely patterns, change processes, and lessons from the past. Scenarios are best built by bringing ideas from the co-sensing phase to develop the worst-case scenario, and from the co-presencing to develop the best-case scenario. Work is best done in a group of diverse stakeholders to refine the three scenarios to accommodate the best- and worst-case scenarios.

Conditions that need to be in place for the group vision to be realized are important and involve identifying the type of mechanisms, level of interaction, types of policies, and types of measures that would allow participants to manage the potential constraints or put in place enablers to success of their vision.

Prototyping is the next stage of learning. A series of questions allow the learner to practice this skill: how can you prioritize to ensure you spend time on outcomes that matter most? What are the prioritized actions and roles, and what is time line by which you would like to achieve your objectives?

What can be ignored or where can failure be tolerated? Answering such questions helps the learner develop trade-offs (cost, speed, attribution) and select a set of approaches to deal with each of the scenarios.

The learner needs a process of triage to identify areas of least priority, least risk, or least buy-in. All of these actions would provide the basis to select a risk measurement approach to assess the risks taken and the residual risks to tolerate.

Sharing experiences with others in similar situations can round off learning. The practice block summarizes key points to aid the self-learner and for future use (Box 5.1).

Box 5.1   Practice Block V: Co-sensing and Co-creating a Superior Risk Management Strategy

Premise: A team of participants, facing a common challenge, would bring different perspectives to the table, allowing them to devise a better set of actions to handle emerging risks.

Objective: To practice the skill of co-sensing the key risks and co-creating strategies and actions that could serve as a prototype for handling the challenge.

Approach: Using the case of beer branding, the construction industry or the infrastructure maintenance policies, co-develop a set of three potential scenarios that could play out and their respective course of action. Discuss the relevance of these strategies and actions with a colleague or a member of another team who has faced similar strategic choices in his or her work. Update the suggested prototype, keeping in mind the work done in the team.

Exercise: The exercise is best done when the learner can benefit from working with a partner. The key issue is to listen to the contributions of a variety of stakeholders and to incorporate them in a co-sensing and co-creating effort to solve the problems. Sharing solutions and challenging initial ideas is good for generating options. Testing the solutions against someone who has faced such problems in their day-to-day work or with a group of colleagues who have done the exercise is useful to hone the skills learned.

6
Leadership and Context

Key Lessons from Chapter 6: Leadership and Context

In this chapter we investigate what approaches are suitable for a particular context, with examples from: (1) the logistics industry; (2) spatial and systemic failure in the financial sector in Iceland; and (3) policy decisions around investment in large-scale complex infrastructure.

A special section is dedicated to the science of muddling through and the potential it has for leadership when very little is known and judgment is at a premium. Learning from failure is also important and a section of this chapter uses examples from multiple sectors to uncover the important elements for learning from failure.

Resilience and how leaders can be comfortable with the concept is an area covered in this chapter, as resilience strategies are also context sensitive.

The chapter ends with a practice block that prepares leaders to embody and prepare for superior performance.

Application to Practice

What particular approaches are suitable for your *specific context*?

Leadership challenges vary with context. Approaches to understanding what is going on, developing appropriate responses, or even shaping a potential future are all context specific.

The aim of the chapter is to support the learner in the holistic use of the concepts of complexity and risk in a variety of contexts. It begins by introducing the contexts of industry, geography, and policy, and presents the main spheres, patterns, drivers and impacts of change in these contexts. Lessons for leadership are drawn from choices that were made in a variety of complex and risky environments.

Application to specific contexts

At the industry level the leadership skills that are of particular relevance for strategy are detecting and assessing tectonic shifts, mapping the evolution of risks affecting decision-making, and anticipating the type of revolutionary outcomes that could materialize from emerging patterns and risks. The logistics industry is an excellent example to bring out interactions between tectonic change, risk, and outcomes.

Examining Iceland and the financial crisis is a good way to take a snapshot of the reality just before the crisis and investigate global linkages through contagion in the financial sector. The sentiments of non-state actors before the crisis are useful to determine what may have been shifting at one level of society, but was not detected at another level. Questions around whether co-sensing could have helped predict the outcomes that emerged are considered. The case also brings out recommendations for learners should they face similar challenges in the future.

Investments in large-scale infrastructure are very relevant for studying the challenges of leadership in changing policy contexts. The concept of complexity is applied to deferred maintenance, a phenomenon rarely considered when leaders take decisions around complex infrastructure. Operational definitions of deferred maintenance help the learner see, through a series of examples, what ignorance of the concept can do in generating risks. Instruments for assessing and controlling deferred maintenance risks and their implications for leadership in other areas are also covered.

Industry context: logistics

The logistics revolution is credited with the major transformations in the speed of globalization in general. Considering the key risks affecting transport logistics is an important activity with lessons of value in other spheres of change.

Patterns of global trade

The decade after 2000 witnessed explosive growth in global trade. Merchandise trade grew in all regions, and a deepened differentiation was visible between service and merchandise trade, particularly among Asian economies. Another important phenomenon was the shift in trade flow patterns between developed and developing countries, with Africa exhibiting important changes. The content of exports and imports between and among low-income economies went through an important transformation. Global trade volumes grew threefold from US$ 6.5 trillion in 2000 to over US$ 18 trillion by 2012 (UN, 2012). Sub-Saharan Africa saw its total imports grow nearly fivefold from US$ 79 billion in 2000 to US$ 370 billion in 2012. Exports in Africa grew fourfold from US$ 93 billion to US$ 418 billion during the same period. The balance of payments in Sub-Saharan Africa remained positive throughout this period and grew from US$ 15 billion in 2000 to US$ 48 billion by 2012.

Trade as a share of GDP grew steadily throughout the 2000s in all regions, up until 2008, when the financial crisis caused a decline. Sub-Saharan Africa was the hardest hit, posting a decline of nearly 15% in trade as a share of

Table 6.1   Trade (% of GDP)

Region	2002	2004	2006	2008	2010
East Asia & Pacific	48	57	64	68	62
Europe & Central Asia	69	70	77	80	78
Latin America & Caribbean	46	49	50	51	47
Middle East & North Africa	67	79	85	96	84
South Asia	32	38	46	51	48
Sub-Saharan Africa	65	64	69	76	65
World	48	51	56	60	56

Source: World Development Indicators, available at http://data.worldbank.org/data-catalog/world-development-indicators.

GDP, from a high of 76% in 2008 to 65% in 2010 (Table 6.1). Trade balances were negative for many regions of the world after 2008, with notable exceptions including the ASEAN region, where positive trade balances were posted of US$50 billion in 2000, dipping only slightly in 2008, and falling but remaining positive at US$33 billion by 2012. Other regions not affected included ECOWAS and CEMAC in Africa, and MERCOSUR in Latin America. Some regions saw big dips in their trade balances, including COMESA (Community of Eastern and Southern African States) in Africa and the EU27.

Europe and Central Asia were the least affected, with declines of 2.5% from a high of 80% in 2008 to 78% in 2010. Trade in services as a share of GDP showed a similar pattern of decline after the financial crisis of 2007 in all regions. However, there was a differentiated response in the observed recovery in three regions—East Asia and the Pacific, Europe and Central Asia, and the Middle East and North Africa—where it rebounded in 2010 from an initial decline in 2008.

Patterns of regional trade: the case of Africa

Regional trade and integration have played an important role in shaping trade patterns, particularly in Africa, where the continent is growing its regional trade and it is hence possible to see changes and relate them to the concepts of complexity. Primarily, the logistics revolution and the rising numbers of the middle class drive the changes in trade patterns in Africa and elsewhere. Resource-rich countries were the first in which the shift was visible, and they continue to present a special case for analysis and learning. South–south trade also shows the impact of tectonic change on the previous pattern of behavior of a system and one can draw implications from those trends.

Africa exports to a growing number of countries due to improved South–South cooperation, which is defined in international relations theory as an exchange of resources, technology, and knowledge between developing countries with the objective of improving economic ties (Wanjiru, 2009).

Such cooperation has also been seen as a way of promoting self-sufficiency and strengthening economic ties among various states (Shaw et al., 2011). The political desire to cooperate has been largely aided by the ability to do so as a result of the logistics revolution, which has brought down the costs of trading across long distances dramatically.

All countries in Africa were importing from other developing countries in 2011, with the vast majority of them importing from two or more countries. The structure of imports into Africa has remained relatively steady over the years, with imports of machinery and transport equipment dominating aggregate import volumes, followed by manufactured goods and chemicals. Imports of consumer goods increased after many countries, including Ghana, stopped import substitution policies and entered into more stable foreign exchange regimes (Harvey and Sedegah, 2011). The improvement in macroeconomic management and the rise in the African middle class were largely responsible for this pattern.

The number of middle class Africans had tripled to 313 million by 2010, representing more than 34% of the continent's population (AfDB, 2011). The figure surged between 2000 and 2010, albeit with a large degree of variation in the geographic pattern of the middle class AfDB, 2011; Ncube and Shimeles, 2012). Tunisia (90%) has the highest, followed by Morocco (85%) and Egypt (80%). Other countries with a large middle class include Gabon, Ghana, Botswana, Namibia, Cape Verde, Kenya, and South Africa. More than 50% of the countries ranked as having a high proportion of middle class population also import from more than one country in the South, indicating the sophistication of the import relationships.

The pattern of imports in 2011 indicates that almost all countries in Africa (92%) were bringing in Chinese imports. India at 33% and South Africa at 25% were also important sources of imports from African countries during this period. The rise of the African middle class was driving consumption levels and import patterns, as by 2010 consumption on the continent stood at a third of that of developing European countries (Table 6.2).

Africa's middle classes, who are driving the patterns of consumption that fuel imports, consist of households with salaried jobs as well as small and medium enterprises that are owned by the middle class (AfDB, 2010). The number of Internet users, which is a proxy for middle class lifestyles, according to AfDB (2010) ballooned from 4.5 million people in 2000 to 80.6 million people in 2008. Large consumers of computer products and services include Nigeria, which has seen an explosion in users of the Internet from just 0.1 per 100 in 2000 to 28.4 per 100 people in 2010); while Egypt, with 26.7 internet users per 100 people in 2010 has seen similar growth since 2000 (World Development Indicators, 2012).

Middle class households in Africa import computers, telephones, flat screen televisions, and cars. Vehicle ownership, which is the quintessential middle class consumption good, has shown similar trends. South Africa went

Table 6.2   South–South import trade in Africa: distribution by number of partners importing from

Partners	Countries	Share (%)
>4	DRC, Djibouti, Eritrea, Gambia, Malawi, Sierra Leone, Somalia	14.6
2–4	Algeria, Angola, Benin, Burkina Faso, Burundi, Cameroon, CAR, Chad, Congo, Côte d'Ivoire, Egypt, Equatorial Guinea, Ethiopia, Gabon, Ghana, Guinea Bissau, Kenya, Libya, Madagascar, Mali, Mauritania, Mauritius, Mozambique, Niger, Rwanda, São Tomé and Príncipe, Senegal, Sudan, Tanzania, Uganda, Zambia, Zimbabwe	66.7
At least one	Cape Verde, Guinea, Lesotho, Liberia, Morocco, Nigeria, South Africa, Togo, Tunisia	18.7
None		0.0

Source: Own analysis using data from ITC International Trade Statistics, available at http://www.intracen.org/itc/market-info-tools/trade-statistics/.

from 135 motor vehicles per 1,000 people in 2004 to 162 in 2009 (World Development Indicators, 2012). The rise of the middle class in Nigeria has emerged along with a tremendous expansion in globalized services in the private sector in the banking and telecommunication sectors, and has been happening mostly in the urban areas, particularly in megacities like Lagos (Statistics South Africa, 2009). Imports from South–South trade can be seen in the displays within the abundance of shopping malls in Nigeria's major cities like Lagos and Abuja (Table 6.3).

The rise of the middle class is attributed to many factors, chief among which are the levels of educational attainment (especially at the tertiary level), investments in infrastructure (which have opened up cities to each other and to the rest of the world), and access to information and communications technologies like the Internet and mobile telephones (AfDB, 2010).

Export patterns between Africa and other countries also provide an interesting perspective. In 2012, countries like Brazil, Russia, India, China, and South Africa (known as the BRICS[1]) were all playing an important role in trade with Africa, as were niche players like Turkey, Thailand, Pakistan, Malaysia, and Indonesia. Almost all countries in Africa were capable of exporting in 2011 to another developing country, with most countries exporting to more than two. Only countries like Ghana and Lesotho were not exporting to a single developing country, with their exports destined for the more advanced economies of the West. Despite these shifts, it is a very small club that was able to export to more than four countries, with most trade relations remaining as select niche exports to one or two countries (Table 6.4).

Table 6.3 South–South trade by country of import

Origin	Import destination	Share (%)
Brazil	Angola, Eritrea, Gambia, Guinea Bissau, Mauritania, Somalia	12.5
India	Angola, Benin, Congo, Djibouti, Eritrea, Ethiopia, Gambia, Kenya, Madagascar, Malawi, Mauritius, Mozambique, Sierra Leone, Sudan, Tanzania, Uganda	33.3
China	Algeria, Angola, Benin, Burundi, Cameroon, Cape Verde, CAR, Chad, DRC, Congo, Côte d'Ivoire, Djibouti, Egypt, Equatorial Guinea, Eritrea, Ethiopia, Gabon, Gambia, Ghana. Guinea, Kenya, Lesotho, Liberia, Libya, Madagascar, Malawi, Mali, Mauritania, Mauritius, Morocco, Mozambique, Niger, Nigeria, Rwanda, Senegal, Somalia, South Africa, Sudan, Tanzania, Togo, Tunisia, Uganda, Zambia, Zimbabwe	91.7
South Africa	Angola, DRC, Eritrea, Kenya, Malawi, Mauritius, Mozambique, Sierra Leone, Tanzania, Uganda, Zambia, Zimbabwe	25.0
Turkey	Libya	2.1
Thailand	Benin, Côte d'Ivoire	4.2
Pakistan	Djibouti, Somalia	4.2
Malaysia	Benin, Djibouti, São Tomé and Príncipe, Sierra Leone	8.3

Source: Own analysis using data from ITC International Trade Statistics, available at http://www.intracen.org/itc/market-info-tools/trade-statistics/.

Table 6.4 South–South export trade in Africa: distribution by number of partners exporting to

Partners	Countries	Share (%)
>4	Benin, Mali, Rwanda, Togo	6.2
2–4	Angola, Burkina Faso, Burundi, CAR, DRC, Congo, Côte d'Ivoire, Djibouti, Egypt, Equatorial Guinea, Eritrea, Ethiopia, Gabon, Gambia, Guinea, Guinea Bissau, Kenya, Liberia, Malawi, Mauritania, Mauritius, Morocco, Mozambique, Niger, Nigeria, Senegal, South Africa, Sudan, Tanzania, Uganda, Zambia, Zimbabwe	66.7
At least one	Algeria, Cameroon, Cape Verde, Chad, Libya, Madagascar, São Tomé and Príncipe, Seychelles. Sierra Leone, Somalia, Tunisia	22.9
None	Ghana, Lesotho	4.2

Source: Own analysis using data from ITC International Trade Statistics, available at http://www.intracen.org/itc/market-info-tools/trade-statistics/.

The important role of China in Africa's trade relations has also been driven by twin phenomena. The first is the tremendous growth rates the country has achieved, and the demand it generates for primary resource inputs (oil, rare minerals) to fuel its economy, many of which are found in Africa. The second is the rising middle class (Kharas and Gertz, 2010) and the consequent increase in the capacity of China to export quality goods to other countries. China is Africa's biggest trading partner, with trade volumes exceeding $166 billion (*Economist*, 2013). The structure of the export trade with China includes minerals, metals, wood, stone, and glass while the imports are mostly machinery and electrical goods, transportation equipment, chemicals, textiles, plastics, and rubber. But China is not the only trader with Africa, as other countries like Brazil, Russia, India, Indonesia, and Turkey are also competitors (Table 6.5).

Indeed, by 2011 China had started to compete with the US as the engine for consumption of imports from developing countries (Kharas and Gertz, 2010). As Kharas and Gertz (2010) say: "by 2015, for the first time in 300 years, the number of Asian middle class consumers will equal the number in Europe and North America." Kharas and Gertz (2010) also suggested that such growth in the middle classes of Asia and Africa "would result in a crossover from West to East in the products, fashions, tastes and designs oriented to the mass middle class."

Table 6.5   South–South trade by country of export

Destination	Export origin	Share (%)
Brazil	Algeria, Equatorial Guinea, Morocco, Nigeria	8.3
Russia	Malawi	2.1
India	Angola, Benin, Congo, DRC, Egypt, Malawi, Morocco, Nigeria, Senegal, South Africa, Sudan, Tanzania, Togo	27.1
China	Angola, Benin, Burkina Faso, Burundi, Cameroon, CAR, Chad, Congo, DRC, Equatorial Guinea, Eritrea, Ethiopia, Madagascar, Mali, Mauritania, Mozambique, Rwanda, South Africa, Sudan, Tanzania, Togo, Zambia, Zimbabwe	47.9
South Africa	Malawi, Mauritius, Mozambique, Zambia, Zimbabwe	10.4
Turkey	Burkina Faso	2.1
Indonesia	Benin, Burkina Faso, DRC, Mali	8.3
Thailand	Burkina Faso, Mali, São Tomé and Príncipe, Seychelles	8.3
Pakistan	Burundi, Rwanda	4.2

Source: Own analysis using data from ITC International Trade Statistics, available at http://www.intracen.org/itc/market-info-tools/trade-statistics/.

Table 6.6   Resource exports from select countries in Africa in 2009

Country	Main exports
Burundi	Coffee, tea, sugar, cotton, hides
Central African Republic	Diamonds, tobacco, coffee, timber, cotton
Democratic Republic of Congo	Diamonds, copper, coffee, cobalt, oil
Republic of Congo	Oil, timber, plywood, sugar, cocoa, coffee, diamonds
Rwanda	Coffee, tea, hides, iron ore
Uganda	Coffee, fish and fish products, tea, tobacco, cotton, corn, beans, sesame

Source: Own analysis using data from ITC International Trade Statistics, available at http://www.intracen.org/itc/market-info-tools/trade-statistics/.

The patterns are different when considering imports. Several Asian countries trade with Africa, including China (47.9%), India (27.1%), Indonesia and Thailand (both at 8.3%), and Pakistan (4.2%). Further growth of the middle classes in Africa and Asia could enhance these patterns of trade, or they may shift as consumers seek products in other regions of the world. The exports of luxury goods are useful in explaining some of the potential shifts (Table 6.6).

A few products, mostly from countries rich in natural resources, dominate the growing export trade relationships between Africa and other developing countries. The Great Lakes region is illustrative, with countries like the Republic of Congo exporting oil, while diamonds and other minerals are exported from the Central African Republic and the Democratic Republic of Congo. There is also a growing pattern of non-mineral and oil exports. This includes commodities like coffee and tea from Burundi, Rwanda, and Uganda, but also food products and even fresh food produce.

Textile exports have been important, as have been exports of fresh food, to meet the increasing demands from the growing middle class in Africa and elsewhere. Many of the early textile industries relied on cotton, and the recent advance in preferences for organic and natural products has fueled a revival in the demand for cotton products. Five countries in Africa ranked in the top 20 exporting countries by value in US$ of cotton lint: Egypt (12); Nigeria (13); Burkina Faso (14); Benin (19); and Mozambique (20), according to FAOSTAT (2010). Egypt faces a high demand for its cotton products all over the world. There is also growing trade in textiles from Egypt to the rest of Africa as a result of its membership of COMESA.

Food is another export product undergoing important changes due to the rising middle classes and shifts in consumer preferences. Advances in cold-chain logistics and investments made by countries to improve their infrastructure and reduce inside-the-border constraints have all supported

Table 6.7 Cameroon: gaining leadership in fresh food exports and establishing a role in food processing

Rank	2006	2007	2008	2009	2010
Fresh foods	131	152	144	55	50
Processed foods	149	130	54	19	20

Source: Own analysis using data from ITC International Trade Statistics, available at http://www.intracen.org/itc/market-info-tools/trade-statistics/.

transformation. Cameroon has taken advantage of new possibilities as its business sector has invested in exports in fresh and processed food markets in Africa, Europe, and other parts of the world. Cameroon jumped in 2006 from a rank of 131 out of 184 countries exporting fresh foods to rank 50th in growth per year of fresh food exports (valued in US$) by 2010 (Table 6.7).

The shift in rank resulted from the ability to export fresh foods, benefiting from cold-chain logistics and improved transport links with the rest of the world. The country was also able to grow the level of sophistication in its economy by entering the processed food market as a result of growing its manufacturing capability. Advances in the techniques for processing, warehousing, and transport, which are at the heart of the logistical revolution, are largely responsible for this transformation. Cameroon jumped from 139 out of 162 countries exporting processed food in 2006 as measured by the value of exports in US$ to rank 20th in 2010 (ITC, 2011).

Cameroon is not the only country that was able to raise its sophistication level in the agricultural sector by exporting processed food or to benefit from improved cold-chain logistics to grow exports of fresh food. Other countries, like Ethiopia, have done tremendously well in raising their global ranking in exports of fresh food, while Malawi has done well in exports of processed foods. Burkina Faso, Rwanda, and Senegal reversed declines in fresh food exports between the period 2008 and 2010, but countries like Djibouti and Liberia lost their ability to do so. Ethiopia managed systematic high growth rates in processed food exports, improving its ranking from 146 in 2006 to 63 in 2010. Burkina Faso, Malawi, and Senegal all recovered their growth rates of processed food exports (Figure 6.1).

Sophistication in agriculture has stagnated over the years, as can be seen in the pattern of use of agricultural machinery (tractors) between 1965 and 2005. The pattern looks like a gaggle of "geese taking off" and has not yet formed the pattern of "flying geese" that is typically expected (Akamatsu, 1961) in developing country environments.[2] By 2012, countries in Africa had not advanced much in transforming the agricultural sector, and the examples of Cameroon, Ethiopia, and Malawi remain bottlenecked by the lack of infrastructure and risky supply chains.

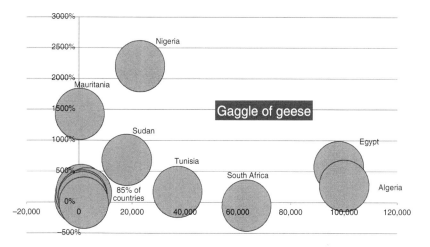

Figure 6.1 Sophistication in the agriculture sector: changes in use of agricultural machinery, tractors 1965–2005
Source: Constructed using data from ADI, World Bank, available at http://data.worldbank.org/data-catalog/world-development-indicators.

Lin (2012) revived the idea of "flying geese" by suggesting that African economies can benefit from the phenomenon by using it as a model to build on comparative advantages to encourage investments in the manufacturing sector and agriculture. Some countries have gone down the path of exploiting their comparative advantages in agriculture, and are leading the transformation. They include Egypt, Algeria, South Africa, Tunisia, Nigeria, and Sudan, visible in their position in the "gaggle of geese." Sophistication in the agriculture sector comes from the improvements in the supply chain made in these countries, including agro-processing that allows them to benefit from the logistics revolution to export more. With better infrastructure and more advanced logistics, the food supply chain from Africa can be greatly enhanced, transforming the gaggle of geese into a skein (Figure 6.2).

The level of sophistication achieved by African countries in the manufacturing sector resembles more the pattern of "flying geese" than a "gaggle of geese" in the case of agriculture. This is not surprising, as manufactured products are less sensitive to failures in infrastructure and other components of logistics. Leading the transformation in manufacturing are countries like Morocco and Tunisia, which have growing manufacturing sectors, followed by countries including Ghana, Lesotho, Kenya, and Madagascar. The ability of Tunisia and Morocco to keep flapping their wings until the next level catches up could prove complicated, as the regional markets that are one of the "wings" that could support a faster speed of convergence of the other countries are not as developed around their neighbors.

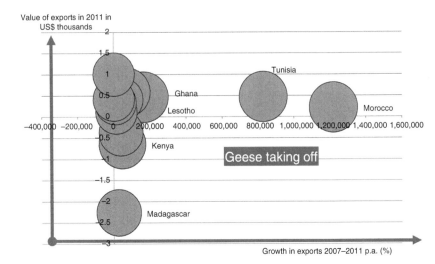

Figure 6.2 Sophistication in the manufacturing sector: value of exports of women's apparel in Africa 2007–2011
Source: Data on value of exports of women's apparel in Africa in Figure 16 come from the African Development Indicators which are a subset of the World Development Indicators and can be found at http://data.worldbank.org/data-catalog/world-development-indicators.

South–South trade and Africa's contribution to an increasingly interconnected world would rely on improved trade within and outside borders. Such improvements are achieved by mitigating geographic characteristics like small country size; insufficient proximity to other countries; few common borders; and being land-locked. Rethinking trade policies in place also helps at the domestic level and is aided by better connectivity through transport and communication investments. More competition across countries in Africa and improved market infrastructure could also help. More favorable international trading agreements with other countries and lower barriers and tariffs are also areas needing attention. At the country level, political leaders and policymakers need policies that adjust for income levels. Such policies include those that would grow the middle class. At the regional level, leaders could come together to ensure policies that encourage richer countries to interact more with other countries through regional trade. Other factors for consideration are import and export policy reforms to remove any other bottlenecks remaining and improving the functioning of the labor markets.

The needs and tastes of new consumers in Asia and Africa could not be met had there not been a logistics revolution to support it. The logistics revolution, and in particular the advancements in cold-chain logistics, has been at the heart of the transformation in trade patterns in Africa and other regions of the world.

The logistics revolution

Recent years have witnessed a tremendous transformation in the logistics industry, commonly referred to as the "logistics revolution." Transportation is largely responsible for this revolution, even though it has been subsumed by other concerns, including the challenges of managing supply chains Allen (1997). Following the logistics revolution, leaders need a good grasp of the approaches to minimize costs and maximize profits. However, leaders are more and more reliant on a qualitative area of logistics, which emphasizes the need to be aware of the entire logistics chain (Allen, 1997).

The logistics revolution is also due to advances in ownership and financing arrangements around the provision of infrastructure and logistics services around the world. The emergence of new approaches for supply chain management is also credited as a driver of the revolution, as are sophisticated event, project, and risk management systems.

The tremendous improvement in access to local land systems is among the achievements in transport infrastructure leading the logistics transformation. The size of the world's highway network and quality of the transport network measured by the share of roads that are paved and hence usable all year round has reduced the constraints in local haul. Such constraints included the ability to use a road only during dry weather, or not having vehicle access to a market, limiting the volume and type of products that can be brought to market. This improvement in access to local land systems is best seen through the growth in railway goods transported between 2002 and 2008, and the effects of the financial crisis on transport in 2009 and 2010 (Figure 6.3).

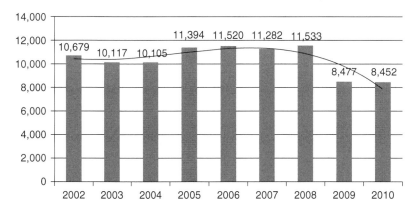

Figure 6.3   Railway goods transported in million ton-km (World Development Indicators)

Table 6.8   Road density (km of road per 100 km² of land area)

Region	2004	2008
OECD members	52	43
Low & middle income	21	21
World	31	30

Source: World Development Indicators, available at http://data.worldbank.org/data-catalog/ world-development-indicators.

Expanding local highway networks requires complex reconciliation between the demands of international trade and domestic interests; a wide range of stakeholders have different interests that cannot always be reconciled. Consider that road density, as measured in kilometers per square kilometer of land area, has declined from 52 in 2004 to 43 in 2008 in OECD countries. The road density has not increased in low and middle-income countries either during the same time period (Table 6.8).

Firms have taken advantage of these reductions and expanded the production frontier accordingly. Growth in individual mobility is another phenomenon with broad implications. The number of vehicles per 1,000 people has grown worldwide. Individual preferences have shifted to favor different modes of transport, each time increasing the demand for motor ownership. Shifts are visible in the increased use of two wheelers commensurate with an increase in vehicle ownership. Such patterns have implications for "Do it yourself" solutions, which are also on the rise in view of higher levels of education that allow individuals to self-provide goods (from prefabricated housing to home assembly of furniture and other such products), further increasing the demand for transport and the use of transport networks. The re-emergence of rail as a clean and reliable service provider has also transformed the logistics arena. The trends where railway lines were being ripped up to make way for other forms of development started to be reversed as early as 2002.

Consider Veolia, a company rooted in trucking and rail, which saw the re-emergence of rail as an opportunity to integrate the supply chains in their business. Their merger with CMA CGM was cleared by the European Union on November 10, 2006 (Europe Intelligence Wire, 2006a). CMA CGM was the third leading container shipping group in the world. Veolia Environnement was the world leader in environmental services. The merger between them was to develop a new rail transportation service for sea containers. The approved merger created two separate companies. The first company was a combined transportation operator (51% controlled by Rail Link and 49% by Veolia Transport) created to organize and market the transportation of sea containers between port terminals and the end customers' industrial sites. The second was a rail company (51% controlled by Veolia Transport and

49% by Rail Link) with all the necessary physical equipment and resources for the actual transportation by rail of the containers. The new company was to serve the heavy business volume corridor to Germany through the port of Marseille. It was such a big player in this transport corridor that it bought its own locomotives to serve the market. Revenues expected from the merger were high, at around €100 million by 2010 for the transportation service operator and €50 million for the rail company.

The merger was deliberately designed to take advantage of the renewed interest in rail while still keeping activity in the trucking business going. The dual strategy was fortuitous, as in less than three years the companies were able to triple their rail-based business; however, they did not succeed in increasing their financial performance (Econostrum.info, 2009).

The companies broke up in 2009 and went back to their primary businesses before the merger. Veolia retreated from rail. CMA CGM remained in rail, with Jacques Saadé, the CEO at the time stating that "rail constitutes the only mode for the future transport of freight over large distances and we will make great efforts to remain in this domain" (Econostrum.info, 2009). The Rail Link Europe Company that CMA CGM continued to operate consolidated its business after the break-up in 2009 on the Le Havre and Marseille-Fos corridor and stopped serving other ports like Zeebrugge. CMA CGM remains one of the major global maritime transport groups to exploit the entire logistics supply chain for a door-to-door service for their clients, offering integrated services of rail, road, and water-based transport.

Patterns of business mergers such as CMA CGM, as well as the increased interest in rail in advanced and developing economies alike, also had an impact on the export and import of railway vehicles. Increased demand for rail services gave countries like Germany, the US, and Japan export markets in new areas.

Evolution in the use of air transport systems has aided the easy transport of perishable goods and has given a wide range of countries options to join the globalized world. The massive growth in air travel in India is one example that has been driven by the rise in the middle class in that country. By 2007, India had more than 20 international airports and more than 12 new entrants in the airline market compared to 2004. This resulted in a large increase in fleet size. Kingfisher Airline became the first Indian carrier to order the Airbus A380 (US$ 3 billion). IndiGo Airlines ordered 100 Airbus A320 (US$ 6 billion) in 2011, while Indian Airlines placed orders for 43 jets from Airbus (US$ 2.5 billion), and Air India placed one for more than 68 jets from Boeing (US$ 7.5 billion) (Sourced from Wikipedia: Transport in India, September 21, 2007).

African countries have had a harder time building a safe aviation industry. Ghana, which had about the same level of development as Korea in the early 1960s, lagged behind in air transport passengers carried, despite the tremendous growth in such travel globally. Such gaps present an

Table 6.9   Top ten exporters and importers of aircraft and associated equipment, spacecraft, space launch vehicles (US$ millions)

Value of exports			Value of imports		
Country	2001	2012	Country	2001	2012
USA	44,688	4,092	Germany	13,979	10,392
France	17,209	47,278	USA	21,180	16,430
Germany	17,174	33,868	France	6,172	14,890
Canada	8,554	6,562	China	4,542	1,771
Italy	2,751	2,163	Canada	5,046	370
Brazil	3,553	4,759	India	260	1,435
Spain	1,342	1,498	Japan	1,970	866
Singapore	850	209	Singapore	3,805	86
Japan	1,729	8	Spain	1,805	5,491
Netherlands	599	1,569	Italy	3,404	975

Source: Own analysis using data from ITC International Trade Statistics, available at http://www.intracen.org/itc/market-info-tools/trade-statistics/.

opportunity for regional solutions. African Heads of State decided to open up space for regional players to come and serve the ECOWAS Region on January 10, 2004 (ASKY, 2012) (Table 6.9).

By September 2005, a regional company known as La Societé de Promotion d'une Compagnie Aérienne Régionale (SPCAR) was created to study the options and analyze the feasibility of bringing operating and financing partners to the table. The SPCAR brought the successful creation of ASKY—an airline serving the sub-region and founded in June 2008 by Ethiopian Airlines, which had a 40% stake (Wikipedia, 2012). By 2012, ASKY was operating 154 flights to 19 destinations in 17 countries, serving the cities of Lomé (where it is headquartered), as well as Abuja, Accra, Bamako, Conakry, Cotonou, Freetown, Lagos, Libreville, Malabo, Monrovia, Ndjamena, Niamey, and Ouagadougou (ASKY, 2012) (Table 6.10).

Scaling-up of maritime transport is also a phenomenon driven by the logistics revolutions. Komadina et al. (2006) show that the maritime sector advanced dramatically—90% of merchandise was being transported by sea and there was a massive increase in the size of vessels. Mergers and acquisitions were on the increase, seeking both vertical and horizontal integration in the supply chain supporting maritime logistics. Port concentration also started to take place (Komadina et al., 2006) with the re-emergence of old ports and the creation of megaports like Singapore. Mergers further raised the demand for feeder networks to big corridors like the Le Havre to Marseille-Fos corridor, as the supply chain complexity of the shipping industry grew with each merger. All these shifts are visible in the patterns of trade related to maritime equipment.

Table 6.10 Top ten exporters and importers of containerized cargo (US$ millions)

Value of exports			Value of imports		
Country	2009	2010	Country	2009	2010
China	26.1	31.3	USA	15.0	17.6
USA	10.2	11.2	China	11.2	12.0
Japan	4.8	5.7	Japan	5.4	6.1
South Korea	4.5	5.2	South Korea	3.9	4.5
Taiwan, China	2.9	3.4	Germany	2.4	2.8
Thailand	3.0	3.4	Other Arabian Gulf	2.3	2.7
Germany	2.6	3.0	UK	2.3	2.5
Indonesia	2.7	3.0	Indonesia	2.1	2.5
Malaysia	2.2	2.5	Taiwan, China	2.2	2.5
Brazil	2.3	2.3	Hong Kong, China	2.3	2.5

Source: World Shipping Council.

Transport of manufactured components for aircraft assembly as well as growth in advanced demands for logistics solutions has shaped the demand for sophisticated transport carriers. Such patterns can be seen in the high growth between 1963 and 2000 of the share of machinery and transport equipment as a percentage of value added in manufacturing. Transport equipment demands have grown—for cranes, conveyors, and industrial trucks. Also grown is demand for commercial trucks with self-loading and unloading capabilities, recreational vehicles with more complex functions, and public transport that serves many differentiated needs—for the elderly, the disabled, and bicycle transport. These developments have closed the gap between transport equipment technology and public use transport vehicles, all contributing to the boom in the manufacturing sector.

Increased sophistication in the freight business has fueled changes. Exports of motor vehicles for transport of goods and special purposes motor vehicles in the EU Zone grew in value from US$ 24 billion in 2001 to over US$ 37 billion by 2005 (ITC, UNCTAD/WTO). Such high growth rates were particularly striking in Asia. China went from US$ 108 million of exports in 2001 to more than US$ 804 million in 2005, while Korea went from US$ 690 million to over US$ 1.5 billion. Japan added more than US$ 2 billion in value of exports between 2001 and 2005, from a value of more than US$ 5 billion to close to US$ 8 billion.

The patterns of import of motor vehicles for transport of goods and special-purpose motor vehicles show different patterns altogether. China, Korea, and Japan, which participated in the export value boom in such freight-related inputs, saw only modest growth in the imports of the same. Such patterns emphasize the varied geographical nature of the effect of tectonic changes like the explosion in demand for sophisticated logistics solutions.

Transport efficiency grew from increased sophistication in the freight service business, but it was also fueled by advances in ownership and financing arrangements. Transport companies took on investment in other areas by transferring capital outside their homes of origin and engaging in M&A activity in transport and logistics.

Lessons on leadership from the logistical revolution

While illustrations have focused on what aspects of the logistical revolution offer lessons for leadership at the firm level, one can also draw lessons for individual leaders. Take the idea of "flying geese" advanced earlier and how policymakers can decide where in the sequence of a flying geese pattern a country wants to be and what it takes to be there. Akamatsu (1961) provided the paradigm for countries to think about choices to keep pushing ahead and battling to stay on top. Policymakers and country leaders can learn from this paradigm to make their strategic choices on what costs in the logistics chain to tackle to position themselves appropriately in the sequencing of players in a given sector, based on their comparative advantages.

At the individual leadership level one can learn from Jack Welch, the CEO of General Electric (GE) between 1981 and 2001 (Welch and Welch, 2009). Mr Welch's father played a role in logistics, having been a conductor with the Boston & Maine Railroad. His son Jack Welch was known for implementing his strategic choices, which are now embedded in business folklore, including in the class he teaches at the MIT Sloan School of Management to a handpicked group of 30 MBA students who have demonstrated interest in leadership (Mitsloan.mit.edu, 2006). His quotes over the years indicate how as a personal leader he referenced the field of logistics, using it in explaining his core strategy to add value to the company he managed. He said in New York in 1981, that GE "will be the locomotive pulling the GNP, not the caboose following it." Many company leaders followed Welch's strategy without paying attention to the meaning of the logistical revolution for their unique businesses. Mergers and acquisition strategies were devised as ways to generate shareholder value in the short run. Mr Welch clarified his perspective in an interview with the *Financial Times* on the Global Financial crisis of 2008–2009, he said of shareholder value: "On the face of it, shareholder value is the dumbest idea in the world. Shareholder value is a result, not a strategy ... your main constituencies are your employees, your customers, and your products." (Guerrera, 2009).

Rapid transformation in logistics also prompted research on logistics and its dependence on large-scale infrastructure (Munnell and Cook, 1990). Others investigated the multiple aspects of interdependency (Pederson et al., 2006). Politicians, however, preferred the simpler world that existed prior, as demonstrated by the famous quote of Margaret Thatcher: "You and I come by road or rail, but economists travel on infrastructure."

Many leaders were caught unaware by these tectonic shifts and did not react to them until they were well on their way. The break-up of the CGM CMA Veolia merger happened only after losses were visible. A leadership lesson in this regard comes from Confucius: "Only after winter comes do we know that the pine and the cypress are the last to fade" (Confucius, *The Analects*, Chapter VII).

Geographical context: the financial crisis and Iceland[3]

The financial sector presents a good opportunity to examine leadership in a globalized world. Finance is possibly one of the most global sectors of the world economy (Foundation, 2011; Gilpin, 2003). It is also widely blamed for recessions and decreases in employment levels. The financial sector is further held responsible for its contribution to global crises such as the one triggered in 2007, lasting into 2012 and beyond, which has been dubbed the longest global financial crisis since the Great Depression (ILO, 2011) (Figure 6.4).

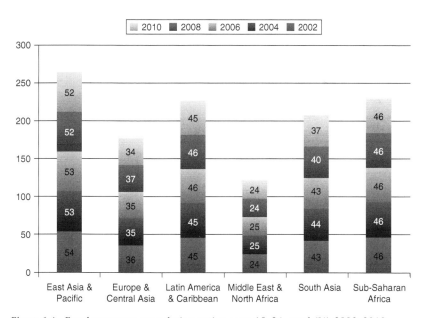

Figure 6.4 Employment to population ratios, ages 15–24, total (%) 2002–2010
Source: Constructed using data from the World Bank Development Indicators, available at http://data.worldbank.org/data-catalog/world-development-indicators.

Iceland is a good country to explore complexity and change; it has been subject to two major tectonic shifts and their related risks—climate change and the financial sector collapse of 2008. Examination of the global context of Iceland's problem is useful to appreciate the tectonic forces, complexity, risk, and the global leadership and governance structures of the solutions tried and proposed.

The case draws on the situation of the 2008 Icelandic commercial bank collapse, and provides background on the Icelandic economy and its institutions, highlighting its monetary policy, loan restructuring, and new institutional design post-2008. Selected strategies to address the financial sector include close monitoring and transparency of monetary policy changes in the short term, as well as capital account liberalization in the long term that targets market diversification, so that foreign direct investment is channeled into green energy and climate change solution technologies.

Iceland and the global financial crisis

The financial crisis of 2007–2009 is described in the literature as a systemic failure of the global financial sector (OECD, 2009a). Aglietta (2000) had anticipated the implications of a globalized financial crisis, which came to bear in 2007. Others have signaled the crisis as a failure of regulation and leadership (Davies, 2010; Vogel, 2010).

Evidence shows that the financial crisis has greatly reduced employment levels, leaving people in many parts of the world deprived of a job (ILO, 2011; OECD, 2009b). The 2007–2009 crisis affected the developed and developing world profoundly (ODI, 2010). Developed economies suffered significant sustained reductions in growth (Davies, 2010; Vogel, 2010). Reductions in GDP per capita were also accompanied by reductions in the amount of capital available for investment in new areas and businesses.

However, some regions of the world have been harder hit, as seen by the lowered prospects for jobs and low employment to population ratios (the proportion of a country or region's population that is employed). The youth population has been hit the hardest. The International Labour Organization (ILO) and the World Bank generally consider ages 15–24 the youth population. This ratio declined in Europe and Central Asia, from 37 in 2008 to 34 in 2010, and the Middle East and North Africa, where it remained flat at 24 in 2008 and 2010. Regions like East Asia and the Pacific and Sub-Saharan Africa seem to have been spared the massive inability to generate jobs.

Iceland's 2008 financial collapse

Iceland was hit hard by the global financial crisis of 2007 to 2009. In 2011, Iceland was still recovering from the collapse of its commercial banks in 2008 and the European and global financial markets in the aftermath of the 2008 sub-prime mortgage crisis. The country was also dealing with the ongoing European sovereign debt crisis within the monetary union of the

EU. Iceland's experience with the crisis has been unlike other countries, as its position was almost unique in that virtually the entire banking system collapsed (Sighvatsson and Daníelsson (2011)). Iceland's three largest commercial banks, Landsbanki, Glitnir, and Kaupthing, collapsed in the fall of 2008, at which point they were nationalized and renamed. By 2011 they made up 90% of all commercial assets held by banks in Iceland (Sighvatsson and Daníelsson (2011)). These banks operated in 2011 almost exclusively within the domestic market and were significantly smaller in size than their predecessors (Sighvatsson and Daníelsson (2011)).

While the banks had decreased in size, their operating expenses had remained consistent at pre-crisis levels (Sighvatsson and Daníelsson (2011)). The Central Bank of Iceland (CBI or the Bank) projected in 2011 that once Landsbanki, one of the three big commercial banks in Iceland, reached settlements with its creditors, including those represented by the Depositors' and Investors' Guarantee Fund (DIGF) and the UK and Dutch governments, there would be little left of the bank (Sighvatsson and Daníelsson (2011), 4). Some bankers who were critically involved in the collapse, such as the former head of Kaupthing Iceland, Ingolfur Helgason, were arrested (Freedom House, 2011).

Iceland: select sentiments of non-state actors credit

The Iceland Nature Conservation Society quoted a famous musician from Iceland on Tuesday, October 28, 2008 in an article headlined "After financial meltdown, now smeltdown." The quote said: "Now we have three aluminum smelters, which are the biggest in Europe; and in the space of the next three years they want to build two more. The smelters would need energy from a handful of new geothermal power plants and the building of dams that would damage pristine wilderness, hot springs and lava fields. To take this much energy from geothermal fields is not sustainable." (Björk)

Non-state actors were quite worried about what was going on in the country, as evidenced by another quote a few years before the crisis headlined "Melting Iceland—Iceland Review" which appeared in the Iceland Nature Conservation Society, Wednesday, April 13, 2005. The quote by Bart Cameron was: "What would you do when your country is located in the world's biggest environmental trouble zone and nations far larger than your own are threatening to destroy your climate and your way of life? During the period 1995 to 2005 the glaciers lost 1m per year evenly distributed over their entire area. Shrinking at this rapid rate they would disappear in 300 years." (Table 6.11)

These two quotes indicate that, before the financial crisis in 2008, the main concerns of civil society in Iceland had to do with the environment. Such sentiment is important to track also, because non-governmental organizations have a high representation in Iceland and their opinion carries a lot of weight in the approach taken to respond to crises. Societal sentiment does have importance in shaping policy decisions in Iceland, as can

Table 6.11　Iceland's major NGOs

ABC Children's Aid
Amnesty International Island
Arctic Council
Environmental and Health Authority of South Iceland
European Kyudo Federation (EKF)
Icelandic Church Aid
Icelandic Environment Association (Landvern) an umbrella organization of 60 Icelandic NGOs
Icelandic International Development Agency (ICEIDA)
Icelandic Mission Society
Icelandic National Committee for UNICEF
Icelandic Youth Council

Source: WANGO available at http://www.wango.org and is supported by data gathered from other Internet searches on Iceland.

be seen in the impact of the strong NGO culture on trade patterns. Net trade in tobacco and plastics was negative in 2007, just before the crisis, while it was positive for natural resources, art and handicraft, and animal products (ITC, 2007).

Iceland's credit ratings and recovery loan packages

The Iceland State Banking Agency (ISBA) was the owner of three banks and was set to disband in the fall of 2014, at which time the restructuring process—including recapitalization and debt repayment schedules—was expected to be completed (CBI, 2009). In a May 2011 report, Standard & Poors noted that it "lowered [their] local currency sovereign credit rating on the Republic of Iceland to 'BBB–' from 'BBB' and affirmed [their] foreign currency ratings at 'BBB–/A–s'" (Standard & Poors, 2011). Standard & Poors also lowered the long-term corporate credit rating on "Icelandic Utility Landsvirkjun to 'BB' from 'BB+'" (Standard & Poors, 2011). The Icelandic Government had partnered with the International Monetary Fund (IMF), receiving its first loan package in 2008 (CBI, 2011). Foreign treasury bonds amounting to €300 million matured in September 2011 and a loan worth €1 billion matured in December 2011 (CBI, 2009). The plan to restructure loans included repayment schedules that were spread out as evenly as possible (CBI, 2009).

Central Bank of Iceland: monetary policy goals and debt position

The Central Bank of Iceland (CBI) is the primary economic institution in Iceland. It uses a "macro-prudential approach" to Icelandic monetary policy (CBI, 2011). Its main policy objective in 2011 was price stability (CBI, 2009). This was achieved by stabilizing the foreign exchange market to ensure a stable exchange rate, which in turn was expected to lead to stable price levels. Stable price levels contain inflation, which thus protects indebted Icelandic households and businesses from having the króna devalue, as such devaluation would increase the cost of borrowing and debt repayment. The financial crisis has led to a great increase in public sector debt. According to a February 2011 Bank publication, in the aftermath of the crisis the "direct and indirect transfer" of private debt to the public sector debt equals approximately 60% of Gross Domestic Product (GDP) (Sighvatsson and Daníelsson (2011), 6). The Bank projected that once the Icelandic economy transitioned to post-crisis stability the public sector debt would be significantly higher (Sighvatsson and Daníelsson (2011), 6). This, however, is not an economic position unknown to Iceland, as it has long been among the most indebted of the world's developed countries (Sighvatsson and Daníelsson (2011)).

The Bank followed strict monetary policy and instituted restrictions on capital flows after the financial collapse of 2008 in order to prevent massive capital outflow (CBI, 2009; 2011). Capital account restrictions limited Icelandic access to foreign credit markets, significantly decreasing the "connection" between foreign and domestic markets in Iceland (CBI, 2011). For example, capital inflow as a percentage of GDP lowered from 33.7% in 2007 to 23.4% in 2011, particularly slumping in 2009 to 0.5% (World Bank, 2011). In 2011, there were very few companies active in Iceland's equity market, making it "extremely weak" (CBI, 2011: 9). For example, only six companies made up the OMX ICE Main List in the year 2011(CBI, 2011: 9).

The CBI planned to eventually liberalize Icelandic markets and reduce capital controls. Generating a surplus of public sector revenues, and increasing Iceland's holdings of foreign exchange reserves were the "first steps" to liberalization (CBI, 2011: 3).

Iceland's loan restructuring

The CBI had been in a phase of restructuring Icelandic banking and debt instruments since early 2009. Restructuring is made difficult due to: i) loss of confidence in the currency, ii) changing regulatory environment due to constant policy changes, iii) contested legality of loan agreements; and iv) lack of knowledge within financial institutions about debt repayment schedules (CBI, 2011: 17). This uncertain economic environment meant that borrowing remained risky and the quality of debt remained poor (CBI, 2011: 5). In 2011 many loans were non-performing as there continued to be delays in the debt restructuring process and many people stopped making interest payments because of the disputed legality of their loans (CBI, 2011: 3; Sighvatsson and Daníelsson (2011)). Less than half of the loans made by Icelandic commercial banks in fiscal year 2011were to service companies, and approximately one fourth of the loans made were to fisheries (CBI, 2011: 16).

Iceland's economic growth, unemployment and interest rates

Economic growth slowed in the aftermath of the financial crisis of 2008. The annual percentage growth of GDP was negative between 2008 and 2011. The economic decline slowed down from –6.9% in 2009 to –3.5% in 2010, yet remained weak by the close of 2011 (World Bank, 2011). There were considerable job losses in Iceland leading to increasing unemployment as a share of the total labor force. This peaked at 7.2% in 2010, the highest unemployment level Iceland that had experienced in 20 years (World Bank, 2011). The government responded to the high levels of unemployment by passing, in June 2010, the Act on Unemployment, which extended unemployment benefits for those who lost their jobs in 2008 until June 2011 (CBI, 2011: 67). During the period of decreased economic output, job loss and growing debt, gross domestic savings as a share of income increased from 17.4% in 2006 to 22.6% in 2009, while Treasury expenditures similarly increased in 2011 due to unemployment and pension benefits, mortgage interest allowances, and agricultural subsidies (CBI, 2011: 74). Short- and long-term interest rates were lowered after the 2008 crisis, despite the Bank's commitment to tight monetary policy (CBI, 2011: 74). The real interest rate level in 2010 was 3.4%, reduced from 9.9% in 2009 and a decade high of 12.9% in 2007 (World Bank, 2011).

Icelandic trade: the service sector, manufacturing and fuel

The service sector remained a strong part of the economy during and after the financial crisis. Before the crisis, the share of trade in services as part of GDP had been steadily increasing over the decade, and was at an all-time high of 37.3% in 2011 (60). The percent of ores and minerals as part of Iceland's merchandise exports peaked in 2008 at 39.9% but decreased to 35% in 2009 (World Bank, 2010).

Manufactured exports as a share of merchandise exports had decreased from 26.7% in 2007 to a steady rate of 19% in 2008 and 2009 (World Bank, 2010). High-technology exports in current US$ have steadily decreased since 2007. In 2007 Iceland exported over US$ 700 million worth of high technology goods, whereas in 2009 this figure had fallen to US$ 224 million. Fuel exports as share of merchandise exports fell to 0.99% in 2009, from 1.5% in 2007. Fuel imports, however, as a share of merchandise imports increased from 8.9% in 2007 to 12.5% in 2009. In December 2009 a Natural Resource Tax was passed, which created an environmental and natural resource tax on fossil fuels, electricity, and hot water, as well as a resource and development resolution, where innovative companies were eligible for a 15% tax break on the research and development costs that make up their operational budgets (CBI, 2011: 75–76).

Iceland's institutions and the financial crisis

Iceland has excellent institutions and is a peaceful country that before the crisis was very connected to the outside world. The Icelandic plan of action to respond to the 2008 collapse of the Icelandic commercial banks involved the institutionalization of financial regulation and prudent fiscal and monetary policy. The CBI's plan to meet its goal of sustained price level and exchange rate stability was created by Icelandic authorities and the International Monetary Fund (IMF). Iceland had a history of excellent institution building; however, in 2011, political and economic institutions remained relatively weak. This weakness was attributed to the financial crisis and the 2009 dissolution of the Independence Party and Social Democratic Alliance coalition government (CBI, 2011: 75–76).

The new Icelandic government, under the leadership of Jóhanna Sigurðardóttir—Iceland's first female Prime Minister and the world's first openly homosexual head of state—established a Parliamentary Special Investigative Commission to report on the 2008 collapse of the commercial banks (Freedom House, 2011). Politicians, including the former Prime Minister, Geir Haarde, were implicated in the crisis (Freedom House, 2011). The government remained a key institution, mediating the deposit insurance agreements with the UK and Dutch governments, after the 2011 referendum when Icelanders rejected the proposed agreement by the British and Dutch (CBI, 2011: 3). The government sought to increase its revenue with fiscal policy. In June 2009, the Parliament passed an act that enforced a variety of fiscal measures, one of which was increased taxes (CBI, 2011: 69). The government made a commitment to support investment in Icelandic business, passing the New Investment in Iceland Act, which is "aimed at promoting investment in business in Iceland" (CBI, 2011: 64).

Iceland's institutions: new government institutions to respond to the financial crisis

The Icelandic government created many new institutions to respond to the 2008 financial crisis, including the Monetary Policy Committee (MPC), created in February 2009 to evaluate and reform Bank policy (CBI, 2009: 5). This body was to evaluate and ensure exchange rate stability in domestic markets (CBI, 2009: 5). A new institution, the Iceland State Banking Agency (ISBA), was established after the crisis to administer the Treasury's ownership of the banks (CBI, 2009: 5).

The Bank also worked in collaboration with the Icelandic Financial Supervisory Authority and the Capital Controls Surveillance Unit (CCSU) to monitor capital account restrictions and with the Icelandic Securities Depository (ISD) as regards security transaction settlements (CBI, 2009: 11, 25). The Central Bank of Iceland Holding Company (ESI) was also created after the crisis and all the assets under dispute from the collapse were transferred to ESI (CBI, 2009: 3). The CBI also has the mandate to "promote the implementation of the economic policy of the government" in so far as such policy does not distort the Bank's main policy objective of price stability (CBI, 2009: 63).

Iceland's institutions: nationalization of private institutions

The government nationalized different sectors in the aftermath of the crisis, including finance and parts of the transportation sector. In January 2009, the Iceland Civil Aviation Administration operating at Keflavík Airport and Leifur Eiríksson International Airport were merged to form the national Keflavík Airport Ltd. Corporation (CBI, 2009: 63). The government centralized its economic holdings within the Ministry of Finance, as illustrated by the August 2009 transfer of the administration of nationalized farms and companies to the Ministry of Finance (CBI, 2009: 71).

Iceland's institutions: global links, inter-governmental,
political and economic links

The Icelandic Government submitted its proposal to join the European Union (EU) in July 2009, despite the "majority of Icelanders" being opposed to EU membership (Freedom House, 2011). In October 2009, the government submitted a questionnaire comprising 2,600 questions as part of its application to the European Union (CBI, 2009: 73). Iceland completed the screening process from November 2010 to June 2011, and was completing the first four chapters of membership negotiations with the EU (EC, 2011) (Table 6.12).

Iceland's strong global links buffered it during the difficult adjustments to the 2008 financial crisis. Merchandise trade held up and even grew from 56.4% of GDP in 2007 to 63.3% in 2009. This was mainly from shifts in trade patterns taking place just before the crisis, favoring fresh food and basic manufactures, which continued to be in high demand after the crisis. However, despite its strong global links (or perhaps because of them), the net inflows of Foreign Direct Investment suffered, declining from a high of US$ 6.7 billion in 2007 to US$ 64 million in 2009. Even Icelanders living abroad remitted less than before, from US$ 41.3 million in 2007 to US$ 24.9 million in 2009.

Iceland partnered with the International Monetary Fund (IMF)—a supranational lender of last resort—to get loans augmented by loan agreements with other countries like Denmark, Sweden, Finland, and Poland (CBI, 2009: 8).

Table 6.12   Iceland's global links and performance after the crisis

Global link indicators	2003	2005	2007	2009
Merchandise trade (% of GDP)	47.5	49.6	56.4	63.3
Foreign direct investment, net inflows (US$ millions)	336.1	3,124	6,679.1	63.6
Remittances received (US$ millions)	96.4	87.7	41.3	24.9

Source: World Development Indicators, available at http://data.worldbank.org/data-catalog/world-development-indicators.

Iceland also established financial links with Nordic and other European countries, such as the UK and Dutch governments. Beyond regional inter-governmental linkages, Iceland was linked up by 2011 with several supra-national organizations other than the IMF. These included the Bank for International Settlements (BIS), and the Organization for Economic and Cooperation and Development (OECD), for example (CBI, 2009: 18).

Iceland thus had well-established global links with governments and supra-national organizations, and had trade and financial links with many of the world's developed economies, with major trading partners in the 27 euro member states, Norway, and the US (EUROSTAT, 2011). While cross-border trade remained open, Iceland's financial links with other countries in 2011 were primarily related to debt obligations.

Causes of global financial crises

The basic causes of financial crises are not easy to ascertain. Much of the lit-erature has not been tested by time with real evidence and much of it is spe-cific and does not examine the full picture. There is also much speculation about the bigger picture that fails to link in well with the specific details. It may be many years before developments in the aftermath of the 2007–2009 crisis are put into a solid theoretical picture. Essentially, the causes of finan-cial crises are many, and few are thoroughly explained and consolidated given the uncertainty that continues to surround the crises that have been global in nature (see Davies, 2011). The consensus in the literature appears in the observation that the crisis stemmed from the complexity of the inter-national financial sector. An illustration of the new regulatory mechanism in the EU (regarded as the simpler of the two when compared with the US) shows much complexity. Leadership in this complex environment of regula-tions is certainly a challenge.

Furthermore, the financial sector has grown in complexity over the years and very few fully understood what was happening. The few that did under-stand were not in a position to act and were not listened to by those who could have acted (see Davies, 2010; Vogel, 2010). Experts have attributed the crisis to the development of global imbalances: the sheer increase in finan-cial assets held by banks, which grew disproportionately (Reinhart, 2009) from a level just above €1 trillion in 1987 to close to €20 trillion at the peak in 2008, before the crisis really took hold. Some scholars point to the mis-match between the high growth rates seen in assets held by non-state actors in the financial sector, which has been paralleled by rising inequalities in many countries (see arguments in Goesling 2004; Sala-i-Martin, 2002; UC, 2011). Some scholars have pointed to the out-of-control consumer borrow-ing (see Davies, 2011; Rogoff, 2009).

Housing is a sector of much focus in the literature because of its boom–bust cycles (Davies, 2010; Rogoff, 2009). Scholars also point to the questionably loose monetary policy that was practiced by countries (Bean, 2009), further exacerbated by mispriced risk (Davies, 2010; S&P, 2011). The credit bubble that developed has also been held responsible for fueling excess leverage of financial institutions. All of these trends were enabled by pro-cyclical regulation and regulatory arbitrage (Davies, 2011). Regulatory capture, where those charged with setting the rules of the game become either incapable of, or too involved within the complexities of the sector, to see the larger context (Rogoff, 2009), has also been seen as a cause of the financial crisis.

The financial crisis can be seen in the context of Theory U in that leaders failed to take the first step, which is to learn from the past (Scharmer, 2009: 33). Pro-cyclical patterns have caused damage in the past, as have housing boom and bust cycles. Addressing policies in the housing sector could have reversed much of the effects that ensued of an ever-snowballing crisis. Much of the literature emphasizes the growth of the financial sector as it magnified risks, and failed to diversify them. Multiple authors argued that it was a case of too much data without the capacity to pull out the correct details, not too little. Globalization is often an issue because it is difficult to adapt to the balance of thinking global, regional, national, and local. The world is changing so dynamically that it is hugely challenging for leaders to pull apart issues. What might appear to be a national question (like the regulation of national financial sectors) can often be an international problem that requires international level oversight.

Patterns and shifts from the financial crisis

The literature illuminates the sub-prime mortgage problem that developed first in the US. It presents how this gargantuan issue snowballed, highlighting that the area was allowed to dilute capital ratios due to low levels of information concerning the scale and imminence of the inability to repay by many borrowers, and the desire to manage "on paper" risks out of existence by many banks (Davies, 2010; Vogel, 2010). The US attempted to cope with the crisis dynamically. The government allowed one of the largest banks to declare bankruptcy and advanced to nationalize the two largest banks that held the majority of toxic debts—namely mortgages (Davies, 2010). Concurrently the Federal Reserve implemented quantitative easing processes (Bernanke, 2009; Wray, 2010). The combination of these responses temporarily seemed to slow the crisis and relax the burden in the US (Davies, 2010), even putting a stopper in the continued downward spiral in the short term. Yet the longer-term issues of increased unemployment and economic stagnation that the US suffered from were harder to resolve (ILO, 2011). The regulatory reaction has been questioned, as instead of rationalizing cumbersome state-level systems split into securities, banking, and investments, the USA sanctioned yet another oversight body (Davies, 2011). This has been widely criticized in the literature, given that the multiplicity of weak oversight bodies was a part of the initial problem (Davies, 2010). Increasing the number and complexity of regulatory systems seems to be a rather unsustainable short-term reaction to the problem (Bradley, 2011; FSA, 2009).

The spread of the crisis to the EU where many governments had unbalanced financial systems resulted in a truly global crisis (Davies, 2010). In Greece, the government was deceptive about the debt levels (Wolf, 2011). In Ireland the banking system was bizarrely disproportionate and the property boom led to a crushing bust (O'Kelly, 2010). Very similarly, Spain had a boom and a resultant property bust (Reuters, 2011), Portugal had debt management issues (Wearden, 2011), as did Italy (BBC, 2011b). In fact, even the largest economies in the EU, France and Germany, struggled, in the aftermath of the 2007–2009 crisis, to manage their own accounts as these other economies continued to spiral downwards (Davies, 2010; G20, 2011).

The EU reaction was to establish a European Financial Stability Fund (EFSF) to allow struggling economies to be bailed out in order to give them time to rectify their macro-economic problems (EFSF, 2010; Davies, 2011). This maneuver was considered workable for some of the economies, those that were not fundamentally flawed (Davies, 2010). However, economies like Greece, where there were structural issues that could not be rapidly remedied, did not react well to this solution and the crisis ground on (ILO, 2011; Vogel, 2010; Wolf, 2011).

The second tier of reactions was a series of political gestures that attempted to reassure international markets (Lall, 2009; Ross, 2011). These had mixed success and no prominent literature describes this crisis as being well handled politically (Reuters, 2010). In fact, the politics arguably grew increasingly adversarial, with multiple consequences. Changes in governments took place across the crisis areas, with most electorates choosing to move to the right of the political spectrum, or to the left with voters clearly indicating that they did not want to have to pay more for the financial crisis in the form of taxes (Chrisafis, 2011; Gallagher, 2011; Roman, 2011). The literature notes the increasing power of technocrats in the management of national politics (BBC, 2011a; Granitsas, 2011). Scholars regarded the increased role of technocrats as the most concerning development in the crisis. Democracy was partially supplanted by technocracy and scholars viewed this move as a highly controversial, and hugely questionable tectonic shift with potential to override the interests of the democratic ideal.

Developing world governments focused on their own economic reactions, including coping with the fallout of the crisis (Islam, 2009; ODI, 2010a). Scholars largely saw them as suffering from the crisis, but relatively powerless to act towards change in the short term (Miller-Dawkins, 2010; ODI, 2010). Many speculations circulated on whether China would reduce the burden held by the US by changing its tight control over exchange rates. China had not opted to do so in previous crises (Tan, 2004) and at the writing of this book had still not opted to do so (Cline, 2011; Morrison, 2009). Most developing countries experienced a sharp reduction in FDI and international demand, and some, like Angola, offered bailout funds to the developed world (Lagarde, 2011; ODI, 2010). Such actions offered an interesting reversal of the historical relationship between the North and South. Certainly, the crisis caused leaders in all parts of the world to tread uncharted waters and entailed many potentialities (Davies, 2010; Vogel, 2010).

At the time of writing the outlook was highly pessimistic, with the intensification of the recession to the point of breaking the euro zone (Wolf, 2011) and international markets frenzied with uncertainty (Giles, 2010a; 2011a). It might prove useful to examine the reasons why the reactions had been deemed inadequate and what the potential lessons for leadership are.

Lessons on leadership from the financial crisis

An assessment of the macroscopic and microscopic patterns of the key observable indicators in the case of Iceland has allowed us to identify the key risks. Such an analysis should have been done before and can be done in the future to avert crises. This would require a study of the agents (people and institutions) and their respective interactions, including the warning signs coming from the civil society segments that were indicating fractures in society with respect to the models selected for development. Investigating patterns of interaction is important to identify the potential for cascading failure, contagion to other systems and countries, and even vulnerabilities within the country itself.

Failure to react appropriately can also been seen as failure to lead. The first observation from the lessons of the 2007–2009 financial crises is that the reactions were seen not to have changed anything central to the problems that were highlighted as the cause of the crisis. The macro imbalances that pervaded the global system were not improved or even fully examined (Cournede, 2011). Loose monetary policy was not alleviated and certainly had not been eliminated. Countries like the US continued the use of quantitative easing, despite criticism that such actions had not been seen to ameliorate the crisis (Bean, 2009; Crotty, 2005). The role of elections that were to be held in November 2012 was not to be underestimated as a driver for the behavior in the use of certain policy measures.

Much of the blame for the continuation of the crisis was also attributed to financial innovations. Very few financial innovations were reduced or restricted in response to the problems that scholars said they created (Chomsky, 1999; Davies, 2011; Economist, 2010). Financial innovation is described by Stiglitz as making no positive contribution to society and guilty of generating very high costs (Park, 1993). Very little was done in terms of regulation to prevent the rapid credit growth that, in some countries, remained an underlying issue at an individual and sovereign level (ILO, 2011). Similarly, the literature illuminates that no solution for asset price bubbles had been created and no analysis of how to better target fluctuations, beyond promises not to make the same mistakes, had been outlined (Davies, 2010; Vogel, 2010). There was also concern in the literature of over borrowing, which was still seen as a fundamental concern for many individuals and governments in the developed world (Dasgupta, 1995; Davies, 2010).

On a broader level, the financial crisis of 2007– 2009 did not result in a change in the number of badly managed and unscrupulous financial firms, nor did it result in a redefinition of flawed assumptions about market efficiency and investor rationality (Chomsky, 1999; Braithwaite, 2011; Vinding, 2006). The ideology of the financial sector did not suffer in the way that many individual's livelihoods have. Last, but not least, is the need to highlight the problem of a global sector without the regulatory or institutional capacity to frame it (Beattie, 2010). The G20 leadership mechanism, which attempted to manage the crisis, was at the writing of this book deemed a failure (*Financial Times*, 2010; Giles, 2011a,b; Hawksworth, 2010). These developments are hugely concerning given the consensus that globalization is a force that it is impossible to restrain or slow. Surely this would mean that we could face more crises, given that many more sectors are globalizing and leadership mechanisms seem to be constantly one step behind.

Theory U could be of relevance, as sensing, presencing, and crystallizing reality might have allowed leaders the space to embrace different perspectives (Scharmer, 2009), thereby averting the crisis. In the context of the financial crisis, international decision-making proves challenging, as it is difficult to arrive at common ground during a crisis, especially when political interests are at play. World leaders have been seen in many ways to struggle to formulate a truly effective response (G20, 2011). The crisis was allowed to snowball and even accelerate, lasting perhaps longer than it would have otherwise.

From a political point of view, and in the context of the workings of international leadership, there are numerous problematic realities. International relations theory supposes that nation states and thereby the political leaders that comprise them act according to self-interest, which takes precedence, for many reasons, regardless of the potential for long-term reduction in welfare and collective losses (TI, 2011). According to this theory the ideal international infrastructure to allow coordination of policies (such as regulation of a complex global industry like finance) would allow leaders (and ministers of whatever branch of individual state governments), to come together in a transparent format and communicate to make informed decisions in the interests of the majority and without harming minorities (Keohane, 2001).

International politics is possibly best explained by Kenneth Waltz, a neo-realist international relations theorist, who proposes a division into three levels or "images": men (conflict oriented); states (institutional infrastructures established for the mutual benefit of men by reducing their capacity for conflict and increasing their capacity to safely interact); and the inter-national realm (in which there are inadequate incentives to coordinate and structure interaction in an institutional way) (Waltz, 1954).

Consequently, what we can observe in the international realm is state-centric anarchy, focused mostly on security dilemmas, using rational behav-ior determined by national domestic interests, molded by the nature of each regime, balanced with military power, and hierarchical in structure (Mearsheimer, 2001; Waltz, 1979). The structure charged with the most power internationally with regard to the financial crisis is the G20, which has worked on approving the Basel III program, consulting with each other on financial issues multiple times. However, in practice it is unwieldy (Beattie, 2010).

The success of the G20 is estimated to be minimal in the context of the failure of their assurances so far (Davies, 2011; Giles, 2011b). They need to look at the issue of globalization and how best to address truly global issues. However, there simply is no capacity when members are grappling with a multiplicity of more pressing short-term issues such as what to do about contagion; the continuation of the European growth slump; and market instability.

Policy context: large scale infrastructure[4]

On November 10, 2007, the Canadian Broadcasting Corporation (CBC) reported that five people were injured following a bridge collapse in Lucknow, some 200 kilometres (190 miles) from Toronto. A year before, on October 1, 2006 similar CBC reports indicated that an overpass had col-lapsed in Laval, Quebec, sending tonnes of concrete onto two cars, crushing five people to death. Over the last 50 years, we have seen an increase in the number of reported catastrophic bridge failures around the world. Bridge failures tend to get more attention because of their catastrophic nature. However, other failures are also on the rise. These are much quieter fail-ures that do not get much attention in the press until they reach gigantic proportions: the continuous failures of all sorts of infrastructure systems, including highways, sewers, and storm drainage systems, which are also on the rise. These failures are so common as to raise important questions about what is happening to decision-making around infrastructure around the world.

Could it be that we are facing an epidemic of infrastructure failures around the world? If yes, what could be causing such an epidemic? Could it be related to collective budget decisions, and how priorities for mainte-nance are set across states? Has it something to do with the globalization of construction standards, inspection procedures, and maintenance practices, since countries and firms are now more interconnected, and are learn-ing faster and more intensely from each other? Could it be a result of the increased interdependence of the myriads of agents making decisions about infrastructure systems? Or could the intensity of failures be caused by the shift in patterns of risks on infrastructure systems as a result of a shift in patterns of climate and usage away from those defined at the design and maintenance stage?

We argue that these patterns of infrastructure failure are manifest as a result of the increased complexity and interconnectivity between people, countries, and systems. Such complexity is rendering decisions about infrastructure more difficult to execute.

Decisions around infrastructure are more challenging for a number of reasons, including but not limited to: (a) *increasing size:* as a result of economic development, we have seen a scaled-up increase in the size and extent of infrastructure networks across the world; (b) *more interdependence*: because of increased trade, travel, and internationalization of production facilities, more of the existing infrastructure networks are becoming more coupled with other systems; (c) *new threats*: more recently evidenced by the global financial crisis, but also through the threats we face as a result of climate change and security risks—we now have a set of new threats requiring appropriate action and management at local, national, and global levels; and (d) *old challenges*: deferred maintenance is looming as a major constraint, challenging the financial and economic stability of some countries and localities, and pressuring decision makers to make tougher trade-offs.

The increase in the sheer size of infrastructure networks presents the twin challenges of affording the higher costs of upkeep and repair while seeking to expand the service networks or even modernize them to be in line with new demands. More important than at any time in history is the need for us to better balance the expansion of our infrastructure systems with the preservation of what systems are already in place. We face the need to simultaneously manage: (a) the balance between financing and preserving existing systems while expanding access or installing new systems; and (b) professionalizing the industry responsible for managing decisions around infrastructure while encouraging a leap-frog to alternate ways of meeting infrastructure service needs. Providing an environment that encourages such trade-offs is complex and requires a level of coordination and coherence rarely practiced before. Such challenges prompt the question of whether there is a need to rethink how we design and construct new infrastructure systems as well as how we make decisions to maintain and preserve existing systems.

Higher interdependence impacts infrastructure systems in different ways. Connectivity between systems of roads, bridges, or energy distribution creates environments in which the demand from one failed system needs to be smoothly transferred to another system. Hence failure in one system changes the probability of failure in the other system, rendering the decision-making environment around the maintenance and operation of a given system more complex. This has consequences, such as creating systems that are more susceptible to large failures or situations where we face increased probability of synchronized failures across multiple systems. The results can be seen particularly in the area of power generation and communication, but also in the shipping industry and ship repair industry, and in the system of bridges serving interconnected highway systems within a given country.

New threats from climate change come from increased risks from flooding, extreme winds, and elongated heat waves that are expected to further challenge the integrity of buildings, storm water and drainage systems, quality of clean water, and reliability of energy transmission and distribution networks, as well as causing increased damage to road, rail, bridge, and airport infrastructure. Assets at risk as a result of security threats are yet another challenge that requires a smart approach to vulnerability assessment and risk management. Because of past decisions to defer maintenance whenever budget constraints were present, we now face an increasingly difficult problem of prioritizing such deferred maintenance in the face of these new threats, such that systems do not fall into irreversible conditions of failure or create unacceptable risks to life and property damage.

The conduct of policy and politics with respect to infrastructure is an area badly in need of rethinking. It is important to create a culture that leads to better decisions around infrastructure. Three key factors make it difficult for such a culture to emerge:

(a) *Election myopia*: where voters reward politicians for visible results (such as large capital projects) and only punish them for visible failures during their tenure in office. In such a culture, politicians find it easy to secure funding for major projects, but can just as easily find themselves taking the rap for massive failures during their tenure that may have been an accumulated effect of poor decisions made by previous administrations.

(b) *Skewed accountability*: where there is budgetary preference for pressing and visible priorities that users and politicians can see, but it is very difficult to win budgets for maintenance spending or preserving existing systems on the basis of technical arguments by professionals who know the real condition of a system.

(c) *Political expediency*: where politicians make decisions to defer financing routine maintenance to later dates, tapping into current maintenance budgets to finance failures that occur under their watch, putting further pressure on finances for routine maintenance or financing innovation.

The shortfall on routine maintenance and the loss from lack of investment in new innovation becomes somebody else's problem in the next round of political competition.

Three important issues stand out:

(a) *Information asymmetry*: ensure that the impact of deferred decisions is more immediately visible, not only to the engineers and technicians who know how the systems behave, but also to the users. This would address the challenge of skewed accountability, but would also require making an effort to render the savings from non-deferred decisions (cost, labor, or material) more visible to the user, voter, and politician.

(b) *Moral hazard*: ensure that managers and politicians are rewarded for visible results such as well functioning systems, but also for avoided risks or supporting projects that are innovative. Such recognition could embolden leaders to take actions supporting massive changes into the future.

(c) *Policy–politics gap*: focus more on developing approaches that better link maintenance needs to the political decision process. This requires going beyond smart data collection and decision-making systems, exploring in addition, political dynamics and policy definition processes.

Resolving the challenges mentioned above would require recasting the infrastructure maintenance problem in the frame of complex adaptive decision-making environments. Such environments would explicitly recognize the variety and *diversity of interests of the agents* involved in the infrastructure provision and production process, the *types of interactions between these agents and the strategies* they choose to undertake, and the *selection from an array of potential courses of action* to manage the risks and remedy the problems related to failing systems. It is paramount to tackle three key challenges to arrive at the appropriate culture for effectively managing infrastructure in an increasingly complex world:

(a) Raise awareness of the risks and opportunities in light of new challenges and how best to handle them.

(b) Enhance the skills and expertise for risk-aware decision-making among policy makers, politicians, users, and engineering professionals.

(c) Develop incentive-based mechanisms for managing long-run risks and encouraging innovation and large-scale change.

Complexity and deferred maintenance

What has made the question of "maintenance" and its more serious consequence of "deferred maintenance" so complex? There are four shifts that have contributed to the difficulty of decisions surrounding infrastructure. First, it is the sheer *increased size* of infrastructure networks that need to be managed around the world. These networks have grown as a result of economic development, increased global integration, and concentration of people and activities in cities. Second, more of the existing infrastructure systems are becoming increasingly interdependent with each other, not only within the same system—such as roads—in a given country, but also across systems—such as energy and communications networks, and across countries—such as interconnected airport and port systems. Third, we face today a series of new threats, ranging from increased security risks to the emerging threats from the effects of climate change. These new threats challenge the old assumptions and tools for managing infrastructure systems. Finally, while we have to deal with these new challenges, we still face formidable old challenges, such as the backlog and effects of deferred maintenance.

Combined together, these four factors are putting pressure on the financial and economic stability of states and countries alike, and call for a different approach to decision-making around infrastructure.

The question of roads is very telling. Between 1990 and 2004 there was a tremendous increase in the size of the global road network as road transport demands grew around the world. The share of roads that are paved also grew tremendously during this period from just above 45% to over 53%. Despite these improvements, major challenges remain, not only in providing access to remote areas and regions of the world through more road construction, but also in tackling the challenges of poor quality road networks and the ever-increasing burden of road replacement and maintenance. This does not include the challenges of modernization to accommodate increasing congestion or to handle more complex traffic patterns.

The McKinsey Global Institute estimates that about US$ 16.6 trillion is needed to meet global road investment needs by 2030 (McKinsey Global Institute, 2013). Replacing existing assets is costly, as is the cost of poor maintenance. It is estimated that every US$ 1 of deferred maintenance leads to US$ 2–3 higher vehicle operating costs (Claffey, 1971). India faces about US$ 4 billion in higher Vehicle Operating Costs due to deferred maintenance.

What are the implications of this massive expansion in road networks? Let us look at a specific case in India—roads in the state of Madhya Pradesh.

The problem facing Madhya Pradesh is quite severe as in 2007 37% of the population lived below the poverty line, a figure significantly higher than the 26% national average.[5] The state has a very low rank in the human development index (ranging from 0.398 to 0.716, compared to the national value of 0.619).

The state decided to expand road access to remote areas, creating a new set of challenges. Madhya Pradesh is located at the center of India, and traffic from the surrounding states passes through it using the existing road and rail networks. Roads are a key investment to connect major towns, improve access to socioeconomic services, increase employment opportunities, and improve means of transport services, thus promoting economic growth and human development, and reducing poverty in the state.

So what is the issue? Madhya Pradesh has 72,000 kilometers of road, 50% of which has deteriorated severely and requires major rehabilitation—largely because of the continuous shortfall in investment on road maintenance in the past and increasing volume of traffic and loads. The state has a backlog of deferred maintenance, including delays in rehabilitating and improving existing roads, strengthening existing culverts and bridges and constructing new bridges and cross-drainage structures.

The second factor generating complexity is the increased interdependence among systems. Complexity theory tells us that when systems are coupled or interconnected, they behave in ways that make them seem as if they are the same system. When one system fails, demands or loads are transferred to the other system and this causes failure in one system to be transferred to the other system. For an example, consider the massive electricity blackout in the north-eastern US (Cleveland area) in 2003, which had impacts not only on electricity networks, but also on water systems, communications, and transport networks. The consequences of increased interconnection are that all systems become more susceptible to massive failures and that there is a greater probability of synchronization of failures across multiple systems.

The shipping industry provides another illustration of the implications of increased interconnectedness. There has been an incredible scaling-up of maritime transport in the past 30 years, with about 90% of merchandise around the world transported by sea. To accommodate the increased demand for shipping, vessel sizes have been increasing. Ship capacity in the 2000s is more than four times what it was in 1970. Because of production and distribution pressures there is a premium on vessel availability. If a vessel is down for repairs, it creates a cost to the shipper and client. Such demands for vessel availability have created secondary impacts on the ship repair industry (Table 6.13).

Because vessel availability is critical, the shipping industry seeks to handle availability of vessels in one of three ways: (1) maximum utilization of the existing fleet; (2) expansion of the size of the fleet; and (3) modernization of the fleet to reduce maintenance needs. All three of these actions result in reducing the offline time of vessels. Evidence shows that the industry applies all three strategies, as the size of purchases of shipping vessels (value of imports between 2001 and 2005) has grown tremendously. The pressure to turn around ship repairs in record time impacts the ship repair industry. Consider this report from Business Market Research: "Some yards claim that they cannot recall the last time they were so busy in terms of occupancy nor had so many months of forward stemming booked. Some have talked of increases in value per contract. However, this may be overoptimistic, many fleets are now very modern and so the maintenance needs are much reduced."

The adaptive strategy of the shipping industry, taken to manage demand better by adjusting the purchase of new capacity and schedules for ship repair, has resulted in reducing the potential benefits to the ship repair

Table 6.13　Risks and interdependence in ship repair

The ship repair industry	Value of imports (US$ millions)		
Vessel availability is key:	**Country**	**2001**	**2012**
• Used to the maximum to lower off-hire time	India	577	6,159
	Poland	713	3,204
	Korea, Republic of	374	2,543
• Repairs and other minor maintenance deferred	Greece	1,133	2,526
	Italy	853	2,352
	Norway	1,491	2,005
• Modern fleets, need less maintenance	France	1,035	1,988
	USA	1,239	1,894
	Spain	685	1,246
"Some yards claim that they cannot recall the last time they were so busy	Belgium	91	525

Top 10 importers of ships, boats, floating structures.

"Some yards claim that they cannot recall the last time they were so busy in terms of occupancy or had so many months of forward stemmings booked. However, this may be overoptimistic, many fleets are now very modern and so the maintenance needs are much reduced."

Source: Own analysis using reports from Business Market Research available at www.BharactBook. com supplemented by data from ITC Trade Statistics, available at http://www.intracen.org/ itc/market-info-tools/trade-statistics/.

industry, which should have been able to benefit from increased maintenance demands. A trader looking only at the growth in shipping demand (as seen through the growth in the maritime fleet capacity) could have lost if betting on the consequent growth in the ship repair business. A shipper, on the other hand, who is hedging in the short-run by keeping the maritime fleet at maximum operation, would be facing higher maintenance costs and even offline time for her fleet. A customer could see sudden swings in unavailability of shipping capacity or sudden price spikes in the cost of shipping as the industry as a whole goes through its maintenance and repair cycles. Most of these outcomes would have an impact on the financial performance of a shipper or customer. All of these factors are now intertwined and it is become increasingly hard to disentangle them.

The shipping industry example shows us how the interconnections between the decisions of various agents (shippers, shipping companies, ship repair shops, customers, traders) leads to unintended consequences in each other's decision outcomes, rendering those very same outcomes even harder to predict in the future. Loss of predictability is a key aspect of complexity that decision-makers around infrastructure need to be aware of.

Another demonstration of the effects of increased interconnection can be seen through the case of bridges. Over the last 200 years, we have seen a very large increase in the number of bridges constructed around the world, but also an increase in the number of catastrophic failures, failures due to disasters, and accidents during bridge construction. These three types of failures have tended to increase together. Bridge disasters are a good example to use, as they create headline news and hence reporting about them is more accurate.

It is likely that a decision to defer maintenance on a bridge in one country can affect the performance of bridges in a neighboring country if the countries share a distributed pattern of traffic. This would be visible in interconnected regions such as Europe or North America, where traffic diversions, especially of loaded vehicles, could put pressure on systems of bridges previously not considered at risk from past traffic load patterns. It is also possible that bridge failures would be correlated if the bridges share the same age profile, design, and construction standards, or maintenance and inspection schedules. All of these factors could interrelate to cause an avalanche of bridge failures in a given state or country.

Canada, which has had its share of bridge disasters, could be used to illustrate this point. Consider the overpass collapse of October 1, 2006 in Laval, Quebec.[6] This was a collapse of a highway overpass, which sent tonnes of concrete on to two cars, crushing five people to death. The bridge was 35 years old and had been open for all traffic loads. The bridge had been inspected less than a year before the collapse. This was the second bridge to come down in Laval in seven years. In 2000, an overpass under construction collapsed, killing one man. Inspectors checked all bridges in the area to make sure they are sound. An independent review of the causes of the collapse indicated that there are multiple and sequential reasons for the bridge disaster: poor workmanship at construction and during repair and rehabilitation, insufficient oversight, and poor maintenance. The province of Quebec inspected over 100 bridges and overpasses following this disaster and closed or repaired many of similar design and age.

Another example in Canada is when five people were injured following a bridge collapse in Lucknow, some 200 kilometres (190 miles) from Toronto on November 10, 2007.[7] The bridge was under construction. Media reports indicate that it was not clear whether the bridge had been open to traffic when it collapsed.

These two cases raise questions when looked at from the lens of complex adaptive systems. Could it be that the collective budget decisions to prioritize the maintenance of bridges at the provincial level is causing coupling between the failure conditions of the bridges? Or is it the fact that construction standards, inspection procedures, and maintenance practices across

Quebec are now so integrated from one road network to the other that the bridges now behave as if they are the same system? What is causing the cascading pattern of bridge failures that we see? Could it be increased complexity and interdependence of the myriads of agents making decisions about the system of bridges? Could the bridges have failed because patterns of climate and environment have shifted away from those assumed at the design and maintenance stage? The findings of the independent review that there were multiple and sequential causes of failure do indeed support the argument of a coupled system of bridges.

There are many other examples of catastrophic bridge collapses in other countries. If indeed decisions made by different agents about transport systems are more interconnected, then we should expect more frequent and even synchronized failures, and perhaps more massive failures, as this is how interconnected or coupled systems behave.

The third factor driving complexity of infrastructure decision-making relates to global discontinuities such as those from climate change.[8] Buildings will be facing increased risks from flooding, extreme winds, and elongated heat waves. Water systems are also expected to see increased risks from climate-related effects. Storm water, drainage, and sewer systems are impacted by increased rain and snowstorms. There could also be a threat to the supply and quality sources of water due to drought and increased risks of fires in already arid regions or during the hot summer months. Energy networks could be more severely impacted by extreme weather events, which could damage transmission and distribution infrastructure. Heat and cold waves could increase peak demand loads for electricity, and extensive drought could challenge hydroelectric systems. Transport systems face risks from extreme rain and wind effects on the potential damage to roads, rail, bridge, airport, port, and tunnel infrastructure. Extreme temperatures could reduce the life of asphalt surfaces of roads and airports, and further stress steel in bridges and rail tracks. Telecommunications systems could face increased damage to access holes and underground facilities due to extreme flooding, and damage to transmission lines from strong winds.

In addition to climate, today's infrastructure systems also face risks related to security.[9] Terrorist attacks could put needed assets at risk: for example, people, facilities, equipment, materials, information systems, and day-to-day activities and operations. Threats could be of different types (insider, terrorist, environmental catastrophe); different motivation; have multiple triggers; or be carried out using different methods (cyber, assault, truck bombs, suicide bombers). It is important to see how past and present trends would affect the risk to existing infrastructure assets (Table 6.14).

Systems face different degrees of vulnerability depending on their physical strength (toughness, strength), technical characteristics (energy surge, cyber attack, contamination), operational factors (policies, practices, procedures), or organizational concerns (business continuity). Being aware of the

Table 6.14   Old challenges in aviation safety

Country	Fatal accidents and casualties	Rank	Aircraft imports (US$ millions in 2011)	Rank
USA	12,683	1	10,080	4
India	2,801	2	605	10
Spain	2,481	3	933	8
France	2,377	4	14,031	2
China	1,971	5	11,649	3
Japan	1,964	6	2,364	5
Canada	1,883	7	2,185	6
Italy	1,449	8	704	9
Germany	1,098	9	16,073	1
Singapore	74	10	1,547	7

Source: Aviation safety network, available at www.flightsafety.org and ITC International Trade Statistics, available at http://www.intracen.org/itc/market-info-tools/trade-statistics/.

consequences of risks is critical, including risks to humans (death/injury), economic activity, environmental quality, national security, or even symbolic activities that are meant to send a signal as a result of the importance of the target. Decision-makers need to seek ways to reduce risks by eliminating threats, reducing vulnerability (say by toughening assets), or dampening the potential impact of consequences (through backup systems and components). Risk reduction strategies are also very important. These need to look at the options for prioritization, cost-effectiveness, irreversibility, reducing specific threat scenarios, managing the geographical spread of risks, and defining acceptable levels of risk.

The fourth factor generating complexity is something decision-makers have been dealing with for many years: the basic problem of maintaining services in the face of increasing or shifting demands while managing risks of service disruption from the potential failure of systems.

The aviation industry has seen an explosion in the number of passengers carried and the size of the aviation fleets. India is a case in point, as it has seen massive growth in air travel. The growth in aviation fleets has posed challenges for airline maintenance and particularly for how airlines balance the costs of fleet maintenance while maintaining travel schedules. While India ranks sixth with respect to growth in aviation imports, it ranks second in the number of fatalities and casualties from aviation incidents and accidents. Poor maintenance practices account for a good share of these results. Airlines in India were responsible for 5% of the 64 global accidents caused by poor maintenance practices. Such practices include: (a) failure to follow proper procedures (17% of global incidents); (b) substandard maintenance practices (9% of global incidents); and (c) wrong installation of parts (3% of global incidents).[10]

Risk and operational definition of deferred maintenance

With the added complexity of decision-making around infrastructure, it is important to have an operational definition of deferred maintenance that can be used to improve the quality and effective of policies and decisions. Three definitions are useful. The first relates to the *deterioration* of machinery, equipment, or infrastructure as a result of postponing prudent but non-essential repair, for example drilling equipment, rigs, or buildings. The second relates to the failure to perform needed repair, maintenance, and renewal at the *optimal time*, for example the ship repair industry, the airline industry, or bridges. The third relates to the *accumulated expenditures* that arise from activities (upgrades, repairs) postponed to later dates, for example roads.

The question of deferred maintenance is not limited to the issue of the appropriate definition, but also to the factors leading to actions to defer maintenance. Five key factors continue to make it difficult to deal with deferred maintenance:

(i) *Economic impact measures*: there is very sparse and contradictory empirical evidence on the long-run economic costs of deferred maintenance; hence it is difficult to make the case for financing maintenance when it is needed;

(ii) *Political risk challenge*: competition for funding between maintenance and other programs leads to appropriations going towards other priorities, as politicians seek to respond to the demands that are more visible or pressing;

(iii) *Risk assessment methods*: there is generally a desire to save cost, labor, or material when undertaking maintenance and repair actions or a desire to limit downtime for operations due to maintenance. This leads to less than desirable outcomes, because more costly maintenance actions could in fact be the more effective ones in the long-run;

(iv) *Risk management approach*: weak maintenance management practices prevent enterprises and organizations from effectively managing key risks, including the risks from deferring maintenance activities; and

(v) *Skills gaps*: insufficient personnel, or personnel without the requisite expertise to perform maintenance, is becoming a key risk today. Some experts believe that the frequency with which failures in infrastructure systems are occurring today is as a direct result of the lack of engineering skills to determine when systems will fail.

There is a very weak directly observable relationship between the condition of the road network and economic performance, despite the theoretical expectation that improved transport access leads to higher economic productivity. Studies to disentangle the effect of well-performing infrastructure

on economic performance are complex and difficult to argue. Data limitations, with very few countries posting a long-run series of data, make it even
more difficult to make a convincing case. Policy makers are left having to
argue through anecdotes to make the case for further attention to investments in roads. Such data shortages also impact decision-making in energy,
large-scale dam infrastructure and other related investments.

Numerous studies measure the impact of infrastructure on economic
productivity and growth (see de la Fuente and Estache, 2004). With the
exception of studies carried out in developing countries, 100% of which
indicate positive effects of infrastructure investment, studies carried out in
other countries are more controversial. A potential reason for divergence
in estimated effects could be the spillover effects that are typical in highly
interconnected systems.

Political decision-making is another factor that further contributes to the
neglect of needed maintenance. There are three challenges that pose particular risks: election myopia, information asymmetry, and political expediency, discussed previously.

Consider the San Francisco sewers. In May 2008 the *San Francisco
Examiner* reported that the Superior Court judge ruled that the City of San
Francisco was liable for sewer overflow damage to at least 30 properties
following massive storm flooding in February 2004.[11] The estimated cost
to taxpayers was estimated at over $3 million. Much of the city's 1,000
miles of brick sewers were built in the 19th century. Flushed waste spurted
up through sinks and toilets and was carried into buildings during the
February 2004 rainstorms that overwhelmed old sewage and storm water
channels. Poor strategies for replacing and upgrading old sewer systems
caused a high expenditure at a later date, creating a legal liability for the
city to private property owners.

Having poor risk assessment methods is another reason why maintenance
decisions are deferred. Maintenance decisions tend to fall below the radar of
senior decision-makers for two main reasons: information asymmetry and
moral hazard, discussed previously.

The *San Francisco Examiner* reported in May 2008 on the outcome of the
watchdog civil grand jury, which castigated the municipal owners of 19
local dams in San Mateo County for failing to meet a March 31 deadline to
prepare coordinated emergency plans.[12] The county's Emergency Services
Council said planning for responses to flash flooding caused by dam failure
in heavily populated areas had to be delayed due to lack of funds. According
to the *Examiner*, applications for state and federal grants were rejected, and
the council had no dam emergency planning budget. "With eight of the
Peninsula's dams rated 'high-risk' by the Army Corps of Engineers, it would
behove local authorities to treat dam failure as a higher priority before they
too, like San Francisco, are ordered by the Superior Court to pay costly flash-
flooding damages," said the *San Francisco Examiner*.

Practices of risk management relating to deferred maintenance are weak because of four key factors:

(i) *Preference myopia*: due to weak links between what users experience and the real pattern of deterioration and failure of equipment, machinery, and infrastructure;
(ii) *Measurement errors*: since there is poor information on what to do and when due to inadequate deterioration models and knowledge of the effectiveness of different maintenance actions;
(iii) *Accountability and incentives*: as a result of poor reporting practices on what needs to be fixed and when; and
(iv) *Policy–politics gap*: because of underdeveloped approaches of linking maintenance needs to the political decision process.

Finally, there are the skills needed to assess maintenance needs. A good infrastructure risk assessment requires personnel with skills to:

(i) Assess user perceptions (satisfaction levels, service demands);
(ii) Appropriately assess the level of asset deterioration (response to usage, condition, time to failure);
(iii) Condition assessment skills (observing failure, measuring failure, assessing current conditions);
(iv) Maintenance decision-making skills (when to maintain, how much to spend, how much is included in budget requests, the effectiveness of maintenance actions); and
(v) Political skills (probability of gaining sustainable funding, arguing for priority of maintenance).

Risks from deferred maintenance

If deferred maintenance is allowed to accumulate, it generates five types of risks for policy makers, politicians, users, and the electorate. These are:

(i) *Deterioration risk*: higher probability of failure, especially when portfolio of equipment, machinery, and infrastructure is aged or aging;
(ii) *Security risk*: increased safety hazards from normal use, made more severe when portfolio of equipment, machinery, and infrastructure is subject to emergency events (floods, storms, tremors, attacks);
(iii) *Serviceability risk*: poor service to the public and consequent higher costs of usage;
(iv) *Financial risk*: higher costs of maintenance and replacement in the future; and
(v) *Operational risk*: inefficient day-to-day operations.

To properly embed decisions around deferred maintenance into decision-making systems we need to resolve a number of methodological challenges. The first one relates to the complexities from the types of failure and their link to deferred maintenance. At present, we lack simple methods for assessing deferred maintenance. In general, there are two types of methods: parametric and non-parametric. Improving the simplicity and usability of such methods is important before they can become more widely used in risk-management and decision-making systems around infrastructure. The second issue relates to the residual risks due to weak knowledge of the effectiveness of action under different failure conditions. In particular, it is important to distinguish between the deferred maintenance risk assessment for discrete failure (such as buildings) and for continuous failure (such as roads).

Inspectors, who tend to be engineering experts, understand the failure of infrastructure systems in a very different manner from the users of the system, who tend to perceive failure in a more discrete fashion (it is working or it is not). Risk management decision systems need to be able to account not only for the time to failure, but also for the probability of failure and the severity of failure. Because users typically are not aware of probabilities, they do not press for maintenance even when it may be the best time to do it. This is even harder for cases of continuous failure, such as roads, where users see the effects only incrementally in increased vehicle operating costs (Table 6.15).

Some simple methods have been developed to improve decision-making around maintenance. These include the use of rapid visual assessments or the practice of using simple coefficients of replacement costs. Prominent examples are those where coefficients of maintenance known as *r*-coefficients (ratio of recurrent to capital costs) are used to better manage long-run fiscal risks at the level of an economy.[13] These methods allow decision makers to plan for deferred maintenance on the basis of the current replacement value of systems and the condition of the system today. We provide an illustration

Table 6.15 Complexities in estimating future maintenance needs

Sector	# of projects	Average *r*-coefficient	Median *r*-coefficient
Energy	14	0.013	0.002
Telecommunications	3	0.003	0.000
Transport	15	0.025	0.009
Water & sanitation	12	0.044	0.021

Source: Taken from World Bank Project estimates provided in Ron Hood, David Husband, and Fei Yu. Recurrent Expenditure Requirements of Capital Projects: Estimation for Budget Purposes. World Bank Research Observer, 2002. These can be found at http://econ.worldbank.org/external/default/main?pagePK=64165259&theSitePK=469372&piPK=64165421&menuPK=64166093&entityID=000094946_0301180436354.

below of such coefficients that are useful to lock in maintenance budgets in difficult and competitive political processes. They are, however, not very suitable for managing risks.

Other approaches include non-parametric methods that calibrate deterioration or use failure models and the effectiveness of maintenance actions, and can be adjusted for usage levels, age of the facilities, and the current condition of the system. For these methods to work, it is critical to have excellent measurement and inspection systems, as well as to have superior and long-run engineering knowledge on the effect of repair activities on the behavior of systems. The highway maintenance models that have been developed over the years provide such information.

Methods for assessing risks also need to be sensitive to the type of failure that could be either continuous or discrete. For every failure type, there is a range of possible responses—replace a part, repair a component, or shut down a facility or service because of total breakdown. When failure is discrete it is easy to see when it happens. When it is continuous, it is gradual and not as visible from one day to the next. Total risk scores are useful tools to use for both types of failure, but it may not be as easy to assign severity of risks to cases of continuous failure.

In the case of discrete failure, one can estimate a total risk score using inputs such as the likelihood of failure (which could be negligible or certain); the estimated time to total failure (more than 25 years, less than 1 year); and the current threats or risks to integrity (accidents, code violations, or reputational risks).

The residual risks can be assessed after accounting for the effectiveness of activities to mitigate risks. These activities could be replacing or repairing a part of equipment, machinery, or an infrastructure component. Other activities could be doing nothing, resulting in a total breakdown of usability of equipment or machinery, or serviceability of infrastructure.

When failure is continuous, another criterion comes into play—when is a facility or service considered unusable? Road surface condition is an example. A road can have many cracks but one can still drive on it. However, after a certain level of cracking, if not addressed, more severe failure can take place, like potholes and the collapse of entire segments that can wash away with the next heavy rain.

Knowing the respective costs of action is also important for decision-making. The residual risk is generally used as an input into other risk control actions. With such assessments, social and political considerations enter into the ranking of actions and estimating the total cost of interventions. It is at this stage that the complexity of arguing for earlier action comes into the picture—how to convince politicians and policy makers about the importance of a high-probability, low-cost event.

Examples of systems that could benefit from this type of assessment are facility management (systems of schools or hospital buildings), equipment (electricity generation and distribution, telecommunications), and fleet management (trucks, buses, taxis, aircraft, shipping vessels).

To illustrate the use of simple ratios, consider the example of deferred maintenance decisions compared to the cost of replacing the entire facility. The Texas Public Universities and Health-Related Institutions have estimated their replacement values, deferred maintenance, and critical deferred maintenance costs (see below). This has allowed them to establish the percentage at risk due to critically deferred maintenance (0.1%), compared to those with deferred maintenance (2.6%). Managing the level of risk from deferred maintenance is possible using such techniques.

Assessing risks in the case of continuous failure requires establishing the failure trajectory of the system. This trajectory is a function of the severity of failure at the start, a user-defined service level, change in the severity level of failure as a result of time and usage, severity at a later time, and the effectiveness of the maintenance policy. The total risk is assessed as the probability of the system being below an accepted service level. The residual risk depends on the effectiveness of the maintenance policies used. Ranking can then be done using social, political, environmental, and financial considerations, which then yields the total risk and the costs of the interventions. Residual risks are then used as an input into other risk control actions. Highway systems can be managed in this manner (Table 6.16).

An application to the case of roads indicates the costs and effectiveness of different activities and the effect of timing of specific decisions. A decision such as routine maintenance, taken early and appropriately, can reduce the future costs of massive failure which is always costly to rehabilitate.

Instruments for controlling deferred maintenance risks

There are numerous examples of risk-based asset management models. These include models for handling security risks as in Moteff (2004), who focuses on assessing, integrating, and managing threats, vulnerabilities, and consequences. Other models include explicitly recognizing the interconnectedness

Table 6.16 Deferred maintenance risk assessment—continuous failure

Example: roads Activity	Cost $/lane-mile	Improvement in performance (0–100)
Rejuvenation	1,900	3–5
Slurry seal	3,300	3–5
Fog seal	570	1–3
Resealing	2,460	25
Surface treatment	3,300	30
Overlay	24,000	>40

Source: Léautier, F. (née Humplick), 1986.

of systems, such as that of Newman et al. (2005) who include assessing risk generated by coupled or interacting infrastructure systems. Yet other models, such as Song et al (2007), focus on rapid risk assessment and decision support for systems at the local level, with specific support to city managers concerned with the performance of urban infrastructure.

Lessons for leadership from the case of deferred maintenance

The examples so far show the importance of increasing the awareness of leaders of the risks of deferred maintenance. Such risks have become more significant because of the interplay between the new and old challenges facing a typical decision maker. It is particularly central to be aware of the scale of the problem we face in infrastructure, in terms of current and future liabilities. Politicians and policy makers need to comprehend the evolution of the deferred maintenance challenge, not only in light of energy constraints, natural disasters, and security needs, but also as a direct result of the increased interconnectivity of systems. The accumulated costs of deferred maintenance are an extra burden to be accounted for.

Enhancing skills and expertise for risk-aware deferred maintenance is critical. This requires going beyond improving the measurement and modelling approaches, but more importantly it requires an assessment of all the agents that interact to provide and produce infrastructure, and the implications of their collective interests and actions on the performance of infrastructure. Knowledge of complex systems theory, and how it can be harnessed for effective decision-making in infrastructure, is essential to improve the quality of policy and political decisions around infrastructure.[14]

Finally, leaders need to be versed in approaches for developing incentive-based mechanisms to manage long-run deferred maintenance risks and to better handle their behavioral and political implications. Methods that could work include price-based regulation with allowable condition levels and service-based regulation with price caps. Other promising techniques include incentive payments linked to predefined performance standards. Such methods allow owners and operators to manage risk effectively, as they are best placed to uncover and handle such risks. Politicians and policy makers can then focus on large-scale risk avoidance by putting in place policies that decouple potentially correlated or sequential risks. Having contingency funds and approaches for handling really severe risks is also a key area of attention for politicians and policy makers.

Leadership and muddling through

A famous quote from Confucius sets the perfect stage to discuss the question of leadership and muddling through when dealing with risks in specific contexts: "Things have their root and their branches. Affairs have their end and their beginning. To know what is first and what is last will lead near to what is taught in the great learning" Confucius (ca 500 BCE), *The Great Learning*. Lindblom (1959) presents the virtues of muddling through in his example of dealing with inflation. Kay (2009a) referred to the article by Lindblom to expound on the virtues of two approaches to problem solving: the root method and the branch method.

The root method relies on the ability to define objectives very well, outline a range of options in a comprehensive manner, evaluate the options, and select the one that maximizes the attainment of the objective. The branch method involves building out step-by-step and in small degrees from the current situation. It is the state of practice used by leaders in political and complex environments. Kay (2010a) illustrates how companies have used these strategies with very different effects. Kay (2010b) further offers learning strategies for individuals to be better at managing portfolio risks by knowing why some companies succeed and some fail.

Two examples from Kay (2009a) stand out: TRW and Saint Gobain. TRW Automotive was originally founded in 1901 as an automotive parts company, headquartered in Michigan, USA (www.trw.com). The name TRW originally stood for Thomson Ramo Woodridge. It was purchased in 2002 by Northrop Grumman, its major competitor, which sold TRW's automotive division to private equity firm The Blackstone Group, which retained a 56.7% share in the company after it went public in 2004 (www.trw.com). After many years of success in automotive parts, the company decided to manage risks by going about the methodical exploration of wide vistas of opportunity to exploit opportunities (Kay, 2009a). Such a strategy led TRW to expand into a three-pronged technology solutions model for problems ranging across urban renewal, mass transportation, and pollution. In this strategy, TRW embraced all aspects of interconnectedness in the ecosystem they were operating in, and tried to define precise ways to deal with it. In doing so, TRW employed "the root method" and aimed to embrace all aspects linked to their business and try to control them. The method had short-term benefits, with a rapid ascent of the company, but resulted in long-term failure, and they were forced to go back to their modest roots as an auto parts supplier (Kay, 2009a). In 2012, TRW was among the world's largest automotive suppliers, employing 70,000 people and with revenues above US$ 15 billion in 2008 (www.boursier.com).

Saint Gobain is a French multinational corporation founded in 1665 in Paris. From a mirror manufacturer it now produces a variety of construction and high-performance materials (www.saint-gobain.fr). Saint Gobain was known for its step-by-step strategy. This approach, also known as the "branch method," was applied mostly by politicians and was deemed useful by Lindblom (1959) in very complex settings. The approach has allowed Saint Gobain to grow organically, through smart purchases and acquisitions, as well as decisions to start or stop producing certain materials. Saint

Gobain has become a globalized multinational with over 180,000 employees in 2010 (www.saint-gobain.fr).

One can critique the outcome of these two strategies only after many years of performance. The trick with leadership is being able to know in advance which one would be relevant and when to switch strategies. The practice block at the end of this chapter provides the learner with the tools to investigate the complex space of decision-making. The learning at each stage supports the learner in deciding whether muddling through from a base case scenario is the best one can do.

Leadership and learning from failure

This chapter would not be complete without discussion on learning from failure. We draw on three motivations to bring up the question of learning from failure. The first is from Chialvo and Bak (1999), who show that mistake-driven neuronal learning can outperform other more complicated and sophisticated models using positive reinforcement. They argue that negative reinforcement, such as what comes from having failed in the past, is essential for adaptation, and that positive reinforcement reduces the ability to adapt. When looking at the ability of leaders to adapt to failure, one is interested in how failure is interpreted by the human brain.

Chialvo and Bak (1999) suggest that the brain functions somewhat like "sand models" of complexity. In sand models, each site receives sand grains from neighboring sites and when the height exceeds a critical threshold, there is a toppling event where grains of sand are sent to neighboring sites. Their argument is that brains function more like tilted sand models, where instead of adding sand, change starts at the steepest site. Such a model is known as "extremal dynamics" and is used in many areas of study, including "winner-take-all" models. In addition to the idea of negative feedback (learning from mistakes) as being important in adaptation, Chialvo and Bak (1999) also have a useful lesson for how much can be done at a given point in time. They show that only a relatively small number of neurons can be associated with a certain task for effective functioning of the brain and hence the learning process. Such a constraint provides us with the starting point to link "learning from failure" covered in this section to the "root and branch method" we discussed in the last section.

The branch method is step-by-step (few neurons firing at the same time) and hence does not overload the decision maker with too many pieces of information with which to render a choice. As such, failures or potential weaknesses can be seen faster, and learning from them can be embedded in day-to-day adaptation, almost in a self-organized way with no need for too much external influence. Organizations (such as Saint Gobain) can learn from within and do not need a major crisis to adapt. The root method subjects the decision maker to a lot of information and choice points, overloading the neuronal network. Seeing flaws and adapting is hard, and change can only take place following massive failure or catastrophe (as in TRW's case).

The second motivation for bringing in learning from failure comes from a quote from Confucius: "In all things success depends on previous preparation, and without such previous preparation there is sure to be failure," Confucius (ca 500 BCE). This quote appeals to us as it posits two aspects in learning from failure—learning from failures in the level of preparedness for catastrophes that have happened in the past and learning from the process and assumptions that led to failure in previous instances.

The third motivation is from reflection following the 2007–2009 financial crises, which was a cause for much consideration on learning from failure. Acharya et al. (2009) stands out in the attempt to extract lessons for finance from the fate of Concorde following its crash in 2000.

Concorde was the most sophisticated airliner of the 20th century, flying at twice the speed of sound. On July 25, 2000 a Concorde aircraft crashed. Speculation as to the causes of the crash were debated, but mostly surrounded the issue of maintenance. The Concorde was very costly to maintain. When it crashed, one school of thought was that a fragment from another aircraft had been left on the runway (faulty maintenance) and the other was that the aircraft was overweight and unbalanced (pilot error). After the crash, lessons were drawn that were relevant for short-term and longer-term strategy. In the short term, efforts were made for temporary design modifications. These did not work, so eventually the technology was jettisoned.

New technology was adopted with sub-sonic aircraft, which are slower but easier to maintain (maintenance strategy) (Table 6.17).

Acharya et al. (2009) draw parallels to the financial system before the sub-prime crisis in 2007. The global financial sector was fiercely innovative, growing at record pace for two decades. After the sub-prime crisis, there was speculation on the cause. Leaders of the financial sector were one group that was blamed (pilot error). The other group receiving blame were the regulators of the system (maintenance failure). Calls were made for reform of capital allocation in complex financial institutions (fix maintenance). Acharya et al. (2009) argue that bankers and insurers underestimated long-run risk–return tradeoffs (pilot error). Government guarantees (FDIC) and "too big to fail" policies caused too much risk-taking (regulator's fault). A number of solutions have been recommended, including a change in the compensation and incentive structure; quantifying systemic risks better; charging for socialized risks; and enforcing greater transparency of financial products. All these solutions look at the leaders in the financial sector (pilots of the industry) and suggest that they need to make changes to fix the problem.

Learning from failure can be useful in the processes that led to failure (maintenance processes) or the agents responsible for decision-making and

Table 6.17   What can we learn from failure? The case of Concorde

Concorde pre-crash:	**Financial system pre sub-prime in 2007:**
• Most sophisticated airline of 20th century flying at twice the speed of sound, very costly to maintain • Crash in Paris on July 25, 2000 with speculation on cause: fragments from other aircraft (faulty maintenance), overweight and unbalanced (pilot error)	• Fiercely innovative, grew at record pace for two decades • Sub-prime crisis, speculation on cause: leaders of the financial sector (pilots error), regulators of the system (maintenance failure) • Calls for reform of capital allocation in complex financial institutions (fix maintenance)
Concorde post-crash:	**Global financial crisis after 2009:**
• Temporary design modifications were made, but eventually the technology was jettisoned • New technology was adopted with sub-sonic aircraft, which is slower but easier to maintain (maintenance strategy)	• Bankers and insurers under estimated long-run risk return tradeoffs (pilot error) • Government guarantees (FDIC) and "too big to fail" policies caused too much risk taking (regulators fault) • Change compensation and incentive structure; quantify systemic risks; charge for socialized risks; enforce greater transparency of financial products

Source: Developed from Acharya, Richardson and Roubini (2009): "Concorde's fate offers a lesson for finance" FT, April 2009, available at www.ft.com.

implementation (pilot's actions). In the next section, we look at a practice module based on Scharmer's Theory U that helps the learner become comfortable with defining experiments and pilots that allow them to learn from failure and adapt in a day-to-day process.

Customization enabled by logistics: case of Philips-UPS[15]

This case focuses on Philips and UPS and their 2006 partnership to run the Global Logistics Network of Philips Medical, and takes different aspects of the logistics industry into account.

Philips has been a leader in its approach to outsourcing logistics services, and provides an excellent example to illustrate the emergence of new approaches to supply chain management. Philips had an in-house system of logistics management prior to the contract that it signed with UPS. The in-house system operated with 12 logistics providers in about 40 locations, and was based on ensuring next business day service to its customers. So why did Philips engage in such a contract with UPS?

Evolution of Philips from 1891 to 2007

Philips was founded in 1891 in Eindhoven, the Netherlands, to make carbon-filament lamps. From 1891 to 1900 Philips was in the Start-up and

Specialization phase. By the turn of the century, it was one of the largest producers in Europe. From 1901 to 1939 the company focused on Innovation and Diversification. In 1914 it created a research laboratory to stimulate product innovation. By 1918 its medical X-ray tube was a product selling across the world. Patents for X-ray radiation and radio reception are the key indicators of the company's successful innovation during this period. In 1925 Philips engaged in the first experiments in television. It branched off in 1927, when it began producing radios, and by 1932 it had sold one million of them. In 1933 Philips started production of medical X-ray equipment in the US and launched in 1939 the first Philips electric shaver.

The company shifted strategy in the 1940s and 1950s with the tremendous developments in science and technology. Inventions included rotary heads, which led to the development of the Philishave electric shaver; groundbreaking work in transistors and integrated circuits; and recording, transmission, and reproduction of television pictures.

The 1960s were a period of exciting new products and ideas. In 1963 Philips came out with the Compact Audio Cassette. 1965 was particularly lucrative, with the company seeing value from its investment in science and technology. That year saw the first integrated circuits; PL and SL energy-saving lamps; and major technological development and advances in the processing, storage, and transmissions of images, sound, and data (LaserVision optical disc, the compact disc and optical telecommunication systems).

Philips went into an acquisitions phase in the 1970s and 1980s. In 1972 it established PolyGram; in 1974 it acquired Magnavox; and in 1975 it acquired Signetic. These achievements were followed in the 1980s when Philips acquired GTE Sylvania's television concern and Westinghouse's lamps business. In 1983 the company reached a technological landmark with the launch of the compact disc.

In the 1990s Philips undertook restructuring and partnerships. It started off by releasing the DVD. This period also saw the creation of 21st century Healthcare, Lifestyle and Technology, which marked the more recent change this case study is focused on.

In 2004 the new brand promise of Philips was focused around "sense and simplicity," with a real alignment to the lifestyle demands of its customers in more advanced economies. In May 2006 it contracted UPS to run its global logistics network and in September 2006 it sold 80.1% of its semiconductor business, creating NXP.

Tectonic shifts impacting Philips

A number of tectonic shifts have impacted Philips, forcing the company to shift its strategy between 1891 and 2007. First, consumer behavior changed, with demand for shorter transport times and more efficiency. Consumers got used to the idea of "same day delivery" and suppliers to large companies have to function with complex contracts of "next business day service."

Higher population growth has led to increased demand for all sorts of products that Philips makes.

Philips operated in 50 countries or more in 2007, where it interacted with local populations who have lower wages and incomes than many of the consumers it serves in more advanced countries. Such disparities often cause tension in the relationship between where goods are produced and where they are consumed. This shows up in the pressure to seek lower and lower wages in manufacturing, while at the same time seeking to be more and more relevant to the local populations in the sourcing countries. Some companies solve this tension through mergers; others through a larger workforce in the sourcing countries. Philips sought to do it by removing the logistics challenges and focusing on cost efficiency and being the best at what it does, branding itself as a lifestyle company that offers products for well-being.

Urbanization is another tectonic change facing Philips. Crowded cities in developing countries, while causing more traffic jams and congestion, also mean, rising middle-income families. Such trends present opportunities for companies like Philips that produce end-user products, which face a growing demand for their goods and services. The company is better served meeting these demands than worrying about headaches in the logistics services.

Changes in mentality around climate change and the way in which it has become commercially desirable for shareholders and civil society groups to demand "green products" has forced companies to advertise their environmental policies, and at times to brand products that are "green" and that follow some form of "fair trade" principles. Philips has engaged in branding itself a green lifestyle company.

Increased individual mobility throughout the world is another tectonic change facing Philips. Consumers can travel more easily to discover tastes and preferences for goods in other countries, sometimes even without leaving the comfort of their homes. They can search on the Internet and engage in conversations on Facebook and Twitter than can move brands and products in minutes rather than days, especially with online shopping and banking. Philips needs to meet these demands, and UPS, with a long history of delivery on time, is better placed to do this.

On the resource side, energy and fuel prices soar and ebb depending on the discovery of new resources or global constraints on extraction and transportation of natural resources. Alternative energy resources that are less reliant on fossil fuels are also being found due to innovations in this sector. Climate change concerns also impact the logistics industry, as consumers and regulators see differentiated pollution levels from different transportation means used by the logistics industries.

It is difficult for a company that is mostly involved in manufacturing to find the right technology choices or model of operating to handle all these shifts. Outsourcing to a specialized company becomes attractive to companies like Philips.

With regard to the economy, tectonic changes hitting the industry include concerns for efficiency. More mergers take place, enabled by increased efficiency in transport services. The shifting private sector role enables movement of finances, which supports further mergers and acquisitions in manufacturing, and also in transport and logistics. All these impacted on the choices for Philips to engage UPS (Table 6.18).

Philips is subject to shifts in the burden of disease and opportunities to innovate for unique markets. The need for medical equipment to solve growing needs from increased risks makes Philips focus and specialize, leaving input-level activities to partners like UPS.

All these shifts can be seen in the evolution of Philips over the years. The contract Philips signed with UPS in May 2006 covers five years, with UPS redesigning and operating a global services parts logistics (SPL) network for Philips Medical. UPS was engaging to offer Philips Medical customers a service level that contrasts with the previous practice of next day business service. The UPS-designed network replaced one operated by Philips Medical. UPS was well placed to offer logistical services, as it is an expert in material storage and inventory management, as well as order fulfillment. UPS is the

Table 6.18 Why is this happening? Drivers of demand for medical imaging

	Year 1990		Year 2010
1	Lower respiratory infections	1	Ischemic heart disease
2	Diarrheal diseases	2	Unipolar major depression
3	Conditions arising during prenatal period	3	Road traffic accidents
4	Unipolar major depression	4	Cerebrovascular disease
5	Ischemic heart disease	5	Chronic obstructive pulmonary disease
6	Cerebrovascular disease	6	Lower respiratory infections
7	Tuberculosis	7	Tuberculosis
8	Measles	8	War
9	Road traffic accidents	9	Diarrheal diseases
10	Congenital anomalies	10	HIV
16	HIV	11	Conditions arising during prenatal period
		25	Measles
		26	Congenital anomalies

Disease burden measured in disability-adjusted life years.
Source: Adapted from "The Global Burden of Disease: A comprehensive assessment of mortality and disability from diseases, injuries, and risk factors in 1990 and projected to 2020." Harvard University Press, available at https://extranet.who.int/iris/restricted/bitstream/10665/41864/1/0965546608_eng.pdf.

master of inbound and outbound transportation and had global visibility and reporting that could be verified online minute by minute. UPS was also able to offer a cheap and fast alternative to repackaging and labeling, as picky customers shopping on line chose to return or exchange products they purchased from Philips. UPS had developed a sophisticated solution for hold-for-pickup and return services in a number of countries and was engaged in solutions for critical parts distribution for other clients.

Evolution of UPS 1907 to 2007

UPS was created in 1907 as a messenger errand service on foot and bicycle. Between 1907 and 1929 the company went on to consolidate package delivery for retail clients, serving them by motorcycle, even contributing to the demand for two-wheelers during this period (Table 6.19).

Common carrier services included daily pickup and streamlined billing and payment. All this time UPS was serving the California market. The company expanded outside of California during the period after 1930 and until 1980 it was engaged in building its air service in addition to the ground service. The completion of the Interstate Highway System to 48 states was a big boon to UPS. The company went on to create its own airline in the period 1981 to 1990 and to grow to serve 175 countries. Between the period

Table 6.19   Evolution of UPS 1907–2007

1907 to 1929	1930 to 1980
• Messenger errand service on foot and bicycle	• Expansion outside of Califronia
• Consolidated package delivery for retail clients by motorcycle	• Air service in addition to ground service
• Common carrier services daily pick-up, streamlined billing & payment	• Interstate service "Golden Link" to 48 states in America
1981 to 1990	**1991 to 1999**
• UPS airlines	• Embracing new technology
• Growth to 175 countries	• Expanded services
	• New York Stock Exchange listing
2000 to 2007	
• Global supply chain management services to others	
• Franchising of retail shipping, postal and business services	
• Expansion of air hubs (Louisville, Cologne), growth in Europe	
• Entry into China and Latin America	
• Growth in heavy freight	

Source: Data from www.ups.com.

1991 and 1999, UPS focused on embracing technology. It expanded its services and also listed on the New York Stock Exchange. The period from 2000 to 2007 was focused on building global supply management services to others, such as the case of Philips. The company went into franchising arrangements for retail shipping, postal, and business services.

UPS procured other air hubs—Louisville in the US and Cologne in Germany—to supporting its expansion in Europe. This period also saw the entry of UPS into China, with non-stop delivery service and joint venture to reach 23 cities in the country. UPS entered the Latin American market with the acquisition of Challenge Air. UPS also entered the heavy freight market, having focused previously mostly in light packages.

Tectonic changes impacting UPS

The transformation in transport technology as well as the Internet has provided fast moving information and ideas at the fingertips of logistics companies. This has allowed easier tracking of shipments, making specialized companies like UPS more competitive in producing unique solutions to companies like Philips. More energy efficient technologies have also emerged for the logistics industry. Better infrastructure for transportation, such as better roads and airports being built, has helped, as has the re-emergence of rail as a clean and reliable service provider (Table 6.20).

Scaling up of various transportation systems, such as maritime and aviation, is also aiding companies like UPS to offer unique logistics solutions. Sharing of databases and experiences within companies as well as throughout industries, especially when mergers occur, has been of tremendous importance in shaping changes across a wide range of industries.

Table 6.20 Exports of pharmaceutical products (medicament mixtures in dosage)

Top ten by value of exports			Asia's best by value of exports		
Country	2001	2012	Country	2001	2012
USA	8,552	24,721	Singapore	224	5,079
Germany	13,209	45,345	Hong Kong, China	545	1,170
Ireland	6,200	19,079	Malaysia	40	174
Netherlands	3,703	12,014	Korea, Rep	104	573
Mexico	720	1,501	Thailand	63	244
UK	10,937	23,227	Pakistan	29	101
Belgium	6,674	29,699	India	764	8,404
France	10,257	27,282	Philippines	17	56
Japan	1,432	2,043	Vietnam	7	44
China	266	2,361	Indonesia	44	297

Source: ITC International Trade Statistics, available at http://www.intracen.org/itc/market-info-tools/trade-statistics/.

Tremendous improvements in access to local land systems also contributes to shifting patterns of congestion and pollution and their corresponding impact on the routing and warehousing choices of companies like UPS.

Position before the logistics outsourcing

Philips contracted UPS for its medical business. At about the time of the merger, medical systems made up 12% of its earnings before interest and taxes. Philips was successfully improving its sustainability bottom line, with the Dow Jones Sustainability Index Score for the company growing from 77% in 2005 to 82% in 2006.

Gross margins were also up for Philips, from €7.9 billion in 2005 to €8.3 billion in 2006. The company had the cash to engage in large-scale contracting with UPS.

At the time of the contract with UPS there was tremendous growth in the exports of instruments for medical, surgical, dental, and veterinary uses. In the US exports grew in value by 42% from above US$ 8 billion in 2001 to close to US$ 12 billion in 2005 (today the value is even higher in the US at close to US$ 25 billion). In the Netherlands, the home of Philips, the value of exports grew by 112% from US$ 1.8 billion to US$ 3.8 billion during the same period (in 2012 exports in the Netherlands were estimated at more than US$ 12 billion). Countries like India saw their exports grow by 223% from US$ 44 million in 2001 to US$ 142 million in 2005 (in 2012 India's exports surpassed US$ 8 billion). Such growth patterns portended very well for a specialized logistics company seeking to offer unique solutions to customers serving the medical instrument business around the world (Table 6.21).

Table 6.21 Financial implications for Philips

Sales and EBIT 2006 in millions of EUR

Sector	Sales	EBIT	As % of Sales
Medical systems	6,742	795	11.8
DAP	2,645	386	14.6
Consumer electronics	10,576	416	3.9
lighting	5,466	635	11.6
Other activities	1,547	(448)	(29.0)
Unallocated	–	(601)	–
Philips group	26,976	1,183	4.4
Gross margin (€ millions)		Dow Jones sustainability index scores	
2006	8,295	2006	82%
2005	7,941	2005	77%

Source: Philips sustainability report, available at www.philips.com.

Stakeholders in the logistics services for medical equipment solutions

A number of stakeholders could have an interest in the business of special-ized logistics services for medical equipment that Philips is engaged in. These include the final consumers of medical equipment (such as hospitals); road users (such as truck drivers serving UPS); environmental NGOs; govern-ments; representatives of local transport industries who compete or partner with UPS; the CEOs of online shopping services like Amazon.com who could be used to order such equipment; trade unions representing labor in the various countries where UPS would serve the contract for logistics services for Philips; supply chain managers at Philips and UPS; fuel suppliers to UPS; and financiers for local transport companies that would grow in a country where UPS is interested in finding specialized solutions. Such stakeholders typically care about different issues, but could also have some transversal areas of common interest such as (fuel prices, consumer satisfaction, reli-able delivery system, developing transport markets, safety in infrastructures, workers' wages, social well-being, etc). Two issues have progressively become the center of focus in the area of multi-stakeholder dialogues in logistics, namely: the questions of energy (fuel prices) and environmental concerns present at every stage of the supply chain.

Embodying and preparing for superior performance

The four cases of the logistics industry, Iceland's financial sector, deferred maintenance, and the Philips and UPS logistics outsourcing, are excellent for role-playing in multi-stakeholder dialogue. The practice block captures Theory U's focus on skills to perform effectively on a daily basis, bringing together lessons from previous learning modules (Box 6.1).

Box 6.1   Practice Block VI: Embodying and Preparing for Superior Performance

Premise: Decision-makers facing a co-developed strategy would bring different solutions to the table, allowing them to achieve superior performance in implementation.

Objective: To practice the skill of embodying the perspectives, under-standings, and solutions of other stakeholders into a collective set of actions leading to higher performance.

Approach: Case studies of the financial sector in Iceland, the logistics case, the case of Philips and UPS, or the deferred maintenance pre-sent an opportunity to learn from large-scale global change. Lessons come from the details of the cases, the time at which they took place, the history and trajectories of the agents concerned, their location before and after important decisions, what was going on globally at the time, and the outcome of their decisions or choices. Leaders in all cases needed to co-develop a set of potential actions and embody them into actions for implementation.

Exercise: Working with a group of stakeholders (or a simulation with role-play), develop a common strategy and execute together for results. The roles and interests of stakeholders are defined and discussed using a group process that ensures that all participants are listened to and their contributions incorporated in an embodying effort for a co-created strategy and set of actions. Care is taken to note areas of confrontation and common interest.

Recommendation: Such an approach would be useful for the leaders of a city or region or those looking to shape and influence policy proposals. The cases could aid the development of political campaigns where the electorate is sophisticated or the coalitions in place change dynamically over short periods of time.

7
Conclusions

This book evolved from the experiences of the author working in a variety of leadership positions in complex environments around the world. Typical challenges facing decision makers in light of complexities from the increased interactions and interconnections in a globalized world were presented. Through a series of real-life case studies the book has introduced the degree of interconnectedness and how it affects the process of decision-making and, indeed, the outcomes of key decisions.

Learning from others and from experience

The book has focused on learning from others and from past experiences to sharpen one's ability to deal with complex decision-making environments. Analytical work done purposefully for the book was used to show the pitfalls of making decisions on the basis of what is visible (surface phenomena) and how ignoring key elements of complexity often leads to costly mistakes and irreversible effects.

Understanding the main spheres of change related to people, economy, resources, and technology and identifying the patterns and underlying drivers of change around these spheres is necessary not only for shaping strategy, but also for developing effective risk management approaches and selecting from a series of potential courses of action.

The role of complexity science and its practical use for decision-making has been introduced, with a special focus on risk and adaptive strategies that can lead to superior decision-making. The nature of interactions and risk also put front and center the question of global governance and how it interrelates to national and local governance and the special role of individuals and their preferences in shaping outcomes on scales beyond their geographical confines.

Hopefully the book has shown that "how" we engage is as important as "what" we engage with in decision-making. Analytic content and case studies are structured to help the learner practice skills and approaches from complexity science, economics, management, and international affairs, which help them navigate better in a complex world.

Navigating through six key questions

The book started off with the importance of asking the right questions. A set of six key questions is proposed to link the key issues in complexity of relevance to decision-making in a globalized world. The first question covers what is changing, and it aims at focusing the learner on the deliberate link between objective areas of data and observations that are complex to explain yet are critical for the competitive advantage of one agent over another.

The second question goes after drivers of change and offers the learner the opportunity to extract the effects of significant drivers of change, many of which are transportable to the decision-making environments they may face. The learner is also introduced to what it takes to work with others to understand how they sense problems and relate different perspectives to their own.

The third question supports leadership learning and provides guidelines on how to use general concepts of "complexity" for effective decision-making under uncertain and risky scenarios. The book introduces the behavioral skills that are desirable to succeed in risky and uncertain environments, including those that grow the comfort level of individuals in dealing with uncertain or incomplete information. Such skills are essential to identify convergent interests and adopt a fair consensus on the objects of negotiations at the international and national levels, and also at the level of interactions between public debates internal to organizations *vis-à-vis* international commitments.

The fourth question brings the learner to consider the role of leadership in ensuring good governance environments. Through analysis and examples from practice, evolution of governance systems around the world is presented with attention to governance changes taking place on the global level and their effect on local and national governance. Security and social cohesion are given important emphasis due to their interactions with decision-making in a critical and sensitive manner in countries that are in and out of conflict. The case of territorial governance gets singular attention because of the importance of geography in leadership and the growing importance of cities in a globalized world. Other elements impacting governance, such as ethnic diversity, language, beliefs, religion, and culture, are treated with specific examples, but not in as much depth as the spatial questions of geography, territory, and cities. I hope the learner benefits from the rehearsal that comes from interacting with this question and related case studies. Insight gained from such rehearsal is important for developing a vision and collective set of intentions that take note of the future as it emerges from group work or from self-reflection.

The fifth question focuses on understanding risks, and in particular how perceptions of risk vary and their implications for decision-making. Complexity reasoning is applied to help the learner become skilled at identifying the most important interactions to expect in a particular context, identifying constraints, deciding where to enact barriers to prevent certain outcomes from materializing, and defining and selecting from a suite of strategies.

The sixth question helps the learner see, through a variety of applications, how all the lessons in the book come together. I hope the section on the science of muddling through has provided guideposts of what to do when very little is known and judgment is at a premium. Learning from failure is also important and is exposed using examples from multiple sectors. The other takeaway from this question is on resilience and how leaders can be comfortable with the concept and become skilled at building context-sensitive resilience strategies.

Being a leader in a complex world

Most people I have interacted with who are in leadership situations around the world have highlighted that their main challenge is the loneliness they sense when it comes to taking difficult decisions. People who report to them rarely come with what is not working until it is too late and often the leaders I have spoken to are absorbed in time-consuming activities that leave them little time for study and reflection. The main challenge is to set up a process that allows them to get the most elements for a decision in the shortest amount of time possible. The answer on how to succeed in such environments varies with each leadership situation, particularly in the country and industry sectors, and more importantly with the culture and governance environments. However, I offer a few guideposts that have wide transferability and that have helped me personally.

First, experience has shown that starting from a better understanding of patterns leads to superior outcomes in a decision process, but the key issue is how to come to a good understanding of patterns. I found it possible to get better at understanding patterns through practice with the understanding that Lucius Annaeus Seneca had in saying:

The way is long if one follows precepts, but short ... if one follows patterns.[1]

People remember more of what they are engaged in analyzing, defining, creating, and evaluating. Furthermore, complex systems require special skills to analyze what is going on. Combining lessons from complexity science with those from the science of working together, as in Theory U, can help ensure better identification and understanding of patterns. So look for patterns and get really good at identifying them in people and their behavior, in systems and their performance, and in outcomes of decisions.

Second, it is not enough to just see the patterns and understand them. As globalization advances, the complexity of decision-making increases, and one needs to have a proper identification of the drivers of change. I have found it particularly helpful to use a process of dialogue to refine my understanding or uncover ones that fell in my blind spot. I gather courage for this approach from the quote attributed to John F. Kennedy:

> *Change is the law of life. And those who look only to the past or present are certain to miss the future.*[2]

When many things are changing at the same time and they are interconnected it can become challenging to identify all the important drivers of change. Furthermore, anticipating change and sensing it as it emerges is a critical skill highlighted in the book, requiring readiness for the future. Practicing by observing how others have solved similar problems can help; so get connected and networked with people who have faced similar challenges and engage with them. Also, practice the skill of extracting drivers using the tools in this book to become good at anticipating the future. You can also create a team of people with good sensing skills that you can work with and engage them with a series of questions, not unlike the six we have covered in this book, to get at what they have experienced and known that could be useful for your situation.

Third, there is a lot of attention to complexity and an effort to make the science usable for day-to-day decision-making. The practical approach in the book encourages the reader not to be stymied by complexity, reminding me of a quote from Nelson Mandela:

> *I have tried not to falter; I have made missteps along the way. But I have discovered the secret that after climbing the great hill, one only finds that there are many more hills to climb.*[3]

Being able to search out what is changing helps us to become good at identifying *variation*, a key aspect of functioning under complexity, as decisions are linked to types of change. Identifying, through observation, analysis, or dialogue, the main *interaction* amongst spheres of change supports effective definition actions to deploy. Using the tools for *selection* among alternative strategies makes the final decision more achievable and the actions doable.

Fourth, I have come across many leaders who struggle in the face of governance challenges. This book provides an approach to understanding governance, buttressed by the values that underpin good governance. Confucius said:

> *In a country well governed, poverty is something to be ashamed of. In a country badly governed, wealth is something to be ashamed of.*[4]

This quote is very fitting for our times, because leaders define the parameters and set the incentive structure that generates governance outcomes. The role of leadership in governance is paramount. Bad governance, as in corruption, power mongering, and greed, have particularly negative impacts on people and nature. Equipping oneself with tools for functioning under diverse potential futures can be a big help, but at the core, embracing the values and behaviors that can serve as a guide in making choices in challenging circumstances is most important.

Fifth is the work around risk analysis, assessment, and management. I came to the practice of risk management after many years of working in development at the World Bank and in founding and leading my own company. But the question of risk came front and center when I spent four years reforming a Foundation in Africa that was aimed at building capacity to manage development affairs effectively. I like to be guided by quotes that one cannot forget easily, and the one from Rosalind Carter is very appropriate for summarizing my learning on risk:

> *You must accept that you might fail; then, if you do your best and still don't win, at least you can be satisfied that you've tried. If you don't accept failure as a possibility, you don't try – you don't take the risk.*[5]

Learning from failure and the whole science around evaluation from past experiences is very useful as a comfort blanket to try new things. Getting comfortable with trying and not seeing results for a long time, and even facing harsh challenges along the way, has been tremendously useful for me. This is why I put a lot of emphasis on learning from failure—personal or from the failure of others. We focus too much on success and with complex systems, where the outcomes can be indeterminate and indeed quite different, with some desirable and many undesirable ones, it falls on the shoulders of a person in a leadership position to set the tolerance for failure and the parameters for risk taking. Set too tight no learning takes place; set too loose and one can cause risks that are hard to recover from. But trying is at the heart of it all, and learning from what didn't work takes a bite out of your soul if you are not prepared to fail.

For leaders, the horizon may be concealed, the path windy and steep, but with the desire to vision a better outcome, the journey would be worth the effort. We must take the first step of many steps to go toward the horizon and beyond.

Notes

Introduction

1. Taken from a recorded interview of Simon Compaoré on August 21, 2012 in Ouagadougou on the occasion of the signing of the Grant from the African Capacity Building Foundation to CIFAL Ouagadougou. The Mayor agreed to share the leadership lessons learned during his tenure as Mayor.
2. Fact-checked from a publication of the Unité d'Enseignement et de Recherche en Démographie (UERD) titled "Les migrations à Ouagadougou: tendances récentes (1990–2000). Ouaga Focus. No. 30, Octobre 2002.
3. Fact-checked from a publication by Södeström, O., Fimiani, D., Glambalvo, M. And Lucido, S. (2009): Urban Cosmographies, Roma: Meltemi; and Guggenheim, M. and Södeström, O. (eds) (2010): Reshaping Cities: How Global Mobility Transforms Architecture and Urban Form. London: Routledge.
4. Lin (2012: p. 112) argues that industrial structures vary with a country's level of development and the need for correspondingly different tangible and intangible infrastructures to facilitate operations and transactions in those economies. This idea is used to explain how countries develop strategy and adapt to global changes. Lin (2012: p. 14) further argues that while each level of development is along a continuum, the policies for upgrading economies cannot just be borrowed from those countries more advanced along the continuum. This idea fits well with the notion of learning, particularly from failure. The third idea, from Lin (2012: p. 25), featuring in several chapters, is the need to balance the role of state, private sector, and civil society institutions. Such a balancing role is particularly needed to achieve the level of coordination sufficient to manage the positive and negative externalities to firms in transaction costs and returns to capital when there are many social, environmental, and economic considerations to account for.
5. For a good analysis of the contribution of Cleveland (1972) to the understanding of the role of governance in public administration see Frederickson, H. George (2004): "Whatever Happened to Public Administration? Governance, Governance Everywhere," Institute of Governance Public Policy and Social Research, Queens University, Belfast. Working Paper QU/GOV/3/2004.
6. "Tectonic" is defined in the *Oxford English Dictionary* as an adjective of a change or development that is very significant or considerable (as in "the last decade has witnessed a tectonic shift in world affairs"). Merriam-Webster defines "tectonic" as having a strong and widespread impact (as in a tectonic shift in voting patterns). The use of "tectonic shifts" and discontinuities is relevant for those changes that are of significant important to policy decision-making as a result of globalization Drucker (1992) and Fariboz and Petersen (2005).
7. Fact-checked from an OECD publication titled "Inondations au Burkina Faso," Club de Sahel et l'Afrique de l'Ouest, which has an interview of H.E. M. Luc Tiao, Ambassador of Burkina Faso to France dated end September 2009.

1   Setting the Stage

1. There are a number of authors who have covered the subject of international migration. To learn more about the historical reasons for migration see Hatton, Timothy J. and Jeffrey G. Williamson (1998): *The Age of Mass Migration: Causes and Economic Impact.* Oxford University Press. For good coverage of international migration in the age of globalization see Solimano, Andrés (2010): *International Migration in the Age of Globalization: Historical and Recent Experiences.* New York: Cambridge University Press. We would also recommend the book review of the Solimano (2010) by Raymond Cohen at http://eh.net/book_reviews/international-migration-age-globalization-historical-and-recent-experiences (posted Mon, 2010-12-06 17:13 by whaples) who gives a good critique of the public policy implications of international migration from a lay perspective.
2. This case study was developed by Kateryna Semchuk for the Leadership in a Globalized World Course offered by Dr Frannie A. Léautier at Sciences Po, Paris in the Fall of 2011. The author has edited the case study for relevance to this chapter and to demonstrate more coherently the choice set possible by a variety of decision-makers.
3. For a good discussion of emotional intelligence I have found a very useful book by Goleman, Daniel (1997): *Emotional Intelligence: Why It Can Matter More than IQ,* Bantam Books.

2   Dynamics of Change

1. Calculations made using data from the World Development Indicators published by the World Bank.
2. Data taken from *The Economist: World in Figures.*
3. There are many analyses of brands, but the one that has the most usable database for long-term analysis is that done by Milword Brown Optimor.
4. Data is from the World Bank Indicators on the investment in transport with private sector participation in current US$.
5. Dr Frannie Léautier prepared this case study while at the World Bank in partnership with Jonathan Lehrich of the MIT Sloan School of Management. It does not represent the views of the World Bank or its Board of Directors. It is based in part on an amalgam of documents available to the public and personal knowledge of the project and project negotiation procedures by the authors. It is intended for discussions and debates on issues of leadership in development.

3   Complexity and Risk

1. The world's largest beer brewers are AB InBev and SABMiller, who collectively market hundreds of brands. The next two largest brewers are Heineken and Carlsberg, as they produce about half of the beer sold worldwide. Source: MilwardBrown (2013): "Brewers Expand Globally While Satisfying Local Tastes." Top 100 Global Brands published in 2013 BrandZ Top 100. http://www.millwardbrown.com/BrandZ/Top_100_Global_Brands/Categories/food_and_drink/Beer.aspx.

2. The Arab Spring according to Oxford Dictionaries is "a series of anti-government uprisings in various countries in North Africa and the Middle East, beginning in Tunisia in December 2010." It is a name given to the revolutionary wave of demonstrations and protests occurring in the Arab World that began on 18 December 2010. The protests have common techniques of civil resistance like strikes, rallies, demonstrations and organized marches, and have also used social media. Some, like Springborg (2011), have questioned the uniqueness of the Arab Spring compared to previous uprisings.

3. This case study was prepared by Dr Frannie A. Léautier for use in the course titled "Leadership in a Globalized World" offered at Sciences Po during the Fall of 2011. The Case material has benefitted from inputs from Chiarra Rosselli, Imen Boussaha, Nelly Hatem, Filipe Pelepka, Pierre Coeffe, Pierre Marie Viville and Moritz Zyrewitz, all of whom were my students in the 2010–2011 class at Sciences PO.

4. WHO *Weekly Epidemiological Record* 2003, 78, 73–80: http://www.who.int/ docstore/wer/pdf/2003/wer7811.pdf, rev. 20/11/10.

5. Wang, M.D. and Jolly, A. M. (2004).*Changing virulence of the SARS virus: The epidemiological evidence.* Bulletin of the World Health Organization, 82, 547.

6. Sarsreference.com: http://sarsreference.com, rev. 20/11/10.

7. Smith, R. D. (2006): Responding to global infectious disease outbreaks: lessons from SARS on the role of risk perception, communication and management, in: *Social Science & Medicine* 63:3114.

8. *The Pharma Letter* (2003-20-06): "SARS boost for Chinese Pharma in May. www. thepharmaletter.com.

9. Smith, R. D. (2006): Responding to global infectious disease outbreaks: lessons from SARS on the role of risk perception, communication and management, in: *Social Science & Medicine* 63:3118.

10. Wang, M.D. and Jolly, A. M. (2004).*Changing virulence of the SARS virus: The epidemiological evidence.* Bulletin of the World Health Organization, 82, 548.

11. http://www.guardian.co.uk/uk/2011/jun/01/e-coli-germany.

12. FAO (2007), Key Statistics of Food and Agricultural Trade.

13. http://www.meatprocess.com/Industry-markets/Sars-outbreak-boosts-Thai-chicken-industry.

14. An example of tracking using social media is Flu Detector, which uses content from Twitter to nowcast flu rates in several UK regions (www.geopatterns.enm. bris.ac.uk).

4   Leadership and Governance

1. The review indicates that the application of such policies varies by region, with the most challenges and violations of the policy being in Africa and in the transport and mining sectors. Application of the policies is best in Latin America and in rural, agriculture, and environmental projects. For a critique of the policies of multilateral institutions in this regard see Mackay, 2002.

2. Analysis using data from the World Bank Governance Indicators and Growth in GDP over time was conducted to study the relationship between governance and economic growth. The results uncovered a U-shaped pattern of change, where early reforms in governance do not result in visible improvements in economic growth, but countries make huge jumps into higher economic performance after sustained governance improvements. Countries can move from a low level of

governance with low economic performance to high levels of governance and high economic performance over time.
3. Data on per capita GDP growth were taken from the World Bank Development Indicators.
4. This section has been developed from a lecture in 2011 by Prof. Cristina D'Allessandro-Scarpari, who participated as a special guest in the course titled "Leadership in a Globalized World" offered at Sciences Po, Paris in 2011 and a paper in 2012 she developed for this book entitled "Territorial governance: A geographical approach of leadership in the contemporary world."
5. Discourses are actions: even if symbolic and not material, their consequences are usually practical and visible. So, actors building and expressing their discourse in public contexts are acting: they are changing the reality. Even if their discourse is inefficient for some reason, the attempt made and the lack of results is already an action with consequences.
6. This perspective has been made possible by trying to use in human geography some findings and theoretical insights of sociology of science (an example is November et al., 2004). Such multidisciplinary attempts remain very limited. Much remains to be done to better investigate these complex dynamics.
7. Scharmer (2007) pages 255–260 are particularly helpful in orienting the learner to be conscious of these types of knowledge and how they can be effective in different settings.
8. The news was reported on March 10, 2009 in a communiqué titled "Activities of Secretary-General in United Republic of Tanzania, 26–28, February 2009. The full text can be found at the following website: http://www.un.org/News/Press/docs/2009/sgt2657.doc.htm
9. A definition inspired by Bernard Debarbieux in Lévy, Lussault (2003), p. 910.
10. People of Cameroonian descent can be found in many countries, including Belgium, Canada, France, Germany, Hong Kong China, Mexico, Romania, Russia, Togo, Turkey, UK, and USA (www.wikipedia.org/wiki/Category. People_of_Cameroonian_descent).

5   Risk Management Approaches

1. The 20th century marked a time of change in the social, political and economic world, in addition to change in the art world. Claude Monet and Paul Cézanne were two revolutionary artists who each found a way of representation, but with greatly different styles. Monet used a technique to represent outdoor light on nature that was not precise, yet always clear, especially when seen from a distance—his paintings represented nature as we see it, yet fuzzy in its detail. Cézanne's paintings were more abstract, analytical and calculating, and had an element of disorder, representing the basic elements that made up nature and a loose form of how they are related. For an interesting comparison of Monet and Cézanne, see Walton, K. (2007): "Contrasting the Work of Cézanne and Monet: Two Unique Paths to Modernism," published on November 8, 2007 at www.empyeasel.com.
2. Data was taken from the ITC (International Trade Center).
3. For more detail see the report on successful apparel brands that can be found in http://www.millwardbrown.com/BrandZ/Top_100_Global_Brands/Categories/consumer_and_retail/Apparel.aspx.

6   Leadership and Context

1. BRICs was a term coined by Jim O'Neill of Goldman Sachs in 2001 in a paper titled "Building Better Global Economic BRICs" in his reference to Brazil, Russia, India, and China, as they were seen to be at stage of newly advanced development (see Kowitt, Beth (2009-06-17). "For Mr. BRIC, nations meeting a milestone." CNNMoney.com. Retrieved 2009-06-18. The term was expanded later to include South Africa and became the BRICS.

2. The "flying geese paradigm" is a view of Japanese scholars on the pattern of technological development, first published by Kaname Akamatsu (1961, p. 208) in his paper titled "A Theory of Unbalanced Growth in the World Economy," *Weltwirtschaftliches Archiv* 86 (2), 192–215. In this paper Akamatsu posits the notion of a pattern with sequential positioning of developing countries lined up behind advanced nations they can emulate, learn from, or capitalize on for their own development.

3. This section of the book benefitted from research work done by Ciara Begley, Kayleigh McElligot and Lara Yeo in 2011 as part of the preparation of case materials for the course I taught at Sciences Po Paris entitled "Leadership in a Globalized World."

4. This chapter was prepared as a paper that was presented to the CERIU INFRA2008 Conference in Quebec, Canada by Frannie A. Léautier under the title "Complexity and deferred infrastructure maintenance: Risk Management Implications" from November 17–19, 2008.

5. Source: Madhya Pradesh Human Development Report for 2007.

6. *Engineering News Record.* 10/23/2007. Laval Bridge Collapse Report Fingers Multiple Culprits. www.enr.com.

7. CBC News. November 11, 2007. Ontario Labour Ministry investigates bridge collapse. www.cbc.ca.

8. For a good analysis see Pauk Holper and Michael Nolan (2007). "Infrastructure and climate change risk assessment for Victoria." GREENHOUSE 2007. October 5, 2007. www.csiro.au

9. For an example see John Moteff (2004). "Risk Management and Critical Infrastructure Protection: Assessing, Integrating, and Managing Threats, Vulnerabilities and Consequences." (RL32561). Washington DC: Congressional Research Service.

10. Data from the Aviation Safety Network indicate that there were 64 incidents and accidents caused by maintenance-related factors. Airlines in India featured in the failure to follow procedures (ABs and BDs), substandard maintenance practices, and wrong installation of parts. There were no airlines from India with causes related to failure of repair from previous damage of engine deficiencies or inspection, which are the two other categories of maintenance-related causes. Two of the airlines are listed with such incidents of accidents: Indian Airlines and Air India. So far, there are no mentions for Kingfisher or IndiGo airlines. Source: www.flightsafety.org.

11. Source: *The San Francisco Examiner.* 2008-05-05 17:51:13.0.

12. Source: *The San Francisco Examiner.* 2008-05-05 17:51:13.0.

13. For a good definition and use of r-coefficients for fiscal risk management see Peter Heller (1979). "Underfinancing of Recurrent Development Costs." Finance and Development. 16: 1:38-41. March 1979. World Bank and IMF.

14. For a good reference see Axelrod, Robert and Michael D. Cohen. *Harnessing Complexity: Organizational Implications of a Scientific Frontier.* The Free Press. New York. 1999.

15. The material in this section was adapted from a case study on the logistics indus-try prepared by William Eschalier, Will Fitzgibbon, Anna Gaarde, Clara Garcia Parra, Maria Rebecka Jonsson, Kornel Koronowski, Nathalie Nahas, Claire Nassiet, José Alberto Navarro, Nora Soussan, Pap Talla, and Noah Turner. The case was part of the learning materials for the course on Leadership in a Globalized World at Sciences Po in the Fall of 2010.

7 Conclusions

1. Source: Moral letters to Lucilius/Letter 6. On Sharing Knowledge: Paragraph 5. http://en.wikisource.org/wiki/Moral_letters_to_Lucilius/Letter_6.
2. Source: John F. Kennedy, XXXV President of the United States: 1961–1963. 266–Address in the Assembly Hall at the Paulskirche in Frankfurt. June 25, 1963.
3. Nelson Rolihlahla Mandela (1994): *Long Walk to Freedom*, The Autobiography of Nelson Mandela, Boston: Little, Brown and Company, p. 1006.
4. Dawson, M.M. (1915): *The Ethics of Confucius*, Chapter V: The State, Nourishment of the People, Analects, bk. Viii, c. xiii., v. 3., p. 190.
5. Carter, R. (1984): *First Lady from Plains*. Boston: Houghton Mifflin Company, p. 45.

Bibliography

Aberdeen (2007): *Winning Strategies for Transportation Procurement & Payment*. Boston: Aberdeen Group Inc.

Acharya, V., Cooley, T., M. Richardson and I. Walter (2009): "Market Failures and Regulatory Failures: Lessons from Past and Present Financial Crises," New York: Stern School of Business, New York University.

AfDB (2011): The Middle of the Pyramid: Dynamics of the Middle Class in Africa," Market Brief, April 20, 2011, Tunis: www.afdb.org.

Africa Report (2007): "Cote d'Ivoire: Can the Ouagadougou Agreement Bring Peace?" Crisis Group Africa Report No. 127, 27 June 2007, pp. 1–31.

Aglietta, M. (2000): "La Globalisation Financiére." Retrieved 11/11/2011, from L'economie mondiale. http://www.cepii.net/francgraph/publications/ecomond/dossierstrat/2000ch5.pdf.

AGRO BIO TEST (2012): "Zakaz stosowania GMO," Certyfikacja Produkcji i Przetwórstwa w Rolnictwie Ekologicznym, AgroBioTest. http://www.agrobiotest.pl.

Akamatsu, K. (1961): "A Theory of Unbalanced Growth in the World Economy," *Welwirtsschaftliches Archiv*, 86 (2), 192–215.

Alicia H. Munnell, Editor, Proceedings of a Conference Held at Harwich Port, Massachusetts, June 1990, Sponsored by the Federal Reserve Bank of Boston, pp. 69–112.

Al Jazeera (2010): "Riots reported in Tunisian City – Africa – Al Jazeera English," Accessed December 20, 2010 http://www.aljazeera.net. Retrieved on 17/12/2012.

Aljazeera (2011): "Icelanders reject debt repayment plan," Aljazeera Europe, 10-4-2011, www.aljazeeranews.com.

Allen, B. (1997): "The Logistics Revolution and Transportation," *Annals of the American Academy of Political and Social Science*, 553, 106–116, Annenberg, Philadelphia.

Anderson, P. (1999): "Complexity Theory and Organization Science," *Organization Science*, 10 (3), 216–232.

Anderson, S. P., de Palma A., and Thisse, J. F. (1992): *Discrete Choice Theory of Product Differentiation*. Cambridge, MA: MIT Press, pp. 66–69.

Andersen, T. M. and Getsson M. H. (2010): "Longevity, Growth and Intergenerational Equity—The Deterministic Case." Central Bank of Iceland Working Paper No. 52.

Anheier, H. K. (2004): *Civil Society: Measurement, Evaluation, Policy*. Sterling: Earthscan.

Antheaume, B., Blanc-Pamard, B., Chaleard, J. L., Dubresson A., Lassailly-Jacob, V., Marchal, J. Y., Pillet-Schwartz, A. M., Pourtier, R., Raison, J. P., and Sevin, O. (1989): *Tropiques lieux et liens: Florilège offert à Paul Pellisier et Gilles Sautter*. Paris: IFRS & CNRS.

Appel, H. (1997): "Voucher Privatization in Russia: Structural Consequences and Mass Response in the Second Period of Reform," *Europe-Asia Studies*, 49 (8), 1433–1449.

Areba, T. (2012): "It is my Time to Build Africa," Published as the Cover Story in MANAGEMENT, A Journal of the Kenyan Institute of Monetary Studies, Auguts 2012. Nairobi.

Aristotle (350 BCE): Politics, Book I & III. Translated by Benjamin Jowett. http://classics.mit.edu/Browse/browse-Aristotle.html.

Arnett, J. J. (2002): "The Psychology of Globalization," American Psychologist, Vol. 57, No. 10, pp 774–763, Washington D.C.: American Psychological Association.

Arrow, K., Bert B., Constanza, R., Dasgupta, P., Folke, C., Holling, C. S., Jansson, B. O., Levin, S., Mäler, K. G., Perrings, C., and Pimentel, D. (1995): "Economic Growth, Carrying Capacity, and the Environment," Policy Forum. *Science*, 268, 520–521.

ASKY (2012): "Un réseau dense construit autour d'un hub." http://www.flyasky.com/asky/15-Un-reseau-dense-construit-autour-d-un-hub.html.

Aviation Safety Network (2013). Latest Safety Occurrences. An exclusive service of Flight Safety Foundation. www.flightsafety.org.

Axelrod, R. and Cohen, M. D. (1999): *Harnessing Complexity: Organizational Implications of a Scientific Frontier*. New York: The Free Press.

Ayangafac, C. (2007): "Peace in Cote d'Ivoire: An analysis of the Ouagadougou Peace Accord," *Conflict Trends* 3, 25–31.

Balance, A. (2002): "Climate change and vulnerability in Africa." UNEP/GRID-Arendal. http://maps.grida.no/go/graphic/climate_change_vulnerability_in_africa.

Bar-Yam, Y. (1997): *Dynamics of Complex Systems*. Reading: Perseus Books.

Bar-Yam, Y. (2005a): *Making Things Work: Solving Complex Problems in a Complex World*. Cambridge, MA: Knowledge Press.

——— (2005b): "Global Control, Ethnic Violence and Terrorism," in *Making Things Work*, Cambridge, MA: Knowledge Press.

BBC (2005): "Monsanto fined $1.5m for bribery," January 7, 2005. http://news.bbc.co.uk.

——— (2010): "Monsanto GM seed ban is overturned by US Supreme Court." http://www.bbc.co.uk.

——— (2011a): "Q and A Monti's technocratic government for Italy." http://www.bbc.co.uk/news/world-europe-15762791.

——— (2011b): "The Italian Crisis." http://www.bbc.co.uk/news/world-europe-15637486.

——— (2010): "Iceland volcano ash continues to ground aircraft." http://news.bbc.co.uk/2/hi/8623806.stm.

——— (2010): "A Guide to Iceland's Volcanoes." http://www.icelandtouristboard.com/index.php?page=about-iceland.

Bean, C. (2009): "The Great Moderation, the Great Panic and the Great Contraction." London: Bank of England.

Beattie, A. (2010): "The New Era: A Big Unwieldy Diverse Body Moves Upstage," *Financial Times*: http://www.ft.com/intl/cms/s/0/881c0e9e-7d8c-11df-a0f5-00144feabdc0,dwp_uuid=34d69372-7da4-11df-a0f5-00144feabdc0.html#axzz1aUAXWgpW.

Benedettini, S. and Nicita A. (2010): "Towards the Economics of Comparative Law: the "Doing Business" Debate. *Comparative Law Review*. http://www.comparativelawreview.com/ois/index.php/article/view/4/8.

Bennet, A. and Bennet, D. (2008): "The Decision-Making Process for Complex Situations in a Complex Environment," in Burstein, F. and Holsapple, C. W. (eds) *Handbook on Decision Support Systems*. New York: Springer-Verlag.

Bennett, D., Chiang, C. F., and Malani, A. (2011): "Learning during a Crisis: The SARS Epidemic in Taiwan," NBER Working Paper No. 16955, Issued in April 2011.

Bergendorf, S. (2007): "Cultural Complexity and Development Policy," *The European Journal of Development Research*, 19 (2), 195–209.

Berhane, D. (2012): "Ethiopia Could Now Become Food Exporter," Danielberhane's Blog: wordpress.com.

Bernanke, B. S. (2009): "The Crisis and the Policy Response." http://www.federalreserve.gov/newsevents/speech/bernanke20090113a.htm.

——— (1983): "Nonmonetary Effects of the Financial Crisis in the Propagation of the Great Depression," *The American Economic Review*, 73 (3), 257–276.

Beyer, A. (2004): "La numérotation des routes françaises. Le sens de la nomenclature dans une perspective géographique," *Flux*, 55, 17–29.

Birch, S. (2011): "Luxury Brands Must Wake Up to Ethical and Environmental Responsibilities," GreenLiving Blog. *The Guardian*. www.theguardian.com.

Borraz, O. and Le Galès, P. (2010): "Urban Governance in Europe: The Government of What?," *Pôle Sud* 1 (32), 137–151.

Bowen, A. and Fankhouser, S. (2011): "Low-Carbon Development for the Least Developed Countries," World Economics, Vol. 12, NO.1, January-March 2011, Economic & Financial Publishing: London, UK.

Bowen, A., Fankhauser, S. et al. (2009): "Policy Brief. Grantham Research Institute on Climate Change and the Environment."

Bowen, A., Forster, P. M., Gouldson, A., Hubacek, K., Martin, R., O'Neill, D. W., Rap, A., and Rydge, J. (2009): "The Implications of the economic slowdown for greenhouse gas emissions and targets," Policy Paper, Center for Climate Change Economics and Policy, November, University of Leeds.

Bowersox, D., David, J., Closs, J., and Stank, T. P. (1999): "21st Century Logistics: Making Supply Chain Integration a Reality," Monograph, Oak Brook: Council of Logistics Management, p. 264.

Bradley, C. (2011): "Intersections in Financial Regulation after the Crisis?" *Blender Law*. http://blenderlaw.umlaw.net/wp-content/uploads/2007/07/crisisresponse-talk.pdf.

Braithwaite, B. M. (2011): "Tighter Rules on Capital: Bankers versus Basel," *The Financial Times*. http://www.ft.com/intl/cms/s/0/852fe7a4-eb4b-11e0-9a41-00144feab49a.html.

Brooks, M. R. and Ritchie, P. (2006): "Mergers and Acquisitions in the Maritime Transport Industry 1996–2000," *Transportation Journal*, 45 (2), 7–22. http://www.jstor.org/stable/20713631.

Brown, S. L. and Eisenhardt, K. M. (1997): "The Art of Continuous Change: Linking Complexity Theory and Time-Paced Evolution in Relentlessly Shifting Organizations," *Administrative Science Quarterly*, 42, 1–34.

Bullmore, J. (2000): "Alice in Disneyland, a Creative View of International Advertising," in Jones, J. P. (ed.) *International Advertising: Realities and Myths*, Thousand Oaks: Sage, pp. 41–56.

Bharat Book Bureau (2014): Logistics & Shipping Industry in India - Identifying Opportunities in Modes, Services & Infrastructure, Transportation & Logistics, www.bharatbook.com.

Cassman, K. G. and Liska, A. J. (2007): "Food and Fuel for All: Realistic or Foolish?" *Biofuels, Bioproducts and Biorefining*, 1 (1), 18–23, doi 10.1002/bbb.3.

Castles, S. and Miller, M. J. (2009): *The Age of Migration: International Population Movements in the Modern World* (4th edition). Basingstoke: Palgrave MacMillan.

CBI (2011): "Financial Stability." The Central Bank of Iceland, 8.

——— (2009): "An Outline of the Case for a Green Stimulus," *Annual Report 2009*. The Central Bank of Iceland.

CBC (2007): "Ontario Labour Ministry Investigates Bridge Collapse," www.cbc.ca.

Cecchetti, S. G., Kashyap, A., and Wilcox D. W. (1997): "Interactions between the Seasonal and Business Cycles in Production Inventories," *American Economic Review*, 87 (5), 884–892, American Economic Association.

Chan, J., Knutsen, S. S., Blix, G. C., Lee, J. W., and Fraser, G. E. (2002): "Water, Other Fluids, and Fatal Coronary Heart Disease: The Adventist Health Study," *American Journal of Epidemiology*, 155 (9), 827–833.

Chen, D. and Dahlman, C. J. (2005): "The Knowledge Economy, the KAM Methodology and World Bank Operations." World Bank Institute Working Paper No. 37256. *Social Science Research Network*: SSRN.

Chialvo, D. R. and Bak, P. (1999): "Commentary: Learning from Mistakes," *Neuroscience*, 90 (4), 1137–1148. Pergamon: Elsevier Science Ltd.

Cho, S. Y. (2012): "Integrating Equality—Globalization, Women's Rights, and Human Trafficking." Economics of Security, Working Paper No. 69. DIW Berlin.

Chomsky, N. (1999): *Profit over People: Neoliberalism and Global Order*. New York: Seven Stories Press.

Chong, M. (2010): "A Crisis of Epidemic Proportions: What Communication Lessons Can Practitioners Learn from the Singapore SARS Crisis?" *Public Relations Quarterly*, 51, 6–11.

Chrisafis, A. (2011): "Greece Debt Crisis: The 'we won't pay' Anti-austerity Revolt," *The Guardian*: http://www.guardian.co.uk/world/2011/jul/31/greece-debt-crisis-anti-austerity.

Chua, A. (2002): *World on Fire: How Exporting Free Market Democracy Breeds Ethnic Hatred and Global Instability*. New York City: Doubleday.

Claffey, P. J. (1971): "Running Costs of Motor Vehicles as Affected by Road Design and Traffic." Transportation Research Board. NCHRP Report No. 111.

Cleveland, H. (1972): *The Future Executive: A Guide for Tomorrow's Managers*. New York: Harper & Row.

Cline, W. (2011): "China's Currency Continues to be Undervalued." http://www.iie.com/publications/interviews/interview.cfm?ResearchID=1849.

CNN (2009): "Iceland Applies to Join European Union." *CNN World*.

Cohen (1997): "The Choice" by William Cohen, US Secretary of Defense, *Washington Post*.

Cohen, J. L. and Arato, A. (1992): *Civil Society and Political Theory*. Cambridge, MA: MIT Press.

Cohn, T. H. (2007): *Global Political Economy: Theory and Practice* (4th edn), Pearson International Edition, Longman: Pearson USA.

Collier, P. (2006): Economic Causes of Civil Conflict and their Implications for Policy. Oxford, UK: Centre for the Study of African Economies, Department of Economics, Oxford University.

COMESA (2013): International Trade Statistics Bulletin No. 12, Common Market for Eastern and Southern Africa, Lusaka: COMESA Statistics Unit.

——— (2007): *The Bottom Billion: Why the Poorest Countries Are Failing and What Can Be Done about It*. Oxford University Press, Emerald Group Publishing: Bingley, UK.

Cooper, M. C., Lambert, D. M, and Pagh, J. D. (1997): "Supply Chain Management: More Than a New Name for Logistics," *The International Journal of Logistics Management* 8 (1), 1–14.

Cournede, P. S. (2011): "Macroeconomic Impact of Basel 3," http://www.oecd-ilibrary.org/docserver/download/fulltext/5kghwnhkkjs8.pdf?expires=1318362606&id=id&accname=guest&checksum=0E7EE526517379B6D4B1FED1C37EA1FF.

Cox, A. and Bragadottir, K. A. (2008): "Iceland: Life on Global Warming's Front Line," *Environmental News Network*.

Crotty, J. (2005): "The Neoliberal Paradox: The Impact of Destructive Product Market Competition and Impatient Finance on Nonfinancial Corporations in the Neoliberal Era." *IDEAS*. http://ideas.repec.org/p/uma/perirb/rb2003-5.html.

Dahlman, C. (2007): "China and India: Emerging Technological Powers," *Issues in Science and Technology*, National Academy of Sciences, National Academy of Engineering, Institute of Medicine, University of Texas Dallas.

Daily News (2012): "Kikwete to Flag Off Kilimanjaro Expédition," *Daily News*: Local News. http://www.dailynews.co.tz/index.php/local-news/2548-kikwete-to-flag-off-kilimanjaro-expedition.

Danielsson, J. (2009): "Waking Up to Reality in Iceland." *BBC*. Energy in Iceland. Iceland Official Trade Directory, http://www.icelandexport.is/english/industry_sectors_in_iceland/energy_in_iceland/.

Dasgupta, K. A. (1995): "Economic Growth Carrying Capacity and the Environment," *Science*, 520–521.

Davies, H. (2010): The Financial Crisis – Who is to blame?, Cambridge: Polity Press, pp. 229.

Davies, H. (2012): "Financial Crisis and the Regulatory Response: An Interim Assessment," *Journal of Disclosure and Governance* 9 (3), 206–216 (11).

——— (2010): *The Financial Crisis*. London: Polity Press.

Davies, K. (2011): "The Australian Financial System in the 2000s: Dodging the Bullet," Conference Volume, Sydney: RBA Conference.

Dei, H. K., Rose, S. P., and Mackenzie, A. M. (2007): "Shea Nut (*Vitellaria paradoxa*) Meal as a Feed Ingredient for Poultry," *World's Poultry Science Journal*, 63 (4), 611–624.

de la Fuente, A. and Estache, A. (2004): "A Survey of the Evidence on the Growth Effects of Infrastructure." World Bank, Washington DC.

Dematteis G. and Governa F. (dir.) (2005): *Territorialità, sviluppo locale, sostenibilità: il modello SLoT*. Milano: Franco Angeli.

De Mello (1984): "The Golden Eagle," Excerpt from "The Song of the Bird." Garden City: Image Books.

Dennie, M. N. (2012): "Medical Benefits of the Shea Nut Tree." Biology Student Research, Department of Biological Sciences, Tennessee State University.

de Tocqueville, Alexis (1835), De la démocratie en Amérique I, GF Flammarion, Paris, 1981.

Diop, A. (ed.) (2008): *Développement local, gouvernance territorial. Enjeux et perspectives*. Paris: Khartala.

Djankov, S., La Porta, R., Lopez-de-Silanes, F., and Shleifer, A. (2002): "The Regulation of Entry," *The Quarterly Journal of Economics*, 117 (1), 1–37.

Dostoevsky: The Brothers Karamazov, "The Grand Inquisitor." Fyodor Dostoevsky. 1821–1881.

Drozdz, M. and Tabarly, S. (2005): "Places marchandes, places migrantes dans l'espace saharo-sahélien," *Géoconfluences*, brève No. 5, http://geoconfluences.ens-lsh.fr/doc/breves/2005/5.htm.

Drucker, P. (1992): Managing for the future, Truman Talley/E.P. Dutton, New York, NY.

Du Marais, B. (2008): "Methodological limits of 'Doing Business' reports." May 2009, SSRN:http://ssrn.com/abstract=1408605.

Durrenmatt, F. (1994): *The Visit*. New York: Grove Press.

EC (2011): "Successful start of Iceland's membership negotiations with the EU." Press Release. European Commission.

Economist (2013): "Africa and China: More than Minerals," The Economist. www.economist.com.

Econostrum.info, March 2009: "CMA CGM et Véolia mettent fin à leur partnenariat dans le fret ferroviare," http://www.econostrum.info/CMA-CGM-et-Veolia-mettent-fin-aleur-partenariat-dans-le-fret-ferroviaire_a867.html.

EFSF (2010): "About EFSF," http://www.efsf.europa.eu/about/index.htm.

Elinaza, A. (2013): "Tanzania: Kikwete Welcomes Foreign Agricultural Investors." *Tanzania Daily News*, allafrica.com.

Europe Intelligence Wire (2006): "Veolia Cargo, CMA CGM Rail link JV cleared by EU."

——— (2006): Veolia Cargo, CMA CGM Rail link JV cleared by EU.

European Commission (2011): "Report from the Commission to the European Parliament and the Council on the Implementation of the Single Sky Legislation: Time to Deliver." Brussels.

EUROSTAT (2011): "Iceland EU Bilateral Trade and Trade with the World," EUROSTAT.

——— (2006): "Iceland's Fourth National Communication on Climate Change Under the United Nations Framework Convention on Climate Change and Iceland's Report on Demonstrable Progress Under the Kyoto Protocol." The Ministry for the Environment in Iceland.

——— (2011): "Icelanders reject debt repayment plan." Aljazeera.

Evans, Peter, B. (2004): "Development as Institutional Change: The Pitfalls of Mono-cropping and the Potentials of Deliberation," Studies in Comparative International Development 38: pages 30–53.

Iceland (2006): "Iceland's Fourth National Communication on Climate Change: Under the United Nations Framework Convention on Climate Change and Iceland's Report on Demonstrable Progress Under the Kyoto Protocol," Iceland: The Ministry for the Environment.

IMF (2011): "Iceland's Unorthodox Policies Suggest Alternative Way Out of Crisis," November 03, 2011, IMF: Washington DC.

Fall, J. (2007): "Lost Geographers: Power Games and the Circulation of Ideas within Francophone Political Geographies," *Progress in Human Geography*, 31(2), 195–216.

FAO (2007): Key Statistics of Food and Agricultural Trade. WHO Weekly epidemiological record 2003, 78, 73–80: http://www.who.int/docstore/wer/pdf/2003/wer7811.pdf, rev. 20/11/10.

FAO (2007): Statistics of Food and Agricultural Trade, http://faostat.fao.org/site/406/default.aspx.

FAOSTAT (2010): FAO Statistical Yearbook 2010, Food and Agriculture Organization of the United Nations, Rome 2010.

Faucheux, S., Coulbaut-Lazzarini, A., and Nemoz, S. (2013): L'éco-innovation au prisme du développement durable: regarde et contributions des sciences sociales, sous la direction d'Armélie Coubaut-Lazzarini et Sophie Némoz; préface de Sylvie Faucheux, Paris: l'Harmattan, p. 129.

Feenstra, R. C. (2004): *International Trade: Theory and Evidence*, Princeton University Press, Princeton NJ. pp. 174–208.

Finch, P. (2004): "Supply Chain Risk Management," *Supply Chain Management: An International Journal* 9 (2), 183–196.

Finley, M. I. (1985): *Athens (Greece); Politics and government; Democracy; History*. New Brunswick: Rutgers University Press.

Firebaugh, G. and B. Goesling (2004): "Accounting for the Recent Decline in Global Income Inequality," *American Journal of Sociology*, Vol. 110, No. 2, September 2004, pp. 283–312.

Fisher, R., Ury, W., and Patton, B. (1991): *Getting to Yes: Negotiating Agreement without Giving in*. Harvard Negotiation Project, Penguin Books USA, New York NY.

Foundation, W. A. (2011): "Index of Economic Freedom World Rankings." The Heritage Foundation, http://www.heritage.org/index/topten.

Frederickson, G. H. (2004): "Whatever Happened to Public Administration? Governance, Govenace Everywhere." Institute of Governance Public Policy and Social Research, Queens University, Belfast. Working Paper No. QU/GOV/3/2004.

Freedom House (2011): *Freedom in the World 2011—Iceland*. www.unhcr.org.

FSA (2011)" The Turner Review: A Regulatory Response to the Global Financial Crisis. http://www.fsa.gov.uk/pubs/other/turner_review.pdf.

G20 (2011): About G20: http://www.g20.org/about_what_is_g20.aspx.

Gabriel, R. A. (2011): *Hannibal: The Military Biography of Rome's Greatest Enemy*. US: Potomac Books, Inc., pp. 83–100.

Gallagher, M. (2011): *How Ireland Voted 2011*. Dublin: Palgrave.

Garner, M. (ed.) (1992): *Best Remembered Poems*. "The Blind Man and the Elephant," John Godfrey Saxe, 1816–1887. New York: Dover Publications, pp. 149–150.

Ghadar, F. and E. Peterson (2005): *Global Tectonics: What Every Business Needs to Know*. The Penn State Center for Business Studies, Smeal College of Business, University Park, PA.

Giles, C. (2011): *Financial Times*: G7 Struggles to Find Common Ground: http://www.ft.com/cms/s/0/af7e08fe-daf9-11e0-bbf4-00144feabdc0.html#axzz1aUAXWgpW.

—— (2010): *Financial Times*. Pressure is on to Reverse Latest Slide. http://www.ft.com/intl/cms/s/0/8d9e7aa0-7d8c-11df-a0f5-00144feabdc0,dwp_uuid=34d69372-7da4-11df-a0f5-00144feabdc0.html#axzz1aUAXWgpW.

—— (2011). *Financial Times*. G7 Faces Grim Outlook with Resignation. http://www.ft.com/intl/cms/s/0/21accee6-da15-11e0-b199-00144feabdc0.html#axzz1aUAXWgpW.

Gilpin, R. (2003): "The Challenges of Global Capitalism: The World Economy in the 21st Century," in Clark, J. (ed.) *Globalization and the Poor: Exploitation or Equalizer?* New York: International Debate Education Association, pp. 61–67.

Giugale, M. (2011): "Globalization: Has It Helped or Hurt Women?" *Huffington Post*.

Glaser, B., Strauss, A. (1967): The Discovery of Grounded Theory. Aldine Publishing Company. Hawthorne, N.Y.

Goleman, D. (1997): *Emotional Intelligence: Why It Can Matter More than IQ*. Bantam Books, New York, NY.

Governa F. and Salone C. (2004): "Territories in Action, Territories for Action: The Territorial Dimension of Italian Local Development Policies," *International Journal of Urban and Regional Research*, 28 (4), 796–818.

Govindarajan, V. and Trimble, C. (2005): *10 Rules for Strategic Innovators: From Idea to Execution*. Harvard Business School Press, Cambridge MA.

Guerrera, F. (2009): "Welch Condemns Share Price Focus," *Financial Times*, http://www.ft.com/intl/cms/s/0/294ff1f2-0f27-11de-ba10-0000779fd2ac.html#axzz256vnHcIU, Financial Times, London UK.

Guggenheim, M. and Södeström, O. (eds) (2010): *Reshaping Cities: How Global Mobility Transforms Architecture and Urban Form*. London: Routledge.

Granitsas, C. P. (2011): "Greek Government Wins Confidence Vote": http://online.wsj.com/article/SB10001424052970203699404577041840493906540.html.

Grimsey, D. and Lewis, M. K. (2004): "Public and Private Partnerships: The Worldwide Revolution in Infrastructure," Transportation *Research Board*, Northhampton: Edward Elgar Publishers.

Harvey, S. and Sedegah, K. (2011): "Import Demand in Ghana: Structure, Behaviour and Stability." AERC Research Paper 233, African Economic Research Consortium, Nairobi.

Hatton, T. J. and Williamson, J. G. (1998): *The Age of Mass Migration: Causes and Economic Impact*. Oxford University Press, Oxford, UK.

Haufler, V. (2001): *A Public Role for the Private Sector: Industry Self-Regulation in a Global Economy*. Washington DC: Carnegie Endowment for International Peace, pp. 12–15, Carnegie Endowment for International Peace, Washington DC.

Havel, V. (1991): *Open Letters: Selected Writings, 1965–1990*. New York: Knopf, Distributed by Random House.

Hawksworth, J. (2010): "Shift in World Economic Power Means a Decade of Seismic Change": http://www.ukmediacentre.pwc.com/content/detail.aspx?releaseid=3547&newsareaid=2.

Heifetz, Ronald, A. (1994): Leadership Without Easy Answers, The Belknap Press of the Harvard University Press, Cambridge MA.

Heywood, A. (2011): *Global Politics, Houndsmills, Basingstoke Hampshire*. New York: Palgrave Macmillan.

Hilsenrath, J. and Sparshott, J. (2011): "Central Banks Move to Calm Fears: Markets Rally After Joint Action Aimed at Cushioning Global Effects of Euro Crisis; Fed 'Prepared' to Do More if Needed," *The Wall Street Journal*, Economy, December 1, 2011.

Holmstrom, B. and Tirole, J. (1997): "Financial Intermediation, Loanable Funds, and the Real Sector," *Quarterly Journal of Economics*, 112, 663–691.

Holper, P. and Nelson, M. (2007): "Infrastructure and Climate Change Risk Assessment for Victoria," www.csiro.au.

Hood, R., Husband, D., and Yu, F. (2002): "Recurrent Expenditure Requirements of Capital Projects: Estimation for Budget Purposes." World Bank Policy Research Working Paper, December 2002.

Hornsey, I. S. (2003): *A History of Beer and Brewing*. Cambridge: The Royal Society of Chemistry.

Howard, J. A. and Jagdish N. S. (1969): *The Theory of Buyer Behavior*, New York, Wiley.

Heller, P. (1979): "Underfinancing of Recurrent Development Costs," *Finance and Development*, 16 (1), 38–41. World Bank and IMF.

Humplick, F. (1983): Predicting Pavement Expenditures in Highway Lifecycle Costing. Masters Thesis. Massachusetts Institute of Technology.

Huxley, T.H. (1948): "The faith of a scientist," address at Priestley Hall Leeds, December 1948. Copy of address, comments from colleagues on draft and on published version (Lindsey Press), Oxford University, Bodleaian Library, Special Collections and Western Manuscripts, Oxford, UK. It was an excerpt used in a book prepared for the World Bank on "Values and Ethics" by the Center for Global Leadership.

ILO (2011): *The Challenge of a Jobs Recovery Global Employment Trends*. Geneva: International Labour Office.

Islam, A. D. (2009): *Financial Liberalization in Developing Countries*. New Delhi: Springer.

IPAR (2009): "Implementation of the EAC Customs Union and Its Impact on Rwanda and Burundi's Economic Development." Improving Policy, Impacting Change. Institute for Policy Analysis and Research—Rwanda. www.ipar-rwanda.org.

ITC (2006): International Trade Indicators. ITC-UNCTAD/WTO.

ITC (2007): International trade in goods – Exports 2001-2007, Geneva: www.intracen.org.

ITC (2010): Trade Statistics. http://www.intracen.org/itc/market-info-tools/trade-statistics/.

ITC (2011): International trade in goods – Exports 2001-2011, Geneva: www.intracen.org.

Jan K. (2008): "Changes in the U.S. Financial System and the Subprime Crisis." The Levy Economics Institute of Bard College. Working Paper No. 530.

Johnson, S. (2011): Iceland to return most of UK local authorities' money. FT.com.

———— (2011): "Key Figures," Statistics Iceland, http://statice.is/Pages/1390.

———— (2008): "Macroeconomic Environment and Financial Markets: Financial Market Conditions Have Deteriorated." Central Bank of Iceland Financial Stability 2008.

———— (2005): "Melting Iceland—Iceland Review." Iceland Nature Conservation Society. Online.

Kaufmann, Daniel, Aart Kraay, and Massimo Mastruzzi (2008): "Governance Matters VII: Aggregate and Individual Governance Indicators 1996-2007," Policy Research Working Paper 4654, The World Bank, Washington D.C.

Kahneman, Daniel, Paul Slovic and Amos Tversky (1982): Judgment under Uncertainty: Heuristics and Biases, Cambridge University Press.

Kaufmann, K. and Mastruzzi, R. (2008): "Governance Matters VII: Aggregate and Individual Governance Indicators, 1996–2007." World Bank Policy Research Working Paper No. 4654.

Karasanyi, M. (2012): "The significance of Agaciro," Commentary. *New Times*. http://www.newtimes.co.rw/news/index.php?i=15121&a=58520.

Kar-Gupta, Sudip (2008): "Jerome Kerviel: "genius" or mediocre backroom boy?, Reuters, Paris, Saturday January 26, 2008 1:54 pm EST.

Kasperson, R. E. (1992): "Social Amplification of Risk: Progress in Developing an Integrative Framework," in Krimsky, S. and Golding, D. (eds) *Social Theories of Risk* Connecticut: Praeger, pp. 153–178.

Kasperson, Roger, E., Ortwin Renn, Paul Slovic, Halina S. Brown, Jacque Emel, Robert Goble, Jeanne X. Kasperson, and Samuel Ratick, March (1988): "The Social Amplification of Risk: A Conceptual Framework", Risk Analysis, Vol. 8, No. 2, Society for Risk Analysis.

Kasperson, R. E., Pidgeon, N., and Slovic, P. (2003): "The Social Amplification of Risk: Assessing Fifty Years of Research and Theory," in Pidgeon, N., Kasperson, R.E., and Slovic, P. (eds) *The Social Amplification of Risk*. Cambridge: Cambridge University Press.

Kay, J. (2009a): "History Vindicates the Science of Muddling Through." Columnists. *Financial Times*, http://www.ft.com/intl/cms/s/0/adab4a7c-2927-11de-bc5e-00144feabdc0.html#axzz25CsShH5Z.

———— (2009b): *The Long and Short of It: A Guide to Finance and Investment for Normally Intelligent People Who Aren't in the Industry*. London: Erasmus Press Ltd.

Kellner, D. (2002): "Theorizing Globalization." *Sociological Theory*, 20 (3), 285–305.

Keohane, R.O. (2001): "Governance in a Partially Globalized World," American Political Science Association, Volume/Issue 1, March 2001, pp. 1–13.

Kharas, H. and Gertz, G. (2010): 'The New Global Middle Class: A Cross-Over from West to East." Draft Version of Chapter 2 in *China's Emerging Middle Class: Beyond Economic Transformation* Cheng Li (ed.), Washington DC: Brookings Institution Press.

Komadina, P., Cisic, D., and Hlaca, B. (2006): "Globalization in the Maritime Transport Industry." Morsko Brodarstvo. ISSN 0469-6255 (183–189).

Kose, M.A., Otrok, C., and Whiteman, C.H. (2003): "International Business Cycles: World, Region, and Country-Specific Factors," American Economic Review, Vol. 93, pp 1216–1239.

Kotabe, M., Srinivasan, S. S., and Aulakh, P. S. (2002): "Multinationality and Firm Performance: The Moderating Role of R&D and Marketing Capabilities," *Journal of International Business Studies*, 33 (1), 79–97.

Kregel, J. (2008): "Changes in the U.S. Financial System and the Subprime Crisis." The Levy Economics Institute of Bard College. Working Paper No. 530.

Krishnamurthy, J. (2009): "Learning from the 1997–1998 Asian Financial Crises: The ILO Experience in Thailand and Indonesia." Employment Sector—Employment Report No. 3. ILO, http://www.ilo.org/employment/Whatwedo/Publications/employment-reports/WCMS_107637/lang--fr/index.htm.

Lagarde, C. (2011): "Global Action for Global Recovery." Project Syndicate: http://www.project-syndicate.org/commentary/lagarde4/English.

Lall, R. (2009): "Why Basel 2 Failed and why Basel 3 is Doomed. Global Economic Governance": http://www.globaleconomicgovernance.org/wp-content/uploads/GEG-Working-paper-Ranjit-Lall.pdf.

Lall, S., Weiss, J., and Zhang, J. (2005): "The 'Sophistication' of Exports: A New Measure of Product Characteristics." Working Paper No. 123, Queen Elizabeth House, Oxford University.

Léautier, F. (1986): "Predicting Pavement Expenditures in Highway Lifecyle Costing." Master Thesis, Massachusetts Institute of Technology.

Léautier, F. A. (2006): *Cities in a Globalizing World: Governance, Performance and Sustainability*. Washington DC: World Bank.

—————— (2013): "The Role of Gender in Development: Where Do Boys Count?" Mimeo. Harare: Zimbabwe.

Léautier, T. O. (2007): *Value Creation from Risk Management: A Guide to Real-Life Applications*. London: Risk Books.

Le Galés, P. (2010): *European Cities: Social Conflicts and Governance*. New York, Oxford: Oxford University Press. Paris: Presses de Sciences Po, 2003; second edition.

Le Figaro (2011): "Le Conseil d'État annule la suspension de culture du maïs OGM de Monsanto," Le Figaro, http://www.lefigaro.fr.

Le Monde (2011): "La France peut-elle rétablir le moratoire sur le maïs OGM?" http://www.lemonde.fr.

Lévy, J and M. Lussault eds. (2003): Dictionnaire de la géographie et de l'espace des sociétes, Publisher Belin: Paris.

Lewis, W. W. (2004): *The Power of Productivity: Wealth, Poverty and the Threat to Global Stability*. The University of Chicago Press.

Licari, L., Nemer, L., and Tamburlini, G. (2005): *Children's Health and Environment: Developing Action Plans*. Denmark: World Health Organization.

Lin, J. Y. (2012): New Structural Economics: A Framework for Rethinking Development and Policy. Washington DC: World Bank.

Lindblom, C. E. (1959): "The Science of Muddling Through," *Public Administration Review*, 19 (2).

Llewellyn, N. (2001): "The Role of Storytelling and Narrative in a Modernisation Initiative," *Local Government Studies*, 27 (4).

Lusk, J., House, L. O., Valli, C., Jaeger, S. R., Moore, M., Morrow, J. L., and Traill W. B. (2003/2004): "Effect of Information about Benefits of Biotechnology on Consumer Acceptance of Genetically Modified Food: Evidence from Experimental Auctions in the United States, England, and France," *European Review of Agricultural Economics*, 31 (2), 179–204.

Macartan Humphreys (2003): "Aspects économiques des guerres civiles," Revue Tiers Monde 174 (April–June 2003).

Machiavelli, N. (1966): *The Prince, Chapters XIV–XVIII*. New York: Bantam Dell.

Mackay, F. (2002): "Universal Rights or a Universe unto Itself? Indigenous Peoples' Human Rights and the World Bank's Draft Operational Policy, 4.10 on Indigenous Peoples," *American University International Law Review*, 17 (3), 527–624.

Madhya Pradesh (2007): Madhya Pradesh Human Development Report 2007, Directorate of Institutinal Finance, Government of Madhya Pradesh, www.dif.mp.gov.in.

Majeed, R. (2012): "Enhancing Capacity, Changing Behaviors: Rapid Results in Gashaki, Rwanda." http://resourcecentre.pscbs.gov.rw/content/reports-and-studies.

Manson, K. (2011): "Pro-democracy Protests Reach Djibouti." *Financial Times*.

Mearsheimer, J. J. (2001): The Tragedy of Great Power Politics, New York: Norton.

McKercher, B. and Chon, K. (2004): "The Over-Reaction to SARS and the Collapse of Asian Tourism," *Annals of Tourism Research*, 31 (3), 716–719.

McKinsey Global Institute (2013): Infrastructure Productivity: How to Save a $1 Trillion a Year, McKinsey 1 Company.

McLaughlin, A. and Woodside, D. (2004): "Rumblings of War in Heart of Africa," *Christian Science Monitor*, 23.

Meatprocess.com (2010-11-10): http://www.meatprocess.com/Industry-markets/Sars-outbreak-boosts-Thai-chicken-industry.

Miller-Dawkins, D. G. (2010): "The Global Economic Crisis and Developing Countries Impact and Reaction." Oxfam: http://www.iadb.org/intal/intalcdi/PE/2010/04613.pdf.

Milward Brown Optimor (2007): 2007 BrandZ. Top 100 Most Powerful Brands. Milward Brown Optimor. http://www.millwardbrown.com/Libraries/Optimor_BrandZ_Files/2007_BrandZ_Top100_Report.sflb.ashx.

Milward Brown Optimor (2013): Brandz Top100 most valuable global brands 2013, Milward Brown Optimor, http://www.millwardbrown.com/brandz/2013/Top100/Docs/2013_BrandZ_Top100_Report.pdf.

MIT (2006): "Corporate icon Jack Welch to Teach at MIT Sloan." NEWSROOM. http://mitsloan.mit.edu/newsroom/2006-welchclass.php.

MIT (2012): "Connectivity, Traffic and Geography Determine How Diseases Spread through Air Transportation Network." *CEE on Balance*. MIT Department of Civil and Environmental Engineering. http://cee.mit.edu.

Mitsloan.mit.edu (2006): "Corporate icon Jack Welch to teach at MIT Sloan," NEWSROOM, MIT Sloan Management, mitsloan.mit.edu.

Mishkin, F. F. (1999): "Lessons from the Tequila Crisis." *Journal of Banking & Finance*, 23, 1521–1533. Elsevier. www.elsevier.com/locate/econbase.

Moderwell, H.K. (1917): "The Epic of the Black Man," The New Republic, September 8, 1917, pp. 154–155.

de Mooij, M. and Hofstede, G. (2002): "Convergence and Divergence in Consumer Behavior: Implications for International Retailing," *Journal of Retailing*, 78, 61–69. New York University. Monsanto: http://www.monsanto.com.

Morens, D. M., Folkers, G. K., and Fauci, A. S. (2004): "The Challenge of Emerging and Re-Emerging Infectious Diseases," Insight Review Articles. *Nature*, 430. www. nature.com/nature.

Morrison, W. (2009): *China and the Global Financial Crisis: Implications for the United States*. Washington DC: Congressional Research Service.

Moteff, J. (2004): *Risk Management and Critical Infrastructure Protection: Assessing, Integrating, and Managing Threats, Vulnerabilities and Consequences. (RL32561)*. Washington DC: Congressional Research Service.

Mulder, R. W. A. and Hupkes, H. (2007): "European Legislation in Relation to Food Safety in Production of Poultry Meat and Eggs," *The Journal of Applied Poultry Research*, Poultry Science Association pp. 92–98, http://japr.fass.org.

Murray, C.J, and A.D., Lopez (1996): The Global Burden of Disease: a comprehensive assessment of mortality and disability from diseases, injuries and risk factors in 1990 and projected to 2020. Cambridge MA, Harvard School of Public Health, (Global Burden of Disease and Injury Series, Vol. 1), 1996.

NCHRP (1997): *Quantifying Congestion*. NCHRP 398.

Ncube, M. and A. Shimeles (2012): "The Making of the Middle Class in Africa," African Development Bank, Tunis: October 2012.

Newman, D.E., Carreras, B.A., and Dobson, I. (2005): "Risk Assessment in Complex Interacting Infrastructure Systems," Thirty-eighth Hawaii International Conference on System Sciences, Hawaii, January 2005.

November V., D'Alessandro-Scarpari C., and Rémy E. (2004): "Un lieu en controverse: une controverse qui fait lieu(x)," *Norois* 4 (193), 91–102.

Nye, J. S. Jr. (2004): *Soft Power: The Means to Success in World Politics*. New York: Public Affairs.

O'Brien, K., Leichenko, Kelkar, R.U., Venema, H., Aandahl, G., Tompkins, H., Javed, A., Bhadwal, S., Barg, S., Nygaard, L., and West, J. (2004): "Mapping vulnerability to multiple stressors: climate change and globalization in India." *Global Environmental Change*, 14, 303–313.

O'Kelly, G. C. (2010). The U.S. and Irish Credit Crises: Their Distinctive Differences and Common Features. http://www.irisheconomy.ie/Notes/IrishEconomy Note10.pdf.

ODI (2010): "Global Financial Crisis." http://www.odi.org.uk/resources/download/4784.pdf.

—— (2010): "Theme: The effects of the global financial crisis on the economic growth." http://www.odi.org.uk/resources/search.asp?database=resources&theme=345.

OECD (2009a). Short-Term Economic Statistics and the Current Crisis—The International Perspective. Paris: OECD.

—— (2009b): "Inondations au Burkina Faso," Club de Sahel et l'Afrique de l'Ouest, interview of H.E. M. Luc Tiao, Ambassador of Burkina Faso to France.

—— (2010): Regulatory Policy and the Road to Sustainable Growth. OECD: Paris.

Oishi, S. (2010): "The Psychology of Residential Mobility: Implications for the Self, Social Relationships, and Well-Being," *Perspectives in Psychological Science*, 5 (1), 15–21.

Park, J. S. -V. (1993): The role of the state in financial markets. UAD: http://www.uad-philecon.gr/UA/files/1924580762..pdf.

Pederson, P., Dudenhoeffer, D., Hartley, S., and Permann, M. (2006): *Critical Infrastructure interdependency Modeling: A Survey of US International Research*. Idaho Falls, Idaho: Idaho National Laboratory, INL/EXT-06-11464.

Pegg, S. (2006): "Can Policy Intervention Beat the Resource Curse? Evidence from the Chad-Cameroon Pipeline Project." *African Affairs*, 105 (418), 1–25.

Pellegrino, E.D. (1989): "Character, Virtue and Self-Interest in the Ethics of the Professions," *Journal of Contemporary Health Law and Policy*, 5, 53–74.

Pellegrino, E. D. and Gray, R.A. (1994): "Character, Virtue and Self-Interest in the Ethics of the Professions." Part i: The erosion of virtue and the rise of self interest," *Reference Service Review*, 22 (1), 29–55.

Pepin, N., W. Duane, and D. Hardy (2010): "The montane circulation on Kilimanjaro, Tanzania, and its influence on the summit ice-fields: comparison of surface mountain climate with equivalent reanalysis parameters," Global and Planetary Change, Vol. 74, Issue 2, pp. 64–75.

Peterson, S. (2011): "Egypt's revolution redefines what's possible in the Arab World," Christian Science Monitor, Boston MA.

Pierre, J. (2000): *Debating Governance: Authority, Steering, and Democracy*, Oxford University Press: Oxford, UK.

Pine, J. B. II and Gilmore, J.H. (1999): *The Experience Economy: Work Is Theatre and Every Business a Stage*. Cambridge: Harvard Business School Press.

Plato, Allan Bloom (1968): The Republic of Plato:Book III Translated with Notes, An Interpretive Essay, and A New Introduction, Second Edition, pp. 63–96.

Plato, Allan Bloom (1968): The Republic of Plato:Book VII: The Allegory of the Cave, Translated with Notes, An Interpretive Essay, and A New Introduction, Second Edition, pp. 193–220.

Presencing.com (2010): http://www.presencing.com/presencing-theoryu, rev. 20/11/10.

Pritchett, L. (2011): "One Size Doesn't Fit All: Lant Pritchett on Mimicry in Development," Global Prosperity Wonkcast, March 14, 2011.

Pritchett, L., Woolcock, M., and Andrews, M. (2010): "Capability Traps? The Mechanisms of Persistent Implementation Failure, Working Paper No. 234," Center for Global Development.

Raffestin C. (1980): Pour une géographie du pouvoir, Litec, Paris.

Ramzi, N. D. Jr. (2013): *Who Owns the Land? Cameroon's Large-Scale Land-Grabs*, Think Africa Press. www.thinkafricapress.com.

Reardon, T.C., Timmer, P., Barrett, C.B., and Berdegué, J. (2003): "The Rise of Supermarkets in Africa, Asia and Latin America," *American Journal of Agricultural Economics*, 85 (5), 1140–1146.

Reinhart, K. R. (2009): The Business Desk. PBS Newshour: http://www.pbs.org/newshour/businessdesk/2009/11/ask-rogoff-and-reinhart-questi.html.

Reuters. (2010): "G20 progress on financial regulation," http://www.reuters.com/article/2010/05/27/g20-regulation-idUSLDE64N0NC20100527.

—— (2011): "Spain's real estate boom and bust." http://www.reuters.com/article/2011/11/18/spain-property-idUSL5E7MI30Q20111118.

Rodrik, Dani (1999): "Institutions for High-Quality Growth: What Are They and How to Acquire Them," Paper presented at IMF Conference, "Second-Generation Reforms," Washington D.C.: November 8–9.

Rogoff, C. R. (2009): The Aftermath of Financial Crises. NBER Working Paper No. 14656.

Rooy, A. (2004): *The Global Legitimacy Game: Civil Society, Globalization and Protest*, Lavoisier.

Roman, J. H. (2011): Conservatives Ride Crisis to Victory in Spanish Vote. WSJ: http://online.wsj.com/article/SB10001424052970204443404577049731117915226.html.

Rosenkopf, L. and Tushman, M.L. (1998): "The Coevolution of Community Networks and Technology: Lessons from the Flight Simulation Industry," *Industrial and Corporate Change*, 7, 311–346.

Ross, C. (2011): *The Guardian*. Basel III: business as usual for bankers: http://www.guardian.co.uk/commentisfree/cifamerica/2011/jun/06/basel-iii-banking-volcker.

Scholte, J.A. (2001): "Civil Society and Democracy in Global Governance," Centre for the Study of Globalisation and Regionalisation CSGR Working Paper No. 65/01.

S&P (2011): Case-Shiller Lists. Standard and Poors. http://www.standardandpoors.com/indices/sp-case-shiller-home-price-indices/en/us/?indexId=spusa-cashpidff--p-us----.

Sala-i-Martin, X. (2002): The Disturbing "Rise" of Global Income Inequality. NBER Working Paper No. 8904.

Samama, P. (2013): "Devant Nokia et Apple, Samsung domine l'ensemble du marché des téléphones mobiles." Olnet. Actualités: Business. http://www.01net.com/editorial/601237/devant-nokia-et-apple-samsung-domine-l-ensemble-du-marche-des-telephones-mobiles/.

Sanchez, C. and Andrews, D. (2011): "Residential Mobility and Public Policy in OECD Countries," *OECD Journal: Economic Studies*, Vol. 1. http://dx.doi.org/10.1787/eco_studies-2011-5kg0vswqt240.

Schabas, R. (2003): "SARS: prudence not panic," *CMAJ*, 168 (May), 1432–1434.

Scharmer, O. C. (2007): Theory U: Leading from the Future as it Emerges: The Social Technology of Presencing. SOL. Cambridge MA: The Society for Organizational Learning.

Scharmer, O. C. (2009): *Theory U: Leading from the Future as It Emerges*. San Francisco: Berrett Koheler Publishers, pp. 33, 45.

Sen, Amartya (1999): Development As Freedom. New York, NY: Knopf.

Sen, A. (2006): Identity and Violence: The Illusion of Destiny (Issues of Our Time). New York: W.W. Norton & Company, Inc.

Senge, P., Scharmer, O.C., Jaworski, J., and Flowers, B.S. (2004): *Presence: Human Purpose and the Field of the Future*. Cambridge MA: The Society for Organizational Learning Inc., pp. 21–70.

Shaw, A. (2010): Gender and Trade in East Africa—A Review of Literature. DfID: London.

Sheffi, Y. (2005): *The Resilient Enterprise: Overcoming Vulnerability for Competitive Advantage*. Cambridge, MA: MIT Press Books.

Sheffi, Y. and Rice, J. (2005): "A Supply Chain View of the Resilient Enterprise", MIT SLoan Management Review, Vol. 47, No. 1, p 41-48, fall 2005.

Sherwood, J. (2008): Iceland Seen Turning to IMF.‖ Wall Street Journal. October 17, 2008. Online.

Schiraldi, P. (2010): "Automobile Replacement: A Dynamic Structural Approach," London School of Economics Working Paper, London, UK.

Shoraka, H., A. J. Ghodousi, and M. Kavianifar (2009): "Malaysia's 2020 Vision," Center for Strategic Research, www.csr.ir.

Sighvatsson, A., A. Danielsson, D. Svavarsson, F. Hermannsson, G. Gunnarsson, H. Helgadóttir, R. Bjarnadóttir, and R. B. Rikarösson (2011): "What does Iceland owe?", Economic Affairs, No. 4, Sedlabanki Islands: Iceland, pp. 1–44.

———— (2011): "Successful start of Iceland's membership negotiations with the EU." European Commission.

Silk, M. (2002): "'Bangsa Malaysia': A global sport, the city and the mediated refurbishment of local identies," *Media Culture & Society*, 24 (6), 775–794.

Slovic, P., Fischhoff, B., and Lichtenstein, S. (1982): "Facts and fears: Understanding perceived risk;" Judelent under uncertainty: Heuristics and biases. Edited by Daniel Kahneman, Paul Slovic and Amos Tversky. Cambridge University Press, p. 463.

Slovic, Paul and Lichtenstein, S. (1971): "Comparison of Bayesian and Regression Approaches to the Study of Information Processing in Judgment," *Organizational Behavior and Human Performance*, 6, 649–744.

Smith, R. D. (2006): Responding to global infectious disease outbreaks: Lessons from SARS on the role of risk perception, communication and management, in: *Social Science Medicine*, 63, 3114.

Södeström, O., Fimiani, D., Glambalvo, M., and Lucido, S. (2009): Urban Cosmographies, Roma: Meltemi.

Solimano, A. (2010): *International Migration in the Age of Globalization: Historical and Recent Experiences*. New York: Cambridge University Press.

Song, J., OK, S.Y., and Chang, L. (2007): "Rapid Risk Assessment and Decision Support for Urban Infrastructure Networks by Matrix-Based System Reliability Method," Inaugural International Conference of the Engineering Mechanics Institute, Urbana-Champaign, IL.

Springborg, R. (2011): "Whither the Arab Spring? 1989 or 1848?" The International Spectator: *Italian Journal of International Affairs*, 46 (3), pp. 5–12.

Standard & Poors (2011): "Iceladic Utility Landsvirkjun Downgraded to 'BB' After Similar Action On Iceland Local Currency Rating; Outlook Neg," May 18, 2011, www.standardpoors.com/ratingsdirect.

—— (2011): "Icelandic Utility Landsvirkjun Downgraded to -BB After Similar Action on Iceland Local Currency Rating; Outlook Neg," Standard & Poor's Global Credit Portal RatingsDirect®.

Statistics Iceland (2010): Tourist Industry, Online http://www.statice.is/Statistics/ Tourism,-transport-and-informati/Tourist-industry.

—— (2010) "Travel and Tourism in Iceland" Iceland Official Trade Directory. Online http://www.icelandexport.is/english/industry_sectors_in_iceland/travel_and_touris m_in_iceland/.

Statistics South Africa (2009): Profiling South African middle-class households, 1998-2006, Pali Lehohla, Statistician General, Report No. 03-03-01.

Sudip, K.G. (2008): "SocGen reels from record $7 billion rogue trader fraud." Reuters. Paris, Reporting from Paris for Reuters. http://uk.reuters.com/article/2008/01/24/ us-france-socgen-wrapup-idUKL2492199220080124

Sufi, A. (2007): "Information Asymmetry and Financing Arrangements: Evidence from Syndicated Loans," *The Journal of Finance* LXII (2).

Tan, A. H. (2004): Monetary and financial management in Asia in the 21st century. London: World Scientific Publishing.

The Arbinger Institute (2000): Leadership and Self-Deception: Getting Out of the Box. San Francisco CA: Bennett-Koehler Publishers Inc.

The Economist (2008): "Cracks in the crust." *The Economist.*

—— (2010): "The banks battle back," *The Economist.* http://www.economist.com/ node/16231434.

—— (2012): "Is the financial system better prepared for a crisis than it was in 2008?" http://www.economist.com/economics/by-invitation/questions/financial-system-better-prepared-crisis-it-was-2008.

—— (2013): "Why are sales of non-alcoholic beer booming?"

The Examiner (2014): "Deferred maintenance is expensive," The San Francisco Examiner Newspaper (2014), www.sfexaminer.com/sanfrancisco/deferred-maintenance-is-expensive/Content?oid=2153376.

The World According to Monsanto, March 11, 2008. http://topdocumentaryfilms. com/the-world-according-to-monsanto/.

Thucydides (431 BCE): "The History of the Peloponnesian War." http://classics.mit. edu/Browse/browse-Thucydides/pelopwar.html.

Toni (2006): "French Monsanto subsidiary found guilty of GMO contamination," By Toni on December 18, 2006. http://www.laleva.org.

Turco A. (2009): *Governance, culture, sviluppo. Cooperazione ambientale in Africa occiden-tale.* Milano: Franco Angeli.

Tushman, M.L. and Anderson, P. (1986): "Technological Discontinuities and Organizational Environments," *Administrative Science Quarterly*, 31, 439–465.

Tversky, A. and Kahneman, D. (1971): "The Belief in the Law of Small Numbers," *Psychological Bulletin*, 76, 105–110.

UC (2011): Is Global Income Inequality Increasing or Decreasing? UC Atlas of Global Inequality. http://ucatlas.ucsc.edu/income/debate.html.

UERD (2002): "Les migrations à Ouagadougou: tendances récentes (1990–2000). Ouaga Focus. Unité d'Enseignement et de Recherche en Démographie (UERD),. No. 30.

UN (2012): 2012 International Trade Statistics Yearbook, Vol. I—World Trade Tables. New York: United Nations.

UNCTAD (2012): World Investment Report 2012: Towards a New Generation of Investment Policies. United Nations New York and Geneva, 2012.

UNCTAD (2013): World Investment Report 2013: Annex Tables. http://unctad.org/en/Pages/DIAE/World%20Investment%20Report/Annex-Tables.aspx.

United Nations (2009): "Activities of Secretary-General in United Republic of Tanzania, 26–28, February 2009." http://www.un.org/News/Press/docs/2009/sgt2657.doc.htm.

—— (2000): *World Population Prospects: The 2000 Revision.*

—— (2001): *World Urbanization Prospects: The 2001 Revision.*

—— (2011): *World Urbanization Prospects, the 2011 Revision.* http://esa.un.org/unup/.

L'Usine Nouvelle (2006): "Veolia et CMA-CGM conjuguent leurs forces," L'Usine Nouvelle No. 3022. http://www.usinenouvelle.com/article/veolia-et-cma-cgm-conjuguent-leurs-forces.N52943.

Van Rooy, A. (2005): *The Global Legitimacy Game: Civil Society, Globalization and Protest*, London: Palgrave Macmillan.

Vinding, A. L. (2006): Absorptive capacity and innovative performance: A human capital approach. Economics of Innovation and New Technology, 507–517.

Vogel, I. G. (2010): Global Governance and Systemic Risk in the 21st Century: Lessons from the Financial Crisis. Global Policy, 4–16.

Walkenhorst, P. (2006): "Uganda's Access to Global and Regional Markets." Background paper prepared for the "Uganda: Diagnostic Trade Integration Study." Kampala and Washington DC: Ministry of Tourism, Trade, and Industry and World Bank.

Waltz, K. (1954): Man, the State and War: A Theoretical Analysis, New York: Columbia University Press.

Waltz, K. (1979): Theory of International Politics, Reading: Addison Wesley.

Wang, M.D. and Jolly, A. M. (2004):*Changing Virulence of the SARS Virus: The Epidemiological Evidence.* Bullet in of the World Health Organization, 82, 547.

Wanjiru, R. (2009): "Is The South-South Cooperation Achieving its Intended Outcomes? Critical Analysis of the South-South Cooperation Based on the Finding of the UNDP Study of 2009," Centre for Economic Governance and AIDS in Africa (CEGAA) mimeo.

Ward, A. (2011): "EU talks hinge on debt resolution, Iceland told." FT.com. April 11, 2011. Online.

Ward, A., Barker, A., and Steinglass, M. (2011): "Legal action looms as Icelanders vote No." www.ft.com.

Warra, A. A. (2011): "Cosmetic Potential of African Shea Nut (Vitellaria Paradoxa) Butter." *Current Research in Chemistry*, 3, 80–86.

Washington, G. (1796): "Farewell Address" September 19, 1796. http://www.presidency.ucsb.edu/ws/?pid=65539.

Wearden, G. (2011): Portugal bailout details boost euro and bond markets. *The Guardian*: http://www.guardian.co.uk/business/2011/may/04/portugal-bailout-euro-rises-bond-markets.

WEF (2013): Global Agenda Council on Water Security 2013. http://www.weforum.org/content/global-agenda-council-water-security-2013.

Welch, J., and Welch, S. (2009): *Winning.* HarperCollins.

Wikipedia (2012): ASKY Airlines, en.wikipedia.org/wiki/ASKY_Airlines.

Wilson, B.G. (ed.) (1996): Constructivist learning environments: case studies in instructional design. Englewood Cliffs, NJ: Educational Technology Publications, Inc., pp. 17–20.

Wen-Ti Sung (2011): "Non-Traditional Security Challenges and Regional Cooperation in East Asia: An Outcomes Paper from the 2011 Emerging Leaders Dialogue," Beijing, 28-29, July 2011.

Wolf, M. (2011): "The eurozone's journey to defaults." http://www.ft.com/intl/cms/s/0/f3f54cd6-7b36-11e0-9b06-00144feabdc0.html#axzz1eN7meBgk.

Wood, L. (2000): "Brands and Brand Equity: Definition and Management." *Management Decision*, 38 (9), 662–669.

Wolnemedia (2009): "Monsanto—największy producent genetycznie modyfikowanej żywności…," *Wolne Media*, http://wolnemedia.net.

World Bank (1998): Assessing Aid. New York: Oxford University Press.

World Bank (2000): "Anti Corruption in Transition: A Contribution to the Policy Debate," World Bank: Washington D.C.

World Bank (2009): Doing Business 2009, The World Bank: Washington D.C.

World Bank (2010): "Ores and metal exports (% of merchandise exports)", Washington: data.worldbank.org.

World Bank (2010): World Development Indicators 2010, International Bank for Reconstruction and Development/The World Bank, Washington D.C.

World Bank (2010): World Development Indicators 2010, World Bank: Washington DC.

World Bank (2011): Iceland. The World Bank. http://data.worldbank.org/country/iceland.

World Bank (2012): Cameroon Economic Update, Issue No. 3, World Bank: Washington D.C., January 2012.

Wray, S. F. (2010): "Quantitative Easing and Proposals for Reform of Monetary Policy Operations." Bard College Levy Economics Institute Working Paper No. 645.

WTO (2012): Trade Policy Review: East African Community. Report by the Secretariat, World Trade Organization. WT/TPR/271. October 17, 2012.

www.thecb.state.tx.us/reports (2006): "Deferred Maintenance to Replacement Value Ratios."

www.wikipedia.com (2003): "North Eastern United States Blackout."

Zippelius, R. (1986): "Exclusion and shunning as legal and social sanctions." *Ethology and Sociobiology*, 7 (3–4), 159–166.

Index

risk management, 271
skills, 16, 17
territorial, 164–5
learning
  by doing, 13
  holistic, 13–21
  interactive, 13–21
  modular, 13–21
  by modules, 13
Lebanon, 149
Leifur Eiríksson International Airport,
  232
Lesotho
  manufacturing sector, sophistication
    in, 217, 218
  South–South export trade in, 212
Levi's, 187, 188
Liberia, food exports in, 216
logistics, 3–4, 15
  industry, 20
    customization in, 258–65
    global trade patterns, 209–10
    regional trade patterns, 210–18
    revolution, 210, 219–25
  management, 27, 56
  management, defined
  revolution, 2, 57, 58
  as turning point, emergence of, 27,
    55–8
Lucknow, bridge collapse in, 245
lululemon, 187, 188

macroeconomic management, 142
Madagascar
  manufacturing sector, sophistication
    in, 217, 218
Madhya Pradesh, road network mainte-
  nance in, 242–3
Malawi
  agriculture sector, sophistication in,
    216
  food exports, 216
Malaysia
  South–South export trade by, 212, 214
  South–South import trade by, 213
  Vision 2020, 169
Mali
  karité nuts production in, 92
  territorial governance, 151
maritime transport, 222

Marks & Spencer, 185
Martha Stewart Living, 185
mass customization, 59
Mauritinia
  agriculture sector, sophistication in,
    217
Mayard-Paul, Thierry, 193
McKinsey Global Institute, 242
measurability, 199–200
measurement errors, 250
MERCOSUR, 105, 210
Mergers and Acquisitions (M&A), 62, 64
metropolitization, 163
Mexico, cotton lint production in, 93
Middle East, trade patterns in, 210
migration, 87–9, 152
  patterns of change, impact of, 30
Milward Brown Optimor, 61, 188, 273n3
mobility, 4, 15, 27, 58–62, 87–9, 152
  physical, 59
  residential, 59
Monaco, migration in, 31
Monet, Claude, 275n1
Monsanto, 13, 14–15, 43–8
  anti-globalization activities against, 48
  environmental organizations against,
    48
  implications for strategy, 50–1
  learning from, 44–5
  new ownership, 45
  organic production, legal require-
    ments for, 46–8
  reactions to change, 49–50
  scientific innovations, benefits and
    risks of, 45–6
  spheres of change, 49
moral hazard, 200, 241
Morocco
  manufacturing sector, sophistication
    in, 217, 218
  South–South import trade in, 211
motor vehicle industry, evolution
  of, 223
Mubarak, Ismail, 74–8
Museveni, 172

Namibia, South–South import trade in,
  211
natural disasters, 71
nepotism, 144